America's Frozen Neighborhoods

America's Frozen Neighborhoods

The Abuse of Zoning

Robert C. Ellickson

Yale UNIVERSITY PRESS
New Haven and London

Published with assistance from the Louis Stern Memorial Fund.

Yale University Press books may be purchased in quantity for educational, business, or promotional use. For information, please e-mail sales.press@yale.edu (U.S. office) or sales@yaleup.co.uk (U.K. office).

Set in 10.5/14.5 Galliard by Newgen North America.
Printed in the United States of America.

Library of Congress Control Number: 2022930667
ISBN 978-0-300-24988-0 (hardcover : alk. paper)

A catalogue record for this book is available from the British Library.

This paper meets the requirements of ANSI/NISO Z39.48-1992 (Permanence of Paper).

10 9 8 7 6 5 4 3 2 1

To the memories of Charles M. Haar,
Jane Jacobs, and Raymond Vernon

Contents

Preface and Acknowledgments

Local zoning measures, to the surprise of many, may be the most consequential regulatory program in the United States. Numerous social scientists have found that local barriers to housing production elevate housing costs and distort household migration decisions. Nonetheless, members of the mass media tend to regard anything that happens at a city hall as unworthy of attention. Thanks to the efforts of many of those cited in this book, zoning seems finally to be drawing the scrutiny it deserves. This work describes local zoning practices in three metropolitan areas: Silicon Valley, Greater New Haven, and the northwestern sector of Greater Austin, Texas. The internet, and the big data that it has spawned, enabled the undertaking.

Lynsey Gaudioso, a former Yale Law School student, inspired this work. In spring 2014, I taught at Yale Law School, for the first and only time, a seminar named *Suburbs*. Lynsey, then a first-year student, enrolled. She wrote a paper that empirically examined the zoning practices of New Haven suburbs. Her paper opened my eyes to what a scholar could accomplish, after the advent of big data, in depicting zoning patterns. But for Lynsey, I would never have undertaken this book.

I have resided for many years in two of the three metropolitan areas that I ended up studying. During most of the 1980s, I was a member of the Stanford Law School faculty and lived in Silicon Valley. My family resided in a Palo Alto neighborhood known as Old Palo Alto. In 1988, I accepted an invitation to join the faculty of Yale Law School, a school from which I had graduated in 1966. Since the move to Yale, I have lived a majority of my adult life in Greater New Haven, Connecticut. On arriving from the West Coast, I first moved to Woodbridge, one of New Haven's most exclusionary suburbs, and later to East Rock, a neighborhood in the City of New Haven itself.

Greater Austin, outside of a few visits, I knew far less well. I am especially grateful to Lynn Baker and Andrew Kull, members of the faculty at University of Texas Law School, for helping open doors in Greater Austin. Two of my Yale Law colleagues, Daniel Markovits and Gerald Torres, lived in Austin for many years. They also helped introduce the area to me.

Most books, even those by a single author, are largely group efforts. I received help on many fronts. As has become a law school tradition, I have presented portions of this book at various law school workshops. Participants at each provided valuable feedback. Three were law-and-economics workshops. I thank Steve Shavell, coordinator of the Harvard Law School Law and Economics workshop, who rightly prodded for improvements in the paper I presented there. Thanks also to Lee Anne Fennell, coordinator of the University of Chicago Law and Economics workshop, and Mitch Polinsky, coordinator of Stanford Law School's workshop. Two of my presentations were to general faculty workshops. Lynn Baker helped arrange one at the University of Texas Law School, and Gideon Yaffe did the same at Yale Law School. I also presented some of my findings at a superb conference on exclusionary zoning that John Infranca convened, in November 2019, at Suffolk University Law School in Boston.

Three colleagues at Yale Law School—Anika Singh Lemar, Jay Pottenger, and David Schleicher—are intensely interested in the issues that exclusionary zoning poses. I have benefited from conversations with each. David strives, as few law professors do, to keep up with developments in both economics and political science. In fall 2021, he at last is offering a Yale Law School course in Property law, a course suited to his central substantive interests. As chapter 4 mentions, Anika and Jay's clinics are engaged in a lawsuit that seeks to strike down some of Woodbridge, Connecticut's exclusionary barriers. I often have bounced ideas off yet another colleague, Zach Liscow, a scholar with exceptionally broad interests. Carol Rose, my longtime compatriot at Yale, provided especially helpful comments on the chapter on covenants, as did Stephanie Stern on the chapter on state land use reforms. Rich Schragger, who supports unfettered local government discretion far more than I do, provided feedback on the entire manuscript.

Several former Yale Law School students have authored many of the best recent works on exclusionary zoning. Eric Biber and Chris Elmendorf have emerged as leading analysts of the complex legal situation in California, the state with the most astronomic housing prices in the United States. In early 2021, Sara Galvan, invariably indefatigable, published the *Connecticut Zoning Atlas,* a landmark study of local practices throughout the state. Owen Jones and Lior Strahilevitz also offered useful advice along the way. Douglas Melamed and Alex von Hoffman, two scholars without Yale Law School ties, provided help as well.

The staffs of local zoning agencies were consistently willing to let me examine copies of their early zoning ordinances and maps. I limit my thanks to two especially helpful individuals in each of the three metropolitan areas: in Silicon Valley, William Chui of Redwood City and Amy French of Palo Alto; in Greater New Haven, Harry Smith of Branford and Kristine Sullivan of Woodbridge; and in northwestern Austin, Paul Frank of the City of Austin and Megan Will of Bee Cave.

Bob Nelson of Accomac, a rustic town on the Eastern Shore of Virginia, prepared the five maps. My thanks to Bill for his admirable patience in educating me about the mapmaking process.

I carried out about half of my research on, of all places, the Left Bank of Paris, France. Because the internet has made big data available worldwide, geographical constraints matter far less than they once did. I am indebted to the series of French scholars who generously provided me a Paris desk in the late 2010s. They were, in order, Christophe Jamin of the Sciences-Po Law School, Etienne Wasmer of LIEPP and the Sciences-Po Economics Department, Denis Baranger and Olivier Beaud of Paris II School of Law, and Rozen Noguellou of GRIDAUH and the Paris I School of Law.

Law faculty tend to be laggards in technology. Yale map librarian Stacey Maples first introduced me to ESRI's ArcGIS program, and Miriam Olivares later trained me in the basics of that system. Chris Rappa of the South Central Connecticut Regional Council of Governments provided a database that greatly simplified my analysis of zoning in Greater New

Haven. Jordan Peccia, of the Yale University Civil Engineering department, advised on decentralized methods of wastewater treatment.

The book cites many obscure sources. The staff of Yale Law School library consistently provided yeoman service in uncovering them. Among many others, I pay special tribute to Julian Aiken and Maryellen Larkin. I could not have completed the book without the services of Gerard Armoogam of Yale Law School's IT department. Gerard regularly updated the laptops that I took to Paris when conducting the research, and he rescued me from crises on numerous occasions.

The Oscar M. Ruebhausen Fund at Yale Law School helped fund the costs of visits to both Silicon Valley and Greater Austin. That funding enabled me to deliver talks to faculties at both Stanford and the UT Law Schools and to visit numerous city halls in both regions.

Brian Chen, of the Yale Law School class of 2021, provided truly exceptional research assistance. Brian had been a student of Bill Fischel's at Dartmouth College, and he came to Yale with a sophisticated understanding of both the potential upsides and downsides of zoning.

The book has twelve chapters. I have separately published a version of nine of them in a law review. Cardozo Law Review published an early version of chapters 2 through 5 and chapter 12. That work appears as "Zoning and the Cost of Housing: Evidence from Silicon Valley, Greater New Haven, and Greater Austin," 42 *Cardozo Law Review* 1611 (2021). I also published much of chapter 2 in *Cityscape*, a journal edited by Mark Shroder of the Department of Housing and Urban Development. Mark arranged for valuable anonymous reviews of an early draft of that chapter. Much of chapters 6 and 7 appeared in "The Zoning Strait-Jacket: The Freezing of American Neighborhoods of Single-Family Houses," 96 *Indiana Law Journal* 395 (2021). A version of chapter 8 appears as "Stale Real Estate Covenants," 63 *William & Mary Law Review* 1831 (2022). I am grateful to the staffs of all these journals for the many improvements they suggested and for their consent to the publication of this book.

At Yale University Press, Seth Ditchik shepherded my outline and eventual manuscript through the shoals of publication approval. I owe to Seth the book's title. Among Seth's many services was the recommendation that Bill Nelson undertake the mapmaking. Thanks also to the Press's Karen Olson and Margaret Otzel, who helped assure completion of the manuscript, and to Liz Casey, the superb copyeditor. Thanks also to Dustin Kilgore, who helped select the book's cover.

Lynn Hammer, my wife, has patiently tolerated my many travails with this book, both in New Haven and Paris. I could not have completed the project without her unfailing support.

Finally, I should affirm that I am willing to share all underlying data with other researchers.

1

Leviathan Goes Local: The Abuse of Zoning

Thomas Hobbes and George Orwell both associated a powerful government with sway over a large territory. Leviathan, however, can go local. Low-visibility zoning controls constitute what may be the most consequential regulatory program in the United States. Many localities have created barriers to the development of less costly forms of housing. In numerous regions, most notably California, this has sent housing prices skyward. Economists unanimously find that current zoning practices inflict major damage on the national economy. This book describes, in unprecedented detail, how the zoning system works and recommends steps for its reform.

In the 1950s, Joseph Eichler of Eichler Homes was a major developer of tract houses in the area now known as Silicon Valley, the region a few dozen miles southeast of San Francisco. In 1952, Eichler sold houses in the Fairmeadow neighborhood of south Palo Alto for about $16,000 ($160,000 in 2020 dollars).[1] Over the next two decades, their market value grew, but slowly. In 1970, despite the draw of the Bay Area's mild Mediterranean climate, Silicon Valley house prices exceeded national prices by only around 20 percent.[2] By 2020, however, the sale price of a

1. See *San Francisco Examiner*, Dec. 13, 1952, 30 (advertising houses in Eichler's Fairmeadow project in south Palo Alto at prices between $15,300 and $17,500). CPI-U is the price deflator.
2. Ellickson, "San Francisco Peninsula" (1982b): 5–8.

Figure 1. Portion of the Fairmeadow neighborhood of south Palo Alto. Eichler Homes developed the neighborhood in the early 1950s, when Palo Alto's zoning required a house-lot of at least 6,000 square feet. Joseph Eichler's lots commonly slightly exceeded that mandate. Note the sidewalks. (mauritius images GmbH/ Alamy Stock Photo)

Fairmeadow house in south Palo Alto had risen to $2.6 million. This was ten times the median house value nationwide.[3]

Why these astronomic prices? A principal cause has been the tightening of local land use regulations. As the book documents, Silicon Valley has become a poster child of zoning abuse. Suburbs such as Palo Alto adopted local regulatory measures, including zoning rules and historic preservation regulations, which have strangled the production of housing. Proposals to permit greater residential density, particularly in neighborhoods of existing single-family houses, are politically doomed at city

3. In November 2020, the Zillow Home Value Index placed the median price of a house in the Fairmeadow neighborhood of south Palo Alto at $2.6 million and a house in all of Palo Alto at $3.1 million. Zillow estimated the national median at $260,000.

hall. After 1970, the State of California itself aggravated the various local abuses, enacting statutes that piled additional constraints on housing supply.[4]

Several other causes, of course, also have helped generate the explosion of house prices in neighborhoods such as Fairmeadow in south Palo Alto. Buildable land is relatively scarce in Silicon Valley, aggravating the effects of local zoning restrictions. Silicon Valley also has become a magnet for national and international talent in the well-paid field of information technology (IT). House prices reflect the forces of demand, as well as those of supply.

Local zoning abuses, coupled with unsound California policies, however, have been the main reason for the astronomic cost of shelter in Silicon Valley. During the 1950s and 1960s, the region's population had grown much faster than California's. Between 1970 and 2010, by contrast, despite the surge in demand to live in the region, Silicon Valley grew at less than half the rate that California did and even substantially lagged the United States as a whole.[5] By 1999, scholars were asserting that the "zoning tax" on the production of single-family houses was higher in San Jose and San Francisco than in any of the other nineteen metros they analyzed.[6]

This book is not critical of all forms of local zoning, but only of regulations that flunk benefit-cost analysis.[7] In 1900, local governments in the United States did too little to regulate land uses. In that era, a developer might erect a factory or high-rise apartment building that courts would not deem noxious enough to constitute a nuisance to nearby landowners. In Chicago, con artists, to shake down neighbors, sometimes threatened to open a livery stable.[8] In 1900, this laissez-faire approach to land use gave rise to overly dynamic real estate markets. In that era, for example, industrial plants could too easily invade a residential neighborhood, and owners of historic buildings could too readily demolish them.

4. See chapter 3.
5. Between 1970 and 2010, the populations of the fifteen cities in Silicon Valley depicted in figure 3, located at the outset of chapter 3, increased by 39 percent. California's population increased by 87 percent, and the nation's by 52 percent.
6. Glaeser et al., "Manhattan So Expensive?" (2005): 359.
7. See chapter 9.
8. Bosselman, "Illinois' Unique Zoning Standards" (1992): 569–70; Kelly, "Strategic Spillovers" (2011): 1645–46.

Today, especially in areas like Silicon Valley, the vice is no longer excessive dynamism, but excessive stasis. Overregulation, not underregulation, has emerged as the basic problem. Two notable corporations, Oracle and Tesla, Inc., the automaker, have recently decided to move their headquarters from Silicon Valley to the Austin area.[9] Why Austin? A major reason, as the book documents, is that Austin localities largely refrain from the excessive regulation of land uses. To reduce their housing costs, specialists in information technology also are increasingly inclined to migrate from Silicon Valley to Austin, one of the fastest-growing metropolitan areas in the United States.

Most of this book focuses on zoning practices in three quite different regions—Silicon Valley; Greater New Haven, Connecticut (where the author lives); and the northwestern portion of Greater Austin. Part I offers metrics for measuring zoning abuse and applies them to these three regions. Part II marshals evidence proving the rigidity of local zoning practices. Especially in an existing neighborhood of detached houses—most of urban America—local politics tends to place land uses in a legal straitjacket. Part III makes specific recommendations for reform. Local governments have many reasons to exclude, and they are unlikely to alter their ways. I urge state governments to take the lead in zoning reform, supported by specific federal initiatives.

Introduction to Zoning

In the 1910s, first Los Angeles, and later New York City, pioneered the use of zoning, an import from Frankfurt-on-Main, Germany.[10] A city's zoning ordinance divides its territory into a number of mapped districts and varies, from zone to zone, regulations on the use of land and the bulk of buildings. By 2020, perhaps fifteen thousand local governments in the United States had adopted zoning ordinances.[11] Many localities also apply complementary tools of land use control, such as

9. Elliott and Copeland, "Tesla to Move Headquarters" (2021).
10. Ex parte Quong Wo, 118 P. 714 (Cal. 1911); Talen, *City Rules* (2012): 22–36.
11. This is an estimate. In 2012, the Census Bureau tallied 35,879 general-purpose local governments in the United States. A national survey in 1968 reported 9,595 localities with zoning ordinances. National Commission on Urban Problems, *Building the American City* (1969): 208. See also Pendall et al., "Land Use Regu-

regulations that govern the subdivision of land and the preservation of places of historic value. An adroitly drafted public land use regulation can address the risk that a new land use will impose what economists call "negative externalities"—adverse effects that bargaining would be unlikely to internalize. In 1900, a Chicago livery stable threatened to inflict this sort of harm.

Herbert Hoover, secretary of commerce under Presidents Harding and Coolidge, gave zoning a major boost. He convened a committee that drafted a model act that encouraged state governments to authorize their local governments to engage in zoning.[12] During the 1920s, many cities joined the bandwagon. In that era, some, perhaps many, public land use controls benefited the nation.[13] Ideal zoning, by controlling obnoxious land uses, can increase a city's or suburb's aggregate land value.

Public regulations, however, also entail costs. Some early supporters, for example, had wanted to use zoning to promote racial segregation.[14] This book focuses on a closely related abuse. A few suburbs, as early as the 1930s, had begun to engage in *exclusionary* zoning—that is, prohibition of the building of least-cost forms of housing. Exclusionary practices tend to raise housing prices to the detriment of regional consumers. Many of the individuals harmed are not eligible to vote in the elections of the government that is restricting their options. Exclusionary zoning thus transforms a program originally designed to *internalize* the negative spillover effects of unwelcome land uses into a program for *inflicting* externalities on housing consumers. Virtually all of the hundreds of legal scholars who have assessed exclusionary practices have condemned them.[15] This book

lations" (2006): 11 (reporting that 8.5 percent of responding localities lacked zoning ordinances).

12. U.S. Department of Commerce, Advisory Committee on Zoning, "A Standard State Zoning Enabling Act" (1924).

13. One team of researchers asserts that Chicago's initial zoning ordinance, by segregating industrial uses, raised the value of houses in the city. Shertzer et al., "Economic Geography of Cities" (2018): 34.

14. Ellickson et al., *Land Use Controls* (2021): 109–10, 635–37.

15. A half-century ago, the primary exceptions were Nolan and Horack, "Minimum Space Requirements" (1954): 985 (asserting virtues of local control), and Bergin, "Price Exclusionary Zoning" (1972) (stressing value of "local decisional autonomy"). In a forthcoming article, "The Perils of Land Use Deregulation," Schragger echoes these authors' themes. But compare Schleicher, "Constitutional Law

documents the severity of current exclusionary practices, especially in Silicon Valley and Greater New Haven.

Greenwich, Connecticut, Embraces Large Lots

The Town of Greenwich occupies the entirety of the southwestern thumb of Connecticut, the portion of the state that intrudes into Westchester County, New York. The town's land area is forty-eight square miles, more than twice that of Manhattan Island. For many decades, Greenwich was a contender for the title of the wealthiest locality in the United States. Connecticut did not enact an income tax until 1991, later than most other states. Greenwich, the part of Connecticut closest to New York City, long served as a tax haven for commuters to Manhattan.

Prior to the 1930s, most housing in Greenwich was concentrated in the southern third of the town, the portion that abuts Long Island Sound. A commuter railroad, now called Metro-North, crosses that portion, as does the Boston Post Road (U.S. 1), then the main highway into New York City. Greenwich first adopted zoning in 1926. Its initial zoning scheme authorized a density of five households per acre in most of the town's largely undeveloped northern sector, which constituted two-thirds of its land area.[16] Neighborhoods developed at that density would have been walkable.

Change, however, was in the offing. In 1938, the Connecticut highway department opened the first segment of the Merritt Parkway, a historic and beautifully designed thoroughfare. The Merritt roughly bisected the mostly undeveloped northern two-thirds of Greenwich. In 1947, just prior to the postwar building boom, Greenwich chose to brake population growth, particularly in its underdeveloped northern area.[17]

---

for NIMBYs" (2020): 886–90; 899–909 (criticizing unconstrained local government discretion).

16. Greenwich, Conn., Building Zone Regulations, adopted Feb. 1, 1926. The town's 1926 map allowed in that region "five families" per acre.

17. Greenwich appears to have been a latecomer to large-lot zoning in Connecticut. In its nearly ubiquitous single-family zone, the Town of Woodbridge, a New Haven suburb, in 1932 required a minimum lot of 20,000 sq. ft., and in 1938 it tripled that requirement. See chapter 2.

A 1947 Greenwich zoning ordinance limited buildings in most of the town's middle third to single-family dwellings on a house-lot of either one or two acres. Compared to the 1926 zoning, the 1947 ordinance's one-acre requirement reduced potential population growth by 80 percent. In its northernmost third, north of Merritt Parkway, the town was even stricter. There Greenwich, with minor exceptions, required a minimum house-lot of four acres. Compared to the 1926 ordinance, this measure reduced residential density by 95 percent. So much for walkable neighborhoods.

By 2020, subdividers had developed most of the northern two-thirds of Greenwich. They marketed large, commonly even palatial, single-family lots that comply with the town's regulations. Local politics now freezes this zoning in place. Between 1947 and 2014, the date of the town's latest map, Greenwich had rezoned virtually none of the northern two-thirds of town to permit greater density.[18] In 1965, a landowner did challenge the constitutionality of the four-acre minimum, but without success.[19]

Greenwich's 1947 large-lot zoning policy generated some benefits. It enhanced, for example, the quality of the foliage observed by motorists driving on Merritt Parkway. Greenwich's decision to engage in large-lot zoning, however, had many negative consequences. People flock to cities to enjoy what economists call agglomeration benefits, the advantages of being close to others. High-tech migrants to Silicon Valley, for example, rightly anticipate gains from residing in a more specialized labor market and having the ability to rub elbows with others like themselves. Greenwich's large-lot zoning decreased the agglomeration benefits that Greater New York can offer. It also lengthened the commutes of numerous suburbanites, increased the region's auto-dependence, and worsened the nation's carbon imprint. Perhaps most seriously, by stifling housing production, Greenwich's policies eventually pushed up the price of shelter in Greater New York.

18. Town of Greenwich, Building Zone Regulations Map, Dec. 19, 2014.

19. Zygmont v. Planning & Zoning Comm'n of Town of Greenwich, 210 A.2d 172 (Conn. 1965) (rejecting substantive due process and takings claims). The opinion asserted, "The courts do not and should not substitute their judgment for that of the local authority." Id. at 175.

A central thesis of this book is that a state, in this instance Connecticut, should sharply constrain the zoning choices that a town such as Greenwich is entitled to make. Just as markets can fail, so can governments at every level. State constraints on local land use policies can themselves be problematic.[20] Connecticut, however, would have been more likely than Greenwich itself to consider the regional consequences of Greenwich's decision to require large house-lots in most of the town. Herbert Hoover's model act had called for states to delegate largely unlimited zoning powers to local governments. Defenders of that approach might invoke the principle of subsidiarity—the advantages of a political system that delegates a responsibility to the smallest government capable of addressing the problem at hand. Compared to residents of the state of Connecticut, Greenwich residents on average unquestionably have greater local knowledge of the town's terrain. Greenwich residents, however, lack incentives to take into account the effects of the town's policies on those who live beyond its borders. Herbert Hoover's model zoning legislation, which had granted local governments largely unconstrained powers over zoning, turned out to be a major mistake. Hoover's drafting committee failed to anticipate that suburbs would abuse zoning powers. The mission of this book is to correct that mistake.

The Costs of Exclusionary Zoning

There is broad agreement that, especially since around 1970, the national costs of local zoning have escalated.[21] Prior to 2000, economists, with a few exceptions, most notably William Fischel, largely ignored the problem of exclusionary zoning.[22] After 2000, many more urban economists began to show interest. In the first decade of the current century, Edward Glaeser and Joseph Gyourko emerged as leading scholars of the effects of public land use controls. They asserted that localities were in-

20. Seifter, "Countermajoritarian Legislatures" (2021) (describing shortcomings of state legislatures).
21. Fischel, "Rise of the Homevoters" (2017): 13–14 ("the 1970s represented a sharp break with the past"); Ganong and Shoag, "Regional Income Convergence" (2017): 89 ("In 1965, land use was permissive everywhere . . . ").
22. See, e.g., Fischel, *Economics of Zoning Laws* (1985).

flicting a "zoning tax" on housing consumers, and they provided estimates of its severity in different metropolitan areas.[23] Beginning around 2015, several other teams of economists, employing vastly different methodologies, published much-heralded papers estimating the magnitude of exclusionary zoning's national burden.[24] Each team agrees that the costs are monumental. Herkenhoff, Ohanian, and Prescott claim that U.S. labor productivity would be 12.4 percent higher if U.S. states were to move halfway toward Texas's current level of land use regulation.[25] Duranton and Puga estimate that relaxing land use regulations in the three most productive cities to that of the median city would raise average real income by 8.2 percent.[26] Hsieh and Moretti assert that land use regulations reduced U.S. growth by 36 percent between 1964 and 2009.[27] Albouy and Ehrlich estimate the welfare loss at 2.3 percent.[28] Ganong and Shoag conclude that restrictive land use controls have halted the migration of low-skilled households from relatively poor states to relatively wealthy states, thus misallocating the national labor force and increasing inequality.[29]

Economists standardly adopt the premise that the greater production of a commodity--in this case, housing--tends to bring down its price. Because housing markets "filter," the construction of luxury housing may assist those who possibly cannot afford a luxury unit. The households who move into new luxury units vacate their previous dwellings, thereby loosening the supply of housing across the board.[30] Some opponents of densification have contested this filtering theory, but few housing experts find their counterarguments convincing.[31] In general, the way to reduce housing costs is to permit the construction of more dwellings.

23. Glaeser and Gyourko, "Zoning's Steep Price" (2002): 26–28; Glaeser et al., "Manhattan So Expensive?" (2005): 359 (estimating "zoning taxes" on the production of single-family houses in various metropolitan areas).
24. See Schleicher, "Stuck!" (2017b): 102–3 (summarizing various findings).
25. Herkenhoff et al., "Land-Use Restrictions" (2018): 90.
26. Duranton and Puga, "Urban Growth" (2019): 37–38.
27. Hsieh and Moretti, "Spatial Misallocation" (2019).
28. Albouy and Ehrlich, "Cost of Land-Use Restrictions" (2018): 101.
29. Ganong and Shoag, "Regional Income Convergence" (2017).
30. See, e.g., Rosenthal, "Filtering" (2014).
31. See, e.g., Been et al., "Supply Skepticism" (2019); Mast, "New Market-Rate Housing" (2021) (finding production of higher-priced housing tends to free up

Motivations for Exclusionary Zoning

What motivated Greenwich, in 1947, to tighten its zoning requirements? Exclusionary practices have many catalysts. Among the most defensible are environmental considerations. In some instances, land development can endanger the quality of air, water, and habitat. Greenwich's large-lot zoning succeeded in making a drive on the Merritt Parkway more pleasant. The net environmental effects of exclusionary zoning, however, commonly tend to be negative.[32] Denser living is more energy-efficient. Large-lot zoning increases automobile dependence and wastes land through sprawl.[33] Each year between 1955 and 1960, about 15,000 more people migrated from Texas to California than vice versa. By 2006–2015, the net flow between the two states had reversed, to an annual flow of 25,000 in Texas's favor.[34] Policies that shift population from temperate regions of California to sweltering Texas increase the nation's carbon footprint.[35]

Fiscal advantage can be another motivation for exclusion. As Bruce Hamilton and others have shown, exclusionary policies can raise home values.[36] Where schools are funded mostly by local property taxes, measures that prevent the construction of least-cost housing deter entry by those who would not pay their own way. Moreover, when a suburb has few close counterparts, exclusion can enable homeowners to drive up the value of their houses by preventing the construction of competing units. In 1947, when Greenwich greatly tightened its zoning controls, some homeowners may have recognized the advantages of suppressing the construction of competing houses elsewhere in the town. Prospects of gain may tempt a homeowner who is neither a classist nor a racist to support exclusion.

---

lower-cost housing); Li, "New Housing Units" (2020). But cf. Freemark, "Upzoning Chicago" (2020).

32. Boudreaux, "Lotting Large" (2016): 12–28.
33. Fischel, "Too Spread Out?" (1999) (asserting that zoning impedes optimal densification of U.S. suburbs). On the measurement and incidence of sprawl, see Lopez and Hynes, "Sprawl in the 1990s" (2003).
34. U.S. Bureau of the Census, "State-to-State Migration Flows" (2020b).
35. Glaeser and Kahn, "Greenness of Cities" (2010).
36. Hamilton, "Zoning and Property Taxation" (1975).

Classism and racism, of course, may also be present, if commonly beneath the surface. Parents of public-school children might favor a zoning policy that would boost the fraction of college graduates moving into their neighborhood. They might think, not implausibly, that restricting the development of multifamily housing, for example, would increase the relative capabilities of their children's classmates. Residents' devotion to the welfare of their children powerfully influences zoning outcomes. Exclusionary zoning, although hardly the sole cause of residential segregation by social class, certainly aggravates it. A team of economists working with Raj Chetty has found that children under the age of thirteen benefit significantly from growing up in a non-poor neighborhood.[37] A nation that prizes equality of opportunity might give high priority to zoning reform.[38]

Racism, most conspicuously against Blacks, unquestionably was once a central motivator of zoning policies. Today, speakers at zoning hearings are unlikely explicitly to raise issues of race, although this factor may hover unspoken. As the American population has become more racially diverse, this motivation probably is less central than it once was. Racial segregation in U.S. neighborhoods has declined significantly since 1970.[39] Nonetheless, in some contexts, researchers continue to find that racism spurs exclusionary practices.[40]

Most local policymakers, and those who lobby city hall, instinctively favor maintaining things as they are. Cognitive psychologists refer to this as status quo bias. Residents of Greenwich, knowing that the northern two-thirds of the town was undeveloped, were naturally tempted to keep it that way. Local eyes tend to undervalue the benefits of land use change and exaggerate its costs. This is a recurring theme of what is to come.[41]

37. Chetty et al., "Exposure to Better Neighborhoods" (2016).

38. On the benefits and costs involved, see Downs, *Opening Up the Suburbs,* 26–60 (1973).

39. Logan, "Persistence of Segregation" (2013): 162 (acknowledging decline over time in Black-White segregation); Vigdor and Glaeser, "End of Segregated Century" (2012): 2–3.

40. Rolleston, "Restrictive Suburban Zoning" (1987): 19; Trounstine, "Geography of Inequality" (2020).

41. See chapter 7.

The Plan of the Book

Part I is the descriptive heart of this volume. It includes data on the zoning practices of forty-one mostly contiguous localities in Silicon Valley, Greater New Haven, and the northwestern Austin area. All forty-one have a zoning ordinance, including those in Texas, where the City of Houston has famously refused to zone. This material, much of it largely unprecedented, brings to light the reality of local zoning practices.

Chapter 2 offers metrics for measuring the extent of exclusionary zoning. All the metrics are based on the contents of localities' zoning ordinances and zoning maps. The first metric examines the incidence of a locality's large-lot zoning, the technique that Greenwich used in 1947. Of the three regions, Greater New Haven is the clear leader in lotting large. The second metric measures whether a locality permits development of single-family houses on small lots. The suburbs of Greater New Haven, reflecting New England tastes, again are found to be particularly hostile to walkable single-family neighborhoods. The third metric measures localities' willingness to allow the construction of multifamily housing, commonly the most affordable of shelter options. Applying the metrics, chapter 2 reports findings for not only each of the three metropolitan areas as a whole but also specific suburbs within them. A final metric measures how suburbs zone 20- to 40-acre tracts of undeveloped private land. This last metric best confirms what most would expect: Austin localities are far less exclusionary than those in the other two regions.

Chapters 3 through 5 turn to thick descriptions of the three metropolitan areas studied. They treat, in turn, Silicon Valley, Greater New Haven, and Greater Austin. The Silicon Valley chapter reveals the strictness of the local zoning imposed on the region's largest landowner, Stanford University, and identifies the few locations where developers have been able to supply housing to meet pent-up demand. Chapter 4, on the zoning practices of New Haven suburbs, includes a discussion of the supply of water and of sanitary sewers, critical facilities in any developing area. It also addresses efforts to protect open space and a Connecticut statute intended to open the suburbs to denser development. Chapter 5 introduces Greater Austin. It demonstrates that Texas laws that govern the structure of local governments have greatly contributed to the receptiveness of Texas cities and suburbs to dense housing development. The Austin chapter also provides demographic data on trends in the racial composition of the populations of the three metropolitan areas. All three, particularly Silicon Valley, are becoming racially more diverse. Greater New Haven, although less racially segregated than previously, is now the most segregated of the three regions studied.

Part II underscores a basic finding of the research for this book: local politics tends, as it did in Greenwich and Palo Alto's Fairmeadow neighborhood, to freeze the zoning of an established neighborhood of single-family houses. These neighborhoods blanket not only much of suburbia but also many central cities. Before 1910, when zoning first became popular, residential real estate markets, a large component of the American economy, were, if anything, changing too fast. No longer. The problem now is overregulation, not underregulation. The freezing of zoning prevents a market economy from responding to changes in the forces of supply and demand. Frozen zoning prevents homebuilders from offering households new residential options.

Chapter 6 marshals evidence, from the three metros and elsewhere, to demonstrate that local politics tends to freeze zoning classifications. The chapter that follows explores the dynamics of local zoning politics. Political scientists used to ignore land use regulation, but more have begun to address the topic. Chapter 7 asserts that, when a local government is in charge, zoning politics actually tends not to be local, but hyperlocal. When a zoning issue arises in an established neighborhood, local officials tend to defer to the preferences of the residents living closest by. Those neighbors standardly prefer to maintain the status quo. Thus the familiar acronym: NIMBY (Not In My Backyard).

Private covenants, the subject of chapter 8, constrain a landowner's choices among land uses. Covenants saddle a large majority of recently developed land in urban America. Although potentially valuable, covenants threaten to aggravate the freezing of existing land uses. The chapter explores how drafters of covenants, courts, and legislatures could deal with the reality that covenants may become obsolete.

Part III turns to what is to be done. Chapter 9 emphasizes the virtues of applying benefit-cost analysis to assess the quality of zoning practices. Although benefit-cost analysis does not pay heed to some relevant considerations, it remains the most useful tool of policy analysis. For decades, the federal government has applied the technique to assess proposed federal programs. Most commentators on land use controls, including supporters of prevailing zoning practices, implicitly use benefit-cost analysis as their method of assessment. Chapter 9 identifies various benefits and costs that should be included in the analysis, such as environmental effects, and others, such as the promotion of racial segregation, that should not.

The ensuing chapters suggest specific federal and state policies to remedy current local zoning abuses. Chapter 10 asserts that the federal government has only a secondary role. Congress would be wise to increase the funding of housing vouchers, a form of housing assistance far more efficient and equitable than project-based housing assistance. The federal government also should provide grants-in-aid to state agencies established to address local zoning abuses.

Chapter 11 argues that state legislatures are the key to zoning reform. History suggests that a state judiciary can do little without a state legislature's support. A legislature has ample power to correct Herbert Hoover's initial mistake, the one that enabled Greenwich, Connecticut, to zone without considering the effects of its policies on regional housing consumers. A state therefore should selectively preempt local governments' powers to zone. In a state where exclusionary zoning has been a problem, the state should establish an agency dedicated to the goal of reducing local barriers to the construction of least-cost housing. The chapter identifies components of a political coalition that might come together to support this reform.

Chapter 12 concludes by addressing the advantages and disadvantages of a denser urban America. Many urban economists used to regard density as disadvantageous. More recently, they have come to emphasize the benefits that individuals and households obtain from living near one another. I endorse a future America that is both more dynamic and somewhat denser than the current frozen urban landscape.

With the stage set, we plunge into how, in three dramatically different regions, zoning actually works.

PART I

Zoning in Action

2

Measuring a Zoning Ordinance's Exclusionary Effects

Part I empirically examines land use policies in largely contiguous regions of three metropolitan areas. It depicts, in their entirety, the zoning policies of thirty-seven suburbs—fifteen in Silicon Valley, fourteen in Greater New Haven, and eight in Greater Austin. Most of the tabulations also reflect the zoning practices of two large cities and two counties. The aggregate data for Greater Austin include the City of Austin's zoning of the northwestern sector of the city. The aggregate data for Silicon Valley similarly include how the City of San Jose zones two of its neighborhoods, North San Jose and West San Jose, and how San Mateo and Santa Clara counties zone their various unincorporated areas.[1] The lightest portions of figures 3, 5, and 7, found at the outset of chapters 3, 4, and 5, precisely indicate the territories where I examined zoning practices.

An alternative research strategy would have entailed random selection of several dozen suburbs nationwide. Focusing on zoning practices in three specific urban regions, however, has several advantages. It helps reveal, for example, the critical influence of state policies, such as those that govern the incorporation of cities.[2] It also enables deeper inquiry into region-specific issues, such as racial demography and the policies that govern the supply of utility services.

1. Footnotes to the various tables indicate exclusions from coverage.

2. See chapter 5.

Scholars have bemoaned the lack of metrics to quantify the stringency of local zoning restrictions.[3] This chapter proposes five separate metrics and a sixth that aggregates the five. It applies these to the zoning practices of localities in the three metropolitan regions. Each metric attempts to boil down a complex set of local policies to a simple number. The first three metrics measure the presence (or absence) of large-lot single-family zoning, of small-lot single-family zoning, and of zoning to permit multifamily housing. In combination, they do much to reveal a locality's zoning intentions. The fourth and fifth metrics focus on the zoning of *undeveloped* sites. The fourth measures local tolerance of new multifamily housing at those locations. The fifth metric is particularly revelatory. It measures how localities zone privately owned, largely undeveloped, tracts that have an area of twenty to forty acres. As mentioned, the sixth metric aggregates the prior five.[4]

For the first three metrics, the chapter presents results not only for each of the three metros as a whole but also for some localities within them. The metrics enable comparison of zoning practices across space and time. A researcher could use them to generate comparable data for Greater Indianapolis or Greater Tucson. The suburbs in Greater Austin may become less friendly to developers in future decades.[5] The metrics provide an objective test for determining whether this will have occurred.

All of the metrics gauge a locality's land use policies from two of its published documents, its zoning ordinance and zoning map. The ordinance indicates the regulations applicable in each of the various zones, and the map identifies zone locations. All forty-one localities selected

3. See, e.g., Gyourko and Molloy, "Regulation and Housing Supply" (2015): 1294, 1298; Herkenhoff et al., "Land-Use Restrictions" (2018): 90, 92.

4. Another conceivable metric would gauge a locality's tolerance of "missing middle" housing—duplexes, triplexes, and other low-density buildings potentially compatible in scale with nearby single-family houses. See Parolek, *Missing Middle Housing* (2020). On that front, the standouts proved to be East Haven and West Haven, two cities that abut New Haven, Connecticut. See chapter 4.

5. A concern articulated in Harris, "Lone Star Slowdown?" (2018). As this book was going to press in 2021, there were reports of spikes in Austin-area house prices. See Sparber "Selling at Super Premiums" (2021). At yet, the causes and significance of these price boosts are unclear.

for study in the three metros have elected to engage in zoning. Each of the forty-one also posts an online version of both its zoning map and zoning ordinance. The availability of these electronic resources, seldom exploited by researchers, greatly facilitates investigation into zoning practices.[6] I selectively read the texts of all forty-one zoning ordinances, some 10,000 pages in aggregate, and measured the acreage that each locality had placed in its various residential zones. Total research time averaged over eight hours per locality.

I treat the current zoning map and zoning ordinance as sincere expressions of local policy. For those unfamiliar with zoning maps, figure 2 reproduces a portion of a 2021 zoning map of Leander, Texas, one of the Austin suburbs studied.

The presumption that a locality's map and zoning ordinance are sincere is hardly above criticism.[7] A suburb obviously retains authority to amend its zoning map and zoning code (and governing general plan, if it has one). Local zoners indeed might see advantages in adopting a wait-and-see approach.[8] Officials pursuing that strategy would initially impose stringent zoning requirements and later relax them once they had received better information about the details of a proposed development. A wait-and-see strategy might better enable officials to extract benefits from developers, such as design concessions, on-site exactions, and impact fees. Moreover, zoning ordinances increasingly make land use decisions discretionary.[9] A locality may expressly retain, for example, the power to approve or reject a final site plan, subdivision map, or permit for a multifamily project. When this sort of discretion is built-in, zoning policies become harder to divine from published documents.

6. A few legal scholars have made detailed examinations of zoning ordinances. See, e.g., Arnold, "Planning Milagros" (1998): 77–89, and Bronin, "Comprehensive Rezonings" (2019).
7. Most analysts treat localities' announced zoning policies as sincere. See, e.g., Glaeser and Ward, "Evidence from Greater Boston" (2009): 267–68.
8. See National Commission on Urban Problems, *Building the American City* (1968): 206–8. For documentation of the trend toward dealmaking, see Rose, "Planning and Dealing" (1983), and Selmi, "Contract Transformation" (2010) (expressing skepticism about trend's desirability).
9. Schuetz, "Multifamily Housing" (2008): 560–61.

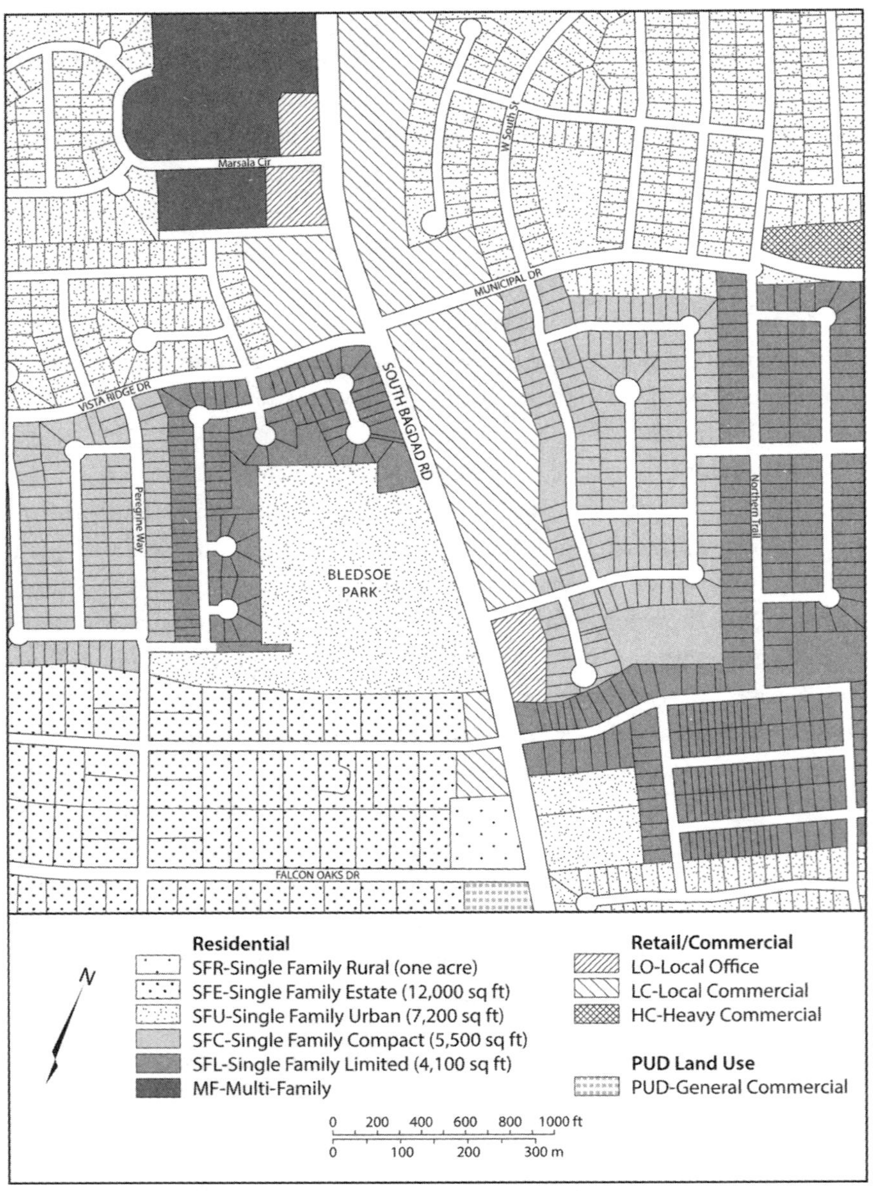

Figure 2. Excerpt from zoning map of Leander, Texas, March 19, 2021. In 2019, Leander's population was 62,608, up from 7,596 in 2000. The entire mapped area is relatively flat. A darker tone indicates a zone where Leander permits greater residential density. In 2017, a multifamily developer built 22 North Apartments in the darkest zone in figure 2. Leander permits the building of single-family detached houses on unusually small lots. The suburb requires a minimum area of only 4,100 square feet

In some instances, the methodology used unquestionably distorts political realities, both by exaggerating restrictions and by understating them. The Connecticut town of Orange, for example, has repeatedly increased its minimum house-lot requirement in the single-family zone that covers most of the town.[10] As a result, many existing Orange houses have become nonconforming uses, because their lots are now too small. Orange lacks both the power and the political inclination to phase out these nonconformities.[11] All of Orange's current zoning rules nonetheless are treated as sincere, which, prospectively, they indeed may be. Conversely, a staunchly pro-growth suburb may have rules on its books that understate its willingness to accommodate denser residential development. Officials in Round Rock, Texas, historically have been likely to approve a developer's application to rezone a large undeveloped tract from the city's basic single-family zone to a denser Planned Unit Development (PUD). The Round Rock data ignore that propensity.

The mass of data assembled in this research indicates, however, that zoning is far less dynamic than generally thought.[12] The thirty-seven suburbs studied set aside 91.0 percent of their residentially zoned land (70.7 percent of their total land area) exclusively for detached single-family use. Of the three metros studied, the suburbs of Greater New Haven were most likely to restrict uses to single-family houses (96 percent of residentially zoned land) and Silicon Valley, the least (85 percent). Even Mountain View, the Silicon Valley suburb with the lowest percentage, restricts 52 percent of its residentially zoned area to detached houses. Once

10. See chapter 2.

11. Connecticut flatly forbids localities from eliminating nonconforming uses. Conn. Gen. Stat. § 8-2 (2019).

12. See also Bronin, "Comprehensive Rezonings" (documenting infrequency of comprehensive rezonings by cities with a population above 100,000).

---

in its SFL zone, where homebuilders in fact have built many houses. By contrast, in the Falcon Oaks subdivision, in the lower left along Falcon Oaks Drive, Leander's SFE zone requires a minimum lot size of 12,000 square feet. In 2014, Leander annexed Falcon Oaks, a lower- to middle-income neighborhood where mobile homes are common and most existing lots have at least that size. Leander's choice of this particular zone illustrates the strong influence of status quo bias on zoning politics. Once large lots, always large lots. (Cartography by Bill Nelson)

houses have actually been built in a single-family neighborhood, local politics, even in Round Rock, Texas, virtually always prohibits a rezoning for greater residential density.[13] Other developed nations are far less likely to treat the detached house as royalty.[14]

The denominator in each of the first three metrics is the locality's total residentially zoned area, that is, the acreage in which one of its various zones would permit some residential use as of right.[15] In the three metros combined, the residentially zoned area constituted 78 percent of total land area, with the remaining zones solely permitting industrial, public-facility, commercial, or other nonresidential use. The most exclusionary suburbs tend to restrict far more than 78 percent of their land area to residential use. The percentage dips, sometimes even below 50 percent, in a suburb that zones large areas exclusively for industry, such as the Silicon Valley cities of Santa Clara and Sunnyvale.

Most contemporary zoning ordinances, including all forty-one studied, are "noncumulative." A noncumulative ordinance bans residential uses in a zone set aside for other uses.[16] Some suburban zones are mixed-use, allowing, for example, commercial use as well as residential. In this study, I treat these as residential zones.

The proffered metrics, despite their potential distortions, in most applications are superior to those that researchers currently employ. The most cited and esteemed is the Wharton Residential Land Use Regulatory Index. In 2008, Joseph Gyourko, Albert Saiz, and Anita Summers

13. See chapter 6.
14. Hirt, *Zoned in the USA* (2014): 6–7, 17–25.
15. Another possible denominator, the entire land area of the locality in question, would have been less revealing. Suppose a suburb was to have zoned exactly half its land exclusively for nonresidential uses and the remaining half solely for single-family detached houses on lots of one acre or more. In calculating the frequency of the one-acre requirement, the denominator used generates a result of 100 percent. If total land area instead had been the denominator, the result would have been 50 percent. Because the goal is to expose exclusionary tendencies, in most contexts 100 percent is the more informative figure.
16. By contrast, the Supreme Court's famous decision in Village of Euclid v. Ambler Realty Co., 272 U.S. 365 (1926), involved a cumulative zoning ordinance. Euclid then permitted, as it no longer does, the erection of houses and apartment buildings in its commercial and industrial zones. See chapter 6.

published the first Wharton Index, and Gyourko is working with another set of co-authors to update the findings (Gyourko et al., 2019).[17] Among the many strengths of the Wharton Index are its national scope, the breadth of its inquiry into barriers to housing production, and its sophistication. Although of unquestioned value, that index has shortcomings. The 2008 questionnaire that the Wharton team used to identify local practices generated a 38 percent response rate, and the authors did not check the accuracy of reports of the localities that replied.[18] No metric for exclusionary zoning is free of shortcomings.

A Primer on Lot Sizes and Neighborhood Grain

Minimum lot-size zoning requirements, especially in the single-family neighborhoods that largely blanket U.S. zoning maps, determine much of the ambiance of an urban area. In 2014, France, hardly a nation averse to regulation, flatly prohibited its municipalities from setting minimum lot sizes for houses.[19] In the United States, by contrast, municipalities invariably impose these regulations. These mandates largely determine the grain and population density of an urban or suburban neighborhood.[20] A larger lot offers greater privacy, gardening opportunities, play space for children, and room for house expansion. But small-lot subdivisions also have advantages. A fine-grained neighborhood typically means more playmates nearby, more visual and social variety, and a higher "walk score."[21]

17. Gyourko et al., "Wharton Index" (2008); Gyourko et al., "New Wharton Index" (2019). See also Kok et al., "Land Use Regulations" (2014): 144 (using as a metric the number of local reviews required prior to final issuance of a building permit).

18. Gyourko (2008): 696 (indicating response rate). In the 2008 Wharton study, 2,649 localities sent in responses. Gyourko et al., "Wharton Index" (2008): 696. In the update, the authors report that responses fell to 2,450 (Gyourko et al., "New Wharton Index" [2019]: 3), but do not indicate the response rate.

19. Code de l'urbanisme, § 123–1-5 (2019), as amended by loi ALUR (2014). This provision also forbids the setting of maximum floor-area-ratios. See Noguellou, "La règle d'urbanisme" (2016).

20. See Lynch, *Good City Form* (1981): 265–68 (elaborating the notion of grain).

21. See Oppenheimer, "It's a Wonderful Block" (2008) (lauding virtues of two blocks in the City of New Haven, where lots are rectangular and about 7,000 sq. ft. in area). On walk scores, see Speck, *Walkable City* (2012): 25–28. All else equal,

It is worth repeating that the thirty-seven suburbs studied restricted 91 percent of their residentially zoned land solely to the construction of single-family detached houses. Of the thirty-seven, the two most zone-happy were Redwood City, California, and Guilford, Connecticut. They both had seven or more distinct single-family zones, each with a different lot-size minimum. Six of the thirty-seven suburbs, by contrast, had only a single single-family zone. Of the six, East Palo Alto, California, required the smallest lot (5,000 square feet) and Orange, Connecticut, the largest (1 ½ acres). An acre comprises 43,560 square feet (0.40 hectare), almost the size of a regulation American football field excluding the end zones. East Palo Alto's 5,000-sq.-ft.-lot requirement thus translates to slightly less than one-eighth of an acre. Using an unpowered lawnmower would be feasible for a 5,000-sq.-ft. lawn but laborious for a 10,000-sq.-ft. lawn. To mow a one-acre lawn, a sit-down power lawnmower is practically a necessity.

Drafters of zoning ordinances typically regard minimum lot-size requirements as the most salient of their zoning controls. Milford, Connecticut, for example, uses *R-5, R-10,* and *R-30* as the names of three of its zones. In Milford's case, the number that follows *R-* refers to the minimum thousands of square feet required for a house-lot within that zone. Other types of zoning controls, such as height limits, parking requirements, and minimum front-yard setbacks, also vary and may significantly affect house designs. In contrast to lot sizes, however, suburbs almost never incorporate these controls into the name of a zone.

Many readers may find it hard to comprehend the meaning of an abstract number of square feet of lot area. To capture the spirit of this research, an inquisitive reader might open Google Earth, an app that provides aerial and street views of neighborhoods worldwide; enter into the search box the name of a locality that contains a familiar single-family neighborhood; and then figure out how to employ the ruler in the upper toolbar to measure the square footage (polygons) of that neighborhood's lots. For many readers, going through this simple exercise would greatly enhance the import of what is to come.

---

home purchasers appear to be willing to pay more to live in a walkable neighborhood. Hamilton and Dourado, "Premium for Walkable Development" (2018). Cf. Couture and Handbury, "Urban Revival in America" (2020) (contending that restaurants and nightlife increasingly draw college graduates to city centers).

Several municipal zoning ordinances in northwestern Greater Austin explicitly refer to 10,000 sq. ft. (0.23 acres) as a "large" lot for a detached house.[22] Census Bureau data support that choice of adjective. In 2019, 33 percent of new single-family houses completed in the United States had a lot area of less than 7,000 sq. ft.; 53 percent, less than 9,000 sq. ft.; and 62 percent less than 11,000 sq. ft.[23] In New England, a bastion of exclusionary zoning, however, the median house-lot of a new detached dwelling is roughly twice what it is nationally.[24]

Cities' choices of the required minimum lot size for a detached single-family house vary widely. The subdivision ordinance of pro-growth Houston, Texas, requires a minimum lot of 3,500 sq. ft., even less than East Palo Alto's 5,000 sq. ft.[25] In the 1950s, Palo Alto's minimum in its basic single-family zone was 6,000 sq. ft.[26] This constraint did not bind Joseph Eichler, then a preeminent builder of tract houses in the Bay Area. Eichler commonly voluntarily chose to provide 7,000- or 8,000-sq.-ft. lots in his many developments in the southern portion of Palo Alto, including Fairmeadow.

22. See City of Austin, Tex., Land Dev. Code, § 25–2-55 (2019); City of Round Rock, Tex., Zoning Code, § 2–14 (2019).
23. U.S. Bureau of the Census, "Characteristics of New Housing" (2020a). In 2019, of the single-family houses "sold," a category that excludes houses that owners built on lots they owned, 64 percent were on lots less than 9,000 sq. ft. in area.
24. Siniavskaia, "New Record Low" (2017) (drawing on census data to estimate a median of 0.4 acre in New England; 0.3 in the Middle Atlantic; and 0.2 nationally).

John Hasse and his co-authors have tallied actual lot sizes in new subdivisions in several counties in New Jersey. They found that house-lots exceeding one acre had constituted 24 percent of the newly developed acreage prior to 1986 but had increased to 46 percent by 1986–2007. Hasse et al., "Monmouth and Somerset Counties" (2011). Hasse attributes this pattern to exclusionary zoning practices, id. at 3, and does not mention site conditions or market demands that might have induced subdividers to create larger lots.

25. Houston, Tex., Code of Ordinances § 42–181(a)(2) (2019) (applicable only to sewered areas of the city). In 1922, New York City permitted the development of Gerritsen Beach in Brooklyn, a subdivision where single-family lot sizes are a remarkable 2,000 sq. ft. Campanella, "Long Before Levittown" (2018).
26. Palo Alto, Cal., Zoning Ordinance § 6.11 (1956) (applicable to R-1 zone). In 2018, a survey of California localities found that the median minimum lot size required in their most mapped single-family zone was a mere 6,000 sq. ft. Terner Center, "Policies Across California" (2018).

In a neighborhood where house-lots are less than 10,000 square feet, as was common in most Eichler developments, local officials commonly compel a subdivider to install sidewalks on both sides of an internal street. In these relatively dense neighborhoods, children can walk to schools and shops. Especially where small lots are rectangular and deep, neighborhoods of 5,000 to 9,000 square-foot lots are heaven for trick-or-treaters. After collecting a handout of goodies, they know that the next stop is only a short amble away.

In the early decades of the twentieth century, developers of several renowned upscale subdivisions, recognizing that some homebuyers prefer spacious lots, voluntarily offered lots of 10,000 square feet or more. This famously occurred, for example, in parts of Shaker Heights, a suburb just east of Cleveland, Ohio, and the Country Club District of Kansas City, Missouri.[27] When lots exceed 10,000 square feet in area, sidewalks, pedestrians, and trick-or-treaters begin to disappear. Where house-lots are 20,000 square feet (one-half acre) or more, dependence on automobiles becomes close to total.

Guilford, the largest New Haven suburb in area, now requires a four-acre minimum house-lot on 61 percent of its residentially zoned territory.[28] Greenwich, Connecticut, also had chosen a four-acre minimum for most of its area north of the Merritt Parkway. A lot this size is twenty times larger than the lots Eichler offered in his subdivisions in south Palo Alto. Fifty miles due north of Silicon Valley lies Napa County, California, site of celebrated vineyards. Napa County currently requires, in the relatively flat areas where most vineyards lie, a minimum house-lot of forty acres. In the hilly regions that comprise most of Napa County, the county insists on a minimum lot size of 160 acres (one-quarter square mile) per house.[29] The thirty-seven suburbs analyzed in this study have an average land area of 18.4 square miles. If subject to Napa County's 160-acre minimum, the average-sized suburb would have room for 74 houses.

27. See respectively Harwood, *Van Sweringen Brothers* (2003): 15–16, and Worley, *J. C. Nichols* (1990).

28. Guilford's minimum actually is 160,000 sq. ft., a bit less than four acres. This book treats a 40,000-sq.-ft. minimum-lot requirement as equivalent to a one-acre requirement (43,560 sq. ft.).

29. Napa County Code of Ordinances § 18.104.010 (2019). Hat-tip to Yume Hoshijima.

Once a locality has specified a particular minimum lot size for a single-family zone, does it ever change it?[30] In Silicon Valley and Greater New Haven, a political ratchet seems to bar any softening of requirements. In portions of Portola Valley, California, where San Mateo County had imposed a one-acre minimum prior to the town's incorporation, the town eventually increased the minimum to 3.5 acres.[31] At the other end of the lot-size spectrum, Palo Alto, California, gradually raised the minimum required in its most-mapped single-family zone from 4,700 sq. ft. in 1928, to 5,000 sq. ft. in 1945, and to 6,000 sq. ft. in 1951. Between 1954 and 1964, eleven of fifteen Connecticut towns increased their minimum house-lot requirements, and none decreased them.[32] The exclusionary New Haven suburbs of Guilford, Orange, and Woodbridge have all jacked up their minimums on three or more occasions, at least tripling their original requirements.[33]

In Greater Austin suburbs, however, this political ratchet seems not to exist. In 1978, for example, Leander, Texas, established a required minimum lot of 12,500 square feet in its primary single-family zone but by 2018 had reduced it to 7,500 square feet. Leander also permits 5,500-sq.-ft. lots in its SF-Compact zone, and, remarkably, 4,100-sq.-ft. lots in its SF-Limited zone. See figure 2. In 2004, Cedar Park, Texas, lowered, from 6,000 to 5,000 square feet, the minimum house-lot requirement in its SF-3 zone, about one-eighth of its residentially zoned land.[34]

30. In 1922, Euclid, Ohio, site of a famous Supreme Court decision, established a minimum of 5,000 sq. ft. for its U1 single-family zone, and it has stuck with that requirement ever since. See chapter 6.

31. Davis, "Portola Valley" (1982): 46–47 and n.27.

32. American Society of Planning Officials, *Connecticut Planning Legislation* (1967): 197 tbl. 12.

33. In the zone that governs most of its northern section, Guilford increased its required minimum house-lot from 10,000 sq. ft. in 1953 to 40,000 in 1955, 60,000 in 1969, and 160,000 in 1978. Orange's "Residence" zone blankets most of the town. For that zone, Orange imposed a minimum of 20,000 sq. ft. in 1938, 30,000 in 1951, 40,000 in 1959, and 60,000 in 2004. The minimum in Woodbridge's nearly ubiquitous A zone was 20,000 sq. ft. in 1932, 60,000 in 1938, and 65,000 in 1966. In 2001, Woodbridge's minimum became two acres in the public watershed areas that constitute a majority of the zone.

34. Cedar Park, Tex., 2004 Code of Ordinances, § 11.03.001. In 1977, when Cedar Park first adopted zoning, it had required a minimum lot of 7,000 sq. ft. for a single-family house.

Table 1. Metric One: Percentage of Residentially Zoned Land Requiring a Lot-Size Above a Specified Minimum

	≥ ½ *acre*	≥ *1 acre*	≥ *1 ½ acres*	≥ *2 acres*
Silicon Valley	52.8%	51.0%	36.1%	36.1%
Greater New Haven	76.1%	74.0%	47.7%	32.0%
Northwest Austin Area	32.3%	32.1%	13.7%	13.7%

Metric One: The Incidence of Large-Lot Zoning

A simple metric for measuring exclusionary zoning is the percentage of residentially zoned land that a locality places in zones that require house-lots greater than, or equal to, a particular size. A focal choice is a minimum lot of one acre, a size that usually obviates the presence of sidewalks and trick-or-treaters. Table 1 presents, for the three metropolitan areas in the aggregate, zoning data not only for a minimum of one acre but also for other minimums.[35]

The New Haven area, where 74.0 percent of the residentially zoned land in the suburbs is restricted to single-family detached houses on lots of one acre or more, leads the three metros in large-lot zoning. Municipalities in the Austin area are, by this measure, the least prone to exclude. No surprise there. Silicon Valley's results are middling. The huge lot-size requirements that San Mateo and Santa Clara counties impose in Silicon Valley's foothill and mountain areas greatly affect that region's figures.[36]

Many of the forty-one localities authorize cluster development.[37] In a suburb that does, a subdivider who has dedicated land as open space is entitled to credit that acreage toward satisfaction of minimum house-lot requirements. Clustering thus greatly expands design options and helps conserve wetlands and forests. Clustering, however, commonly does little

35. A regression analysis has found that large-lot requirements are associated with higher housing prices. Glaeser et al., "Eastern Massachusetts" (2006): 23. This outstanding study, in several dimensions more ambitious than this one, was pioneering in many respects. See Appendix.

36. See chapter 3.

37. Whyte, *Cluster Development* (1964) inspired this innovation. Many Greater Boston suburbs have adopted cluster zoning. Glaeser and Ward, "Evidence from Greater Boston" (2009): 270, fig. 3.

Table 2. Municipalities with the Highest, Median, and Lowest Percentages of One-Acre Minimum House-Lot Zoning in Their Residential Zones

	Highest percentage	*Median percentage*	*Lowest percentage*
Silicon Valley*	Atherton (100%), Los Altos Hills (100%) [most acres: Portola Valley]	Cupertino (24%)	Five cities with 0%, including Menlo Park and Sunnyvale
Greater New Haven	Bethany (100%) [most acres: Guilford]	Hamden (61%)	West Haven (0%)
Northwest Austin Area*	West Lake Hills (99%) [most acres: Georgetown]	Leander (38%)	Rollingwood (0%)

* Excludes unincorporated areas and neighborhoods in cities of San Jose and Austin.

to mitigate the wastefulness of large-lot minimums. Unless accompanied by a density bonus, a cluster design has little or no effect on average population density.

Table 2 indicates variations in the zoning practices of individual suburbs in the three metropolitan areas. Each metro has at least one suburb that places over 99 percent of its residentially zoned land in ≥1-acre zones, and each also has one or more that do not place any in that category. Table 2 also indicates for each metro, in brackets, the municipality with the greatest amount of acreage in ≥1-acre zones.

Of the thirty-seven municipalities studied, Atherton, California, first made efforts to exclude. In 1928, it mandated, on either side of a house, a minimum setback of forty feet, a huge distance.[38] By 2020, Atherton's zip code contained the highest-priced houses in the United States.[39] Woodbridge, Connecticut, New Haven's wealthiest suburb, employed a different regulatory technique, lotting large.[40] In 1932, Woodbridge required, virtually throughout town, a house-lot of 20,000 square feet or more, and, in 1938, it upped that requirement to 60,000 square feet.[41] Large lot requirements quickly became a standard means of suburban exclusion.[42]

38. Atherton, Cal., Ord. No. 87, § 2(c) (Dec. 3, 1928).
39. PropertyShark, "Most Expensive Zip Codes" (2020).
40. Boudreaux invented this verb in "Lotting Large" (2016).
41. Woodbridge, Conn., Zoning Ordinance of Dec. 24, 1932; Woodbridge, Conn., Zoning Ordinance of Aug. 4, 1938.
42. See, e.g., Flora Realty & Inv. Co. v. City of Ladue, 246 S.W.2d 771 (Mo. 1952)

In 1938, Orange, Connecticut, followed Woodbridge's lead and imposed a 20,000-sq.-ft. minimum.[43] Atherton's leaders also eventually recognized the advantages of lotting large. In 1947, Atherton imposed, town-wide, the requirement of a one-acre minimum house-lot, a signature policy that it has not altered since.[44] West Lake Hills, Texas, incorporated in 1953, has long been the king of one-acre zoning in the Austin suburbs.

Metric Two: Allowing Detached Houses on Small Lots

Exclusionary zoning is popularly thought to be synonymous with requirements for multi-acre single-family lots. This is not correct. Another finding of this study is the sharp variation in suburbs' willingness to allow single-family detached houses on lots ranging from 5,000 to 8,000 square feet, that is, Eichler-grained subdivisions.[45] A suburb requiring 15,000-sq.-ft. lots in all of its single-family neighborhoods might be able to exclude homebuyers of modest income as successfully as a suburb requiring five-acre lots. This is the exact zoning strategy of Rollingwood, Texas, Greater Austin's wealthiest suburb.[46] Larger house-lots tend to command higher prices, but, beyond 8,000 square feet or so, less and less at the margin.[47]

Metric Two identifies a locality's tolerance of relatively small lots for detached houses. The denominator, as usual, is the total acreage in zones

---

(involving 3-acre minimum enacted in 1934); Honeck v. County of Cook, 146 N.E.2d 35 (Ill. 1957) (upholding 5-acre minimum imposed in 1940); Fischer v. Bedminster Tp., 93 A.2d 378 (N.J. 1952) (sustaining 5-acre minimum adopted in 1946).

43. Orange, Conn., Zoning Ordinance of Jan. 12, 1938.

44. Atherton, Cal., Ord. No. 151 (Jan. 18, 1947), codified at Atherton, Cal. Mun. Code, §§ 17.32.020, 17.33.020 (2020).

45. "By changing only a small percentage of Connecticut's land now zoned for a minimum lot size of 20,000 square feet or more, to permit 5,000-square-foot single-family dwellings and medium-low density apartments, the rezoned land alone would house a 100 percent increase in the State's population." American Society of Planning Officials, *Connecticut Planning Legislation* (1967): 32.

46. See chapter 5.

47. See Glaeser and Gyourko, "Zoning's Steep Price" (2002): 26–28; White, "Subdivision Costs" (1988): 380 (providing a graph showing the falloff in value as lot size increases); see also Fischel, *Homevoter Hypothesis* (2001): 232.

Table 3. Metric Two: Percentage of Residentially Zoned Land Permitting House-Lots Below a Specified Minimum

	≤ *6,000 sq. ft.*	≤ *8,000 sq. ft.*	≤ *10,000 sq. ft.*
Silicon Valley	20.5%	24.9%	32.3%
Greater New Haven	0.2%	1.0%	3.6%
Northwest Austin Area	24.8%	39.5%	49.0%

that allow some residential use as of right. The numerator is the zoned acreage that would permit house-lots as small as the stated size. Table 3 presents gross findings for the three metros for three relatively modest minimums: 6,000, 8,000, and 10,000 square feet.

Table 3 identifies a stunning outlier. New Haven suburbs, honoring a distaste widely shared in New England, are the harshest by far on would-be developers of subdivisions of modestly sized house-lots.[48] Milford, Connecticut, allows 15 percent of its residentially zoned territory to be developed into Eichler-sized 8,000-sq.-ft. lots, the only New Haven suburb above 2 percent. For Cedar Park, Texas, Round Rock, Texas, and East Palo Alto, California, the equivalent figure is over 80 percent, and for the California cities of Santa Clara and Sunnyvale, around 65 percent.

Table 4 helps unpack the gross data presented in Table 3. It reports only on suburbs' tolerances of houses on 8,000-sq.-ft. lots. Most localities in Silicon Valley and Greater Austin allow house-lots of that size in some zones, but only three of the fourteen New Haven suburbs do.

Metric Three: Permitting Multifamily Housing as of Right

In a canonical 1926 decision, *Village of Euclid v. Ambler Realty Co.*, the United States Supreme Court sustained the federal constitutionality of selective local prohibitions on the construction of multifamily

48. On the exceptionalism of New England, see Glaeser and Ward, "Evidence from Greater Boston" (2009): 269 (reporting that 57 percent of Boston suburbs have an average minimum house-lot requirement of 35,000 sq. ft. or greater); Gyourko et al., "Wharton Index" (2008): 695 (ranking New England states among the most exclusionary); Siniavskaia, "New Record Low" (2017).

Table 4. Percentage of Residentially Zoned Land Permitting ≤ 8,000-Sq.-Ft. House-Lots

	Highest percentage	*Median percentage*	*Lowest percentage*
Silicon Valley*	East Palo Alto (81.6%) [most acres: Sunnyvale]	Palo Alto (36.1%)	Four tied at 0%: Atherton, Los Altos, Los Altos Hills, Woodside
Greater New Haven	Milford (14.7%) [most acres: Milford]	0%. Only 3 of the 14 suburbs have a single-family zone allowing 8,000-sq.-ft. house-lots.	Eleven tied at 0%.
Northwest Austin Area*	Round Rock (79.5%) [most acres: Georgetown]	Leander (24.9%)	Three tied at 0%: Bee Cave, Rollingwood, West Lake Hills

* Excludes unincorporated areas and neighborhoods in the cities of San Jose and Austin.

buildings.[49] Some state supreme courts immediately indicated their discomfort with this holding.[50] Particularly condemning was Judge Offutt's dissenting opinion in a Maryland case involving a Baltimore zone that had prohibited the construction of row houses: "The ordinance is nothing more nor less than a vast, comprehensive, and complete plan or scheme of segregation, under which the population of the city in respect to their dwelling places are graded and classified according to their means. . . . Heretofore that result has been possible only by contract, by incorporating restrictions in deeds. . . . "[51]

Denser residential developments do tend to be more affordable. Metric Three tallies, for the various localities, the percentage of residentially zoned land on which a developer, as of right, could build mul-

49. 272 U.S. 365 (1926); see also Miller v. Board of Public Works, 234 P. 381 (Cal. 1925).

50. See, e.g., Altschuler v. Scott, 137 A. 883 (N.J. 1927) (locality that allowed multifamily housing in some zones could not constitutionally prohibit them in other zones).

51. R. B. Constr. Co. v. Jackson, 137 A. 278, 286 (Md. 1927) (Offutt, J., dissenting).

Table 5. Metric Three: Percentage of Residentially Zoned Land Permitting Multifamily Use

Silicon Valley	10.0%
Greater New Haven	1.4%
Northwest Austin Area	6.0%

tifamily housing at a density of at least eight gross dwelling units per acre.[52] Examples of these potentially lower-cost structures are apartment buildings, townhouses with party walls, and parks for mobile homes ("manufactured housing" is the contemporary euphemism). *Multifamily housing,* for current purposes, refers to any of these denser forms of development, provided the zoning ordinance permits at least eight gross units per acre.[53] In all three metros, localities' zoning ordinances commonly state that a would-be developer of a multifamily project has to apply for and receive a discretionary permit. This study assumes, however, that if a locality had gone so far as to name its zone "multifamily," "apartments," "townhouse," "mobile home," or the like, it would grant the permit.

Table 5 indicates the percentage of residentially zoned land where local authorities in the three metros permit multifamily use, so defined. As table 5 implies, residential development in Silicon Valley is more than two times denser than that in Greater New Haven and northwest Greater Austin.[54] In 2010, Silicon Valley had a population density of 3,700 per square mile. Austin's northwestern sector, as defined in this study, averaged 1,600, and the New Haven suburbs averaged 1,300. Table 5 reveals that New Haven suburbs are especially hostile to multifamily housing.

To provide more texture, table 6 indicates variations in municipal policies governing the building of multifamily housing. This table confirms that Silicon Valley suburbs are, at least superficially, the most tolerant of apartment buildings.

52. On the exclusion of multifamily housing, see Babcock and Bosselman (1963); Schuetz, "Rental Housing" (2009); Schuetz, "Multifamily Housing" (2008).

53. Most high-rise apartment buildings have a density far greater than eight dwelling units per gross acre. I chose my breakpoint to help reveal the hostility of most suburbs to even low-density multifamily housing.

54. Metropolitan areas in California are among the densest in the United States. Cox, "California's Dense Suburbs" (2018).

Table 6. Municipalities with the Highest, Median, and Lowest Percentages of Multifamily Zoning in Their Residentially Zoned Area

	Highest percentage	*Median percentage*	*Lowest percentage*
Silicon Valley*	Mountain View (41.4%) [most acres: Sunnyvale]	Palo Alto (8.4%)	Tied at 0%: Atherton, Los Altos Hills, Woodside
Greater New Haven	Meriden (8.9%) [most acres: Meriden]	North Haven (1.0%)	Tied at 0%: Bethany, Branford, Madison, North Branford, Orange
Northwest Austin Area*	Bee Cave (12.8%) [most acres: Cedar Park]	Leander (4.1%)	Tied at 0%: Rollingwood, West Lake Hills

* Excludes unincorporated areas and neighborhoods in cities of San Jose and Austin.

Metrics Four and Five: Zoning Undeveloped Land

The fourth and fifth metrics measure the zoning policies that localities apply to undeveloped land. Both require a researcher to make a judgment about the extent of a particular parcel's development. For both Metrics Four and Five, the aerial photographs available in Google Earth were used to decide the matter.[55] The decision rule, at times difficult to apply, was whether buildings, asphalt, or intensive landscaping covered at least 50 percent of the area of the parcel. If so, it was deemed "developed" and, if not, "undeveloped." The payoff to this extra work is deeper insight into the realities of zoning policies. To ease comparison of localities' zoning practices on developed and undeveloped multifamily land, the first column in table 7 repeats data reported in table 5.

Undeveloped Parcels in Areas Zoned for Multifamily Use

Although localities in Silicon Valley show the greatest willingness to zone for multifamily development, nearly all of the lands that they have zoned in this fashion already have multifamily structures on them. The most notable finding in table 7 is that undeveloped multifamily land is

55. An alternative, not used for this study, would be the National Land Cover Database (2016).

Table 7. Metric Four: Percentage of Residentially Zoned Land Permitting Multifamily Use

	Both developed and undeveloped sites	*Undeveloped sites only*
Silicon Valley	10.0%	0.2%
Greater New Haven	1.4%	0.3%
Northwest Austin Area	6.0%	2.2%

roughly ten times more commonly available in the northwestern Austin sector than in the other two metros.

The municipalities with the highest percentages of undeveloped residential land currently zoned for multifamily use were, in the three metros, East Palo Alto, California (2.8 percent); Meriden, Connecticut (2.7 percent), and Bee Cave, Texas (7.3 percent). A multifamily housing developer looking for a permissibly zoned and undeveloped site would find fewer acres in the entire Silicon Valley than in any one of four suburbs northwest of Austin: Cedar Park, Georgetown, Leander, and Round Rock.

Zoning Large Undeveloped Tracts of Land

In a developed neighborhood of detached houses, local politics virtually freezes existing single-family zoning.[56] When a largish tract of land is mostly undeveloped, by contrast, zoning officials have greater political freedom. Table 7 reveals how localities in the three metros zone a tract of land that satisfies all of the following four criteria: (1) it is mostly undeveloped; (2) it is zoned to permit residential use as of right; (3) it has an area of between 20 and 40 acres; and (4) it is owned privately, but not by a nonprofit. The owner of a tract meeting these four criteria might not have developed it for good reason, of course. From a supply-side perspective, it might disproportionately contain steep hillsides, ledge, and wetlands.[57] On the demand side, it might be remote from utility services and employment opportunities.

56. See Part II.

57. A slope in excess of 15 percent typically makes a tract undevelopable. Saiz, "Geographic Determinants" (2010): 1256.

Table 8. Metric Five: Zoning of Privately Owned, Residentially Zoned, and Mostly Undeveloped Tracts of 20–40 Acres

	Silicon Valley	*Greater New Haven*	*Northwest Austin Area*
Number of qualifying tracts	57	242	123
Zoned for house-lots of at least one acre	96.5%	90.9%	41.5%
Zoned multifamily or for house-lots ≤ 8,000 sq. ft.	3.5%	0.4%	50.4%
Zoned multifamily	1.8%	0.4%	17.1%

Tracts that satisfy all four criteria are present in only four of the fifteen Silicon Valley suburbs. In that metro, 81 percent of these largish, privately owned, and undeveloped tracts lie high in the upper-foothill and mountain areas of Portola Valley, Woodside, and unincorporated Santa Clara County. None of those localities permits, in these locations, a house-lot of less than five acres.

The fourteen suburbs in the long-settled New Haven area have far more undeveloped private land. On average, they have seventeen of these privately owned, residentially zoned, and undeveloped tracts. The New Haven suburbs require a house-lot of at least one acre on 90.9 percent of these 20- to 40-acre undeveloped tracts (see table 8). That figure far exceeds 74.0 percent, the overall large-lot proclivity of New Haven suburbs (see table 1). Having fired the first barrel of the exclusionary shotgun, New Haven suburbs also fire the second. They permit house-lots of 8,000 square feet or less on only 0.4 percent of these largish private tracts.

The data in table 8 perhaps best demonstrate the relatively pro-growth policies of municipalities in Austin's northwestern sector. Of their privately owned, undeveloped parcels of twenty to forty acres, they zone 33.3 percent to permit subdivisions of house-lots no larger than 8,000 square feet and an additional 17.1 percent to permit multifamily construction. This combined percentage of 50.4 percent is roughly ten times the combined percentage for Silicon Valley and one hundred times that for Greater New Haven. Georgetown, Texas, is the oldest and least pro-development of the four suburbs studied in Williamson County, north of

Austin. Yet Georgetown plainly favors walkable single-family neighborhoods. It authorizes the subdivision of 35 percent of its 48 largish, undeveloped private tracts into house-lots as small as 5,500 square feet.

Of the 299 qualifying 20- to 40-acre tracts in Silicon Valley and Greater New Haven, three are zoned to permit the construction of multifamily housing, two in North San Jose, California, and one in Hamden, Connecticut. Austin localities, by contrast, are particularly prone to authorize multifamily development on largish undeveloped private tracts. They authorize multifamily use on 17 percent of them, a percentage almost triple of what they allow on their residentially zoned land in general.[58] In Williamson County, Texas, the suburbs of Cedar Park, Leander, and Round Rock each contain four or more of these large, densely developable, but currently underdeveloped, tracts.

Metric Six: Aggregating the Five Metrics

The five metrics just introduced can be combined in numerous ways. My method of aggregation gives equal weight to each of the five metrics presented: the percentage of residentially zoned land requiring house-lots of at least 40,000 square feet (just shy of one acre); the incidence of zoning permitting 8,000-sq.-ft. lots (or of even higher residential density); the acreage zoned for multifamily development; the availability of undeveloped multifamily land; and the zoning of residentially zoned, undeveloped, private parcels of twenty to forty acres. For each of the five metrics, I ranked the thirty-seven suburbs from most exclusionary to the least exclusionary. A suburb's aggregate metric is the average of its rankings.[59] Table 9 presents results for each of the thirty-seven suburbs examined.

This system of aggregation, one of many possible, identified two Silicon Valley suburbs, Atherton and Los Altos Hills, as the most exclusionary of

58. See table 5 above, indicating a northwest Austin percentage of 6.0 percent.

59. Eleven Silicon Valley suburbs and three in Austin lack undeveloped tracts of 20 to 40 acres. In these instances, I divided the rankings on the other metrics by four, not five. Another approach, more time-consuming but arguably more accurate, would have averaged a suburb's standard deviation on the first five metrics.

Table 9. How the Thirty-Seven Suburbs Rank on the Various Metrics

	Metric 1: residential zoned land requiring ≥40,000-sq.-ft. house-lot	*Metric 2: residential zoned land allowing lot of ≤8,000 sq. ft. or denser*	*Metric 3: zoned multifamily ≥8 dwelling units per acre*	*Metric 4: vacant land in multifamily zones*	*Metric 5: median zone, private, undeveloped tract of 20-40 acres*	*Metric 6: average rank on the five metrics*
Silicon Valley						
Atherton	100%	0%	0%	0%	-	1.5
Campbell	0%	88.7%	21.9%	1.0%	-	36
City Santa Clara	0.1%	99.9%	26.3%	0.8%	-	32
Cupertino	23.5%	60.8%	7.4%	0.1%	3 acres	20
East Palo Alto	0%	99.9%	15.1%	2.8%	-	37
Los Altos	0%	2.6%	2.3%	0%	-	16
Los Altos Hills	100%	0%	0%	0%	-	1.5
Menlo Park	0%	54.3%	21.4%	0.8%	-	30
Mountain View	1.5%	85.2%	41.4%	1.0%	-	33
Palo Alto	51.5%	46.1%	8.4%	0.02%	-	21
Portola Valley	96.7%	1.1%	0.05%	0.03%	7.5 acres	7.5
Redwood City	0.03%	87.1%	25.2%	0.2%	-	28
Saratoga	56.4%	1.1%	1.1%	0.04%	2 acres	13.5
Sunnyvale	0%	99.9%	28.4%	0.3%	-	35
Woodside	97.3%	0%	0%	0%	5 acres	4

Greater New Haven						
Bethany	100%	0%	0%	0%	65,000 sq. ft.	5
Branford	44.7%	10.1%	3.0%	0%	20,000 sq. ft.	17
East Haven	23.2%	44.1%	3.2%	0%	40,000 sq. ft.	18
Guilford	92.7%	1.7%	0.07%	0.03%	160,000 sq. ft.	9
Hamden	60.8%	6.3%	3.0%	0.9%	40,000 sq. ft.	19
Madison	99.8%	0.2%	0.1%	0%	80,000 sq. ft.	7.5
Meriden	35.2%	16.0%	6.7%	1.0%	40,000 sq. ft.	24
Milford	20.2%	23.4%	4.6%	0.5%	1 acre	23
North Branford	98.5%	1.3%	0%	0%	40,000 sq. ft.	10
North Haven	59.5%	1.4%	1.0%	0.1%	40,000 sq. ft.	15
Orange	99.6%	0.2%	0%	0%	60,000 sq. ft.	6
Wallingford	63.7%	3.3%	1.0%	0.1%	120,000 sq. ft.	13.5
West Haven	0%	31.8%	7.2%	1.3%	20,000 sq. ft.	29
Woodbridge	97.8%	0.7%	0.5%	0.2%	2 acres	12
Northwest Austin Area						
Bee Cave	47.9%	12.8%	12.8%	7.3%	-	26
Cedar Park	4.2%	81.4%	10.2%	5.0%	5,000 sq. ft.	34
Georgetown	47.9%	52.0%	2.8%	1.7%	2 acres	22
Lakeway	2.6%	28.5%	1.5%	0.7%	10,000 sq. ft.	25
Leander	38.4%	29.2%	4.1%	3.5%	9,000 sq. ft.	27
Rollingwood	0%	0%	0%	0%	-	11
Round Rock	7.5%	89.1%	6.8%	2.0%	5,500 sq. ft.	31
West Lake Hills	98.8%	0%	0%	0%	-	3

the thirty-seven. Silicon Valley also contains the three least exclusionary municipalities. In order, they are East Palo Alto, Campbell, and Sunnyvale. East Palo Alto requires a house-lot of only 5,000 square feet, while Atherton and Los Altos Hills uniformly require one acre, more than eight times larger. East Palo Alto, however, is hardly a pushover for developers. East Palo Alto is firmly opposed to the densification of its existing single-family neighborhoods.[60] In both suburbs and central cities, NIMBYism arises almost everywhere.

The aggregate rankings present few surprises to those who have perused the prior tables. Five of the eight Austin suburbs rank in the bottom third of exclusionary bent, as do seven of the fifteen in Silicon Valley. Of the fourteen New Haven suburbs, only West Haven falls in the bottom third, and Bethany ranks as the most exclusionary.

But enough, for a time, of tables. The next three chapters provide verbal descriptions of the geography, governance, racial demography, and zoning history of the three metropolitan areas.

60. See chapter 6.

3

Silicon Valley: Slamming the Door on Growth

The zoning histories of the three regions differ. As early as the 1930s, some New Haven suburbs were committed to exclusion, and, by the end of the 1950s, a majority were. Most suburbs northwest of Austin, by contrast, continue to have policies that affirmatively favor housing development. The history of zoning in Silicon Valley has been more volatile. During the postwar period, many Silicon Valley suburbs were pro-development. Between roughly 1965 and 1975, however, most of them withdrew their welcome mats.

This shift had two main causes. The first was the pronounced drop in the undeveloped but readily buildable acreage in Silicon Valley. Albert Saiz has provided estimates of geographic constraints on housing supply in the ninety-five most populous U.S. metros. He ranks San Jose the ninth most geographically constrained, New Haven-Bridgeport-Stamford the seventeenth, and Austin-San Marcos the eighty-fifth.[1] During the 1950s and 1960s, the paucity of buildable land in Silicon Valley did not much matter. Joseph Eichler and other homebuilders then were able to transform much of the region from agricultural fields into neighborhoods of single-family detached houses. As elsewhere in the United States, suburban homebuilding transformed the politics of local zoning. Homeowners in the new neighborhoods came passionately to oppose denser development near

1. Saiz, "Geographic Determinants" (2010): 1258–59.

their residences.[2] Their NIMBYism combined with Silicon Valley's inherent geographic constraints to pinch the supply of building sites.

The second reason for Silicon Valley's shift toward antidevelopment policies was the advent of the environmental movement. This cause was particularly fervent in the Bay Area. Stanford graduates Denis Hayes and Pete McCloskey, the latter a local congressman, were key organizers of Earth Day 1970, an event that helped trigger a nationwide surge of environmentalism.[3] Responding to this shift in voters' priorities, California legislators enacted several measures that strengthened the legal toolkits of antidevelopment forces. The most important was the California Environmental Quality Act of 1970 (CEQA).[4] Jennifer Hernandez asserts that "The top CEQA lawsuit targets [became] infill housing and local land use plans to increase housing densities and promote transit."[5] A second significant legal hurdle was the California requirement that the zoning ordinance of a general law city conform to its comprehensive plan.[6] Attorneys for antidevelopment interests became adept at wielding these barriers to building. As early as the 1970s, Bernard Frieden found that proposed housing developments in the Bay Area increasingly were encountering fervent opposition, whatever their location.[7]

Between 1965 and 1975, many of Silicon Valley's local governments also turned antidevelopment. Representative was the rise of the Residentialists in Palo Alto, the epicenter of Silicon Valley and one of its relatively upscale suburbs.[8] Politicians even in suburbs that had long been havens of the less wealthy also cooled on supporting housing development. In

2. See chapter 6.
3. Rome, *Genius of Earth Day* (2013). On the influence of the flowering of environmentalism on the growth of NIMBYist sentiments, see Fischel, *Zoning Rules!* (2015): 203–5. The history of zoning in Silicon Valley might be Fischel's Exhibit A. For a review of causes of the rise of opposition to growth, see Altshuler et al., *Regulation for Revenue* (1993): 19–33.
4. Cal. Pub. Resources Code §§ 21000–21154 (2016).
5. Hernandez, "CEQA Lawsuits" (2018): 23.
6. Cal. Gov't Code §§ 65860(a) (2009). On the effects of both statutes, see Ellickson, "San Francisco Peninsula" (1982b): 14–15.
7. Frieden, *Environmental Protection Hustle* (1979): 9, 120–21.
8. On the history of Palo Alto land use policies, see Coyle, "Far Cry from *Euclid*" (1982) (decrying Palo Alto's exclusionary turn).

the 1970s, Mountain View drastically scaled back its plans to develop the North Bayshore.[9] By 1975, Redwood City had committed itself to barring construction of multifamily housing in single-family neighborhoods.[10]

Between 1965 and 1975, members of the California state judiciary similarly shifted course. Prior to 1967, California judges had tended to defer to a locality's zoning choices, whether pro- or anti-development. After 1967, however, the California Supreme Court began to side with the anti-development party "as if nothing else in a case mattered."[11] This change in judicial policy, coupled with legislative changes at the state and local levels, helped stifle new housing supply. When demand by well-paid tech workers to live in Silicon Valley surged, housing prices soared.

Introduction to Silicon Valley

Silicon Valley imperfectly describes the region that bears that name.[12] *Silicon Slope* would be a more accurate designation for the territory chosen for study, the lightest portion of figure 3. This territory forms an incline that ascends southwesterly, over the course of eight to twelve miles, from the San Francisco Bay to the 2,000-foot-high ridge of the Santa Cruz Mountains. Along the ridge's crest runs Skyline Boulevard, the western border of the region examined. The local governments in the area include fifteen municipalities, the City of San Jose (two of whose neighborhoods are included), and San Mateo and Santa Clara counties, which both zone various unincorporated areas.

9. Ramniceanu, "Mountain View" (1982): 54, 58–61. In the late 2010s, the city would authorize a huge Google residential complex at a North Bayshore site.
10. Cook, "Redwood City" (1982): 76–77. The authors of the essays cited in the last three footnotes wrote an initial draft for a seminar I taught at Stanford Law School in 1981. In 1982, the *Stanford Environmental Law Annual* published the collection.
11. DiMento et al., "California Supreme Court" (1980): 868. Cf. Ybarra v. Town of Los Altos Hills, 503 F.2d 250 (9th Cir. 1974) (rebuffing Equal Protection Clause challenge to large-lot zoning policy).
12. In 1971, journalist Don Hoefler, a writer for *Electronic News,* first coined *Silicon Valley.* He probably intended *valley* to refer to the larger area between the Santa Cruz Mountains on the west and the Diablo Range, located east of San Francisco Bay.

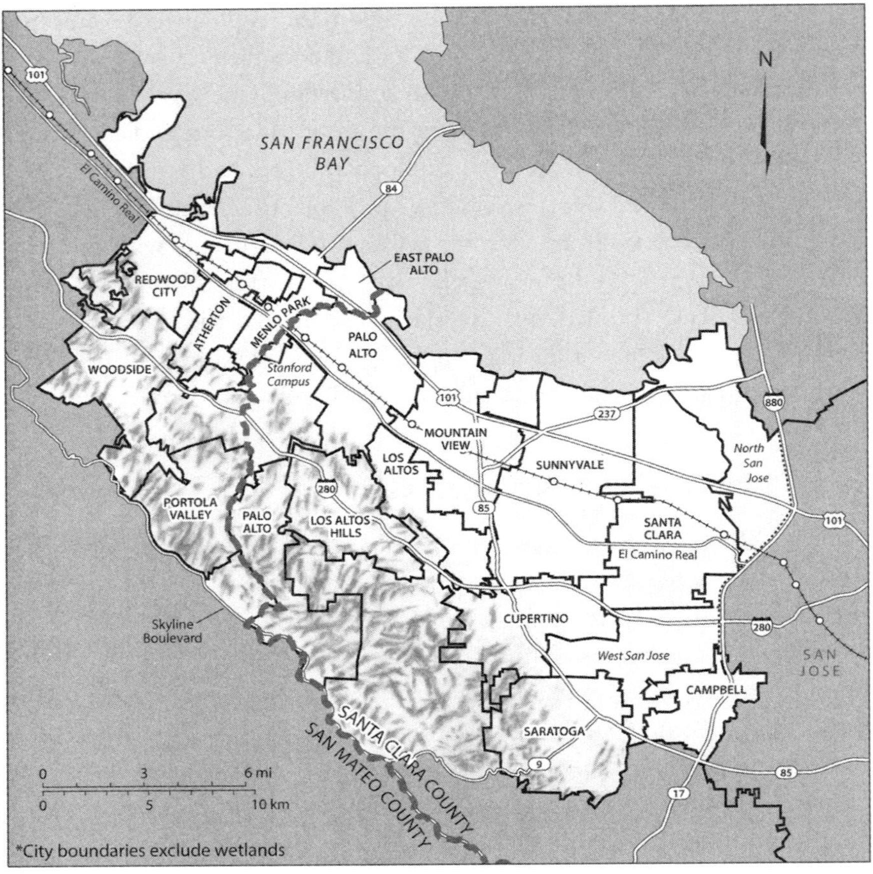

Figure 3. Silicon Valley (Cartography by Bill Nelson)

As figure 3 indicates, the Silicon Slope in fact rises not to the west, but to the southwest. The region's residents understandably perceive that San Francisco Bay lies to their east, although it actually lies northeast of most of Silicon Valley. The erroneous impression that the Bay is easterly gives rise to the conception that the mountains are to the west. This distortion of geography results in oddities, such as the name East Palo Alto, a city located due north of downtown Palo Alto. Here we follow local usage and treat the slope as rising to the west.

The lands within this sloped terrain lie in four bands, largely parallel. Each of the four warrants a shorthand. The band furthest east, usually the narrowest, is the *Bayshore*. Much of it consists of formerly filled tidal mud flats and salt marshes. Figure 3 shows the Bayshore Expressway (U.S. 101), the highway that serves as the Bayshore's western border. Next to the west lies the band of *Plains,* roughly three miles in width in the north, but, like the Bayshore, widening toward the south. This is the most densely settled portion of Silicon Valley. Through the heart of the Plains runs El Camino Real, the area's oldest road and now predominantly a commercial strip. Further to the west lie the *Foothills.* The approximate boundary that separates the Plains from the Foothills is the aptly named Foothill Expressway, two of whose northern extensions are Junipero Serra Boulevard and Alameda de las Pulgas. Figure 4, presented later in this chapter, shows portions of these thoroughfares. In the part of Silicon Valley that extends north from Cupertino, the scenic Junipero Serra Freeway (I-280) roughly bisects the Foothills band. Near that freeway runs the San Andreas Fault, whose presence understandably has affected building designs in the region. The last of the four bands is the *Mountains,* the generally steep section leading up to Skyline Boulevard.

To an observer concerned with future housing production in the region, the zoning histories of the Plains and the Foothills warrant the greatest attention. The Mountains, rugged and remote, hold scant promise for housing development. The relative smallness of the Bayshore band makes it less important, although, since 1990, the Bayshore in fact has been the site of many of Silicon Valley's densest housing developments

During the 1950s and 1960s, the combined populations of San Mateo and Santa Clara counties rose by over one million, evidence of robust housing demand. Yet, by 1970, housing prices around Palo Alto were only 20 percent above the national average.[13] The 1950s, however, provided early omens that local land use regulations, particularly in the Foothills, would become more stringent. As the 1960s progressed, the omens multiplied and spread to the Plains. By 2020, house prices in Palo Alto had risen to roughly ten times the national median.[14] The next sections show how, during this period, legal constraints on homebuilding multiplied.

13. Ellickson, "San Francisco Peninsula" (1982b): 5–8.

14. See chapter 1. In retrospect, the modesty of the increase in Silicon Valley housing prices during the 1970s is puzzling. Perhaps homebuyers underestimated

Zoning in the Foothills

Because few tracts in the Foothills are flat, lands there tend to be more expensive to develop. Where demand for housing is robust, however, the presence of slopes does not obviate residential development. Immediately east across the Bay from San Francisco, houses pepper the steep hills above Berkeley and Oakland up to an elevation of 1,000 feet. Many of these Berkeley and Oakland hillside houses sit on lots less than 8,000 square feet in area, a size that the zoning officials who control Silicon Valley's Foothills virtually never permit. Local governments authorize multifamily development on less than 1 percent of the residentially zoned land in Silicon Valley's Foothills band. In the Plains, that figure is vastly greater, 22 percent.

Beginning in the mid-1950s, housing development in Silicon Valley's Foothills became far more difficult. Of the many pertinent local legal events, three warrant emphasis. The first was the incorporation of a new set of suburbs. Prior to the mid-1950s, most of Silicon Valley's Foothills had lain in unincorporated areas of San Mateo and Santa Clara counties. In the 1950s and early 1960s, Foothill residents accomplished a handful of incorporations that shifted zoning powers from these counties to newly created municipalities. Three of these new suburbs encompassed lands mostly in the Foothills: Los Altos Hills (1956), Woodside (1956), and Portola Valley (1964).[15] Some of the world's richest individuals, among them Steve Jobs, would later buy houses in these suburbs.[16] These towns' zoning practices generally came to be more exclusionary than county policies had been.[17]

---

the later intensity of demand to live in the region or anticipated that the anti-growth turn would prove not to be permanent. The high transaction costs of acting as an arbitrager in a housing market also undoubtedly limited the number of speculative purchasers.

15. Beginning in 1963, California lawmakers greatly modified state statutory procedures governing local boundary changes. They sought to deter the incorporation of new cities and to prevent cherry-stem annexations such as Palo Alto's annexations in the Foothills. See Martin and Wagner, "Local Agency Formation Commissions" (1978).

16. See Uphold Our Heritage v. Town of Woodside, 54 Cal. Rptr. 3d 366 (Cal. App. 2007) (involving a Jobs house).

17. Portola Valley, for example, increased the minimum lot size that San Mateo County formerly had imposed. Davis, "Portola Valley" (1982): 46–47 and n.27.

The three towns have a combined area of thirty square miles but zone only two acres (0.01 percent) for multifamily housing. Two incorporations further south created Cupertino (1955) and Saratoga (1956), cities whose lands lie in both the Foothills and Plains. The homeowners who pushed for these five incorporations primarily were seeking to prevent annexation by a neighboring city, whose residents might have been less inclined to prevent the construction of less costly housing. The incorporators of Los Altos Hills, for example, had feared annexation by either Los Altos or Palo Alto, and they had been traumatized by a Santa Clara County rezoning that had permitted 10,000-sq.-ft. lots.[18]

The second notable occurrence was Palo Alto's set of annexations, between 1959 and 1968, of ten square miles of Foothill and Mountain land. The city undertook these efforts to provide open space and retard housing development in the annexed area. After the first annexation, Palo Alto opened a two-square-mile park, later named Foothill Park. In combination, these annexations almost doubled Palo Alto's land area but made its shape bizarre. The city's northern half is in the Plains, just east of the campus of Stanford University (most of which lies in unincorporated Santa Clara County). As figure 3 reveals, a narrow strip connects Palo Alto's northern half to the Foothill and Mountain areas that it annexed to form its southern half.

During the decade after Palo Alto's completion of these annexations, events transformed the city's politics. In the 1950s, Palo Alto's city manager had been Jerome Keithley, whose overtly pro-growth policies had seldom provoked opposition. During the 1960s, however, a potent coalition of Residentialists came into being, with the central aim of slowing development.[19] To Residentialists, Keithley symbolized the pro-growth Establishment. The struggle to control the Palo Alto City Council turned bitter, and, in 1966, Keithley resigned to become Oakland's city manager. Over the ensuing handful of years, the Residentialists became politically

---

See Ellickson, "Suburban Growth Controls" (1977): 404–9 (attributing these more stringent practices to the greater degree of local control).

18. Mensinger, "Los Altos Hills" (1982): 21–22. See also, e.g., Davis, "Portola Valley": 40 (reporting that control of zoning had motivated the incorporators of Portola Valley). The creators of Saratoga had feared that the City of San Jose would annex their lands. See Saratoga, California, History (2020).

19. Winslow, *Palo Alto* (1993): 53–57; Thorp, "Palo Alto 101" (2014).

dominant. By 1971, Palo Alto had begun buying land in the city's Foothills for open space and had imposed a minimum ten-acre house-lot requirement on Foothill tracts that it did not acquire. Both fiscal and environmental incentives underlay Palo Alto's motives.[20] The city's efforts to slow development proved largely successful. In 2020, the half of Palo Alto that lies in the Foothills and Mountains contained fewer than one hundred housing units, compared to the more than 20,000 in the city's Plains.

The third notable events were Santa Clara and San Mateo counties' decisions to ban residential development on nearly all of Stanford University's nine square miles of undeveloped Foothill land.[21] Figure 4 depicts Stanford's entire land holdings, which include, in the Plains, its main campus and the Stanford Research Park. Most of Stanford's holdings in the Foothills lie west of the main campus, beyond Junipero Serra Boulevard. Aerial photographs reveal that the University's lands are conspicuously emptier than neighboring Foothill lands.

During the past century, San Mateo County's zoning of Foothill lands generally has been less restrictive than Santa Clara County's. During the 1920s, San Mateo County permitted, at an elevation of 1,000 feet, the subdivision of Los Trancos Woods, a community of houses on roughly half-acre lots.[22] In the late 1940s, the county gave a green light to Ladera, a subdivision of 520 houses on 9,000- to 15,000-sq.-ft. lots at a site wedged between, but outside, Stanford's Foothill holdings (see figure 4).[23] Despite these early precedents, San Mateo County has permitted Stanford to build virtually no housing on its four square miles of unincorporated

20. See Frieden, *Environmental Protection Hustle* (1979): 107–18. In at least one instance, a court ruled that Palo Alto's large-lot requirements had unconstitutionally taken the private land affected, compelling Palo Alto to provide compensation. Arastra Ltd. Partnership v. City of Palo Alto, 401 F. Supp. 962 (N.D. Cal. 1975), *vacated* 417 F. Supp. 1125 (N.D. Cal. 1976). Palo Alto eventually bought the Arastra site for $7.5 million. Frieden, *Environmental Protection Hustle* (1979): 117. See also Eldridge v. City of Palo Alto, 129 Cal. Rptr. 575 (Cal. App. 1976).

21. Stanford's website asserts that the University's total landholdings amount to 8,180 acres, or almost 13 square miles. Stanford Lands (2020). A map depicting the various localities with zoning power over Stanford lands appears at Stanford Community Plan Issues and Policies, p. i (undated).

22. Softky, "Los Trancos Woods" (2005).

23. Ladera, California (2020).

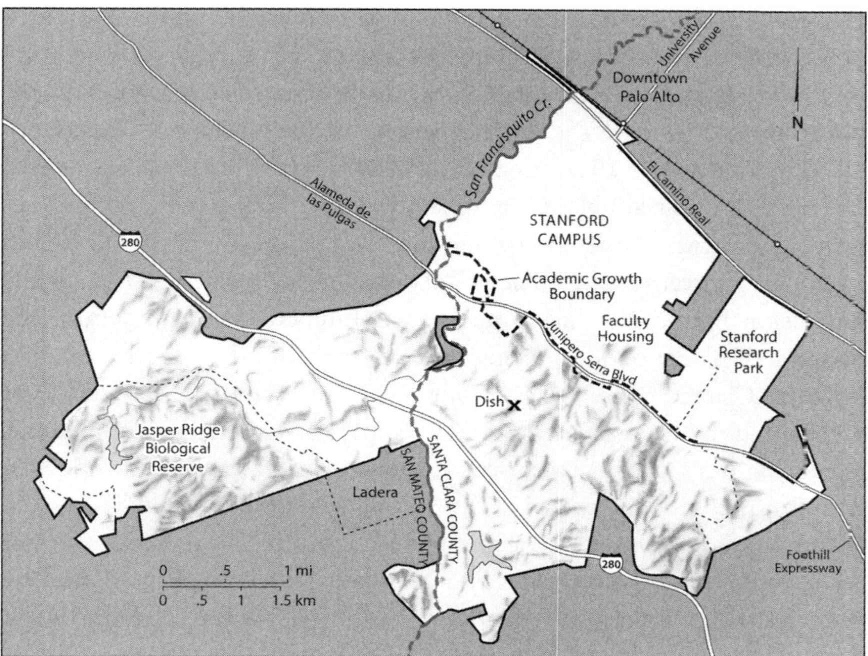

Figure 4. Map of Stanford University lands (Cartography by Bill Nelson)

land in the county. In 1973, Stanford's trustees voluntarily set aside the most elevated one-third as the Jasper Ridge Biological Preserve. On the remaining two-thirds, San Mateo County's zoning essentially limits uses to single-family detached houses on lots of at least one acre, triple the size of lots in nearby Ladera.[24] Most of these Stanford lands are devoted to the Stanford linear accelerator (SLAC) and various equestrian facilities.

Santa Clara County's zoning regulations on Stanford Foothill lands have long been tighter than San Mateo County's. In the 1950s, Santa Clara County imposed a one-acre minimum house-lot requirement on much of its unincorporated Foothill areas, including Stanford's lands.[25]

24. County of San Mateo, Cal., Zoning Regs. § 6300.1 (Aug. 2019) (minimum lot required in an R-E, S-11 zone).

25. E-mail to author from Colleen A. Tsuchimoto, senior planner, Santa Clara County Planning Department, Nov. 28, 2018. In the 1950s, the county also had required one-acre house-lots in the area that became Los Altos Hills. Interview with Steve

County regulations then would not have permitted a subdivision there as dense as nearby Ladera in San Mateo County, whose terrain is similar. By the 2010s, Santa Clara County's controls on the use of Stanford's Foothill lands had become the strictest of any in Silicon Valley. The county places two-thirds of these lands in a zone that flatly forbids residential structures. For almost all of the remainder, it requires a minimum houselot of twenty acres, the largest minimum-lot requirement of any Silicon Valley local government.[26] The county also has delineated an "Academic Expansion Boundary" that largely tracks Junipero Serra Boulevard (see figure 4).[27] This boundary helps assure that Stanford's building projects in Santa Clara County will be confined to its traditional campus area, eastward in the Plains. The most famous spot on Stanford's Foothill holdings is the Dish, a radio telescope that serves as a destination for joggers. A run to the Dish currently is a run through undeveloped land.

Although Stanford has objected to some of the land use controls that the counties have placed on its Foothills lands, it has acquiesced in many of them. When dealing with Santa Clara County, Stanford's primary goal, understandably, is to win approvals of projects proposed for sites near its traditional campus. Santa Clara County's implicit deal with Stanford permits the university to proceed with projects east of the Academic Growth Boundary only if, to the west, it keeps its Foothills lands undeveloped. The primary lobbyists for this basic bargain have been advocacy organizations for open space, chief among them the Committee for Green Foothills. In recent years, the main person this group has had to persuade is Supervisor Joe Simitian, whose district includes the Stanford portion of Santa Clara County.[28]

Padovan, consultant planner to the Los Altos Hills Planning Department, Nov. 13, 2018.

26. County of Santa Clara, Cal., Ord. Code § 3.10.030 (2020) (lot area required in an A1–20s zone).

27. The 2000 Stanford Community Plan and the interconnected Santa Clara County General Use Permit can be located at Stanford Community Plan Issues and Policies (undated). The plan includes a map that designates nearly all of Stanford's Foothill lands as either "Open Space and Field Research" or "Special Conservation." Id. at 27.

28. A California county has five supervisors. Prior to 2012, San Mateo County had elected its supervisors at-large. By 2020, both it and Santa Clara County were electing supervisors by district.

The internal politics of any university are complex. Some factions within Stanford, such as fundraisers and administrators involved in recruitment, likely would want to weaken the counties' zoning controls. Other factions, perhaps joggers to the Dish and the faculty members who currently own houses in the region, might support perpetuation of the counties' current zoning.

The bottom line is that next to none of Stanford's nine square miles of land lying in the accessible lower Foothills currently is devoted to housing. In light of Silicon Valley's astronomic housing prices, the value of these holdings, if developable, might be $2 million per acre.[29] If so, they would be worth around $12 billion, about half the university's endowment. To enable agglomeration efficiencies, an urban area requires density. The setting aside of the Stanford Foothills as open-space viewsheds is in obvious tension with the affordability of Silicon Valley housing.

Zoning in the Plains

The stakes of housing consumers are greatest in the Plains, the natural location of Silicon Valley's densest residential developments. The Caltrain railroad and several highways make this band the most accessible, and infrastructure there is relatively cheap to provide. In 1945, orchards covered much of the Plains, particularly its southern section. Especially between 1950 and 1965, Eichler and other homebuilders turned many of these formerly agricultural lands into residential neighborhoods. A dozen Silicon Valley cities zone most of this territory (see figure 3 at the beginning of this chapter). Their tastes for new housing development vary, sometimes sharply.

Single-Family Detached Houses

Cities in the Plains are far less likely to engage in large-lot zoning than cities in the Foothills. The three suburbs entirely in the Foothills require house-lots of at least one acre on 98 percent of their residentially

29. One source estimates that, in 2017, land in San Mateo County was worth $5.7 million per acre and, in Santa Clara County, $5.2 million per acre. Joint Center for Housing Studies, "Residential Land Prices" (2019). Because many of Stanford's Foothill lands are hilly, I adjusted these estimates downward.

zoned land. In the other twelve Silicon Valley cities, most of them in the Plains, that figure plummets to 24 percent.

Three Plains municipalities are the most exclusionary. In the order of descending strength of this inclination, they are Atherton, Saratoga, and Los Altos. Atherton was born to zone. In 1923, six years after California had first granted zoning power to municipalities, local residents incorporated Atherton to ward off annexation by neighboring Menlo Park.[30] Atherton began its exclusionary efforts in 1928, and, since 1947, has required, throughout town, a one-acre minimum house-lot. In November 2020, Zillow estimated the median value of an Atherton house at $6.5 million.[31] Saratoga was incorporated in 1956 to forestall annexation by the City of San Jose.[32] Saratoga requires a house-lot of at least one acre in 56 percent of its residentially zoned territory, and 10,000 square feet or more in 98 percent. Los Altos, the least fancy of these three Plains suburbs, mostly requires a 10,000-sq.-ft. lot in its single-family zones. Together, these three suburbs zone a combined 1 percent of their lands for multifamily housing.

The other nine cities in the Plains generally are less restrictive. Indeed, until around 1965, their zoning practices seldom constrained a developer shopping for single-family land. In the 1950s, Palo Alto, the most upscale of the remaining group, required a house-lot of only 6,000 square feet in south Palo Alto. That lot size equals a mere 1.5 percent of the ten-acre minimum that Palo Alto currently mandates in its Foothills section. In 2015, six other Plains suburbs were choosing 6,000 square feet, or less, as the minimum for their most-mapped single-family zone. On this front, the suburbs in the Plains of Silicon Valley are similar to those northwest of Austin but distinctly dissimilar from those of New Haven.[33]

Future housing production in the Plains of Silicon Valley necessarily will entail redevelopment. By 2015, there remained in the Plains not a single 20- to 40-acre tract that was privately owned, undeveloped, and

30. *See* 1917 Cal. Stat. 1419; Ex Parte White, 234 P. 396 (Cal. 1925); History of Atherton (2020).

31. See www.zillow.com/atherton-ca/home-values/ (visited on Nov. 10, 2020).

32. Saratoga, California, History (2020).

33. See chapter 4.

residentially zoned. Established neighborhoods of single-family houses instead predominate. Relief for housing consumers will require the densification of the zoning of some of them.

Zoning for Multifamily Housing

The nine non-exclusionary Plains suburbs traditionally have been relatively generous in permitting apartment construction.[34] In 2015, they together zoned 24 percent of their residentially zoned land for some form of multifamily housing, including townhouses and mobile home parks, at a density of at least eight dwelling units per acre. Mountain View, the suburb just south of Palo Alto and home of Google, zones 41 percent of its residential land in this fashion, the highest percentage of any Plains city. Redwood City, the City of Santa Clara, and Sunnyvale each allow multifamily development on over a quarter of their residentially zoned lands. Households looking for relatively inexpensive housing have disproportionately flocked to these cities, as well as to North San Jose.

New multifamily projects, however, are far from easy to build in the Plains of Silicon Valley. Of the many sites zoned for multifamily use, 97.8 percent have already been developed in that manner.[35] Many of the existing multifamily structures are no more than two stories high.[36] Effective relief for housing consumers will require somewhat taller buildings and, in some cases, densities greater than thirty dwelling units per acre. Few Plains cities, with the notable exception of Redwood City, have made significant moves in that direction. Developers consequentially have built many of the densest recent multifamily developments in Silicon Valley not in the Plains, but, as we shall see, in the Bayshore.

34. With regard to "missing middle" housing, the three most tolerant Plains cities are Redwood City, which allows the building of triplexes on 13.5 percent of its residentially zoned land, and Sunnyvale and Mountain View, which respectively allow duplexes on 8.5 percent and 6.3 percent.

35. Derived from data used to generate table 7 in chapter 2.

36. The City of Santa Clara, traditionally a suburb that has welcomed apartment buildings, limits their heights to two stories in its two most ubiquitous multifamily zones (R3–18D and R3–25D). Santa Clara, Cal., City Code §§ 18.16.060, 18.18.060 (2019).

The history of high-rise apartment buildings in Palo Alto, the heart of Silicon Valley, is particularly instructive.[37] Palo Alto's downtown centers on University Avenue. In 1929–1930, when Palo Alto's zoning was still young, entrepreneurs erected, within two blocks of University Avenue, three six- to seven-story apartment buildings. The next Palo Alto apartment buildings equal or greater in height went up between 1960 and 1965, when the city approved four more, including the 101 Alma Street condominiums, the city's tallest at fourteen stories.

By the early 1970s, the anti-growth Residentialists had won political control of Palo Alto from the pro-growth Establishment. The Residentialists promptly imposed a maximum height-limit of fifty feet, roughly five stories, on *all* new buildings in Palo Alto.[38] A half-century later, this 50-foot limit, with minor exceptions, remains on the books.[39] In 2018, each of Palo Alto's multifamily zones was even more restrictive, limiting heights to forty feet or less.[40] The actual heights of buildings in the city tend to be far lower. In 2018, 74 percent of the buildings fronting on University Avenue in the heart of downtown Palo Alto had heights of two stories or less, and a mere 3 percent exceeded four stories.[41] Transit nodes typically are conducive to dense development. Palo Alto nonetheless imposes a forty-foot height limit in its sole "transit-oriented" zone near the

37. The Emporis website provides data on the tallest buildings in various cities worldwide. The list for Palo Alto can be found at Emporis, Palo Alto (2020).
38. Sheyner, "Palo Alto Height Limit" (2016).
39. Several provisions in Palo Alto's zoning ordinance reflect this policy. See, e.g., City of Palo Alto, Cal., Zoning Regulations § 18.16.060 tbl. 4 (2019) (maximum height of fifty feet in mixed-use zones, including the downtown commercial area along University Avenue); § 18.20.040, tbl. 2 (maximum height of fifty feet in industrial zones). Palo Alto, however, can waive this height limit in return for the donation of public amenities. In 2014, for example, Palo Alto authorized Stanford to erect a 130-foot tall hospital building for children at its on-campus medical complex. Sheyner, "Stanford Offers City" (2011) (describing preliminary discussions).
40. Palo Alto's RM-15 zone limits building heights to 30 feet; its RM-30 zone, to 35 feet; and its RM-40 zone, to 40 feet. City of Palo Alto, Cal., Zoning Regulations § 18.13.040, tbl. 2 (2019).
41. Author's tally, in November 2018, of structures on the five blocks on University Avenue between Cowper and Alma streets. This is the heart of downtown Palo Alto.

California Avenue Caltrain station.[42] Palo Alto's immediate neighbors are more tolerant of tall buildings. In 2002, Mountain View permitted the opening of the ten-story Avalon Towers on El Camino Real. In 2018, Menlo Park's Bayshore saw the opening of the eleven-story Hotel Nia.

An incident in the early 1980s illustrates the Residentialists' aversion to dense multifamily housing in the Plains of Palo Alto. Stanford University then proposed to erect in the city an 1,100-unit mid-rise apartment development, Stanford West, for members of the university's administrative staff. Stanford planned to situate the project within walking distance of both the center of campus and the Stanford Shopping Center. None of Palo Alto's many existing single-family neighborhoods lay within a mile of the proposed site. Stanford nonetheless came away with nothing. In the words of the university official who managed the Stanford West proposal, "we got blown out of the water."[43] The scale of Stanford West may partly have doomed it. In recent decades, Stanford has persuaded Palo Alto to approve a handful of less massive housing developments. In 1999, one was a different Stanford West, a dense two- and three-story 628-unit apartment complex on Sand Hill Road. To succeed, the university had to survive a Palo Alto referendum challenge and a CEQA lawsuit by Menlo Park, a city abutting the site.[44] Stanford has had to site all its apartment developments, however, at least one block, and often far more, from any existing Palo Alto single-family neighborhood.[45]

Zoning in the Bayshore

This narrow band lies between U.S. 101 on the west and San Francisco Bay on the east. Historically, many U.S. cities, perhaps Boston

42. City of Palo Alto, Cal., Zoning Regulations § 18.34.040 tbl. 2 (2019). In November 2018, in the four-block commercial section south of the California Avenue station, 85 percent of the buildings actually were two stories or fewer. Author's tally.
43. Bird, "Stanford Faces Demand" (1985): 6.
44. Stanford News Service, "Sand Hill Road Project" (1998).
45. In the late 2010s, for example, Stanford set back its new mid-rise University Terrace condominiums a full block from existing single-family houses in College Terrace. See Stanford University Terrace (2020).

most notably, expanded their footprints by filling wetlands. Prior to 1965, Bay Area governments did as well. They authorized landfills in the Bay, for example, ten miles north of Silicon Valley, to expand the site of the San Francisco Airport. South of the airport, early 1960s landfills created Foster City and Redwood Shores, two ambitious housing developments, the latter in Redwood City. After 1965, however, fillings of the Bay essentially stopped and indeed reversed. In that year the California legislature approved the creation of the San Francisco Bay Conservation and Development Commission.[46] Because credible environmental concerns are likely to stem additional filling, the small size of the Bayshore limits its potential for housing development.

Seven cities control zoning in the Bayshore. Except in East Palo Alto, the lands in this band tend to be distant from the downtowns of the cities that zone them. Although the Bayshore includes a handful of single-family-house neighborhoods, these are far less common than in the Plains and Foothills.[47] This has enabled Bayshore cities to zone to permit two uses that few homeowners would want in their backyards. Particularly numerous are office buildings occupied by high-tech firms, typically surrounded by parking lots for employees. Also abundant in the Bayshore, perhaps surprisingly, are mobile home parks. Developers created dozens of these, especially between 1955 and 1975. In 2018, spaces in Silicon Valley mobile home parks totaled 7,500, more than enough to house twice the population of Atherton.[48] Almost three-quarters of the spaces lie in the Bayshore, with the balance mostly in the close-by Plains. Sunnyvale, home to half of Silicon Valley's mobile home spaces, was once particularly permissive.[49]

46. Smith and Pendleton, "San Francisco Bay Commission" (1998).
47. Examples include Redwood City's Redwood Shores, Menlo Park's Belle Haven, Sunnyvale's Lakewood, North San Jose's Alviso, and several East Palo Alto neighborhoods.
48. Author's count, derived from Google Earth aerials and various mobile home park websites.
49. Mountain View and North San Jose each also have more than a thousand spaces. The nearby City of Santa Clara, by contrast, contains no mobile home parks. Density in the existing Silicon Valley mobile home parks typically ex-

At its southern end, the Bayshore widens to three miles and there encompasses North San Jose, one of the many neighborhoods of that sprawling city. In 1990, most sections of North San Jose were seas of mobile home parks and low-rise office complexes. Homeowners were largely absent. These conditions enabled developers to turn part of North San Jose into a major escape valve for the pent-up forces of housing supply in Silicon Valley. The neighborhood became the site of many of the region's densest multifamily developments, typically complexes of four- to five-story buildings. Since 1990, developers have built twenty or more huge apartment projects in North San Jose north of Montague Expressway.[50] Among the largest have been the 2,700-unit North Park (2007), the 1,750-unit Crescent Village (2013), the 769-unit Epic (2016), and the 1,308-unit River View Apartments (2016).

A technological innovation provided a boost. In 2012, International Building Code officials approved a new and less costly technology for mid-rise apartment buildings, commonly known as "stick frame over podium." These structures have a deck of concrete for the first floor or two and wood bearing-walls for the three to five stories that extend above.[51] A planning document of the City of San Jose anticipates an additional 32,000 new housing units in North San Jose alone.[52]

Google also has recognized that a project proposed for a Bayshore site is less likely to encounter political resistance. The firm plans to erect as many as 8,000 dense housing units near its Bayshore headquarters in Mountain View.[53] Google's chosen site for the project is the North Bayshore, an area east of U.S. 101 and safely distant from Mountain View homeowners.

Absent the apartment developments in North San Jose and elsewhere in the Bayshore, housing prices in Silicon Valley would be even more

ceeds eight units per acre, enough to qualify them as multifamily housing. See Appendix.

50. Two of the earliest were the two-story Fountains at River Oaks (1990) and the four-story Elan Village of 941 units (1992).

51. Malone, "5-Over-2 Podium Design" (2017).

52. San Jose, California, "North San Jose Development Policy" (undated).

53. D'Onfro, "Google Has Huge Plans" (2018).

astronomic. In terms of urban form, however, there is a downside to what has happened. Dense housing developments are better located near the urban cores of cities, not in remote industrial areas. In Silicon Valley during recent decades, only Redwood City has permitted significant residential densification of its core. Redwood City's Downtown Precise Plan of 2011 triggered the development, primarily along major streets downtown, of a burst of multistory apartments.[54] Demand to reside in Silicon Valley plainly remains intense, if usually frustrated.

California's Efforts to Control Local Zoning Abuses

The phrase *housing crisis* is much overused, but it describes well the current situation in California. This chapter has largely emphasized city and county actions that have pushed house prices in Silicon Valley to ten times the national median. It is worth repeating, however, that some state policies, such as the California Environmental Quality Act of 1970, have contributed as well.

Even in the 2010s, California adopted two new mandates that will tend to boost housing costs statewide. Unlike most states, California has begun to require that a new single-family house come equipped with both solar panels and sprinklers to suppress fire.[55] These initiatives certainly will generate some benefits, but they underscore the state's uncertain devotion to reducing the cost of shelter.

The history of California's efforts to control local zoning is far too tangled to recount. In brief, prior to the 2010s, the State of California made some token interventions.[56] Since 1980, California has required a

54. Kautz et al., "California Conundrum" (2019): 45. Of the thirteen projects with five or more dwelling units that Redwood City approved between 2014 and 2016, however, no more than two replaced single-family housing units and, in those instances, only a couple. Author's examination of addresses generously provided by Moira O'Neill, Giulia Gualco-Nelson, and Eric Biber.

55. Thoubboron, "California Solar Mandate" (2019); Faturechi, "Fire Sprinkler War" (2016).

56. A 1979 California statute requires a local government to provide a density bonus to a developer who has proposed a qualifying mixed-income project. Cal. Govt. Code § 65915 (2019). In response to this enactment, a strategic suburb

locality to estimate its fair share of the Regional Housing Needs Assessment (RHNA). Each locality must submit a housing element (part of its general plan) to the state Department of Housing and Community Development for approval. The element indicates how the locality plans to meet its RHNA targets in various bands of affordability.[57] Especially prior to 2010, this approach was notably ineffective.[58]

Since 2010, however, California has somewhat toughened its constraints. In 2012, Facebook successfully invoked the California fair share statute when pressuring Menlo Park to approve the development of 1,975 new housing units, mostly in the Bayshore.[59] California also has preempted, with increasing vigor, local limitations on a homeowner's right to build an accessory dwelling unit (ADU, or granny flat).[60] In 2017, State Senator Scott Wiener conspicuously took up the cause of reducing local barriers to housing production. Weiner's most controversial bill, yet to be adopted, would preempt local controls that prevent the construction of mid-rise multifamily housing near a transit station.[61] In 2017, however, Wiener did successfully sponsor a California statute that eases local approvals of mixed-income projects proposed for an area already zoned for residential use.[62] In downtown Cupertino, home of Apple, the redeveloper of a shopping mall site has successfully invoked this statute.[63]

The legal situation in California is complex and very much in flux. Several law professors based in the state, such as Eric Biber and Christopher Elmendorf, have helped keep non-Californians abreast of the turbulent events.[64] In general, California legislators have too often opted for the dream of comprehensive planning, as opposed to the simpler expedient,

---

might reduce the densities it initially allowed, a ploy that the statute does not prohibit.

57. Cal. Govt. Code § 65580–89.11 (2020).
58. See, e.g., Field, "Fair Share Housing Laws" (1993).
59. Agatstein, "Suburbs' Fair Share" (2015): 242.
60. See chapter 11.
61. SB 50 (Cal. 2018). See Wick, "Demise of SB 50" (2019).
62. Cal. Gov't Code § 65913.4 (2020).
63. Bitters, "Controversial Vallco Project" (2020).
64. See, e.g., Elmendorf et al., "Making It Work" (2020); Elmendorf, "Beyond the Double Veto" (2019); and O'Neill et al., "California's Housing Policy Debates" (2019).

exemplified by the ADU measure, of selectively preempting local zoning powers.

As noted, developers have succeeded in building batches of mid- to high-rise apartment houses in a few Silicon Valley locations, notably North San Jose and Redwood City. They would have had far more difficulty in most of the suburbs of our next metropolitan area.

4

Zoning in Greater New Haven, Land of Large Lots

We now turn to the zoning policies of the fourteen suburbs that surround the City of New Haven, Connecticut, our Frostbelt representative.[1] The map in figure 5 shows their locations. New Haven is a port city on Long Island Sound. It lies sixty-five miles northeast of New York City, at the far reach of a conceivable commute. I selected this metro because, frankly, it lay conveniently at hand.[2] This proximity facilitated research into suburbs' zoning histories, information rarely available online. Another plus is the reality that the demographics of Greater New Haven mimic those of the median U.S. metro.[3] Greater New Haven, in addition, proves to be a fine setting for introducing two new topics that inevitably affect housing supply: the provision of utility services and the setting aside of land for open space.

Measured by the metrics presented in chapter 2, New Haven's suburbs have traditionally been far more exclusionary than most of their counterparts in Silicon Valley and northwestern Greater Austin. Zoning policies of course vary within the Frostbelt, and there is no claim here that the

1. These towns, and the City of New Haven, are the members of the South Central Regional Council of Governments. See http://scrcog.org/. As the three metro maps indicate, I excluded from the study all downtowns, namely the entire City of New Haven, downtown San Jose, and downtown Austin.
2. Cf. Dahl, *Who Governs?* (1961): v.
3. Kolko, "Normal America" (2016) ("the metropolitan area that looks most like the U.S. is New Haven, Connecticut").

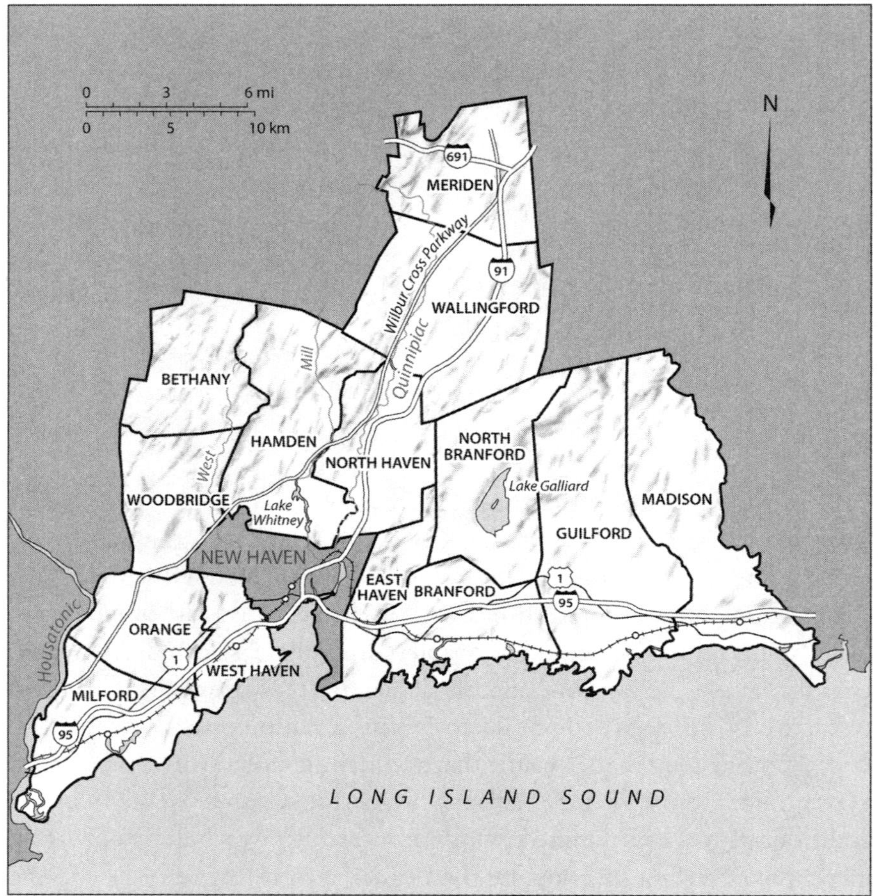

Figure 5. Greater New Haven (Cartography by Bill Nelson)

practices of New Haven's suburbs are typical. Greater New Haven is not, however, unrepresentative of Connecticut. Fairfield County, which lies closer to New York City, is Connecticut's wealthiest county and its towns are likely even more exclusionary.[4] An examination in 1960 of zoning

4. About two-thirds of the population of New Haven County lives in the City of New Haven and its fourteen suburbs. In 2016, Fairfield County's median household income was $92,969, while New Haven County's was $67,128. Exclusionary practices positively correlate with the presence of wealthy households. Glaeser and Gyourko, "Housing Supply" (2018): 19.

policies of localities in the seventeen counties closest to New York City, a list that included Fairfield County but not New Haven County, deemed Fairfield County practices to be the most exclusionary of all seventeen.[5] Several older empirical studies assert that the suburbs of Hartford, the capital of Connecticut, are even more exclusionary than New Haven's.[6] However, the *Connecticut Zoning Atlas*, released in 2021, casts doubt on this.[7] Application of the metrics offered in chapter 2 would more conclusively confirm variations in land use policies, both within Connecticut and throughout the Frostbelt.

Introduction to Greater New Haven

European settlers first arrived in New Haven in 1638, making it handily the first colonized of the three metros studied. Yale College (originally called the Collegiate School) was founded in 1701, almost two centuries before the 1880s, the decade that witnessed the opening of campuses at Stanford University and the University of Texas at Austin. New Haven's suburbs are relatively long-settled. In 1880, the City of New Haven's (then thirteen) suburbs had a combined population of 48,000. In that year, that headcount exceeded the combined population of Santa Clara and San Mateo counties in California, and that of Travis and Williamson counties in Texas.[8] Even by 1920, the population of Greater New Haven, including the central city, exceeded the combined populations of these four California and Texas counties.

5. Regional Plan Ass'n, *Spread City* (1962): 40 tbl. 10.
6. American Society of Planning Officials, *Connecticut Planning Legislation* (1967): 190 tbl. 10 (indicating that towns in New Haven County, during the early 1960s, were less likely than towns in Fairfield and Hartford counties to impose large lot-size requirements on vacant land); Pendall et al., "Land Use Regulations" (2006): New Haven CT NECMA, at 1.
7. Connecticut Zoning Atlas (2021).
8. Exact population figures for 1880: New Haven suburbs, 47,934; the two California counties, 43,708; the two Texas counties, 42,183. In 1880, the City of New Haven's population of 63,000 was five times that of the City of San Jose and five times that of the City of Austin. In 2018, each of the latter two cities, partly because of annexations, had populations that outnumbered the City of New Haven's eight-to-one.

During the nineteenth century, both New Haven and Connecticut were at the forefront of U.S. technology, particularly in fabrication.[9] Eli Whitney, a Yale graduate, is widely thought to have pioneered the use of replaceable-parts manufacturing at a site on the Mill River in Hamden, just upstream from the City of New Haven.[10] By the 1850s, the City of New Haven housed factories specializing in the production of goods such as clocks and rubber boots. Another firm evolved into the mammoth Winchester Repeating Arms Company.[11] Among other accomplishments, in 1878 New Haven became the site of the world's first telephone switchboard.

Connecticut has long been one of the wealthiest states, and, up until the 1970s, was a magnet for upwardly mobile workers.[12] No longer. Over the course of the twentieth century, the Greater New Haven economy shifted away from manufacturing and toward the provision of higher education and health services.[13] In 2016, median household income in New Haven County was $67,000. That figure exceeded the U.S. median household income by 11 percent, but it was less than half that of Silicon Valley and slightly trailed that of Travis County, Texas, home of Austin.[14] Greater New Haven can still boast of having some of the best pizzerias in the nation but, unlike the other two metros, not about being a locational superstar.[15]

New Haven's suburbs almost doubled in population during the 1950s and 1960s. During that era, the City of New Haven's nationally prominent urban renewal program helped spur suburbanization, particularly

9. Higgs, "Urbanization and Inventiveness" (1975): 254–57 (marshaling data indicating that Connecticut was the most inventive state in the late nineteenth century).

10. Some historians contest how interchangeable Whitney's parts actually were. See, e.g., Smith, *American System of Manufacturing* (1990).

11. On Greater New Haven's then comparative advantage in manufacturing, see Rae, *Urbanism and Its End* (2003): 52–54, 108–9. New Haven County's population grew by 48 percent during the 1850s, more than the national figure of 36 percent.

12. Ganong and Shoag, "Regional Income Convergence" (2017): 77.

13. The share of New Haven County jobs in manufacturing fell from 33.1 percent in 1970 to 8.0 percent in 2016. Berube and Murray, "Older Industrial Cities" (2018).

14. In 2016, Palo Alto's median family income was $157,000, around the median for a Silicon Valley suburb. Travis County's was $72,000.

15. Saltonstall, "Best Pizza Places" (2019), ranks Frank Pepe's of New Haven as best in the nation.

paucity of these options likely repels millennials, many of whom prefer walkability.[26]

Connecticut's local institutions are distinctive in other respects. In most towns, the members of a zoning commission are elected, not appointed, as in other states.[27] This selection process may make these members even more responsive to the interests of incumbent homeowners and increase the deference of the state judiciary to local zoning decisions. Also noteworthy in the land use context are two specific Connecticut statutes. The retreat of glaciers after the end of the Ice Age created an unusual number of wetlands in the state. Since 1972, Connecticut has required each town to create an Inland Wetlands Commission, a body with independent permit authority over development proposals.[28] In 1990, Connecticut also enacted the Appeals Act, an anti-snob zoning statute that directly addresses, largely ineffectually, issues of exclusionary zoning. This chapter includes an assessment of its effects.

Zoning in New Haven's Most Exclusionary Suburbs

In 2016, five of the fourteen New Haven suburbs outranked the others in median household income. These five are, according to chapter 2's metrics, also Greater New Haven's most exclusionary.[29] The five—Bethany, Guilford, Madison, Orange, and Woodbridge—each allow only a detached house on at least 99 percent of their residentially zoned land.

26. Lee, "Millennials Coming to Town?" (2020); Hamilton and Dourado, "Premium for Walkable Development" (2018).
27. Conn. Gen. Stat. § 8–1 (2019) (authorizing a local government to create a zoning commission and barring various other municipal legislative bodies from directly exercising zoning powers).
28. Inland Wetlands and Watercourses Act of 1972, Conn. Gen. Stat. §§ 22a-36 to 45 (2019). On the impact of this sort of regulation in a neighboring state, see Sims and Schuetz, "Wetlands Bylaws in Massachusetts" (2009).
29. In 1965, the Connecticut General Assembly approved Special Act 249, which authorized a study of the effects of large-lot zoning and increased subdivision standards on the price of housing. The Ross Hardies law firm of Chicago, specialists in land use law, helped prepare the eventual report, American Society of Planning Officials, *Connecticut Planning Legislation* (1967). As the state legislature had requested, the consultants proposed comprehensive changes in Connecticut's zoning statutes. These the legislature largely ignored.

Figure 6. Google Earth aerial, in 2012, of a portion of Woodbridge, Connecticut. Since 1938, the Town of Woodbridge has restricted the development of over 90 percent of its territory to a single-family detached house on a lot of at least 60,000 square feet, just under 1 ½ acres. By 2001, Woodbridge had twice slightly increased this minimum-lot requirement in a majority of town. Note the absence of sidewalks.

All but Guilford require a house-lot of at least one acre on 98 percent of that acreage. For Guilford, that figure is 93 percent. In fact, these five towns require a two-acre minimum house-lot—roughly ten times the area of an Eichler 8,000-sq.-ft. lot—on 55 percent of their residentially zoned land. Bethany, which did not adopt zoning until 1952, in 1958 decided that the *only* new residential use it would permit would be a single-family detached house on a lot of at least 65,000 square feet.[30]

(In 2020, a Yale Law School clinic challenged Woodbridge's exclusionary practices. The clinic's client owned a detached house on a 1 ½-acre

30. Bethany, Conn., Zoning Ordinance, revision of June 19, 1958, at 10.

lot that the town had zoned single-family-only. The clinic's first gambit was to ask Woodbridge to rezone the lot to permit the development of a fourplex.[31])

New Haven's five most exclusionary suburbs are large in area, with an average of twenty-eight square miles. That figure is six times the size of Atherton, California, and eight times that of West Lake Hills, Texas, two of their exclusionary counterparts in the other metros. All five suburbs suppress walkability. None of their zoning maps depicts a single-family zone where local authorities would permit an 8,000-sq.-ft. lot as of right. Among the five, the zoning maps of only Guilford and Woodbridge include multifamily zones, which take up respectively 0.1 percent and 0.5 percent of those towns' residentially zoned territory.

New Haven's five most exclusionary suburbs all contain an above-average portion of both wetlands/floodplains and slopes in excess of 15 percent.[32] Those conditions make development more costly but hardly prevent it. In bucolic Bethany, the town with the largest fraction of these complicating conditions, developers have subdivided about a fifth of the wetlands and a quarter of the hillsides into lots.[33]

The Effects of Water Supply and Wastewater Treatment on Zoning Policy

Systems for providing utility services, a topic not broached in the analysis of Silicon Valley, profoundly shape patterns of urban growth. In all three of the metros studied, utility agencies are present and influential. Of the many utility services, those used for the supply of water and the removal of wastewater typically have the greatest impact on patterns of residential development. A network of sanitary sewers may be either separate from the network of storm sewers used to dispose runoff from rain or, particularly in an older city, combined with it. For water supply and wastewater removal, three technological options—two widely familiar, one not—warrant mention.

To enable exploitation of potential efficiencies of scale, most states designate a particular utility organization to furnish water and remove

31. O'Leary, "Challenge to Woodbridge Zoning" (2020).
32. Milone & MacBroom, *Regional Build-Out Analysis* (2010): appendixes.
33. Id., Bethany appendix.

wastewater in a given urban area. In all three metros, this process has produced a crazy quilt of interlocking organizations, mostly public, some private. In Williamson County, Texas, a suburban municipality typically maintains a utility department that provides both water and wastewater services. In Greater New Haven, by contrast, distinct entities commonly provide the two services. The South Central Connecticut Regional Water Authority (RWA) supplies water to ten of New Haven's fourteen suburbs. The region's largest wastewater utility, the Greater New Haven Water Pollution Control Authority, by contrast, serves only four towns: a small fraction of Woodbridge and most of the developed portions of East Haven, New Haven, and Hamden.

In some large-lot single-family neighborhoods, such as many in Woodside, California, Orange, Connecticut, and West Lake Hills, Texas, water utilities serve most detached houses, but sewer utilities, whose pipes are costlier to install, serve only a few. In Woodside, California, most homeowners have public water, but mostly use household-scaled septic tanks.[34] Utility organizations typically impose exactions on developers and user fees on consumers to help finance their undertakings. A wastewater utility commonly operates a treatment plant to remove contaminants prior to discharging effluents into a waterway. A local utility that lacks a treatment plant may contract for treatment services with a nearby utility.[35]

At the other extreme from a designated utility is a household-scaled system. Many Greater New Haven suburbanites, as well as some homeowners in the two other metros, use these for both water supply and wastewater disposal. New Haven is the wettest of the three metros, with annual rainfall of forty-eight inches, an amount normally sufficient to replenish aquifers.[36] A house on a spacious suburban lot in the New Haven area commonly obtains its water from an on-site well into which an electric pump has been submerged. To dispose of wastewater, the homeowner typically employs a septic tank. Waste fluids from the tank eventu-

34. E-mail to author from Sage Schaan, principal planner, Town of Woodside, Cal., Aug. 12, 2019.

35. See Shoreline Care Ltd. Partnership v. Town of North Branford, 650 A.2d 142, 143 (Conn. 1994) (noting that North Branford had three sewered areas, from which it sent sewage to three different neighboring towns).

36. Austin receives an average of thirty-four inches, and Silicon Valley, fifteen.

ally flow into a leaching field that distributes them into the soil of the house-lot. Especially when a house-lot is small, the leaching process may contaminate the aquifers that provide well water to the host house or nearby houses. Suburban officials who anticipate that homeowners will use household-scale systems commonly invoke this risk to justify imposition of a large minimum area for a house-lot.[37]

There is, however, a third, and much less familiar, technological option: a "decentralized," or "community," water and/or sanitary sewer system.[38] These operate at an intermediate geographic scale. They serve an area larger than a house-lot but smaller than the service area of a typical public utility. The services of community-scaled systems commonly are superior to those of household-scaled systems. A decentralized "package plant" for treating wastewater, for example, usually is better able than a traditional septic tank to remove nitrates and other contaminants from effluents. A civil engineer designing a decentralized utility system has many options for locating both water wells and outlets for treated wastewater. When properly designed, a decentralized utility system negates the standard public-health rationale for large-lot zoning. To encourage the development of these systems, a suburb's zoning ordinance might automatically relax a minimum–house-lot requirement when a subdivider has provided a sufficiently safe decentralized alternative. Almost none of the zoning ordinances examined, however, offers a developer that option.[39]

Zoning officials, especially those in Greater New Haven, have been eager to protect from development the natural watersheds that feed reser-

37. In addition, Greater Boston suburbs commonly stiffen Massachusetts's standards for septic tank performance. Glaeser and Ward, "Evidence from Greater Boston" (2009): 269.

38. U.S. Environmental Protection Agency, "Decentralized Wastewater Treatment Systems" (2004); Gikas and Tchobanoglous, "Decentralized Strategies" (2009): 149 (fig. 3) (providing illustration of a decentralized wastewater treatment system for a small subdivision of houses); see also Landmark Dev. Group, LLC v. East Lyme Zoning Comm'n, 2011 WL 5842576 (Conn. Super. Ct. 2011), at 12–22 (discussing community wells and community septic tanks).

39. The Austin suburb of Lakeway comes closest. When an "organized sewer" serves a lot, Lakeway reduces the required lot area in its basic single-family zone from one acre to either 10,000 or 15,000 sq. ft. Lakeway, Tex., Code of Ordinances § 30.03.002(d) (2019).

voirs. In a rural area, this policy commonly is cost-justified. When applied close to the urban core, however, a watershed-protection policy reduces population density and is distinctly anti-urban. At a close-in location, a system of post-reservoir water purification commonly is superior.

The South Central Connecticut Regional Water Authority has used, in different locations, both of these means of assuring water quality. In 2018, RWA owned 24,300 acres of land in New Haven's fourteen suburbs, almost 11 percent of these towns' total acreage.[40] In the relatively remote area around Lake Gaillard in North Branford, the largest of the Authority's reservoirs, the dedication of Authority lands to watershed protection likely is cost-effective.[41] In a neighborhood close to the City of New Haven, however, a system of post-reservoir water purification makes more sense. Since 1860, Lake Whitney, a dammed reservoir on the Mill River in the town of Hamden, has been the source of most of the City of New Haven's water supply. In 2018, hundreds of Hamden dwelling units lay within one block of the shores of Lake Whitney. The tap water that the lake provides nonetheless is potable. The Authority has attained this result by repeatedly modernizing, most recently in 2005, its filtration facility just downstream from the lake.[42] The RWA's decision to opt for post-reservoir filtration at this close-to-downtown location was more utilitarian than razing hundreds of dwellings in Hamden.

A town's decision to refuse to provide sanitary sewers can be the cornerstone of an exclusionary land use policy. Connecticut courts have repeatedly accepted the absence of sanitary sewers as an adequate justification for a town's large-lot zoning.[43] Courts in other states similarly

40. South Central Connecticut Regional Water Authority, "Annual Report" (2018): 65.
41. In fact, RWA operates in North Branford a plant to treat Lake Gaillard water. Turmelle, "Fix in North Branford" (2018).
42. Michael Van Valkenburgh Associates, Inc. (undated).
43. See, e.g., Senior v. Zoning Comm'n, 153 A.2d 415 (Conn. 1959) (sustaining increase, from two to four acres, of minimum-lot requirement); De Mars v. Zoning Comm'n, 115 A.2d 653, 654 (Conn. 1955) (rebuffing claim that town's 40,000-sq.-ft. minimum-lot requirement for a house was an unreasonable exercise of police power). But cf. Builders Ser. Corp. v. Planning & Zoning Comm'n, 545 A.2d 530 (Conn. 1988) (holding that minimum *floor* area requirements were

have tended to defer to local minimum lot-size requirements.[44] Perhaps tempted by the opportunity to secure this form of legal cover, three of New Haven's five most exclusionary suburbs decline to provide sanitary sewers anywhere in town. Of the remaining two, Woodbridge provides them in about 7 percent of its territory, and Orange does so in about 15 percent, in both cases mostly in commercial areas.[45] In eight of the remaining nine New Haven suburbs, by contrast, sanitary sewers serve more than half of the town's territory.[46]

A town's decision not to sewer, of course, may be cost-justified. There may be scant demand for dense housing, and hydrological conditions may favor the use of wells and septic tanks. These conditions largely prevail in Bethany and Madison, suburbs remote from the City of New Haven. Three of the suburbs that have chosen to be mostly sewerless, however—Guilford, Orange, and Woodbridge—each include neighborhoods within a ready commute to downtown New Haven. The lack of sanitary sewers in those neighborhoods has sapped Greater New Haven's potential agglomeration efficiencies.

The Connecticut Statute Favoring Projects with Affordable Dwellings

Both Connecticut and California have enacted complex statutes, along different lines, to counter exclusionary zoning. To date, the payoff in both states has been modest. Texas, where the exclusionary policies have been less rife, has done far less.[47] The zoning ordinances and plans

---

not rationally related to the legitimate objectives of zoning outlined in state zoning enabling act).

44. A leading decision is Simon v. Town of Needham, 42 N.E.2d 516 (Mass. 1942). For a review of the case law, see Boudreaux, "Lotting Large" (2016): 20–27.

45. Southern Connecticut Regional Council of Governments, "Plan of Conservation" (2009) (providing, in appendixes, a map of each town's sewered area).

46. Id.

47. But cf. Texas Homestead Protection District and Reinvestment Zone Act, Tex. Local Govt. Code § 373A.001ff, adopted in 2005, which authorizes the creation of tax-increment-finance districts to raise revenue to subsidize mixed-income housing projects.

of the suburbs in Greater New Haven commonly refer to Connecticut's statutes, just as Silicon Valley suburbs frequently allude to California's.

Connecticut's most pertinent initiative, the Affordable Housing Land Use Appeals Act, dates from 1990.[48] The statute specifically seeks to reduce the regulatory obstacles facing a developer who desires to build a mixed-income housing project that would violate local zoning requirements. In a mixed-income development, some occupying households pay market rents (or purchase prices), while other households, whose incomes qualify them as either low- or moderate-income, pay below-market prices for "affordable" units.[49] The Appeals Act, when it applies, enables a developer to overcome the presumption of validity that Connecticut courts have traditionally granted to town zoning decisions.[50] Christopher Elmendorf, whose enthusiasm for the approach is limited, refers to this system as the "Northeastern Model" of zoning reform. His central criticism is that it fails to limit local actions that raise the cost of market-rate housing.[51]

To qualify for the benefits of the Appeals Act, a developer must promise to make at least 30 percent of the units in the proposed project affordable for low- and moderate-income households.[52] When a town has denied a zoning change or other permit necessary for a project that qualifies, the

48. Conn. Gen. Stat. § 8–30g (2019). The Massachusetts Anti-Snob Zoning Act, Mass. Gen. Laws Ann. ch. 40B, §§ 20–23 (West 1994), first enacted in 1969, plainly influenced the drafters of Connecticut's Appeals Act. On the impact of the Massachusetts statute, see Reid et al., "California's Housing Shortage" (2017).
49. See Ellickson, "Mixed-Income Housing Project" (2010).
50. A "fundamental purpose of the affordable housing statute was to eliminate [judicial] deference to [zoning] commission judgments." Quarry Knoll II Corp. v. Planning & Zoning Comm'n of the Town of Greenwich, 780 A.2d 1, 29 (Conn. 2001). A town that permits the building of a sufficient number of inclusionary units may qualify for a four-year exemption from exposure to the act. Conn. Gen. Stat. § 8–30g(a)(6) (2019).
51. Elmendorf, "Beyond the Double Veto" (2019): 99–100.
52. The Connecticut legislature frequently tinkers with the Appeals Act. The text describes the statute as it was in 2016. Amendments enacted in 2000 increased the required percentage of inclusionary units from 20 percent to 30 percent, and for the first time required the set-aside of units for lower-income households. One commentator has asserted that exclusionary suburbs favored these 2000 amendments in order to deter developers from invoking the statute. Carroll, "Connecticut Retrenches" (2001): 1269–72.

developer can appeal that denial to a specially designated court.[53] On appeal, the town's zoning commission bears the burden of proving that its denial was based on a health or safety concern that "clearly outweighs" the town's need for affordable housing.[54] Connecticut judicial decisions in Westlaw databases cite Connecticut's Appeals Act over 250 times.[55] In 70 percent of the decisions rendered between 1991 and 2006, judges rejected towns' rationales for refusing development approval.[56]

The merits of mixed-income housing projects, and of inclusionary zoning efforts more generally, are contested. Critics have long asserted that inclusionary zoning policies may function, counterproductively, as taxes on housing production.[57] The reductions in the sale or lease prices chargeable on affordable units are borne by the developer, not the general taxpayer. If unable to shift these costs, a developer might be less inclined to build.

A developer has two primary means for offsetting the added financial burdens that below-market units pose. First, an Appeals Act developer may benefit from a density bonus that permits the building of more dwelling units. The locality may voluntarily confer the bonus, or the plans that the developer submits may simply envision more units than the current zoning allows.

Second, the developer might successfully apply for benefits available under one of the raft of federal and state housing-subsidy programs. The most prominent is the Low-Income Housing Tax Credit program (LIHTC), currently the mainstay of subsidized housing production in the United States.[58] The federal treasury bears the cost of LIHTC tax

53. Conn. Gen. Stat. § 8–30g(f) (2019).
54. Conn. Gen. Stat. § 8–30g(g) (2019). Reviews of the case law on this issue include Carroll, "Connecticut Retrenches" (2001): 1259–60, and Tondro, "Only Middling Results?" (2001): 121–22.
55. On September 14, 2020, the number of Westlaw cases citing the Appeals Act was 253.
56. Shipman & Goodwin LLP, "Housing Land Use Appeals" (2006).
57. Fischel, *Zoning Rules!* (2015): 280–82; Glaeser and Gyourko, *Federal Housing Policy* (2008): 82; Ellickson, "Irony of Inclusionary Zoning" (1981). See generally Schuetz et al., "Inclusionary Zoning" (2011).
58. On LIHTC, see Weiss, "Locating Affordable Housing" (2018).

credits, but a state agency—in Connecticut, the Connecticut Housing Finance Authority—decides which applicants receive them.

LIHTC has many critics. Edward Glaeser, for example, favors LIHTC's repeal because the program fails to target its subsidies on regions where housing production is constrained.[59] Other critics emphasize LIHTC's failures to promote fair housing goals.[60] The LIHTC database published by the Department of Housing and Urban Development (HUD) indicates that, between 1988 and 2013, twenty-two LIHTC projects opened in New Haven's suburbs.[61] During those years, there were forty-seven projects in the City of New Haven itself. New Haven, with 5 percent of the metro's land area, thus was the site of 68 percent of Greater New Haven's LIHTC projects. Two working-class New Haven suburbs, Meriden, with eight LIHTC projects, and West Haven, with three, were the only suburbs with more than two.

Between 1990 and 2018, the Westlaw database indicates that developers invoked the Appeals Act against at least ten of the twelve New Haven suburbs that are potentially subject to the statute.[62] The most common target was Milford, the New Haven suburb closest to New York City. Milford battled against at least eight different Appeals Act proposals, in three instances with some success in court.[63]

59. Glaeser, "Land Use Restrictions" (2014); see also Glaeser and Gyourko, *Federal Housing Policy* (2008): 102–14, 143 (offering a wide-ranging critique of LIHTC).

60. Boggs and Dabrowski, "Out of Balance" (2017): 23–24 (also complaining that holders of housing vouchers concentrate in poor neighborhoods). But cf. Ellen et al., "LIHTC Program" (2009) (finding little evidence that LIHTC concentrates poverty nationwide).

61. LIHTC Database Access (2020).

62. The act only applies to a town in which affordable housing units are less than 10 percent of total units. Conn. Gen. Stat § 8–30g(k) (2019). This provision exempts three towns in Greater New Haven: Meriden, West Haven, and the City of New Haven.

63. The Connecticut Supreme Court held, for example, that AvalonBay could not compel the Town of Milford to extend sanitary sewers to a 284-unit, partially subsidized, project. AvalonBay Communities, Inc. v. Sewer Comm'n, 853 A.2d 497 (Conn. 2004). On Milford's oppositional attitude, see Ebersold, "Affordable Housing Plan Denied" (2016).

Particularly instructive is the history of the war between AvalonBay and the Town of Orange, Milford's neighbor to the east. Between 1999 and 2007, AvalonBay, one of the largest real estate investment trusts in the United States, systematically used the Appeals Act as a lever to force Connecticut suburbs to accept multifamily housing.[64] During those years, AvalonBay appeared as the named plaintiff in an average of three reported Connecticut cases per year, most of them Appeals Act cases.[65] AvalonBay won its signature success in Orange at a site three blocks south of the Boston Post Road (U.S. 1), one of the major arteries that links Greater New Haven to New York City. The firm proposed to build a 168-unit multifamily project, some of it five stories high, with 20 percent of the units affordable. Orange strenuously opposed AvalonBay's plans. The tussle generated, between 1999 and 2002, seven reported judicial decisions, two by the Supreme Court of Connecticut.[66] In one, the high court invalidated Orange's eleventh-hour bid to use its power of eminent domain to convert the site to a high-tech industrial park.[67]

Despite its triumph in Orange, AvalonBay has stopped invoking the Appeals Act. Between 2007 and 2011, the firm's role as a plaintiff declined, and as of 2012 it ceased altogether. AvalonBay seems to have decided that an alternative business strategy would be more profitable.[68] Invoking the Appeals Act typically imposes additional costs on a developer, such as attorney fees, the hassle of obtaining housing subsidies, and, perhaps, the risk of acquiring a reputation with suburbs as a non-cooperator. In addition, the presence of affordable units in a project may reduce the marketability of the unsubsidized units. Although other Connecticut developers

64. On the firm's strategy, see Charles, "Law in Its Toolbox" (2001).

65. The source of the figures was Westlaw's database of Connecticut judicial decisions, far more expansive than the Atlantic Reporter's.

66. AvalonBay Communities, Inc. v. Plan & Zoning Comm'n of Town of Orange, 796 A.2d 1164 (Conn. 2002) (providing overview of the issues contested).

67. AvalonBay Communities, Inc. v. Town of Orange, 775 A.2d 284 (Conn. 2001).

68. One well-informed commentator suggested that AvalonBay decided to stop building apartment buildings in Connecticut because the company's many existing projects had made it "overexposed" in the state. Interview with Richard Freedman, Garden Homes Mgmt. Corp., Dec. 6, 2018.

continue to invoke the Appeals Act, AvalonBay's decision to withdraw is ominous for opponents of suburban exclusion.

Although the Appeals Act has stirred passion in Connecticut, its impacts on New Haven's five most exclusionary suburbs have been minor. Between 1990 and 2018, no federal LIHTC tax credits were awarded to a project in Bethany, Madison, or Orange. Woodbridge does have a thirty-unit LIHTC project, exclusively for the elderly, and Guilford has two, with a total of thirty-four dwelling units.[69] But these projects all received their tax credits prior to 2001. Between 2002 and 2018, only one Appeals Act lawsuit, decided in 2007, has been successful against New Haven's five most exclusionary suburbs.[70] The Town of Orange's belligerent opposition to AvalonBay, by contrast, seems to have deterred subsequent developers from filing lawsuits. After AvalonBay's triumph in 2002, by 2020 there had been no reported cases brought against Orange under the Appeals Act. The town retaliated for its loss to AvalonBay by rezoning to light industry the entire area around the site where AvalonBay had won the right to build apartments. That action immunized the rezoned region from the reach of the Appeals Act.[71]

Connecticut's pressure on towns to permit denser housing sometimes bears fruit. In 2020, none other than the Town of Orange itself rezoned land near the Boston Post Road to permit development of a mixed-income multifamily project of forty-six units.[72] These outcomes are rare, however, and do nothing to cure the inherent flaws of the Connecticut Appeals Act.[73] The statute does nothing to eliminate local regulations that increase the cost of market-rate housing. The Appeals Act confers

69. LIHTC Database Access (2020).

70. Halter Estates Senior Community, LLC v. Planning & Zoning Comm'n of Town of Bethany, 2007 WL 1417159 (Conn. Super. Ct. 2007). In 2020, a clustered project, Rocky Corner Cohousing, was under development at the site. See http://rockycorner.org/.

71. See Conn. Gen. Stat. § 8–30g(g)(2)(A) (2019).

72. McLoughlin, "Affordable Housing Project Approved" (2020).

73. Richard Freedman of Garden Homes Management Corporation, a knowledgeable source, has asserted that the Appeals Act "hasn't done a lot" in Connecticut. See note 68. See also Freeman and Schuetz, "Producing Affordable Housing" (2017) (contending that inclusionary housing programs and state fair-share programs have yet to significantly boost the nation's housing stock).

project-based subsidies, a method of housing assistance, per dollar spent, substantially more costly than housing vouchers.[74] In practice, Appeals Act projects typically entail major transfer payments to mostly moderate-income households, not to low-income households. The selected beneficiaries are no more deserving than the host of others who receive no support. Connecticut has gone down a blind alley.

Open Space Set-Asides

Future historians of land policies in the United States are likely to stress two massive changes that occurred during the twentieth century. The first, portended by the rise of zoning during the early decades of the century, was the vast increase in municipal regulation of the use of private land. The second trend has been less obvious. Partly spurred by the environmental movement that blossomed around 1970, governments and nonprofit institutions have started to protect an ever-increasing fraction of land from development of any kind.

Greater New Haven has led the three metros in this pursuit, with Silicon Valley a close second and Greater Austin not far behind. To illustrate the magnitude of the change, Connecticut had no system of state parks prior to 1913.[75] In 1997, the state legislature announced the goal of either acquiring or permanently protecting 21 percent of the state's land as open space by the year 2023.[76]

In many contexts, the preservation of open space is meritorious. Especially in a rural setting, the conservation of land can provide habitat for wildlife, preserve endangered species, protect watersheds that feed reservoirs, and offer opportunities for outdoor recreation.[77] Residents of an urban area also unquestionably benefit from parks and other open spaces, welcome forms of relief from asphalt and concrete.[78] During the

74. See chapter 10.
75. Connecticut State Parks History (2016).
76. Conn. Gen. Stat. § 23–8(b) (2019). The legislation contemplates state ownership of about half the acreage, with the balance protected mostly by local governments, land trusts, and water companies.
77. McConnell and Walls, *Value of Open Space* (2005).
78. Turner, "Landscape Preferences" (2005) (emphasizing value of open space in urban areas).

mid-nineteenth century, civic leaders in Manhattan had the wisdom to create Central Park, which provided needed respite from the relentless northerly march of the grid of streets.[79]

The provision of open space in an urban area, however, is not invariably benign. The agglomeration benefits of urban living spring from population density. Open spaces reduce density. From a utilitarian perspective, just as there can be too little open space, there also can be too much. The value of a particular open space may be less than the sum of the forgone benefits of development (the opportunity costs), and the loss of agglomeration benefits. New York City's leaders, for example, would have been foolhardy to have set aside as a park the half of Manhattan lying north of 59th Street, Central Park's southern boundary.

Guilford, one of New Haven's five most exclusionary suburbs, illustrates the variety of institutions that have assisted in the setting aside of open space.[80] In 2014, 33 percent of Guilford had been set aside in this fashion.[81] The percentage is even higher in North Branford, one of Guilford's neighbors to the west. Guilford has a land area of forty-seven square miles, making it handily the largest of New Haven's suburbs. Because it lies east of the City of New Haven and thus farther from New York City, development pressures have been less intense. Guilford's topography has somewhat accentuated the hankering of its residents for open space. Much of the town's coastal area along Long Island Sound consists of tidal wetlands, and its upland regions contain several lakes. Most of the terrain in the northern half of Guilford is rugged and situated beyond an easy commute to downtown New Haven. Guilford's policies regarding its southern half, bisected by I-95, more greatly affect the welfare of the residents of metropolitan New Haven.

Most of Guilford's open spaces lie in the northern portion of town. The South Central Connecticut Regional Water Authority (RWA), owner of 11 percent of the town, is the largest owner of Guilford open space. (Some open-space advocates are wary of the depth of the Authority's

79. On Central Park, see *Greatest Grid* (2012): 118–21.

80. On the underlying motivations for preserving open space, see Bates and Santerre, "Demand for Open Space" (2001).

81. Milone & MacBroom, Inc., "Guilford Plan" (2015): 17. Because the denominator includes street rights-of-way, the percentage of non–right-of-way land in open space would be higher.

commitment to keeping its watershed lands undeveloped. They would prefer belt-and-suspenders protections of these lands, for example, ownership by a first entity committed to open space protection, subject to a conservation easement in favor of a similarly committed second entity.[82]) After RWA came the nonprofit Guilford Land Conservation Trust, with 10 percent of town land, the Town of Guilford itself (7 percent), and the State of Connecticut (4 percent).[83]

The fraction of open space land in Guilford, 33 percent in 2014, was conceivably as low as 2 percent in 1918. In the 1920s, the predecessor of the Regional Water Authority first began acquiring watersheds to protect its major reservoir in nearby North Branford. The Guilford land trust was not founded until 1965. Many of the Town of Guilford's own open-space acquisitions are recent, such as the 588-acre Timberlands Preserve, acquired in 1975. The State of Connecticut's acquisitions for Cockaponset State Forest, its main holding in Guilford, did not begin until the 1920s.

As Guilford illustrates, the flowering of open-space sentiment has prompted actions by governments at all levels. Among the government inducements have been tax subsidies to nonprofit land trusts. Since 1980, the federal income tax code has included a provision governing the deductibility of the donation of a perpetual conservation easement to these trusts.[84] The State of Connecticut has provided additional tax inducements.[85] Since 1991, each of New Haven's fourteen suburbs has had a land trust.[86] Guilford's land trust now owns more acreage than any other in Connecticut.[87]

82. See Serkin, "Entrenching Environmentalism" (2010) (raising concerns about excessive calcification of policy choices). Fischel also has emphasized the inflexibility of conservation easements. Fischel, *Zoning Rules!* (2015): 365.
83. Milone & MacBroom, Inc., "Guilford Plan" (2015): 17.
84. 26 U.S.C. § 170(h) (2000). Federal authorities commonly challenge, as overly generous, appraisals of the value of donated interests. McLaughlin, "Perpetual Conservation Easements" (2013): 703–16.
85. Conn. Gen. Stat. § 12–217dd (2019) (providing as much as a 50 percent tax credit to a donor that owes state corporation business taxes); see also Conn. Gen. Stat. § 12–107(e) (2019) (providing favorable property taxation of land set aside as open space).
86. Connecticut Land Conservation Council (2018). See McLaughlin, "Perpetual Conservation Easements" (2013): 690 (graphing growth of number of land trusts nationally).
87. Guilford Land Trust, Land Acquisition (2020).

The Town of Guilford has no sanitary sewers, and it requires a four-acre minimum house-lot in most of its northern section. These policy choices have driven down the market value of undeveloped land and abetted landowners' willingness to forgo development. In at least five instances since 1997, New Haven's suburbs have acquired an undeveloped tract, with an average area of 150 acres, explicitly to prevent housing development.[88] Although the details of these transactions vary, the following script generally applies. The town employs various exclusionary practices to depress the market value of the undeveloped tract. The landowner then threatens to sell the tract to a housing developer, perhaps one who might invoke the Connecticut Appeals Act as leverage. Bargaining between town and landowner ensues. In the end, to prevent development, the town acquires the tract, either by voluntary transfer or by exercising the town's power of eminent domain.

The Town of Orange, true to its traditionally exclusionary bent, carried out the most memorable of these five purchases.[89] In 2010, Hubbell Inc. owned a 376-acre tract, the largest undeveloped parcel remaining in Orange. The town had successively raised its minimum required house-lot for this property. It started with a ½-acre minimum in 1938, the year of Orange's first zoning ordinance, and, by 2004, had raised it to 1 ½ acres. In 2010, Hubbell proposed to develop 225 houses, some of them subsidized, on the 376 acres. Hubbell eventually agreed to sell the tract to the town for $7.1 million. The town's leaders then asked voters to ratify the purchase in a referendum. Prior to the vote, the town's top elected official advised the electorate that the purchase would serve the fiscal interests

88. On this local strategy, see Schmidt and Paulsen, "Open-Space Preservation" (2009). See also Tondro, "Only Middling Results?" (2001): 159 (stating that five Connecticut towns had acquired lands to squelch proposed Appeals Act projects).

89. The other four instances: In 2000, Woodbridge voluntarily purchased the Elderslie Preserve (198 acres) and, in 2009, the Country Club of Woodbridge (150 acres). Branford and North Haven have exercised their powers of eminent domain. See Branford v. Santa Barbara, 988 A.2d 209 (Conn. 2010) (tract of 77 acres); Peter Rock Assocs. v. North Haven, 756 A.2d 335 (Conn. Super. Ct. 1998), aff'd, 756 A.2d 290 (Conn. App. 2000) (involving 182 acres acquired to expand an adjacent park). Cf. Dana, "Exclusionary Eminent Domain" (2009) (discussing condemnation of buildings in which lower-income households reside).

of Orange households. He predicted that a typical homeowner's annual costs of financing the purchase of the Hubbell site would be far less than the costs of financing services to the new residents were the property to be developed.[90] In July 2011, 83 percent of Orange voters, in a massive turnout, approved the proposed purchase.

Connecticut's system of school finance helped clinch this outcome. Several Connecticut Supreme Court decisions, the first in 1977, compelled the Connecticut legislature to tilt formulas for state aid to schools more sharply in favor of jurisdictions with relatively poor residents and against a wealthy suburb such as Orange.[91] These changes may have deepened anti-growth sentiments in the town. It is unlikely that many Orange voters were eager to add to public open space as such. They mostly dwell in houses on lots of 0.5 to 1.0 acre, and the town already owned several spacious hiking areas.[92] Orange voters appear to have supported the purchase of the Hubbell tract mainly to avoid fiscal burdens and, in some instances, the prospective influx of less prosperous neighbors.

Especially since the 1960s, set-asides of open space also have occurred in Silicon Valley and Greater Austin. In the former, the Midpeninsula Regional Open Space District, founded in 1972, has become a major presence. In 2018, the District held eleven open-space reserves, totaling twenty-one square miles, within the white-colored territory of the map located at the outset of the last chapter.[93] Most of the District's holdings

90. Orange's first selectman estimated that a typical homeowner's annual share of the costs of purchasing the Hubbell site would be $100, far less than $500, the annual costs of providing public services were the site to be developed. McCready, "Hubbell Land Purchase" (2011).

91. See, e.g., Horton v. Meskill, 376 A.2d 359 (Conn. 1977). On the massive effect of these fiscal changes, see Liscow, "Local Government Finance" (2017): 1854–55 (reporting sharp drop in state aid to Orange, Connecticut, relative to the City of New Haven, between 1970 and 1999). While having more students tends to increase local schooling costs, in Connecticut a school system that enrolls more students from lower-income households generally receives more state aid. See School + State Finance Project, "Weights" (2020).

92. Prior to the Hubbell purchase, seven spacious sites in Orange were available for hiking and other recreational use. Orange Conservation Commission, "Open Spaces of Orange" (circa 2012).

93. See Midpeninsula Regional Open Space District (2019) (map). There also

were high in the mountains. The Greater Austin region has three active land trusts, the first created in 1986. Their founders organized these regionally, not, as in Greater New Haven, suburb by suburb. Northwest of Austin, the most pertinent local land trust is the Hill Country Conservancy, founded in 1999. The City of Austin also has undertaken land acquisitions in its northwestern portion, primarily to add to the Balcones Canyonlands Preserve.[94]

Zoning in New Haven's Middle-Income Suburbs

As chapter 2 demonstrated, all New Haven suburbs, not just the five most exclusionary, have a penchant for both large-lot zoning and limiting sites for as-of-right multifamily development. An important empirical question is whether these tendencies have increased over time. In general, they have. Many New Haven suburbs have significantly increased the minimum house-lot requirements in their single-family zones, and none has decreased them.[95] To illustrate this general historical trend, this section invokes the zoning history of Branford, one of New Haven's middle-income suburbs and formerly an important outlet for regional development pressures.

Branford's Green lies six miles east of the New Haven Green. In 1958, the Connecticut Turnpike (now I-95) first connected the two towns and spurred Branford's development. Between 1950 and 1980, when Branford's policies were generally pro-development, its population almost tripled. Daniel Cosgrove, a well-connected construction contractor and political boss, dominated Branford politics during the 1960s and 1970s.[96] Cosgrove headed the local Democratic committee and, more pertinently, Branford's sewer authority. His policies helped fuel a condominium boom. By 1989, the town had granted permits for 47 condominium complexes containing 3,253 units.[97] In 2020, these constituted about one-quarter of

have been municipal acquisitions, notably the City of Palo Alto's purchase of Foothill Park. See chapter 3.

94. See chapter 5.

95. See chapter 2.

96. Chambers, "Boss of Branford" (2006).

97. Schmitt, "Connecticut's Condo Capital" (1989).

the town's housing stock.[98] In the New Haven region, Cosgrove's tolerance of relatively dense development earned Branford the nickname "condo city."[99] To avoid riling nearby homeowners, condominium developers commonly placed a wreath of open space around their complexes, limiting town-wide walkability. In part because living in a multistory condominium tends to be less expensive, in 2016, Branford's median family income ranked eleventh highest among New Haven's fourteen suburbs.

By the 1980s, Branford's politics had begun to green. Residents formed the Branford Land Trust in 1967 and began using it as a vehicle for acquiring open space.[100] In the early 1980s, a grassroots group, the Beacon Hill Preservation Society, came to life and succeeded in scotching a proposed condominium development near one of Branford's traprock ridges.[101] During the 1980s, the Branford Land Trust witnessed an "explosion of energy" as its membership and land holdings both began to climb.[102] Cosgrove, a skeptic of the value of preserving wetlands, had become suspiciously wealthy during the 1960s and 1970s. Cosgrove suffered a key defeat in 1983 when Branford voters elected Judy Gott as First Selectwoman. Gott had run on a platform of slowing the development of high-density condominiums. In 1987, Gott pushed through a zoning amendment that reduced the maximum density of future multifamily developments from eighteen units to six units per acre, a limitation that Branford continues to retain.[103]

The greening of Branford's politics has profoundly dampened housing production. During Branford's 1960s and 1970s phase as condo city, the town had approved 160 units of condominium development per year. During the period 1997–2016, approvals of this sort apparently had fallen by 95 percent to no more than eight per year.[104] Since 1990, when

98. In 2005, Branford had 3,700 condominium units in 50 complexes. Hodara, "Branford, Conn." (2005).

99. Brooks, "Town Reversing Stand" (1982).

100. Branford Land Trust Timeline (undated).

101. Brooks, "Town Reversing Stand" (1982). In 1991, the State of Connecticut, with help from the town and the town's land trust, bought the ridge, known as Beacon Hill.

102. Wanerka, "Branford Land Trust: History" (1994): 27.

103. Branford, Conn., Zoning Regulations § 3.4A (2015).

104. Between 1997 and 2016, Branford granted permits for 153 housing units in structures containing five or more units. Connecticut Department of Economic and Community Development (2020).

developers had built out formerly approved condominium projects, Branford's population has been flat. Many Branford residents now are skeptical of development of any kind. In 2017, after a long battle, opponents caused Costco to scrap plans to erect a store near one of the Branford exits off I-95.[105]

Branford's political turn against development is analogous to Palo Alto's, although it occurred a decade or two later.[106] A valuable counterweight to the main narrative of this book would be the history of a town where YIMBYs (Yes In My Backyard advocates) had taken over from NIMBYs.[107] None of the zoning histories of the forty-one localities included in this study fits that scenario.[108]

Zoning in New Haven's Blue-Collar Suburbs

East Haven, Meriden, and West Haven are, to invoke an arguably anachronistic label, New Haven's blue-collar suburbs. In 2013, the median household income in each lagged the other eleven suburbs but was about 50 percent higher than that of the City of New Haven itself. Yet even these three suburbs engage in a form of exclusionary zoning that the less prosperous suburbs of the other two metros do not practice.

West Haven and East Haven, as their names imply, immediately adjoin the City of New Haven along Long Island Sound. These two towns are the smallest of New Haven's suburbs in area. West Haven came into existence in 1921 when it was carved out of the larger Town of Orange. In that year, downtown West Haven, which had long enjoyed streetcar links to downtown New Haven, was already relatively dense. In 2016, 21 percent of West Haven's population was African American, the second highest percentage for a New Haven suburb.[109] East Haven, by contrast, then was only 3 percent African American. East Haven's percentage of Italian Americans is 43 percent, the highest in the region.[110]

105. Norton, "Costco Gives Up" (2017).
106. See chapter 3.
107. On this countermovement, see chapter 11.
108. Leander, Texas, arguably comes closest. See chapter 2.
109. In 2016, Hamden's population was 25 percent Black.
110. Holahan, "Italian Roots Run Deep" (2016).

Meriden's downtown lies in a flat portion of Connecticut's Central Lowlands, about halfway between the cities of New Haven and Hartford. Meriden developed as an industrial center during the late nineteenth century. By 1900, it had a population of 29,000, at that time 42 percent of the combined populations of New Haven's fourteen suburbs. In 2016, 27 percent of Meriden's population was Hispanic, the highest of any New Haven suburb.

The most striking aspect of these three blue-collar towns' zoning policies is the unanimity of their refusal to allow house-lots small enough to enable walkability. Each of their zoning maps permits, in a solid majority of their residentially zoned area, only single-family development. East Haven requires a lot of at least 20,000 sq. ft. in these single-family neighborhoods; West Haven, 16,000 sq. ft.; and Meriden, 11,250 sq. ft. The average of these lot sizes is roughly twice the national median for a new detached house.[111] This aversion to small house-lots pervades New England. The most likely cause is how New England states structure their local governments. These states lack unincorporated areas and deploy long-established suburbs to hem in their central cities.[112] Conceivably, New Englanders also may harbor different conceptions of ideal suburban densities.[113]

New Haven's blue-collar suburbs are relatively tolerant, however, of both "missing middle" and multifamily housing complexes. East Haven allows duplexes on 39 percent of its residentially zoned land, the most of the thirty-seven suburbs studied. West Haven permits triplexes on 18 percent, and Meriden allows either a duplex or triplex on 8 percent. The three towns permit the construction of apartments or dense townhouses on 5.8 percent of their residentially zoned territory. That figure far exceeds 0.8 percent, the number for the other eleven New Haven suburbs.

111. See chapter 2.

112. Texas, in particular, structures its local governments differently. See chapter 5.

113. See American Society of Planning Officials, *Connecticut Planning Legislation* (1967): 183–84: ". . . [T]he consultants gained the impression that the majority of persons in Connecticut felt that a lot was not 'large' until it exceeded a half-acre, or even one acre. This can be contrasted to many other parts of the United States."

Meriden and West Haven also contain, between them, 56 percent of the undeveloped acreage that New Haven suburbs zone for multifamily use. These greenfield sites amount to 2.1 percent of their combined residentially zoned territory.

For Greater New Haven, these three blue-collar suburbs, although surprisingly averse to walkable single-family neighborhoods, are relatively pro-development. In northwestern Greater Austin, their tolerance of residential density would be well below average.

5

The Booming Municipalities Northwest of Austin

Greater Austin is a plausible choice for the role of Sunbelt boomtown. Between 1970 and 2010, the populations of Travis County, where most of the City of Austin lies, and Williamson County, situated just to the north, grew by a combined 234 percent. This rate of population growth placed Greater Austin in the top handful of U.S. metros.[1] By comparison, over the course of these same four decades the headcount in the United States increased by 52 percent; in Silicon Valley's fifteen suburbs, by 39 percent; and in New Haven's fourteen suburbs, by 19 percent. The Austin suburb of Round Rock, which in the 1990s became the headquarters of Dell Computers, is the most conspicuous of the burgeoning suburbs in Greater Austin's northwestern sector. Figure 7 shows its location. Round Rock's population exploded, partly because of annexations, from 3,000 in 1970 to an estimated 133,000 in 2019. A central contributor to Greater Austin's growth has been Texas's local government law. Texas's policies, far better than both California's and Connecticut's, work to suppress local exclusionary tendencies.

Introduction to the Austin Area

In 1838, the newly formed Republic of Texas chose to site its capital on a lightly settled bluff above the Colorado River. This watercourse

1. Frey, "Population Growth Since 1980" (2012): 4 (placing the population growth rate of the Greater Austin metro in the top six nationally in each of the 1980s, 1990s, and 2000s).

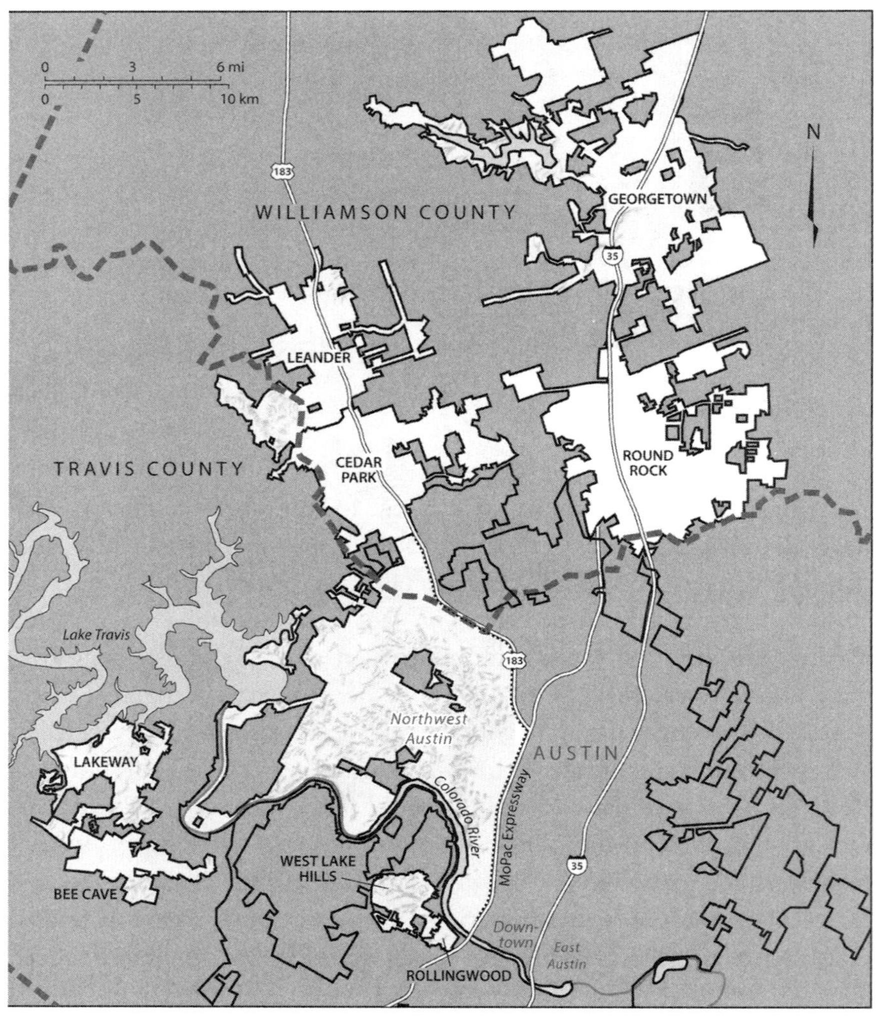

Figure 7. Greater Austin, Northwestern Sector (Cartography by Bill Nelson)

is far less well known than another with the identical name that lies a thousand miles further west. The Austin area is the flattest of the three regions studied, and, unlike Silicon Valley especially, has a plentiful supply of undeveloped land.[2] West and northwest of downtown Austin, the

2. Saiz, "Geographic Determinants" (2010): 1258–59.

terrain gently rises and eventually transitions into the Texas Hill Country, widely perceived as the beginning of the American West. Visible limestone outcroppings and caliche soils are common and limit farming potential, especially in the western portion of Greater Austin. Winters are mild, but summers can be oppressively hot and humid.

As elsewhere, water policies have strongly influenced development patterns. In 1937, a century after the founding of the City of Austin, the area's newly elected congressman, Lyndon Baines Johnson, began a successful campaign to win partial federal funding for a dam on the Colorado River a dozen miles northwest of the city.[3] This dam created a major reservoir, Lake Travis. Lakeway, the westernmost of the Austin suburbs included in this study, abuts its waters. Greater Austin sits above two major sources of groundwater, the Trinity Aquifer and the Edwards Aquifer.[4] Water levels in both are dropping and may eventually retard the pace of the metropolitan area's development.[5]

A century ago, Austin was by far the least populous of the three metros. In 1920, the population of Travis County was 58,000, about one-third that of the City of New Haven alone, and barely one-half that of Santa Clara County. The expansions of both Texas state government and the University of Texas at Austin, one of the largest universities in the United States, have contributed to Greater Austin's surge. IT firms, searching for a metro attractive to techies but cheaper than Silicon Valley, have also contributed to regional growth. Austin loyalists tout many attractions, including the city's reputation as the live-music capital of the world.

Like Dallas, Houston, and San Antonio, the City of Austin is physically vast. It currently encompasses three hundred square miles, fifteen times the area of the City of New Haven. Austin is slightly larger in area than the entire Silicon Valley, the whitish area in figure 3. To lessen computational burdens, this study focused solely on zoning policies in the relatively prosperous northwestern sector of Greater Austin. The light

3. Beach, "Saddling the Colorado" (2018).
4. Texas Almanac, "Major Aquifers of Texas" (2018). On management of the Edwards Aquifer, see Torres, "Groundwater in Texas" (2012).
5. See Hargrove, "Drinking Water" (2019) (assessing possibility of future water shortages).

areas in figure 7 indicate the 213 square miles included in my study of the Austin area. Many of figure 7's dark areas, especially those in Williamson County, are unincorporated and not zoned. More than a quarter of the light area lies within the City of Austin itself, much of it land that the city annexed between 1970 and 1989.[6] The northwestern sector includes some of the City of Austin's most upscale neighborhoods, such as Tarrytown, as well as several of its toniest suburbs, such as Rollingwood and West Lake Hills.[7] In 1992, the City of Austin, working with various partners, created the Balcones Canyonlands Preserve to set aside open space. In 2018, the preserve included about fifteen square miles of city land in the western portion of the area of study.[8]

Of the three metros, Austin has the fewest suburbs, an outgrowth of Texas local government law. The area of study includes eight suburbs in their entirety. Four of these, the smallest in both headcount and area, lie in Travis County south of the Colorado River.[9] The larger four are all situated farther north, in Williamson County (see figure 7).[10]

As a laboratory, Greater Austin promised several advantages compared to other fast-growing Sunbelt metros. One is the presence of the flagship campus of the University of Texas, which enhances scholars' familiarity with the metro. Another is the diversity of political ideologies in Greater Austin. Voters in Travis County, "a blue dot in a sea of red," twice cast over 60 percent of their ballots for Barack Obama in presidential elections. Williamson County, by contrast, traditionally is solidly Republican. There, Barack Obama twice won only about 40 percent.[11] This divide promised to help shed light on whether Republican voting

6. For a map of the city's annexations between 1959 and 2014, see Reddit, "Austin Annexations by Decade" (2014).
7. More precisely, the study area included the portion of the City of Austin that lies north of the Colorado River and west of the MoPac Expressway, extended northwest along U.S. 183 after U.S. 183 intersects MoPac.
8. Balcones Canyonlands Preserve (undated); Travis County, Texas, "Balcones Canyonlands Conservation Plan" (2020).
9. Bee Cave, Lakeway, Rollingwood, and West Lake Hills.
10. Cedar Park, Georgetown, Leander, and Round Rock.
11. In the 2020 election, by contrast, Williamson County voters narrowly supported Biden over Trump. Jankowski, "Suburban Swing" (2020).

tendencies are associated with more restrictive or less restrictive zoning policies.[12]

The Pro-Growth Zoning Policies of Austin and Its Suburbs

Chapter 2 provides summary data on zoning practices in the three metros. According to each of the metrics applied, localities in the northwest quadrant of Greater Austin are by far the least exclusionary. No suburb in the Austin region comes close to rivaling the large lot requirements of the Silicon Valley suburbs of Portola Valley and Woodside. West Lake Hills, the most overtly exclusionary of the northwest Austin suburbs, does require a minimum house-lot of one acre on 99 percent of its residentially zoned area. In two respects, however, West Lake Hills's form of exclusion is mild. On average, New Haven's five most exclusionary suburbs are eight times the area of West Lake Hills, which comprises only 3.7 squares miles. Members of the New Haven quintet also impose a two-acre minimum on 53 percent of their residentially zoned land, twice the one-acre requirement in West Lake Hills.

The northwestern sector of Austin contains a second classically exclusionary suburb, Rollingwood. In 2015, that city's households had the highest median income of any municipality in the Austin area. Rollingwood, with 0.7 square mile, is the tiniest of the thirty-seven suburbs studied. Its standard single-family zone mandates a house-lot of 15,000 square feet, a smaller minimum than the 20,000 required in blue-collar East Haven, Connecticut.[13]

Greater Austin localities also are relatively tolerant, in single-family neighborhoods, of allowing Eichler-sized 8,000-sq.-ft. lots, the bane of every New Haven suburb.[14] The City of Austin and its four northernmost suburbs permit 8,000-sq.-ft. lots on a whopping 55 percent of the area

12. Compare Kahn, "Do Liberal Cities Limit?" (2011) (finding that California cities with more residents registered in left-leaning parties were less likely to permit new housing development); Sorens, "Partisan Geography" (2018) (finding that areas with more restrictive zoning become more Democratic).

13. See chapter 4.

14. See chapter 2, tables 3 and 4.

they restrict to detached single-family development.[15] The northwestern Austin sector, moreover, far outstrips the other metropolitan areas in providing undeveloped sites zoned for multifamily housing. Although Silicon Valley is more than twice as dense on average and contains many more multifamily developments, the Valley's percentage of undeveloped multifamily acreage is one-tenth that of northwestern Austin.[16]

Texas's fiscal structure has helped keep its politics pro-growth. Unlike both California and Connecticut, Texas has no income tax. Property tax rates in Texas, by contrast, are high, averaging 2.18 percent in 2018.[17] Local governments in Texas rely on property tax revenues to fund most local services, including schools. In California, by contrast, voter approval of Proposition 13 in 1976 capped property tax rates at one percent, reducing a suburb's fiscal advantage of permitting new construction.[18]

The Influence of Texas Local Government Law

Texas statutes do not direct a suburb to allow small house-lots and to zone a significant fraction of vacant land for multifamily housing. But that is what most Austin suburbs do. These outcomes reflect not only the policy preferences of suburban officials but also the traditional pro-growth tilt of both the Texas legislature and the Texas judiciary. Texas's local government law has favored the evolution of muscular central cities, such as Austin, and sharply constrained the emergence of exclusionary suburbs. Connecticut, more than California, stands at the opposite pole.[19] Some legal commentators contend that variations among the states are insignificant.[20] This chapter challenges that assessment. Five

15. The four small Austin suburbs south of the Colorado River, by contrast, permit 8,000-sq.-ft. lots on only 10 percent of their total single-family acreage.
16. See chapter 2, table 7.
17. Morris, "Texas Property Tax Rate" (2019).
18. Quigley and Raphael, "Housing in California" (2005): 323. Cf. Schwartz, "Prisoners of Proposition 13" (1997) (contending, because California grants localities a share of sales tax revenues, Proposition 13 has induced municipalities to favor retail uses).
19. See chapter 4.
20. See, e.g., Feeley and Rubin, *Federalism* (2008): 118–20.

Texas policies affecting the structure of local government warrant emphasis. I present them in decreasing order of seeming importance.

A Central City Can Veto the Incorporation of a Nearby Suburb

Texas has granted Austin, and its other most populous cities, the right to prevent the creation of a new municipality within five miles of its borders. The five-mile distance defines the reach of a populous city's Extraterritorial Jurisdiction (ETJ), an acronym familiar to Texas attorneys and planners.[21] In the 1950s, Austin acquiesced in the creation of the small municipalities of West Lake Hills and Rollingwood, each located a few miles west of downtown.[22] Over the decades, however, Austin typically has been hostile to the formation of new suburbs within its ETJ, perhaps because it has aspired eventually to annex the territories involved.

Besides Texas, a few other states, such as Oklahoma and Tennessee, empower their big cities to veto the creation of a nearby suburb.[23] The contrast between these states and the New England states is particularly striking. In Connecticut especially, suburban towns, with fixed borders, hem in central cities. A Texas approach to municipal formation also would have transformed the configuration of local governments in California. The backers of many successful Silicon Valley municipal incorporations were seeking to ward off annexation by a nearby city, such as San Jose.[24] Had California law conformed to Texas law, San Jose could have vetoed the creation of these new suburbs.

21. Tex. Loc. Gov't Code Ann. § 42.021 (West 2008) (setting ETJ of five miles for a city whose population is 100,000 or greater); id. at § 42.041 (conferring veto power).
22. West Lake Hills, developed by Emmett Shelton, Sr., was incorporated in 1953. Rollingwood, a creation of George B. Hatley, was incorporated as a village in 1955 and as a city in 1963. The planning department of neither city was able to provide a copy of its earliest zoning map.
23. Oklahoma prohibits the creation of a new suburb within five miles of a city with a population of 200,000. Okla. Stat. Ann. tit. 11, § 2–104(A) (West 2021). Tennessee generally bars the creation of a new municipality within three miles of an existing city and within five miles of a city whose population exceeds 100,000. Tenn. Code Ann. § 6–18–103(b) (West 2015).
24. See chapter 3.

Counties Lack Authority to Zone

Texas, unlike California and most other states, denies a county the power to enact a zoning ordinance.[25] Texas, however, is hardly anarchic. The state authorizes a county to impose subdivision regulations on its unincorporated territory, and many counties in the Austin metropolitan area have done so.[26] Travis County has hundreds of pages of subdivision regulations. Williamson County has them as well.[27] These regulations may include minimum lot-size requirements, such as Travis County's minimum of one acre for a lot that will rely on a septic tank.[28] These county mandates, however, are typically far less stringent than, for example, San Mateo and Santa Clara counties' restrictions on the development of Stanford's Foothill lands.[29]

Central Cities Can Annex Territory Unilaterally

Prior to 2017, Texas was one of the seven states to authorize its populous chartered cities, such as the City of Austin, to expand unilaterally.[30] Until 2017, a municipality had the power to annex unincorporated territory within its extraterritorial jurisdiction, even over the objection of residents and landowners in the annexed area.[31] Like many of Texas's populous cities, the City of Austin warmly embraced this invitation. By 2017, the northernmost extremity of the City of Austin indeed had pushed beyond Travis County into Williamson County. Annexations have multiplier effects in Texas. By annexing, a city can extend its ETJ and thus expand the geographic reach of its powers both to annex and to veto the creation of a new suburb.

25. Tex. Loc. Gov't Code Ann. § 231 (West 2016) (carving out various exceptions). Connecticut counties have no governing powers.
26. Tex. Loc. Gov't Code Ann. § 232.001 (West 2016).
27. Williamson County Subdivision Regulations (adopted Dec. 17, 2019).
28. Travis County, Tex., Code § 448.032(b) (2018).
29. See chapter 3.
30. Tyson, "Involuntary Annexation" (2012): 318–25. Texas's about-face in 2017, for counties with a population of at least 500,000, appears at Tex. Loc. Gov't Code Ann. §§ 43.0681–43.0699 (West 2017).
31. See, e.g., Allen v. City of Austin, 116 S.W.2d 468 (Tex. Civ. App. 1938). The Texas statutes that govern annexations are complex and much contested. Houston, "Municipal Annexation in Texas" (2012).

Policies That Enable Developers to Obtain Utility Services

In Texas, a government that provides utility services has a duty to serve, typically in return for fees, all lands that it has fully annexed.[32] The four large suburbs in Williamson County each has a utility department that provides both water and sanitary sewer services to most of its residents. In Greater New Haven, in sharp contrast, the centerpiece of some towns' exclusionary policies has been the denial of water and, especially, sanitary sewers.[33]

A Texas municipality ordinarily has no duty to serve lands beyond the boundaries of its "service area," which commonly tracks city boundaries.[34] Texas statutes, however, offer the developer of a tract in an unincorporated area the option of establishing a Municipal Utility District (MUD). Texas MUDs average less than a square mile in area.[35] Their smallness makes some of them potential candidates for the use of decentralized utility technologies.[36] Both the Texas Commission on Environmental Quality and the city whose ETJ includes the proposed MUD have to consent to a MUD's creation.[37] Both routinely do. The City of Austin has twenty-seven MUDs in its planning area. In 2019, Round Rock had fourteen, many of them in territories that the city has since annexed.[38] The legislature's provision of the MUD alternative, long controversial in Texas, is yet another symbol of the state's pro-growth inclinations.[39]

32. Tex. Loc. Gov't Code Ann. § 43.056(c) (West 2019), requiring provision of water and sanitary sewers after an annexation for "full-purposes"; Tex. Water Code Ann. § 13.250(a) (West 2013). Cf. Lukrawka v. Spring Valley Water Co., 146 P. 640 (Cal. 1915) (on duty of a water utility to serve in California).
33. See chapter 4.
34. City of Livingston v. Wilson, 310 S.W.2d 569, 576 (Tex. Civ. App. 1958).
35. Galvan, "Wrestling with MUDs" (2007): 3045 (reporting that a MUD serves 525 acres on average).
36. See chapter 4.
37. 30 Tex. Admin. Code § 293.11(d) (2021); Tex. Water Code Ann. §§ 54.014, 54.016 (2019).
38. Round Rock, Tex., "MUDs" (2019).
39. Defenders of MUDs tout their tax advantages and value in enabling developers to secure financing. Bumgardner and Hemyari, "Dodging Mud Slingers" (2017) (stressing financing advantages). Critics point to instances of corruption and cronyism, lack of democratic oversight, and aggravation of sprawl. Galvan, "Wrestling with MUDs" (2007).

The Texas annexation process commonly produces suburbs with weirdly shaped boundaries. In Connecticut and, to a lesser degree, California, most municipalities are compact. As figure 7 indicates, the shapes of Texas cities can look like portions of a Rorschach test. Northwestern Austin suburbs, particularly those in Williamson County, are full of holes (unincorporated areas) and may include grotesquely shaped arms (typically, extensions along highways or rivers). The latter may reflect municipalities' efforts to extend their ETJs, reap fiscal benefits, and obtain the power to zone the annexed areas. Landowners also may have initiated some of these annexations, especially when creating a MUD would be inferior to belonging to a municipality saddled with a duty to serve.

Independent School Districts Have Their Own Boundaries

In Connecticut, school district boundaries largely track town boundaries.[40] When the boundaries of both are congruent, Connecticut zoning commissioners know that their decisions will significantly influence the socioeconomic status of children enrolling in local public schools. They also are aware that the local portion of the costs of public education will invariably fall on members of the local electorate. In recent decades, Connecticut increasingly has enabled pupils to transfer between local school districts, somewhat weakening the former link between zoning and schools.[41]

In both California and Texas, school district boundaries commonly do not track city boundaries. The high school that serves Atherton, California, the wealthiest town in Silicon Valley, for example, also serves East Palo Alto, California, the region's least wealthy.[42] The adjective "independent" appears in the name of most school districts in Texas, where school district boundaries may spill over city borders.[43] The Eanes Independent School District, one of the highest-rated in the Austin area, includes not only Rollingwood and West Lake Hills but also much of the territory

40. An exception in Greater New Haven is the regional school district that provides middle schools and a high school to Bethany, Orange, and Woodbridge, three of the region's five most exclusionary towns.
41. Suarez, "Educational Outcomes" (2010): 484–87.
42. Menlo-Atherton High, "School Boundaries Map" (2020) (mapping school's service area).
43. See Greater Austin School District Map (undated).

north and west of those suburbs. The Leander Independent School District includes both the City of Leander and the City of Cedar Park. The uncoupling of school district lines from city boundary lines somewhat attenuates incentives for exclusionary zoning.[44]

Racial Demography in the Three Metropolitan Areas

Because Texas formerly was a Confederate state, it is timely to introduce the topic of racial segregation. A century ago, many early supporters of zoning in the United States lauded its potential for segregating households by race.[45] In 1917, however, the United States Supreme Court invalidated an explicit effort by the City of Louisville to zone by race.[46] During the following decade or two, the court reaffirmed that holding, striking down efforts by the cities of New Orleans and Richmond to use zoning to promote residential segregation.[47] Numerous civil rights statutes also now bar zoning by race.[48] Residential racial segregation nonetheless unquestionably continues in the United States, limiting the life chances of members of racial minority groups.[49]

Commentators debate the weightiness of the multiple causes of residential racial segregation.[50] Current public policies, among them exclusionary zoning, certainly have contributed.[51] So have private actions, such

44. See also Ross, "Fiscal Zoning" (2018) (finding that a locality tends to be more pro-development when it can export part of the fiscal burden of financing schools to residents of other localities).

45. Ellickson et al., *Land Use Controls* (2021): 109–10, 635–37; Rothstein, *Color of Law* (2017): 43–54; Trounstine, *Segregation by Design* (2018): 85–97 (using regression analysis to identify attributes of cities that first adopted zoning).

46. Buchanan v. Warley, 245 U.S. 60 (1917).

47. Harmon v. Tyler, 273 U.S. 668 (1927) (per curiam); City of Richmond v. Deans, 281 U.S. 704 (1930) (per curiam).

48. See, e.g., Fair Housing Act of 1968, 42 U.S.C. §§ 3601–31 (2012).

49. On detriments to those excluded, see Card and Rothstein, "Racial Segregation" (2007); Cutler and Glaeser, "Ghettos Good or Bad?" (1997). Cf. chapter 1 (discussing Chetty et al.'s findings on the effects of segregation by social class).

50. See, e.g., Starkey, *Stuck in Place* (2013); Trounstine, "Geography of Inequality" (2020).

51. Rothwell, "Racial Enclaves" (2011): 347 (attributing at least 25 percent of U.S. racial segregation to zoning policies); see also Rothwell and Massey, "Effect of

as steering by real estate brokers. Largely discontinued past practices, such as racially restrictive covenants and overt redlining by mortgage lenders, may have cast shadows whose effects continue.[52] Households' locational preferences also are pertinent. As Thomas Schelling has shown, if the race of neighbors is salient to a dwelling-seeker and individuals generally prefer to live in a neighborhood with many residents like themselves, even a society cleansed of racist practices might end up with neighborhoods that differed by race.[53] Lee Fennell, reviewing studies of individuals' preferences for neighborhoods of varying racial mixes, has stressed that prior patterns of racial segregation may have influenced those preferences.[54]

Trends in Racial Demography

By almost all measures, the incidence of racial segregation has declined in the United States.[55] In 1968, the Kerner Commission famously declared, "Our nation is moving toward two societies, one black, one white—separate and unequal."[56] This statement eloquently reminded the nation of the challenges stemming from a legacy of slavery. But the Kerner Commission badly forecast the nation's actual demographic future. In Silicon Valley in 2014, the sum of those who self-identify as either Asian or Hispanic handily exceeded the sum of those who self-identify as either Black or White.[57] Between 2000 and 2014, the number of Black and White residents in Silicon Valley each declined by 14 percent. Greater New Haven and Greater Austin, like most metros, also have witnessed

---

Density Zoning" (2009); Resseger, "Racial Segregation" (2013) (finding zoning exacerbates racial segregation).

52. Brooks and Rose, *Saving the Neighborhood* (2013).

53. Schelling, *Micromotives and Macrobehavior* (1978): 140–55. See also Bayer et al., "Residential Segregation" (2014) (marshaling data indicating that many college-educated Blacks prefer middle-class neighborhoods that are majority Black); Graham, "Neighborhood Effects" (2018): 465–90 (discussing how voluntary household sorting among neighborhoods might produce neighborhoods different from those that a social planner would choose).

54. Fennell, "Searching for Fair Housing" (2017): 372–75.

55. Lee, "Racial Segregation" (2017); Logan, "Persistence of Segregation" (2013) (lamenting lack of further progress); Vigdor and Glaeser, "End of Segregated Century" (2012).

56. National Advisory Commission on Civil Disorders, *Report* (1968): 1.

57. See table 10.

Table 10. Population by Race, 1950 and 2014

	Silicon Valley	Greater New Haven	Northwest Austin Area
1950			
Total Population	c. 140,000	201,978	c. 22,000
Non-Hispanic White	c. 92.0%	99.1%	c. 86.0%
Black	c. 2.0%	0.8%	c. 2.0%
2014	(24 places)	(14 places)	(9 places)
Total Population	916,684	439,383	394,773
White	41.1%	74.8%	65.1%
Asian	33.4%	4.3%	6.2%
Black	2.3%	7.7%	5.2%
Hispanic	18.7%	11.1%	20.9%
Places more than 80% White	12.5% (3/24)	64.3% (9/14)	11.1% (1/9)
Suburb with highest % of Whites	Woodside 86.4%	Madison 92.6%	Rollingwood 87.1%
Suburb with median % of Whites	Palo Alto 56.3%	Milford 84.6%	Georgetown 73.7%
Suburb with lowest % of Whites	East Palo Alto 7.6%	W. Haven 52.5%	Round Rock 50.3%
Suburb with highest % of Asians	Cupertino 66.3%	Woodbridge 15.5%	Cedar Park 8.8%
Suburb with highest % of Blacks	East Palo Alto 11.9%	Hamden 21.5%	Round Rock 10.1%
Suburb with highest % of Hispanics	East Palo Alto 63.5%	Meriden 25.2%	Round Rock 30.5%

Source: U.S. Bureau of the Census, American Community Survey 2012–2016.
Note: In 2014, Hispanics of all races are tallied solely as Hispanics.

large increases in Asian and Hispanic residents. Table 10 presents snapshots of the racial demographics of the three study areas for two years, 1950 and 2014.[58]

As table 10 indicates, between 1950 and 2014, the percentage of Whites fell the furthest in Silicon Valley, from 92 percent to 41 percent.[59] In the

58. Racial change over time is difficult to measure, in part because the Census Bureau periodically changes, in the decennial census, the wording of the pertinent question.

59. Hereafter, *Whites* refers only to non-Hispanic Whites.

three regions, the New Haven suburbs have the highest percentage of Whites. Yet, even in Greater New Haven, the number of Whites fell over the course of that sixty-four-year period from 96 percent to 75 percent. In 1970, all fourteen of New Haven's suburbs were more than 90 percent White. By 2014, only Guilford and Madison, both east of the city, remained that way. The population of the northwestern sector of Greater Austin, which is 21 percent Hispanic, currently is more racially diverse than the Greater New Haven suburbs. Greater Austin is the only region studied where Americans in all major racial groups have seen a rise in numbers.

More recent demographic trends also are informative. Between 2000 and 2014, the number of Whites in the northwestern sector of booming Greater Austin rose by 84,000. During that same period, by contrast, Silicon Valley lost 59,000 Whites and the New Haven suburbs 27,500.

Myron Orfield has offered a facially plausible definition of a racially integrated suburb.[60] His standard is whether between 20 percent and 60 percent of its residents are other than non-Hispanic Whites. A suburb that meets this test would have a significant, but not preponderant, share of minority residents. In 2010, Orfield found that 44 percent of suburbanites in the fifty largest U.S. metropolitan areas lived in localities that met this criterion. In 2014, by the Orfield standard, the suburbs northwest of Austin were the most integrated of the three areas studied. There, 99 percent of residents (all except those in Rollingwood, which the Orfield standard deems overly White) lived in a racially integrated community. In Silicon Valley and Greater New Haven, by contrast, the percentage of the population meeting the Orfield standard fell to around one-half, but for different reasons. In Silicon Valley, four suburbs flunked the Orfield standard because they had more than a 60 percent minority population (Cupertino, East Palo Alto, City of Santa Clara, and Sunnyvale), and two (Portola Valley and Woodside) flunked it because they had less than a 20 percent minority population. In Greater New Haven, no suburb had too many minorities, but nine of the fourteen suburbs failed the Orfield standard by having over 80 percent non-Hispanic Whites.

60. Orfield, "America's Most Diverse Neighborhoods" (2012).

The residential segregation of African Americans has most troubled social scientists.[61] In 1950, when racial segregation was more pronounced in the United States, each of the three metros had a recognized Black neighborhood with relatively distinct boundaries. In the Silicon Valley of the 1950s and 1960s, many Blacks lived east of the Bayshore Expressway in either East Palo Alto, then unincorporated, or Belle Haven, an adjoining neighborhood in Menlo Park. In the City of New Haven, the Dixwell neighborhood historically was the center of Black settlement, especially before the 1950s, when an urban renewal project decimated it.[62] In the City of Austin in the mid-twentieth century, Blacks were concentrated in East Austin. East Austin then lay east of East Avenue, a street that in 1962 became I-35.[63] In 1928, the City of Austin had contemplated taking affirmative steps, in almost certain violation of Supreme Court precedent, to create a "Negro District" in East Austin.[64]

In all three metros, the residential segregation of African Americans has become less prevalent. In 1950, eight of New Haven's fourteen suburbs had fifty or fewer Black residents. By 2014, none of them did. In 1970, 83 percent of Blacks in the New Haven metro resided in the City of New Haven itself. By 2014, that percentage had declined to 56 percent. If recent trends continue, by 2030 over half of the Greater New Haven's Black population will be living in the suburbs. The Black population in East Austin similarly has plummeted as that area has gentrified.[65] By 2010, more Blacks in the Greater Austin area lived outside the City of Austin than in the city itself.[66] Between 2000 and 2014, the number of Blacks in Williamson County's four booming suburbs—Cedar Park, Georgetown,

61. See, e.g., Intrator et al., "Segregation by Race" (2016).
62. Warner, *New Haven Negroes* (1940): 195–99 (including a map showing areas of concentrated Black residence in City of New Haven); Rae, *Urbanism and Its End* (2003): 339 (describing effects of urban renewal).
63. McDonald, *Racial Dynamics in Austin* (2012): 70 (providing a map showing residence by race, circa 1929); Zehr, "Austin's Racial Divide" (2020) (mapping residence by race from 1940 to 2010).
64. Tretter, "Austin Restricted" (undated): 18; Buchanan v. Warley, 245 U.S. 60 (1917).
65. McGlinchy, "Residents of East Austin" (2017).
66. Goldsberry, "Define Austin" (2015).

Leander, and Round Rock—increased by 10,000, and in the latter year Blacks constituted 4 percent of these suburbs' combined populations. In Silicon Valley, by contrast, between 2000 and 2014 the Black population fell by 3,400 to constitute 2.3 percent of the region's population, a toll of high housing prices.[67] By 2014, East Palo Alto, traditionally a center of Black population, was almost two-thirds Hispanic.

Social scientists standardly employ a dissimilarity index to compute the extent of racial segregation in a particular area.[68] The dissimilarity index indicates the percentage of Blacks who would have to move to equalize the Black/White ratio in every neighborhood. *Diversity and Disparities,* a website that John Logan helps maintain at Brown University, provides dissimilarity indexes over time for all U.S. metros.[69] The website confirms that Black/White segregation continues to exist in the three metros chosen for study but that it declined in each between 1980 and 2010. That source indicates that Greater New Haven is the most racially segregated of the three regions studied and the only one more segregated than the median U.S. metro. Between 1980 and 2010, the Black/White dissimilarity index in New Haven fell from 69 to 62. In the Austin metro, the drop was the largest of the three, from 65 to 48, consistent with the national pattern that a fast-growing metropolitan area tends to be less racially segregated.[70] The Brown University data identify the San Jose metro, where the index dropped from 48 to 39, as the least segregated of the three regions. The most racially segregated metros in the United States, many of them in the northern Midwest, are far more racially segregated than any of the three examined here.

The Logan website also provides dissimilarity data in 2010 for selected sub-metropolitan municipalities and places. It describes a Black/White index of 30 as a "fairly low" level of segregation. (It is far from clear,

67. Romem and Kneebone, "Disparity in Departure" (undated) (documenting that out-migrants from Silicon Valley tend to have lower incomes).

68. Vigdor and Glaeser, "End of Segregated Century" (2012): 2–3 (explaining difference between the dissimilarity index and its chief alternative, the isolation index).

69. *Diversity and Disparities* (undated). This source defines the boundaries of the three metros differently than those used to create table 10.

70. Cortright, "Persistence of Residential Segregation" (2018).

however, whether most members of a racial minority group would regard a dissimilarity index of zero as ideal.[71]) Of the twelve localities in Silicon Valley for which the Logan source provides data, two have an index over 30. They are Menlo Park (65, attributable to Belle Haven) and Redwood City (37). For Greater New Haven, the website reports data for the City of New Haven and seven of its suburbs. Three of the eight municipalities have a dissimilarity index above 30: the City of New Haven (51), Meriden (31), and West Haven (45). The Logan source also provides data for six cities in northwest Austin. The two that exceeded 30 are the region's oldest: Austin (54, for the entire city) and Georgetown (44).

Explicit and Implicit Racial Motivations for Zoning in the Three Metros

In 1920, 20 percent of the residents of the City of Austin were Black, in that year a percentage far higher than that of the City of New Haven (3 percent) and the City of San Jose (0.5 percent). The Blacks who took part in the Great Migration from 1920 to 1970 tended to exit states that had been members of the Confederacy, such as Texas. By 1950, the percentage of Blacks in the City of Austin had fallen to 13 percent and, by 2014, to 7 percent. In the City of New Haven, by contrast, the percentage rose from 3 percent in 1930 to 6 percent in 1950, to 26 percent in 1970, and to 34 percent in 2014.

Racial considerations, perhaps subconscious, almost certainly have influenced the facially race-neutral zoning ordinances of the suburbs in all three metros.[72] Prior to 1950, racial motivations probably were most important in Austin, a region where explicit Jim Crow policies had prevailed. After 1950, by contrast, race arguably was most salient in Greater New Haven. The Great Migration brought large numbers of Blacks to the City of New Haven, which came to fit most closely the exaggerated stereotype of a chocolate city surrounded by vanilla suburbs. In these three metropolitan areas, only the City of New Haven, in 1967,

71. See note 53; Ellickson, "Social Composition of Neighborhoods" (2006).

72. Rolleston, "Restrictive Suburban Zoning" (1987): 19; Trounstine, "Geography of Inequality" (2020). See also Whittemore, "Racial Bias" (2018) (emphasizing period prior to 1985).

was the site of a late-twentieth-century riot with predominantly Black participants.[73]

Silicon Valley unquestionably is the metro where racial animus is least likely to have tarred zoning policy. The western United States has long been the least segregated region in the United States. The Black population has always been small in Silicon Valley. In the City of San Jose, for example, the percentage of Blacks was 0.6 percent in 1950, inching up to 2.5 percent in 1970 and to 3.1 percent in 2014. One of Joseph Eichler's distinctions as a homebuilder was his overt willingness, unusual during the 1950s, to sell houses without regard to a purchaser's race or religion.[74] In Silicon Valley, however, segregation by social class appears to be roughly as pervasive as in the other two regions.

How Extreme Are Texas's Policies?

In 2006, a Brookings Institution team led by Rolf Pendall published the results of a national survey of local land use regulations. The team's report chided not only exclusionary regions, such as the Northeast, but also "Wild Wild Texas," where the authors concluded localities had been regulating too little.[75] Does "Wild Wild" fairly describe the findings for northwestern Austin?

Texas unquestionably fits the stereotype of a business-friendly, small-government state.[76] Some critics bewail the power of the state's homebuilding lobby.[77] Both legislators and judges have nudged Texas toward lightening the burdens of land use regulations. As this chapter has noted, various Texas statutes deny counties the power to zone and authorize a

73. O'Leary et al., "1967 Riots" (2017); Olzak et al., "Race Riots" (1996): 601.
74. Howell, "Eichler Homes" (2016). In contrast to Eichler, William Levitt of Levitt & Sons and J. C. Nichols, developer of the Country Club District in Kansas City, at times affirmatively pursued segregationist policies. Lambert, "Legacy of Bias" (1997); Worley, *J. C. Nichols* (1990): 147–55.
75. Pendall et al., "Land Use Regulations" (2006): 23–24, 31.
76. See, e.g., Echeverria and Hansen-Young, "Democracy's Laboratories" (2009): 519 (referring to Texas's "pro–property rights" culture).
77. Welch, "Containing Urban Sprawl" (2008): 149–53.

developer with land in an unincorporated area to create a MUD to provide utility services. Other Texas enactments limit a municipality's authority to, for example, declare a moratorium on development, delay action on a proposed subdivision map beyond thirty days, or require a homebuilder to sell inclusionary units at below-market prices.[78] And members of the Texas judiciary, compared to California's, probably would be somewhat more sympathetic to a developer's constitutional challenge to the magnitude of a subdivision exaction for parks.[79]

Nonetheless, the Brookings team has exaggerated the permissiveness of Texas's legal culture. The Texas judiciary is not especially hostile to local zoning. The Supreme Court of Texas, like other state supreme courts, has been disinclined to uphold a constitutional challenge to a zoning constraint.[80] The leading Texas decisions on large-lot zoning have sustained the practice.[81] The Supreme Court of Texas has rejected a state constitutional takings claim against a Dallas suburb's zoning measure that almost halved permitted housing density.[82] The Texas legislature also has been

78. Tex. Loc. Gov't Code Ann. § 212.131-.139 (West 2016); id. at § 212.009; id. at § 214.905(a).

79. Compare Associated Home Builders v. City of Walnut Creek, 484 P.2d 606, 611 (Cal. 1971) (referring to "urgent needs" for more parks), with City of College Station v. Turtle Rock Corp., 680 S.W. 2d 802, 807 (Tex. 1984) (requiring "reasonable connection" between exaction and service needs that subdivision had created).

80. City of Pharr v. Tippitt, 616 S.W.2d 173, 175–76 (Tex. 1981) (stating that a zoning ordinance is presumed valid as a constitutional matter). The same presumption applies in Connecticut. Town of Beacon Falls v. Posick, 563 A.2d 285, 292 (Conn. 1989). The California courts have been especially solicitous of zoning. Miller v. Board of Public Works, 234 P. 381 (Cal. 1925) (sustaining, a year prior to *Euclid,* the legitimacy of zoning as an exercise of police power).

81. See, e.g., Mayhew v. Town of Sunnyvale, 964 S.W.2d 922, 934–35 (Tex. 1998) (unanimously rejecting takings claim against Dallas suburb's one-acre minimum-lot requirement and recognizing the legitimacy of an ordinance designed "to protect the character of the community"). But compare Dews v. Town of Sunnyvale, 109 F. Supp. 2d 526 (N.D. Texas 2000) (holding that town's one-acre zoning violated federal Fair Housing Act of 1968).

82. Sheffield Dev. Co., Inc. v. City of Glenn Heights, 140 S.W.3d 660 (Tex. 2004).

unusually supportive of restrictive covenants, another legal device that tends to freeze land uses in single-family neighborhoods.[83] The authors of the 2008 Wharton Index, the most-cited national survey of local zoning practices, found that twenty other states had land use controls that were more lax than Texas's.[84] Moreover, Wharton's 2019 update on the restrictiveness of metropolitan land use regulations places Dallas-Fort Worth, Houston, and San Antonio in the middle half of the nation's restrictiveness, not in the bottom quartile, where it situates Atlanta and Chicago.[85] Contrary to the Brookings team, Herkenhoff and his co-authors have singled out Texas's zoning system as something other states should emulate.[86] Compared to Texas, New England states, where the area of a house-lot for a new house is twice the national average, are greater legal outliers.[87] More fitting than "Wild Wild Texas" would have been "Over-zoned New England."

83. See chapter 8.
84. Gyourko et al., "Wharton Index" (2008): 711.
85. Gyourko et al., "New Wharton Index" (2019): 41 (fig. 1).
86. Herkenhoff et al., "Land-Use Restrictions" (2018): 90, 98 (asserting, inconsistently with the findings in Gyourko et al., "Wharton Index" [2008], that Texas's land use regulations are less restrictive than any other state's).
87. See chapter 2.

PART

Frozen Neighborhoods

6

A Zoning Straitjacket Binds Neighborhoods of Detached Houses

Recall the neighborhood where you spent your childhood. For most Americans, it would have been a neighborhood of detached single-family houses.[1] The thesis of this chapter is simple: if you were to visit the same neighborhood decades from now, it would remain virtually unchanged. One reason is economic. Structures typically are built to last. A second reason, and the focus here, is the impact of law. The politics of local zoning almost invariably works to freeze land uses, especially in a neighborhood of detached houses. This is a significant finding, not yet part of urban lore. I chose the title of the book to emphasize it.

The previous chapters were largely cross-sectional, emphasizing differences in zoning practices in different regions. This part, by contrast, is longitudinal. It stresses change—or the reality of the paucity of change—in legal rules over time.[2] Decades-old zoning maps and ordinances are seldom available online. A local planning office, however, typically has

1. In 2019, the Census Bureau estimated that 63.9 percent of U.S. housing units were single-family detached houses. An additional 5.4 percent were mobile homes, and 5.2 percent single-family attached. U.S. Bureau of the Census, American Housing Survey, "Occupied Units" (2019).
2. An alternative approach to longitudinal analysis of land use policies would entail the study, in specific urban areas, of aerial photographs of varying vintages. For that sort of work, geographers are more likely than legal scholars to have the pertinent skill set. For the potential of this approach, see Hasse et al., "Monmouth and Somerset Counties" (2011).

files that reveal the locality's prior policies. These offices invariably were generous in sharing what they had.[3]

Attorneys associate the U.S. practice of municipal zoning with a watershed case the United States Supreme Court decided in 1926, *Village of Euclid v. Ambler Realty Co.*[4] Ohio district judge David Westenhaver conducted the trial, a property owner's challenge to the validity of a zoning ordinance of a suburb just east of Cleveland. Euclid's zoning map had depicted various zones, and the Village's ordinance regulated permissible land uses, lot sizes, and building bulks in each of them. Judge Westenhaver ultimately held that the ordinance violated, among other constitutional provisions, the Due Process Clause of the Fourteenth Amendment. The Supreme Court, in a decision that has become a staple of American legal education, reversed.[5] In this chapter and the next, I focus less on Judge Westenhaver's legal analysis than on his conception of zoning politics. His opinion stated, "The plain truth is that the true object of the ordinance in question is to place all the property in an undeveloped area of 16 square miles [that is, all of Euclid] in a strait-jacket."[6] Judge Westenhaver wrongly forecast the outcomes of local zoning politics. In a neighborhood where most land is undeveloped, NIMBY forces are relatively weak. But in a developed neighborhood of detached houses, *strait-jacket* perfectly describes the usual upshot of zoning controls.[7] This chap-

3. Local government record keeping is erratic, to put it gently. The City Clerk of Palo Alto, an upscale Silicon Valley suburb, stated that the city no longer had a copy of Ordinance 172, its first zoning ordinance, adopted on Aug. 16, 1918. Minor (2018). Similarly, both Rollingwood and West Lake Hills, Texas, lack copies of their initial zoning ordinances.
4. 272 U.S. 365 (1926).
5. Wolf, *Euclid v. Ambler* (2008) provides a thorough historical account.
6. Ambler Realty Co. v. Village of Euclid, 297 F. 307, 316 (N.D. Ohio, 1924). Judge Westenhaver overestimated the village's land area. In 1924, the Village of Euclid had a land area of roughly eleven square miles, not sixteen square miles. After minor annexations by various neighbors, including the City of Cleveland, in 2019 Euclid's land area had fallen to 10.6 square miles. See Cleveland Annexation Map (undated).
7. The inimitable Jane Jacobs came up with another apt analogy: the taxidermy of urban space. Lemar, "Zoning as Taxidermy" (2015): 1539 n.91, citing Jacobs, *Great American Cities* (1992): 373.

ter draws on the zoning histories of various municipalities, including the City of Euclid's, to support this central thesis. The next chapter explores the dynamics of local zoning politics, the source of the zoning freeze.

The zoning straitjacket binds a large majority of urban land in the United States. Los Angeles and Chicago, two of the nation's densest central cities, permit the building of only a detached house on, respectively, 75 percent and 79 percent of the areas they zone for residential use.[8] In suburban areas, the percentage typically is far higher. The thirty-seven suburbs studied in Silicon Valley, Greater New Haven, and Greater Austin set aside 91 percent of their residentially zoned land (71 percent of their total land area) exclusively for detached houses.[9] For many local officials, only a detached house seems to satisfy the American Dream of homeownership. A townhouse or condominium unit does not suffice. Planners in other developed nations largely disagree. They are far more likely to permit the mixing of different types of dwellings in the same neighborhood.[10]

The single-family zone, ubiquitous in American cities and suburbs, is popular because it generates real benefits. It may protect homeowners' property values and enhance their peace of mind. On balance, however, some single-family zones, perhaps a large fraction, inflict net social harm. Some jurisdictions have begun to recognize this. The State of Oregon and City of Minneapolis have recently abolished the single-family-only zone.[11] In 2020, in a sharp break from prior orthodoxy, the leading U.S. planning journal published two articles that called for abolition of the traditional single-family zone.[12]

8. Badger and Bui, "Cities Start to Question" (2019). New York City, the nation's largest and densest city, had the lowest percentage zoned single-family-only, 15 percent. Id.
9. See chapter 2.
10. Hirt, *Zoned in the USA* (2014): 6–7, 17–25. The literature on comparative land use policy understandably is thin. High-quality comparative work requires a deep knowledge of both the cultures and the institutions of the nations examined.
11. See chapter 11.
12. Manville et al., "End Single-Family Zoning" (2020); Wegmann, "Death to Single-Family Zoning" (2020). The same issue includes brief responses by skeptics.

The costs of the straitjacket are huge. Absent overly strict regulation, suppliers of goods in a market economy are able to adjust to changes in supply and demand. The freezing of land uses in a broad swath of urban America prevents housing developers from responding to changes in consumer tastes about where and how to live. Especially in West Coast and Northeastern states, the zoning straitjacket has stifled the building of denser housing and has aggravated auto-dependence. Moreover, the straitjacket misallocates the national labor force, prompting households to migrate from overregulated regions, such as California and New England, to less regulated regions.[13] Every economist who has investigated the issue has concluded that current local zoning practices inflict massive costs on the national economy.[14]

Three initial clarifications of the scope of the straitjacket thesis are in order. First, in a neighborhood of houses, zoning policies typically do not bar a homeowner from remodeling a detached house or even from razing it to build another.[15] In most urban areas, however, local zoning politics almost never allows a landowner to replace a house with a denser residential use, such as a duplex, set of townhouses, or apartment building.[16] Second, although this chapter emphasizes the freezing of neighborhoods of detached houses, the context in which the thesis best applies, opposition to residential change extends more broadly.[17] In the Brooklyn neighborhood of Carroll Gardens, for example, owners of townhouses supported a rollback of permitted heights for mid-rise apartments.[18] Third, in most U.S. regions, the straitjacket has become tighter over time. This chapter demonstrates that even in the 1920s, shortly after the advent of zoning, suburbs such as Euclid, Ohio, and Palo Alto, California, had begun to freeze single-family zones in neighborhoods where streets already existed.

13. Ganong and Shoag, "Regional Income Convergence" (2017).
14. See chapter 1.
15. Legal barriers to both remodeling and razing are higher, of course, in either a historic district or a covenanted community.
16. A few states, including California, do compel localities to allow a homeowner in a single-family district to construct an accessory dwelling unit. See chapter 11.
17. See chapter 7.
18. Hills and Schleicher, "Balancing 'Zoning Budget'" (2011): 83–85.

The straitjacket, however, became tighter in many U.S. regions roughly around 1970.[19] The environmental movement appears to have heightened urbanites' preferences for policies that perpetuate familiar land uses. Palo Alto's policies, for example, were generally pro-growth prior to 1965. Between 1965 and 1975, anti-growth Residentialists came to dominate Palo Alto politics.[20] Their core credo was "protect the neighborhoods."[21] The Residentialists supported not only stricter zoning of undeveloped land but also tightening the straitjacket in existing single-family neighborhoods. A Palo Alto rezoning to allow greater residential density was rare in those neighborhoods prior to 1965, but it became even rarer thereafter.[22]

A variety of seldom-cited sources support the thesis that zoning politics straitjackets land uses in a settled single-family neighborhood. I marshal evidence that the freeze exists not only in ritzy suburbs but also in less prosperous ones. It prevails even in pro-growth Texas. The final section of the chapter explores possible exceptions to the zoning straitjacket.

Evidence from Four Famous Suburbs

As this chapter indicates, I first induced the existence of the straitjacket from the zoning history of the City of Euclid, site of the landmark judicial decision. I later discovered that Jonathan Levine, a professor at the University of Michigan planning school, had previously expounded the same thesis.[23] I salute him. Levine's book, however, placed little emphasis on the straitjacket finding, and no author of a law journal article has associated him with the idea.[24]

19. Fischel, "Rise of the Homevoters" (2017). In what may not have been entirely a coincidence, around 1970 the rate of U.S. economic growth seems to have begun to slow. See Gordon, *American Growth* (2016). Gordon primarily attributes the decline to a falloff in great inventions. He notes, however, that excessive land use regulations may also have contributed. See id. at 649.
20. See chapter 3.
21. Winslow, *Palo Alto* (1993): 57.
22. See this chapter, text accompanying note 42.
23. Levine, *Zoned Out* (2006): 76–81, 204 n.1.
24. Other precursors worthy of note include Elmendorf, "Beyond the Double Veto" (2019): 88–89 (asserting a "density stasis in extant residential neighborhoods"),

Two sources strongly support the facial plausibility of the existence of the straitjacket. As of 2020, no work in the legal literature had cited either. First, a Massachusetts agency found that more than 99.7 percent of the state's land in single-family use in 1970 remained in single-family use in 1999, almost thirty years later.[25] Second, in an invaluable blog post, Issi Romem, a recently minted Ph.D. economist, tracked housing construction in all major U.S. metropolitan areas between 1940 and 2016.[26] Romem asserts that, in recent decades, most suburban areas have become "dormant"—his term for straitjacketed—while a few have been "pockets of dense construction." The authors of both these studies are fully aware that local zoning and planning practices have led to the rigidities that they document. But neither offers direct evidence of the history of the evolution of land use controls. The next sections tackle that task, marshaling support from selected suburbs in seven states.

Euclid, Ohio

The City of Euclid, a Cleveland suburb on Lake Erie, was a mere "village" during its day in the sun in 1926. Because of its fame, Euclid's 1922 zoning map and ordinance are among the few from that era available online.[27] Both documents illustrate path-dependence in zoning practices. In 1922, the Village of Euclid called its basic single-family detached zone U1. Almost a century later, the 2020 Euclid ordinance retained that exact label.[28] In 1922, the Village required a minimum house-lot of 5,000 square feet in its U1 zone. That figure also remains unaltered.[29] When Euclid first

---

and Rothwell and Massey, "Effect of Density Zoning" (2009): 790 (showing stability of localities' zoning regulations between 1988 and 2003).

25. Levine, *Zoned Out* (2006): 78, using data layers that the Massachusetts Executive Office of Environmental Affairs (2016) later published. The Massachusetts data actually imply even less change. As Levine describes, much of the change occurred in the Town of Sudbury, which allowed the transformation of some low-density single-family neighborhoods into medium-density single-family neighborhoods.

26. Romem, "Dormant Suburban Interior" (2018).

27. Euclid Village Zoning Map (1922).

28. City of Euclid, Ohio, Code of Ordinances § 1351.02 (2020).

29. Id. at § 1381.01 (2020). This provision establishes 5,000 sq. ft. as the usual minimum lot size in an A-1 area zone. Euclid's 1922 zoning map states that all U1 zones are in A-1 area districts.

Table 11. Glacial Change in Euclid's 1922 Single-Family-Detached Zone (U1)

	Euclid still zoned U1 in 2017	*Euclid permitted greater residential density in 2017*
Neighborhoods where streets had been laid out in 1922	99.0%	0.3%
Neighborhoods where streets had *not* been laid out in 1922	75.7%	9.1%

adopted zoning in 1922, over half of the village was undeveloped. Euclid's initial zoning map, foreshadowing the usual devotion of local officials to the prospect of neighborhoods of detached houses, placed 52 percent of the suburb's total land area in the U1 zone. The areas so designated lay primarily in either the Village's northern area bordering Lake Erie or south of Euclid Boulevard, the thoroughfare that the plaintiff Ambler Realty Company's tract abutted.

Since 1922, Euclid has reduced the acreage that it zones U1 by about one-fourth. But the city has made these reductions almost exclusively in neighborhoods where streets had not been mapped or installed in 1922. In 1922, Euclid lots comprising a total of 1,282 acres satisfied all of the following three criteria: (1) they were zoned U1; (2) they lay in a neighborhood where Euclid's 1922 zoning map indicates that developers had already mapped or installed streets; and (3) they did not abut either Euclid Avenue or Lake Shore Boulevard, the city's two principal arterial streets. *In 2017, of the acreage that satisfied these three criteria in 1922, Euclid continued to zone 99.0 percent single-family (U1).* See table 11.[30] By contrast, in neighborhoods where internal streets had not been laid out in 1922, single-family zoning was not nearly as fixed. In these, Euclid had rezoned 24.3 percent of the land area away from U1. Euclid also has virtually abandoned single-family zoning along its two major arteries, paring the U1 acreage along them from 82 percent in 1922 to 7 percent in 2017. See table 12.

30. Two-thirds of the 1.0 percent—the area rezoned away from U1—Euclid placed in a Campus-Institutional zone to enable the opening of the Forest Park Middle School on Elinore Avenue.

Table 12. Euclid's Zoning Along Its Two Major Arteries, Euclid Avenue and Lake Shore Boulevard

	1922 zoning map	*2017 zoning map*
Zoned single-family (U1)	81.7%	6.8%
Permitting multifamily use	9.7%	16.3%

Euclid's zoning history supports several inferences. It strongly affirms the book's central thesis that single-family zoning is encased in a political straitjacket once minor interior streets have been laid out within a neighborhood. Prior to the layout of local streets, a single-family zone is somewhat easier to override. Moreover, when lots front on a major thoroughfare, zoning politics seems to be more fluid.

Euclid has made one major change in its zoning policies during the past century, an amendment with a pronounced exclusionary thrust. The Village's 1922 map placed 27 percent of its total acreage in commercial and industrial zones. The Village's zones then were cumulative, permitting landowners in those zones to erect residential structures, including apartment buildings. Euclid's present zoning ordinance, like most contemporary ones, is noncumulative.[31] Euclid's 1922 ordinance had permitted the construction of multifamily buildings on 1,830 acres. In 2017, Euclid, after switching to noncumulative zoning, had pared its potential multifamily sites by more than three-quarters, to 419 acres.[32]

The Levittowns

To broaden the geographic diversity of the localities examined, I added the three largest Levittowns without knowing what the results would bring. During the postwar period, Levitt & Sons, the developer of these communities, was a successful high-volume homebuilding firm. In the late 1940s, the company started the first of the Levittowns in the Town of Hempstead, Nassau County, New York. This Levittown eventually com-

31. City of Euclid, Ohio, Code of Ordinances §§ 1339.01-.06 (2020).

32. See Hills and Schleicher, "Noncumulative Zoning" (2010): 251–56 (lamenting rise of noncumulative techniques). On the decline of cumulative zoning in Boston suburbs, see Schuetz, "Multifamily Housing" (2008): 559.

Figure 8. Levittown, New York, developed between 1947 and 1951, near the date of its completion. Most of the original houses were similar in design. Homebuyers, with rare exception, strove to individualize the houses. To appreciate the diversity of their undertakings, take a Street View tour on Google Earth. (Ewing Galloway/Alamy Stock Photo)

prised 17,000 detached houses, similar in design, on lots of roughly 6,000 square feet. Many purchasers promptly remodeled their houses to differentiate them. But Levittowners, despite their itch to remodel, were also committed to suppressing deviations from single-family use. In 1975, when some of the covenants assuring single-family use in this six-square-mile territory were about to expire, Levittown, New York, residents successfully lobbied the Town of Hempstead to freeze permanently the single-family character of all Levitt subdivisions.[33] Score one for the straitjacket thesis.

33. The "Levittown Planned Residence District" restricts uses to "single-family detached or senior residence" and imposes a minimum lot size of 6,000 sq. ft., thereby preventing the subdivision of most existing lots. Town of Hempstead, N.Y., Building Zone Ordinance, art. XV §§ 177, 193 (2019).

Mostly during the 1960s, Levitt & Sons developed Willingboro, New Jersey, the last of the company's three most massive developments. Willingboro Township's current zoning map also places all Levittown neighborhoods of detached houses in zones that permit no other use.[34] Score two for the thesis.

Evidence from Levittown, Pennsylvania, is more mixed. Falls, Middletown, and Bristol townships largely control the local zoning. Consistent with the straitjacket thesis, the Falls and Middletown Township ordinances restrict future uses in all Levitt subdivisions to single-family detached houses.[35] But Bristol Township, which encompasses about half of Levittown, Pennsylvania, has placed about three-quarters of its Levittown subdivisions in an R-3 zone that permits, in addition, "multiple-family dwellings."[36] Few, possibly none, have actually been built in that zone.[37] Forays on Google Earth and Trulia-For-Rent turned up no multifamily structures in areas that clearly had been Levitt & Sons subdivisions originally. Of the three Levittowns, the total score supporting the straitjacket thesis thus is at least two and one-half.

Single-Family Neighborhoods in the Three Metropolitan Areas Studied

Silicon Valley

In this region of sky-high housing prices, market pressures to bring townhouses and apartments to single-family neighborhoods are especially intense. Zoning authorities nonetheless seldom bend to these

34. Burlington County, New Jersey, provides the best available zoning map of Willingboro. Willingboro Township Zoning Map (2017).
35. Falls Township, Pa., Code of Ordinances § 209–20 (2019) (adopting a special "Neighborhood Conservation Residential District" to assure this outcome); Middletown Township, Pa., Zoning Map (May 2013) (indicating that all Levitt subdivisions had been placed in single-family zones).
36. Bristol Township, Pa., Code § 205–28(A)(2) (2019); Bristol Township, Pa., Zoning Map (2014).
37. On August 1, 2018, the author sent an inquiry about actual land uses to the head of Bristol Township's Building, Planning, and Zoning department, who declined to answer it.

forces. Moira O'Neill, Giulia Gualco-Nelson, and Eric Biber's valuable empirical study of Bay Area zoning practices included interviews with insiders. The various experts identified the existence of a "grand bargain" on housing issues: zoning officials, as long as they would "leave the low-density residential neighborhoods alone," could approve the densification of other venues.[38] Between 2014 and 2016, the City of San Francisco approved ninety-four projects containing five or more housing units. Reflecting the robustness of the grand bargain, only two of these ninety-four projects replaced prior residential uses.[39]

Silicon Valley's sixteen suburbs also consistently resist densification of their existing single-family neighborhoods. Apartment developers have met with success primarily in either formerly industrial areas, such as North San Jose, or already densely built-up areas, such as downtown Redwood City.[40] Events in Oakland, California, affirm the pattern. West Oakland has witnessed five arson attempts at sites where multifamily housing had been under construction.[41] Of the sites identified, only on Lester Avenue, long zoned for multifamily use, would the new multifamily structures have replaced single-family houses.

The zoning histories of two Silicon Valley suburbs—Palo Alto and the much less wealthy East Palo Alto—strongly support the straitjacket thesis. Palo Alto has many existing single-family neighborhoods, and, especially after the Residentialists won political control in the 1960s, the city's politics has tended to freeze land uses in all of them. Three of Palo Alto's oldest neighborhoods of houses—Crescent Park, Old Palo Alto, and Professorville—lie in the northern part of the city. In 1922, Palo Alto's initial zoning map placed virtually all of these three neighborhoods, even lots abutting collector streets, in single-family zones. There, with exceptions amounting to less than 1 percent of their combined area, they remain a century later. Crescent Park was the site of the most notable rezoning away from single-family. No later than 1955, Palo Alto, then a pro-growth

38. O'Neill et al., "California's Housing Policy Debates" (2019): 68.

39. Id. at 64. The O'Neill et al. data do not reveal whether the prior residential use had been single-family or multifamily.

40. See chapter 3.

41. Goldberg and Dillon, "Arson Probed" (2018).

city, rezoned three blockfronts along University Avenue, roughly 2 percent of Crescent Park, from single-family to multifamily use.[42] After Residentialists took control of city politics, however, their policy of "protecting the neighborhoods" would have squelched rezonings of this sort.

Beginning in 1925, Palo Alto annexed large areas to the south. During the 1950s and 1960s, Joseph Eichler and other homebuilders converted much of south Palo Alto from orchards into tract houses. In those decades, the city placed most of south Palo Alto in an R-1 zone. That designation restricted land uses to a detached house on a lot of at least 6,000 square feet, the area of a typical Levittown, New York, lot. In 2020, these tract houses, more affordable than those in Palo Alto's fancier northern neighborhoods, were selling for more than $2 million each.[43] Six decades after the original development of its southern single-family neighborhoods, Palo Alto continues to zone more than 99 percent of these areas R-1.

California law requires that a city's zoning policies be consistent with its general plan.[44] The general plan that Palo Alto adopted in 2017 indicates the city's intention to continue to bar multifamily buildings in all of its existing single-family neighborhoods.[45] Between 2014 and 2016, Palo Alto approved five projects containing five or more dwelling units. None replaced single-family detached houses.[46]

A recent change in Palo Alto zoning policy reduces the potential population density of its southern section. At the behest of homeowners devoted to preserving Eichler designs and protecting the privacy of their backyards, the city has entitled homeowners in a single-family neighborhood to vote to recommend limiting the heights of houses to a single story.[47] Between 1992 and 2018, Palo Alto approved single-story overlays

42. These blockfronts lie just north of downtown Palo Alto.
43. See chapter 1.
44. Cal. Gov't Code § 65860 (West 2009).
45. Palo Alto, Cal., Comprehensive Plan 2030 (2017). Map L-6, which follows p. 28 of Comprehensive Plan 2030, designates all current neighborhoods of detached houses as "single family res," a category that precludes multifamily housing, although not necessarily duplexes or accessory dwelling units. See id. at 31.
46. Author's examination of project addresses that O'Neill and her co-authors provided.
47. Palo Alto, Cal., Municipal Code § 18.12.100 (2019). Some other Silicon Valley suburbs with Eichler houses have followed suit. See, e.g., City of Sunnyvale Municipal Code § 19.26.200.1 (2019).

of this sort in a dozen small areas, mostly Eichler subdivisions in south Palo Alto.[48]

Events in 2013 demonstrate the depth of Palo Alto's antagonism to dense housing at the fringe of a single-family neighborhood. The non-profit Palo Alto Housing Corporation had proposed the four-story, 62-unit Maybell project, a partially subsidized multifamily development designed primarily for seniors. The city had long zoned the site at issue for multifamily use. Existing houses bordered only one side of the site. The architectural plans called for construction of some two-story single-family houses to buffer the existing houses from the taller building. The Palo Alto city council voted unanimously to approve the Maybell project. The city's approval enraged homeowners in nearby single-family neighborhoods. Citing concerns about traffic and increased density, opponents organized Palo Altans to Preserve Neighborhood Zoning. The group gathered thousands of signatures, enough to place the issue on the ballot. In November 2013, 56 percent of Palo Altans voted to scotch the Maybell development.[49]

In recent decades, Palo Alto has approved a dozen or more proposals for multifamily development, including some that Stanford University has put forward.[50] Local politics, however, has required that these projects be sited at least one block, and typically far more, from an existing Palo Alto single-family neighborhood. Many of the city's recent multifamily projects lie in areas once zoned for industrial uses or along the highly trafficked El Camino Real.[51]

The zoning politics of East Palo Alto, Silicon Valley's least prosperous suburb, has been equally respectful of existing single-family neighborhoods. Incorporated in 1983, East Palo Alto is Silicon Valley's newest city and its only municipality whose territory lies mostly east of the Bayshore Freeway (U.S. 101).[52] In the early 1950s, residents of the area that later

48. Palo Alto, Cal., Map of Single Family Overlay Districts (2016) reveals the locations.
49. Green, "Voters Reject" (2013).
50. See chapter 3.
51. The multifamily projects formerly in Palo Alto industrial zones include those at Berryessa Street, Fabian Way (the Taube Koret development), Feather Lane, and Quail Drive.
52. See map at outset of chapter 3.

became East Palo Alto were almost entirely White. The area had turned majority Black by the mid-1960s and, after 2000, majority Hispanic.[53] East Palo Alto's most recent zoning map places 79 percent of its residentially zoned territory in a zone that permits only a single-family detached house on a lot of at least 5,000 square feet. Land uses in these neighborhoods are as frozen as they are in Palo Alto. East Palo Alto's general plan explicitly declares the goal of "preserv[ing] the character of existing single-family neighborhoods."[54] One such neighborhood is University Village, which lies in the far north of the city. A few blocks to the west, Facebook is planning a 1,500-housing-unit development in the City of Menlo Park.[55] Yet East Palo Alto's specific plan for the University Village area explicitly pledges to protect that neighborhood's single-family character.[56] Hills and Schleicher hope that NIMBYists would be less able to influence a locality's general plan than its zoning ordinance.[57] These nuggets of East Palo Alto evidence suggest otherwise.

Greater New Haven

Fourteen suburbs surround the City of New Haven. In 2015, the five most exclusionary insisted on detached houses on 99.5 percent of their residentially zoned territory.[58] Their tiny zones permitting either duplexes or multifamily housing usually adjoin commercial areas, where homeowners seem to regard those uses to be less threatening. The Connecticut Appeals Act has put pressure on these suburbs to allow denser forms of housing, but rarely with success.[59]

In the next six New Haven suburbs, ranked by exclusionary tendency, the detached house also is king. These municipalities permit only single-family detached houses on 95.5 percent of their residentially zoned territory. That is a touch below 99.5 percent, the figure for New Haven's

53. Cutler, "East of Palo Alto" (2015); East Palo Alto, California (2020).
54. City of East Palo Alto, Cal., General Plan: Vista 2035, Goal LU-5, at 4–22 (March 2017).
55. Wagner, "Facebook Is Building" (2017).
56. East Palo Alto, Cal., Ravenswood/Four Corners TOD Plan 48 (Feb. 22, 2013): "[N]o land use changes are proposed in the University Village neighborhood."
57. Hills and Schleicher, "Planning an Affordable City" (2015).
58. See chapter 4.
59. Id.

five most exclusionary suburbs, but it is far higher than the median for a Silicon Valley suburb, 88.5 percent.

New Haven's three working-class suburbs—East Haven, West Haven, and Meriden—have been far more tolerant of diverse forms of residential living. They permit duplexes or even denser residential uses on 26 percent of their residentially zoned territory, a percentage fifty times greater than what New Haven's most exclusionary suburbs permit (0.5 percent).[60] Nonetheless, even these three least tony suburbs set aside 74 percent of their residentially zoned land exclusively for detached houses. Their single-family zones appear in large, sometimes concentrated, swaths on their zoning maps. West Haven, for instance, permits only detached houses in the southwestern 40 percent of the city, excluding the beachfront. East Haven similarly bars duplexes and apartments in its northern 20 percent. Of the three working-class suburbs, Meriden has been the most flexible. It has frequently approved a developer's application for the equivalent of a Planned Unit Development (PUD), at times including multifamily housing, on a largish tract of undeveloped land.[61] The ultimate form of residential densification would be the replacement of detached houses, in an area formerly zoned single-family, with townhouses or apartments. In New Haven's blue-collar towns, as elsewhere, this almost never occurs.

Greater Austin

Texas generally is a pro-growth state. The disproportionate size of the state's housing industry and the self-sorting of immigrants by ideology may both have contributed to this inclination.[62] A look at the zoning histories of four of the oldest localities in the northwest sector of Austin, however, indicates that zoning politics in Texas, as elsewhere, enables homeowners in an established neighborhood to freeze single-family zoning.

60. Id.

61. The PUD approach entitles a developer who owns a largish tract to propose a mix of land uses, including perhaps multifamily housing and commercial structures. The municipality, of course, must agree to the proposal. See Mandelker, "Planned Unit Developments" (2008).

62. See chapter 5.

The City of Austin, incorporated in 1839, is Greater Austin's oldest city. A century ago, when Texas's capital city was lightly populated, subdividers created, within a mile or two of Austin's downtown core, a number of low-density, largely residential neighborhoods, among them Bouldin Creek, Clarksville, and East Austin. Many lot owners in these neighborhoods built single-family detached houses, a use adapted to the market conditions then prevailing. In 2012, the City of Austin shifted from electing city council members at-large to electing them in separate districts. This structural change, intended in part to enhance the racial diversity of the council, served to strengthen the forces of NIMBYism.

Austin's politicians recently discovered the political clout of homeowners opposed to densification. The City of Austin's population now approaches one million, and its downtown is insufficiently large and dense for a city of its size. Mayor Steve Adler, first elected in 2015, recognized this obsolescence. In the late 2010s, he helped sponsor CodeNEXT, a measure designed to increase permitted residential densities in close-in locations.[63] This proposal stirred opposition in the older Austin neighborhoods near downtown, including the three just mentioned. CodeNEXT's supporters eventually had to water down the proposal, for example, by exempting some neighborhoods from it.[64] In August 2018, Mayor Adler bowed to political realities and pulled the plug on CodeNEXT, at least temporarily.[65]

The history of Tarrytown, an upscale Austin neighborhood a bit west of downtown, also illustrates the constraints of Texas's zoning politics.[66] Excluding Tarrytown's fringes, Austin's zoning rules restrict residential uses in 97 percent of the neighborhood to single-family detached houses.[67] Perhaps because of the pro-growth inclinations of Texas culture, a

63. Shaw, *Generation Priced Out* (2018): 95–102 (describing CodeNEXT, prior to its demise).
64. Theis, "Slams CodeNEXT" (2017).
65. McGlinchy, "Austin's Code Rewrite" (2019).
66. Tarrytown is defined here as the area south of West 35th Street, west of MoPac, north of Enfield Road, and east of Lake Austin.
67. Austin's predominant zone in Tarrytown, SF-3-NP, nominally also permits duplexes. The suffix -NP signals, however, that a neighborhood plan would bar those uses. The Central West Austin Neighborhood Plan (2010) does so, proclaim-

few developers have succeeded in recent decades in winning Austin's approval of PUDs that have brought denser residential uses to Tarrytown. Nonetheless, these PUD developments, taken together, comprise just over 1 percent of the neighborhood's land.[68] Absent state intervention, zoning politics in Austin is likely to freeze single-family uses in Tarrytown nearly as permanently as it would in other metros.

The City of Georgetown, which dates from 1848, is the second oldest of the Greater Austin cities studied. Georgetown's 2017 zoning map includes an "Old Town Overlay," an area of roughly two hundred square blocks.[69] Despite what its name implies, Old Town is hardly a bastion of density. In about 97 percent of that area, Georgetown's zoning permits, as a residential use, only a detached house. The city zones no more than two blocks, roughly 1 percent of Old Town, for multifamily housing. These blocks are the sites of the area's largest apartment complexes, one- or two-story structures built in the 1960s.[70] Since the 1960s, with rare exception, Georgetown's zoning politics has protected Old Town homeowners from not only townhouses and apartments but also duplexes.

In the 1950s, developers created both Rollingwood and West Lake Hills, two tiny suburbs that are among Greater Austin's wealthiest. The founders of both cities plainly foresaw them as havens for life in a detached house. Their housing stocks consist of little else. Rollingwood requires a minimum house-lot of 15,000 square feet on 100 percent of its residentially zoned land, and West Lake Hills requires a minimum of one acre on 98.8 percent. West Lake Hills permits two-family structures on 0.9 percent and multifamily uses on the remaining 0.3 percent. West Lake Hills's two principal existing multifamily structures are both located in extreme corners of the city. These two cities' zoning policies are significantly less exclusionary than those of, for example, Woodside, California, or Guilford, Connecticut. Nonetheless, the devotion of Rollingwood and West Lake Hills to detached-house living is fervent. Their internal politics

ing, at p. 38, an intention to "[p]reserve and protect the historic character and integrity of Central West Austin's predominantly single-family neighborhoods."

68. For the locations of these PUDs, see Austin Zoning Map (undated).

69. Georgetown, Tex., Official Zoning Map, October 2017.

70. These are Alpine Apartments, 806 E. 13th St., and Mid-Century Park, 900 E. 13th St.

would almost certainly doom any rezoning to allow greater residential density. The zoning straitjacket plainly extends to Texas.[71]

A New Transit Node Can Loosen the Zoning Straitjacket's Hold

Nonetheless, there is some play in the joints. In exceptional cases, local politics does permit a suburb to densify a single-family neighborhood. Urban researchers should more thoroughly investigate when and where this is possible.[72] Here are preliminary impressions.

Changes in transportation networks appear to be the events most likely to loosen the straitjacket. When a nearby transit hub or corridor has just opened, or is scheduled to open, the prospect of profit may tempt some nearby homeowners to *support* densification. One of the best-documented cases is the opening, in 1977, of the D.C. Metro's Courthouse station in Arlington, Virginia. In that instance, the new station prompted two dozen nearby homeowners to assemble their lots for eventual sale to a developer and to support the rezoning of their neighborhood for high-density residential use.[73] These moves enabled them to reap roughly three times the pre-station market value of their houses.[74] In New York City, between 1920 and 1960 apartment buildings similarly replaced single-

71. The Travis County Central Appraisal District (2020), like many counties, maintains a database of parcel sizes. A researcher could use it to determine the influence of zoning on the distribution of actual lot sizes.

72. Romem, "Dormant Suburban Interior" (2018) offers an insightful assessment. Valuable studies of patterns of rezonings include Been et al., "Overtaking the Growth Machine?" (2014) (focusing on New York City); Mangin, "Ethnic Enclaves" (2018) (also NYC); and Steele, "Functions of Zoning" (1986) (a study of zoning changes in Evanston, Illinois, a dense suburb north of Chicago).

73. Clary and Rasmussen, "Buyout Phenomenon" (1985). See also Schmitt, "Homeowners Unite" (1985) (describing assemblage and sale, for an office complex, of 144 houses near the MARTA Dunwoody station north of Atlanta). On systems that would enable a majority or supermajority of landowners to compel a joint sale, see Heller and Hills, "Land Assembly Districts" (2008) and Shultz and Schnidman, "Land Readjustment" (1990).

74. Clary and Rasmussen, "Buyout Phenomenon" (1985): 20. On the difficulty of voluntary land assembly, see Brooks and Lutz, "Urban Land Assembly" (2016); Heller and Hills, "Land Assembly Districts" (2008): 1473–74. But cf. Kelly, "Strategic Spillovers" (2006): 23–24 (reporting successes of land assemblers who used

family houses in some neighborhoods near subway lines.[75] State Senator Scott Wiener of California, recognizing the complementarity of mass transit and dense housing, has introduced a much-discussed bill to compel local governments to allow greater residential densities near both new and existing transit nodes.[76]

Some cities in all three metros have adopted Transit Oriented Development (TOD) zoning policies that deliberately raise permitted residential densities near rail or express-bus stations.[77] When a new station on the Metro-North line opened in 2013, the City of West Haven placed the surrounding area in a TOD zone. In this zone, West Haven permits the construction of apartment buildings as tall as eight stories.[78] Austin's TOD district authorizes residential buildings as tall as sixty feet near the East Austin mass-transit station.[79] Palo Alto is more averse to bulk. Its sole TOD district is near, not its downtown Caltrain station, but the less central California Street station. There Palo Alto's TOD policy limits building heights to forty feet.[80]

Densification near a new mass-transit station is far from inevitable. A familiar joke among transportation planners is that every commuter rail line eventually is correctly located because land uses invariably densify near stations.[81] Not so.[82] Atherton, California, permits only single-family uses near its station on the Caltrain commuter line.[83] Three-quarters of the land within one-half mile of the Tacoma Park, Maryland, Metro station

---

secret buyers, such as Disney Corporation near Orlando, Florida, and Harvard University in the Alston neighborhood of Boston).

75. Stern et al., *New York 1960* (1997): 799–830 (Upper East Side of Manhattan): 993–97 (Queens Boulevard).
76. SB 50 (Cal. 2018).
77. See, e.g., Nasri and Zhang, "Transit-Oriented Development" (2014).
78. City of West Haven, Conn., Zoning Regulations, tbl. 35.1.7 (Dec. 31, 2018). By 2019, no TOD projects in the city had actually commenced.
79. Martin Luther King Blvd. TOD Station Area Plan (undated): 8, 39.
80. Palo Alto, Cal., Code of Ordinances, § 18.34.040 tbl. 2 (2019). On the effects of height limitations on builders' costs, see Eriksen and Orlando, "Impact of Building Height" (2020).
81. van Wee, "Transport Interaction Models" (2015): 1.
82. See also Schleicher, "Transportation Innovation" (2017a): 44–45 (doubting that zoning officials permit sufficient densification near transit stations).
83. Atherton, California, Zoning Map (2011).

is zoned solely for detached houses.[84] Many of New York City's recent rezonings have lowered residential densities near mass-transit stations.[85]

Proximity to a major highway also can sometimes change the dynamics of zoning politics. Homeowners near an exit off an interstate highway may support rezonings for denser residential or commercial use.[86] In addition, frontage on a major arterial street may help loosen zoning restrictions, perhaps because residents are already acclimated to noise and traffic congestion. As mentioned, in 1922 Euclid limited 82 percent of the area fronting on Euclid Avenue and Lake Shore Boulevard, two of its major thoroughfares, to single-family use. By 2017, Euclid had reduced the single-family percentage along these arteries to 7 percent and was zoning 16 percent of the frontage for multifamily housing.[87] Frontage on a mere collector street, a roadway not as wide as an arterial, occasionally may also be sufficient. In the 1950s, as noted, Palo Alto, then in a pro-growth mode, rezoned several blocks along University Avenue just northeast of downtown to permit multifamily development.

Exceptions to the straitjacket other than proximity to a transit node may exist.[88] But none seems as plain. Some observers have assumed that homeowners in a neighborhood that is both relatively poor and relatively non-White would lack political power and therefore be more vulnerable

84. Loh, "Growth Near Metro" (2019).
85. Hills and Schleicher, "Balancing 'Zoning Budget'" (2011): 85.
86. Knack and Peters, "Starting to Spread" (1985): 22 (mapping examples along Interstate 285 north of Atlanta); Schmitt, "Homeowners Unite" (1985) (providing example north of Atlanta); see also Shoup, "Graduated Density Zoning" (2008): 172–74 (describing how Simi Valley, California, reduced its required minimum house-lot size from 20,000 to 2,850 sq. ft. at a site several hundred yards from a freeway exit).
87. See table 12 above in this chapter.
88. Two low-probability scenarios warrant brief mention. A neighborhood disaster, natural or manmade, may nudge local politicians to favor densification. See Dericks and Koster, "Billion Pound Drop" (2018); Hornbeck and Keniston, "Great Boston Fire" (2017); van Holm and Wyczalkowski, "New Orleans After Katrina" (2019). Pro-density religious preferences also may alter the outcomes of zoning politics. A group of Hasidic Jews supported the conversion of a Brooklyn neighborhood from single-family dwellings to multistory walkup apartments. Mangin, "Ethnic Enclaves" (2018): 441–42.

to densification.[89] The zoning history of the East Austin neighborhood may support this conjecture. In 2014, however, three of the many suburbs previously discussed were both lower-income and majority-minority: East Palo Alto, Euclid, and Willingboro.[90] In the 2010s, as this chapter indicates, all three were staunchly committed to keeping densifiers away from their single-family neighborhoods.

The straitjacket also might tend to be looser in a locality with a large population, where politics likely would be more pluralistic, than in a lightly populated suburb where homeowners predominate.[91] The City of Minneapolis has garnered headlines by authorizing the construction of triplexes in zones where it formerly had restricted residential uses to detached houses.[92] Some recent studies, however, emphasize the strength of NIMBYist homeowners in central cities such as New York City and San Francisco.[93] And San Mateo and Santa Clara counties, both populous localities, impose the Silicon Valley's toughest land use controls on Stanford University lands in the Foothills.[94] Even in a populous locality, zoning politics tends to be hyperlocal, giving great weight to the opinions of those who reside near the site at issue.[95]

How a city structures its local elections might affect the tightness of its straitjacket.[96] As noted, Austin shifted from electing local officials at-large

89. Romem, "Dormant Suburban Interior" (2018).
90. In 2014, median household income in Euclid was the lowest of all the municipalities studied. Euclid's median was 70 percent of the State of Ohio's and 25 percent of Palo Alto's. In 2014, Euclid's population was 59 percent African American.
91. Ellickson, "Suburban Growth Controls" (1977): 404–9; Marantz and Lewis, "Jurisdictional Size" (2021); see also Oliver, "Civic Involvement" (2000) (finding that an increase in the population of a city or suburb results in less political participation).
92. Blumgart, "Minneapolis Evicts" (2019). Grand Rapids may have pioneered this innovation. Brey, "Zoning in Grand Rapids" (2018).
93. Been et al., "Overtaking the Growth Machine?" (2014); O'Neill et al., "California's Housing Policy Debates" (2019): 68; Schleicher, "City Unplanning" (2013): 1698–99.
94. See chapter 3.
95. See chapter 7.
96. Hills and Schleicher, "Planning an Affordable City" (2015): 111–15; Stahl, "Local Growth Politics" (2010); see also Clingermayer, "Ward Representation"

to electing them by district. Hankinson and Magazinnik confirm that, in California, this sort of switch typically makes a city council more responsive to NIMBYist lobbying.[97] Evan Mast has confirmed the pattern nationwide.[98] The importance of the local electoral system, however, should not be exaggerated. Palo Alto, a paragon of the protection of existing single-family neighborhoods, has long elected its city council at-large.[99]

(1993) (finding mildly positive association between ward, as opposed to at-large, local elections and date a locality first adopted zoning).

97. Hankinson and Magazinnik, "Effect of District Representation" (2019) (finding a 44 percent drop in permits for multifamily housing).

98. Mast, "Warding Off Development" (2020).

99. Kadvany, "Racially Polarized Voting" (2018).

7

Zoning Politics at City Hall

Political scientists, at least traditionally, have showed little interest in the workings of local government. A survey of articles on elections in leading U.S. political science journals found that 94 percent focused on federal elections, 6 percent on state elections, and less than 1 percent on local elections.[1] Social scientists, however, increasingly have come to recognize the massive effects of local zoning practices on both the national economy and household migration choices. This has resulted in a boom, or at least a boomlet, of pertinent scholarship. Zoning decisions are political outcomes. They tend to reflect the ideologies of local officials and the interests of those best able to lobby city hall. This chapter aims to enhance the sophistication of theories of local zoning politics.[2]

Both federal and state laws constrain a locality's choices in how to zone. Both levels of government, in selected cases, have forced localities to accept, even in an existing neighborhood where detached houses predominate, religious facilities, group homes, accessory dwelling units, and other land uses.[3] The effects of these preemptive overrides, however, generally have been modest. State and federal constitutional constraints

1. Berry and Howell, "Local Elections" (2007): 845 n.3.
2. For a concise overview of existing theories, see Been et al., "Overtaking the Growth Machine?" (2014): 230–38.
3. See, e.g., Religious Land Use and Institutionalized Persons Act of 2000, 42 U.S.C. §§ 2000cc to 2000cc-5 (Supp. 2018); Lemar, "Role of States" (2019); and chapter 11 below (on ADUs).

also exist, but they obviate only extreme policies. In the United States, local officials remain largely free to determine permissible land uses.

The first section of this chapter summarizes theories of zoning politics that Harvey Molotch, William Fischel, and Roderick Hills and David Schleicher have advanced. The ensuing sections aspire to develop a theory of zoning politics that makes sense of three of this book's specific findings:

(1) Zoning practices vary significantly by region, with suburbs in Greater Austin generally being far more pro-growth than suburbs in Silicon Valley and Greater New Haven.
(2) Once streets have been laid out in a neighborhood where zoning permits only detached houses, zoning politics, even in Greater Austin, typically bars any form of denser residential use.
(3) The event most likely to loosen this zoning straitjacket is the opening of a new transit node.

The proposed theory is both tentative and eclectic. It assumes that many factors influence the decisions of local politicians. Among them are self-interest, personal political ideologies, neighborhood social pressures, lobbying, and, most importantly, the psychological disposition of both local voters and local officials to favor maintenance of the status quo.

Current Theories of Zoning Politics

In 1976, Harvey Molotch asserted in an influential article, or at least in the article's title, that a "Growth Machine" dominates local land use politics.[4] Molotch's central claim was that "elites," who are inherently pro-growth, have an outsized influence on policy. "Growth Machine," albeit a memorable phrase, has always mischaracterized many zoning realities.[5] For example, Greenwich, Connecticut's decision in 1947 to require four-acre house-lots in the northern third of town was hardly a

4. Molotch, "City as Growth Machine" (1976).
5. Molotch's supporters include Schragger, "Mobile Capital" (2009). Skeptics include Been et al., "Overtaking the Growth Machine?" (2014) (finding evidence of NIMBYism in New York City, the last place an observer might expect it).

pro-growth policy.[6] To his credit, Molotch acknowledged that his title might be claiming too much. The text of his article observed that the very rich had been able to create for themselves some "small, exclusive meccas of low density."[7] (Greenwich, a town of forty-eight square miles, in fact is not small.) Living in the Santa Barbara area during the 1970s, Molotch also indicated that he was aware that political tides in California had emphatically shifted away from pro-growth policies.[8]

William Fischel has advanced a theory of local politics that is far more realistic than Molotch's. Fischel coined a neologism, *Homevoter*, to highlight homeowners' interests in local issues.[9] Many homeowners regard their houses among their principal financial assets. Insurance against a decline in house value seldom is available. The effects of local decisions on matters such as zoning and the quality of public schools are largely capitalized into house values. Fischel hypothesizes that Homevoters, for him implicitly the political heavyweights in local politics, tend to favor decisions that would enhance the value of their abodes.

Recent scholarship generally affirms Fischel's theory that homeowners, not developers, dominate local politics. Owners of residential dwellings are almost twice as likely as renters to vote in local elections.[10] In the suburbs of Greater Chicago, Eric Oliver found that homeowners constituted 99.5 percent of the candidates for local office.[11] Homeowners are particularly likely to rouse themselves on zoning issues.[12] In the Boston region, Einstein, Glick, and Palmer found that homeowners, who constituted 46 percent of the general electorate, were 73 percent of the commentators

6. See chapter 1.
7. Molotch, "City as Growth Machine" (1976): 327.
8. Id. at 326–29 (mentioning anti-growth sentiment in, among other cities, Palo Alto). On the tightening of zoning controls in California between 1965 and 1975, see chapter 3.
9. Fischel, *Homevoter Hypothesis* (2001).
10. Oliver, *Local Elections* (2012): 69; Hall and Yoder, "Does Homeownership Influence?" (2020) (finding that acquisition of a house increases likelihood of voting in local elections); see also Whittemore, "Zoning Los Angeles" (2012b) (describing rise of homeowner influence on Los Angeles zoning between 1960 and 2000).
11. Oliver, *Local Elections* (2012): 99.
12. Id. at 106.

at public zoning hearings.[13] Regardless of ideology, these speakers tended to be skeptical of projects that would densify their neighborhoods.[14] Einstein and her co-authors found that residents offering testimony were disproportionately male, White, older, longtime homeowners, and overwhelmingly opposed to new housing construction.[15] Even renters are potential recruits to NIMBY causes.[16]

Roderick Hills and David Schleicher have offered a theory that nicely supplements Fischel's. As Fischel well understood, members of two other broad factions have a major stake in zoning outcomes.[17] One faction consists of housing suppliers—the individuals and firms that would gain financially from housing production. The second and larger faction consists of housing consumers. Consumers benefit when suppliers offer more dwelling options and housing production is robust enough to dampen increases in regional rents and sale prices.[18] Invoking public-choice theory, Hills and Schleicher observe that the various local factions face different collective action problems.[19] Members of some factions are better able to make financial contributions to local candidates or to induce lobbying activity, such as attendance at a zoning hearing.

To understand the realities of zoning politics, consider Professorville, a neighborhood that Palo Alto zoning restricts to single-family detached houses.[20] Professorville is the prototype of a neighborhood ripe for densification. The neighborhood is within easy walking distance of both down-

13. Einstein et al., *Neighborhood Defenders* (2019): 101.
14. Id. at 106 (finding that 62 percent of speakers opposed new housing, compared to 15 percent supporting it and 23 percent neutral); Marble and Nall, "Opposition to Housing Development" (2020) (finding widespread opposition to neighborhood densification). See also Wong, "Localism Meets Liberalism" (2018) (finding that belief in local control correlates with opposition to housing development).
15. Einstein et al., *Neighborhood Defenders* (2019): 101–14.
16. Hankinson, "Renters Behave Like Homeowners?" (2018) (finding that renters in high-rent cities are likely to oppose a nearby project that might accelerate gentrification).
17. Fischel, *Homevoter Hypothesis* (2001): 15–16, 257–58.
18. See chapter 1.
19. Hills and Schleicher, "Balancing 'Zoning Budget'" (2011): 89–96.
20. Chapter 11 also invokes the Professorville example.

town Palo Alto and the railroad station that serves it. If unconstrained by zoning, a modern-day Joseph Eichler plainly could profit by buying up contiguous house-lots in Professorville and redeveloping the site, perhaps for townhouses or a mid-rise multifamily building.

Local zoning politics, however, assures that the rezoning of a significant part of Professorville would be a nonstarter in Palo Alto. All politics, it is said, is local. As the straitjacket thesis implies, zoning politics in the United States in fact is *hyperlocal*.[21] Palo Alto officials, if asked to consider a zoning proposal that would densify Professorville, would nearly always give priority to the wishes of incumbent Professorville homeowners. Einstein, Glick, and Palmer found that almost half of commentators at public zoning hearings lived on the same block where the new housing was proposed, and they were overwhelmingly opposed to its construction.[22] The instinctive status quo bias of nearby local residents would doom the prospect of a Palo Alto rezoning of even a small portion of Professorville.

Professorville homeowners likely would invoke historic preservation as a central reason for opposition. Around 1980, the U.S. Department of the Interior designated eight square blocks of Professorville a historic district.[23] In 1993, the City of Palo Alto, on its own initiative, almost doubled the size of the protected area.[24] Perhaps 40 percent of the houses in the larger district are individually worthy of historic preservation. Yet even if an Eichler were to propose densifying several Professorville lots that lacked buildings of historic distinction, he would encounter a chorus of NIMBYs opposing the rezoning. In the end, local zoning politics thus would elevate the preferences of Professorville homeowners and historic

21. Cf. Kazis, "Sources of Hyper-Localism" (2021).

22. Einstein et al., *Neighborhood Defenders* (2019): 102–3.

23. In 1979, Palo Alto first applied to the National Register of Historic Places, a division of the Interior Department, for recognition of an eight-block Professorville Historic District. The city's application included a map indicating that buildings of some historical importance were present on roughly 60 percent of the lots in the proposed district. Professorville Historic District, "Application" (1979): 16.

24. See map at Page and Turnbull, "Professorville Design Guidelines" (2016): 3. I used these expanded boundaries when estimating that 40 percent of Professorville's structures have individual historic value.

preservationists over the interests of housing suppliers and, most pertinently, Silicon Valley housing consumers. This bias against change seems to affect local officials more powerfully than lawmakers at the state or national level. NIMBYism flourishes more at city hall than it does at a higher-level government.[25]

Hills and Schleicher's stress on the costs of collective action serves to clarify why this occurs. Incumbent residents of Professorville could readily overcome impediments to acting collectively. The Palo Alto zoning ordinance requires the city to send, at least ten days in advance of the upcoming hearing, a mailed notice to owners of lots within six hundred feet of the land affected.[26] Those recipients could readily rally additional opposition by knocking on the doors of neighbors located a bit farther away. Palo Alto's city hall is a ten-minute walk from Professorville. Neighborhood residents could easily participate in the hearing and confer esteem on homeowners who step forward to defend the status quo in Professorville.[27]

Housing consumers, by contrast, would face colossal collective action problems. A Palo Alto rezoning would affect housing options not only for consumers throughout the Bay Area but also for techies worldwide. A particular consumer's stake in the outcome of a specific Professorville densification proposal is trivial, far less than that of a neighborhood homeowner. For most consumers, the lengthiness of a trip to Palo Alto would preclude attendance at a rezoning hearing. The advent of the internet, however, has slightly reduced housing consumers' costs of collective action. In the 2010s, one outgrowth was the birth of the YIMBY (Yes In My Backyard) movement.[28]

Housing suppliers with a financial stake in a particular Professorville densification project, by contrast, would be intensely motivated to participate in a Palo Alto hearing. Before the start of construction, however, they likely would number no more than a handful. Some, if resident in

25. This chapter later explores why this is so.
26. Palo Alto, Cal., Code of Ordinances, § 18.80.060(a)(2) (2019).
27. McAdams, "Development of Norms" (1997): 355–72.
28. Palo Alto Forward (2020) is the closest equivalent in Palo Alto. On YIMBYs, see also chapter 11.

another city, would be unable to vote in a Palo Alto election. Growth Machine theorists, of course, might stress that outsiders ineligible to vote could still engage in lobbying and make campaign contributions. State and local campaign finance statutes, however, might compel a candidate to disclose political donations.[29] If so, because developers are highly unpopular, a housing supplier's donation might backfire.[30]

Hills and Schleicher's emphasis on the costs of collective action helps reveal why local zoning politics has become hyperlocal and why the zoning straitjacket exists. Absent state reform, a developer of dense housing is likely to avoid a neighborhood such as Professorville. Given the nature of local politics, developers understandably decide that their best targets of opportunity lie not in neighborhoods where houses predominate, but elsewhere.

Why Are Austin Suburbs Relatively Pro-Growth?

The next sections strive to develop a theory of zoning politics that is consistent with the larger study's three principal empirical findings. The first finding is the propensity of localities in the northwestern sector of Austin, compared to those in Silicon Valley and Greater New Haven, both to resist large-lot zoning and to allow multifamily housing and small-lot subdivisions.[31] Why has Greater Austin been different?

Three possibilities stand out. The first may appeal to skeptics of the quality of life in Texas. Greater Austin's undeveloped land, on average, might have less environmental value than land in the other two metros. If so, environmentalist opposition to housing development would be less intense. This is more plausible in the relatively flat portions of Greater Austin, such as Round Rock, than in, say, West Lake Hills. Many Austin residents, however, would dispute the claim that their metropolitan area lacks environmental potential. They might point to a 2017 *Architectural*

29. Gilbert, "Campaign Finance Disclosure" (2013). In California, these donations could not be anonymous. Cal. Gov't Code §§ 84211, 90008 (West 2017). On the merits of compelled disclosure, see Ayres, "Disclosure Versus Anonymity" (2000).

30. Monkkonen and Manville, "Opposition to Developers?" (2019).

31. See chapter 2.

Digest ranking of the nation's ten "greenest" metropolitan areas: Austin topped the list.[32]

The other two possible explanations why Greater Austin is different turn on differences in the dynamics of state and local politics. The second possibility, a stripped-down version of the Growth Machine theory, emphasizes the economic payoffs to housing suppliers when zoning is pro-growth. The relative inattention of voters to local politics eases the burden of putting together a pro-growth coalition capable of controlling city hall. Homebuilders obviously have a huge stake in zoning policy. A wide variety of other specialists, moreover, also profit from increased housing supply: construction workers; subcontractors; civil engineers; real estate brokers; real estate attorneys; mortgage lenders; owners and employees of restaurants, furniture stores, and moving companies; and on and on.[33] A fast-growing metropolis, by definition, has a larger fraction of these diverse suppliers. This increases their political heft. In all but the most elite suburbs, local political control may be within their reach. Where housing demand is strong, pro-growth policies thus may be politically self-perpetuating.

This stripped-down Growth Machine conception also forecasts that the pro-growth inclinations of Austin's suburbs might not endure. If national fertility rates and immigration rates were to plummet, housing development would slow, weakening the housing-supplier coalition nationwide. The defeat of CodeNEXT at the hands of NIMBYists suggests that politics in the Austin metro hardly lies beyond the national mainstream.[34]

The third possibility, and the most plausible theory to explain why municipalities in Greater Austin have been pro-growth, takes into account the political ideologies of both voters and local elected officials.[35]

32. Johnson, "The 10 Greenest Cities" (2017).

33. "From 1960 until 1982 almost every member of the [Redwood City, California] City Council favored continued housing construction. Most council members have been employed in jobs related to the housing industry or in local Redwood City businesses which would benefit from growth." Cook, "Redwood City" (1982): 71.

34. See chapter 5.

35. See, e.g., Béland and Cox, *Ideas and Politics* (2011); Wilson, "How Divided Are We?" (2006).

In contrast to the prior theory, this one implies that the Austin region's pro-growth policies might continue. The ideologies of the median Texas voter and legislator differ from their counterparts in both California and Connecticut. Academic economists, who devote their lives to the world of ideas, ironically have been resistant to the notion that ideas matter. Some economic historians have begun to break ranks and to emphasize the power of ideas to shape events.[36] In the context of land use regulation, several authors have noted the potential influence of political ideologies.[37] William Fischel has associated the rise of suburban growth controls with the rise of the environmental movement in the late 1960s.[38] The chronology of Silicon Valley zoning politics firmly supports Fischel's thesis.[39] Matthew Kahn has found evidence that, controlling for other variables, California cities with more residents registered in left-leaning parties are less likely to approve proposed housing developments.[40]

Stereotypes and statistics both support the notion that Texans tend to favor a government that regulates less. Texas lawyers, for example, are notably more politically conservative than those in California and Connecticut.[41] A predilection for small government likely boosts the popularity of pro-growth policies in Austin suburbs. When asked whether there was an anti-growth faction in Round Rock, Texas, a member of the city's planning staff stated that none existed.[42] Self-selection by migrants may have contributed to this political tilt. Some observers surmise that adults are more likely to move to, and remain in, places where other people share their values.[43] Households with relatively pro-growth inclinations may have been flocking to the Austin area. Even apart from ideology, a metro's

36. See, e.g., McCloskey, *Bourgeois Equality* (2017); Mokyr, *Culture of Growth* (2016).
37. See, e.g., Baldassare and Wilson, "Support for Growth Controls" (1996).
38. Fischel, *Zoning Rules!* (2015): 203–5.
39. See chapter 3.
40. Kahn, "Do Liberal Cities Limit?" (2011).
41. Bonica et al., "Ideologies of American Lawyers" (2016): 299 (inferring ideologies from campaign contributions).
42. Interview with Clyde von Rosenberg, senior planner, City of Round Rock, Tex. (Oct. 30, 2018).
43. Bishop, *The Big Sort* (2008); Cho et al., "Changing Partisan Loyalty" (2018). But see, e.g., Mummolo and Nall, "Partisans Do Not Sort" (2017). On

growth history likely has some effect on who migrates there. A metropolitan area like Greater Austin, where some of the landscape is constantly changing, might put off a person harboring a strong status quo bias.

Why Homeowners Typically Can Freeze Zoning, Even in Greater Austin

Chapter 6 marshaled evidence that a straitjacket binds, even in Greater Austin, most neighborhoods of single-family houses. The foundation for a theory of local zoning politics is provided by Fischel's Homevoter hypothesis supplemented by Hills and Schleicher's emphasis on the costs of collective action. The theory could be further enriched by insights from psychology, sociology, and philosophy.

Psychology: Status Quo Bias

People are wary, an evolutionary trait that may be generally adaptive. As Laurence Siegel puts it, "Our neural network says to us all the time: That could be a tiger, or it could be a rabbit, so let's assume it's a tiger."[44] According to renowned cognitive psychologists Daniel Kahneman and Amos Tversky, individuals choose a reference point from which to evaluate the consequences of a change. From that reference point, they give more weight to losses than to objectively equivalent gains.[45] The Kahneman and Tversky theory is broadly accepted.[46] Humans innately fear that change will bring tigers, not rabbits.[47]

---

political clustering within U.S. metropolitan regions, see Badger et al., "Partisan Segregation" (2021).

44. Zweig, "Why Invest?" (2020), includes the Siegel quote.

45. See, e.g., Kahneman and Tversky, "Prospect Theory" (1979): 279; Kahneman et al., "Anomalies" (1991).

46. See, e.g., Glaeser, *Triumph of the City* (2011): 262; Korobkin and Ulen, "Rationality Assumption" (2000): 1104–13. Cf. Postrel, *Future and Its Enemies* (1999) (contrasting the views of those who favor dynamism and stasism). But cf. Plott and Zeiler, "Exchange Asymmetries" (2007). There is some debate about the universality of the endowment effect, a closely related phenomenon. Apicella et al., "Evidence from Hunter-Gatherers" (2014).

47. Several legal scholars have briefly discussed the possible influence of status quo bias in land use regulation. Doremus, "Takings and Transitions" (2003): 21–24; Spence, "Local Vetoes" (2014): 396–97.

Status quo bias particularly influences land use policy when, as is typical in the United States, a local government makes zoning decisions. Both neighborhood residents and local elected officials plainly choose the existing landscape as their reference point. This enhances the hyperlocal nature of zoning politics and fosters NIMBYism.

The residential densification of a neighborhood such as Professorville in Palo Alto would have both negative and positive effects on residents. The downsides might include more traffic, greater difficulty in finding an empty parking space on the street, bulkier buildings that cast longer shadows, and greater risks in the event of a pandemic. Densification also would bring a variety of benefits. Some would be local, such as greater safety resulting from additional pedestrian traffic and a potential increase in the variety and quality of nearby stores and restaurants. Other benefits would be diffuse, such as greater specialization of Silicon Valley job opportunities and an increase in networking opportunities.[48] Because of status quo bias, Professorville residents would tend to give more weight to each of the prospective costs of densification than to each of its prospective benefits.[49]

A rezoning to permit the building of townhouses or low-rise apartments on Professorville lots might triple the market value of the rezoned lots. In an extreme case, notably near a new transit node, prospects for reaping these financial gains might induce some homeowners to favor densification.[50] Status quo bias, however, reduces the likelihood of this outcome. Because of the bias that Kahneman and Tversky identify, Professorville homeowners likely would undervalue the windfalls they would gain from rezonings.[51]

Status quo bias powerfully affects all aspects of local land use policy. For starters, it supports the perpetuation of existing uses. Many localities that

48. See chapter 1.

49. On the actual arguments used by opponents of proposed housing developments, see Einstein et al., *Neighborhood Defenders* (2019): 87–88, 115–45; Pendall, "Opposition to Housing" (1999). On objections to subsidized housing projects in particular, see Nguyen et al., "Opposition to Affordable Housing" (2013).

50. See chapter 6.

51. Fischel has proposed creation of a market for home-value insurance. Fischel, *Homevoter Hypothesis* (2001): 8–10, 268–70. If NIMBYist fears of worst-case outcomes arise from psychological predispositions and not from rational responses to risk, however, this innovation would be less than completely effectual.

would never approve construction of a new neon sign or billboard strive to preserve an old and familiar one. Notable examples are the CITGO sign adjacent to Fenway Park in Boston and the Hollywood sign high in the Los Angeles hills. Also illustrative is the widespread municipal practice of permitting nonconforming uses to continue even when those uses nominally violate current zoning rules. In Somerville, Massachusetts, an older city with a population of nearly 80,000, one study found that only 22 residential uses conformed to all current zoning requirements.[52] Palo Alto, a municipality hardly likely to permit the opening of a new mobile home park, is making strenuous efforts to prevent the closing of an existing one.[53] Buena Vista, the city's sole mobile home park, dates back at least to the 1940s.[54] A facility with about one hundred spaces, Buena Vista occupies a 5.5-acre site on Los Robles Avenue, a stone's throw from El Camino Real. In the 2010s, Buena Vista's owner sought to close the park. In 2017, after lengthy negotiations, Palo Alto and two other public agencies agreed to buy the facility for $400,000 per space.[55] The buyers plan eventually to replace Buena Vista with subsidized housing that its former residents could afford.

Status quo bias not only favors retention of the familiar but also spurs resistance to the coming of new land uses. It undergirds NIMBYist opposition to change near one's backyard.[56] It accounts for some of the

52. Hertz, "Illegal City of Somerville" (2016). Connecticut flatly forbids its local governments from amortizing (phasing out) nonconforming uses. Conn. Gen. Stat. § 8–2 (2019). On the merits of protecting existing uses, compare Serkin, "Existing Uses" (2009), with Lindsay, "In Praise of Nonconformity" (2021).
53. Kurhi, "Buena Vista" (2017). The City of San Jose similarly fought to slow the redevelopment of a mobile home park in West San Jose. Fernandez, "Winchester Ranch" (2020).
54. In 2012, the City of Palo Alto initially supported the owner's effort to close Buena Vista. In 2016, the issue became more politically salient when a court held that the owner's offer of relocation payments to tenants had been insufficient.
55. The two other purchasers were Santa Clara County and the Santa Clara County Housing Authority. Palo Alto's zoning ordinance permits "mobile homes" as of right in its three multifamily zones. Palo Alto Code of Ordinances § 18.13.030, table 1 (2019). Since the advent of Buena Vista, however, none has opened in the city.
56. Richman and Boerner, "Understanding NIMBY Problem" (2006). On the underlying psychology, see, e.g., Devine-Wright, "Rethinking NIMBYism" (2009).

opposition to the gentrification of neighborhoods.[57] It lies at the heart of the precautionary principle, a credo of environmentalists reluctant to encounter new risks.[58] It triggers popular support for preventing the development of existing open spaces.[59] It helps explain why respondents to a national survey favored, by a margin of 52 percent to 36 percent, maintaining rather than relaxing zoning restrictions on housing production.[60] Courts have frequently ruled on whether a suburb's use of zoning to protect the "community character" of an existing neighborhood is a legitimate exercise of the police power. The supreme courts of California, Connecticut, and Texas all have held that it is.[61]

Status quo bias also generates political support for historic preservation, a cause that some Professorville homeowners certainly would invoke. Historic preservation, although hardly free of costs, commonly is a worthy objective.[62] Central cities worldwide have led efforts to preserve both landmarks and historic neighborhoods. French lawmakers, as Alain Bertaud has asserted, have sought to maintain "Paris streets as they were at the time of the Impressionists."[63] During the nineteenth century, Manhattan was one of the most dynamic U.S. real estate markets. This led to the razing of many buildings worthy of preservation.[64] Times have changed. Today, historic preservation regulations freeze many Manhattan land uses, and New York City zoning procedures tend to favor

57. See, e.g., Dubin, "From Junkyards to Gentrification" (1993); Hwang and Sampson, "Pathways of Gentrification" (2014).
58. Sunstein, "Precautionary Principle" (2003) (warning of the principle's potential paralyzing effect).
59. See chapter 4.
60. Hart Research Associates, "How Housing Matters Survey" (2014).
61. Miller v. Board of Public Works, 234 P. 381, 386–88 (Cal. 1925); Damick v. Planning & Zoning Comm'n of Town of Southington, 256 A.2d 428, 431 (Conn. 1969); Mayhew v. Town of Sunnyvale, 964 S.W.2d 922, 934–35 (Tex. 1998). See also "Developments in the Law—Zoning" (1978): 1450–57 (discussing legitimacy of preserving "community character").
62. See Ellen and McCabe, "Historic Preservation" (2017) (recognizing benefits of preservation efforts but urging attention to associated costs); Glaeser, "Preservation Follies" (2010).
63. Bertaud, *Order Without Design* (2018): 314.
64. Tauranac, "Lost New York" (1999).

NIMBYs.[65] The benefits of densifying some non-historic portions of Professorville now would exceed their costs.

The straitjacket hypothesis supposes that a proposal to densify would encounter more opposition in a neighborhood of detached houses than in one that includes duplexes, townhouses, and apartment buildings.[66] Several sources support this thesis.[67] In San Francisco, the "grand bargain" permits residential densification only in neighborhoods where house owners are few.[68] Eric Steele has observed that Evanston, Illinois, was particularly solicitous of protecting its single-family neighborhoods: "Community opposition is a more potent force than is community support, and both are more powerful in the context of a single-family neighborhood. This conclusion is consistent with what we have seen to be the central impulse of urban zoning—conserving the character of existing residential areas, particularly single-family neighborhoods."[69] In neighborhoods where residential densities are greater, exclusionary practices are hardly unknown. They appear, however, to surface less powerfully and pervasively.

Neighborhood opposition to change may deepen with the duration of a particular homeowner's ownership, the age of the neighborhood, and perhaps even the age of the zoning government.[70] Mancur Olson has asserted that longevity causes institutions to become more rigid.[71] In the

65. Been et al., "Overtaking the Growth Machine?" (2014); Glaeser, "Preservation Follies" (2010); Schleicher, "City Unplanning" (2013): 1695–98.

66. See chapter 6.

67. Levine, *Zoned Out* (2006): 78; Gabbe, "Why Are Regulations Changed?" (2018): 295–96 (finding that upzonings in Los Angeles were far less likely when homeowners lived nearby); see also Glaeser and Ward, "Evidence from Greater Boston" (2009): 266–67 (asserting that a locality where housing density has historically been high is less likely to embrace exclusionary practices); Evenson and Wheaton, "Local Variation" (2003) (similar).

68. See chapter 6.

69. Steele, "Functions of Zoning" (1986): 731.

70. Strahilevitz and Loewenstein's "Ownership History" (1998) is a leading study of the effect of length of ownership on perceptions of loss. The authors found that those who owned an item of personal property for up to an hour valued it more highly than those just given it. Owners of real estate, of course, might behave differently.

71. Olson, *Decline of Nations* (1982).

three metros studied, New Haven's suburbs are by far the longest settled. They also have existed the longest as municipalities, and none of their boundaries has changed since 1921.[72] These forms of seniority may have contributed to New Haven suburbanites' exceptional hostility to both multifamily housing and small house-lots.

Social scientists, including psychologists, have seldom explored the ramifications of status quo bias in the land use arena.[73] On its face, the bias leads to normatively myopic results. After a new land use has replaced an old one, local residents likely would soon regard the new use to be part of the status quo. Manhattanites may now be fully acclimated to Freedom Tower, one of the skyscrapers that replaced the World Trade Center towers destroyed on September 11, 2001. If most individuals indeed do adapt quickly to the advent of new land uses, policymakers should give less weight to prospective fears of neighborhood change.[74]

A key point is that interest in preserving the existing landscape is more salient to local officials than to either federal or state officials.[75] NIMBYism flourishes at city hall but matters less at a higher level of government. National governments tend best to protect the interests of housing consumers. The federal government has put pressure on localities to accept religious land uses, cell-phone towers, and other uses.[76] In France and Japan, where national governments largely control land use policy, exclusionary practices are far less common. France flatly forbids its local governments from setting minimum sizes for house-lots.[77] Japan's policies have enabled the building of high-rise apartments in Tokyo.[78] In the

72. See chapter 4.

73. An exception is Devine-Wright, "Rethinking NIMBYism" (2009).

74. Cf. Sunstein, "Behavioral Welfare Economics" (2020) (exploring implications of behavioral realities for policymaking).

75. Chapters 10 and 11 address, respectively, zoning politics at the federal and state levels.

76. See Religious Land Use and Institutionalized Persons Act of 2000, 42 U.S.C. §§ 2000cc to 2000cc-5 (Supp. 2018); Telecommunications Act of 1996, 47 U.S.C. § 332(c)(7)(B)(i) (Supp. 2019).

77. Code de l'urbanisme, § 123–1-5 (2019), as amended by loi ALUR (2014). See Noguellou, "La règle d'urbanisme" (2016).

78. Sorensen et al., "Tokyo's High-rise Boom" (2010) (describing national government's occasional successes in forcing local governments to permit high-rise multifamily structures); see also Urban Kchoze (2014).

United States, state politics tends to favor housing consumers more than local politics does. Many states require localities to accommodate group homes and other controversial land uses.[79] Oregon, over local protest, has compelled its populous localities to abolish the single-family zone.

Zoning reform at the state level, of course, would be far from easy. But it would not be impossible, as it commonly would be at the local level. City halls are physically closer to the neighborhood defenders, to invoke Einstein, Glick, and Palmer's apt phrase, who are apt to attend local hearings and to lobby against increases in residential density.[80] Professorville residents could lobby Palo Alto City Hall far more easily than Sacramento or Washington. Even a local government large in population is likely to treat a zoning decision as hyperlocal. In 2010, the Silicon Valley counties of San Mateo and Santa Clara both had populations greater than 700,000. Yet, when zoning their scattered pockets of unincorporated land, officials of both counties seemed to give extra weight to the tastes of voters residing near the site in question. San Mateo County requires in North Fair Oaks, a blue-collar area in its plains, a mere 5,000-sq.-ft. house-lot. The county's required minimum in Emerald Lake Hills, an unincorporated area in the foothills, however, is 12,000 square feet, a requirement in line with the zoning policies of surrounding suburbs. Santa Clara County similarly requires 5,000-sq.-ft. lots in Burbank, a blue-collar area in its plains, but 20,000-sq.-ft. lots in Loyola, which lies in the foothills. On Stanford lands, Santa Clara County requires a twenty-acre house-lot.[81] These varying requirements grow out of differences in not only site characteristics but also the hyperlocal dynamics of local zoning politics.

In the 1920s, a Herbert Hoover panel urged state governments to give local governments a largely free hand in developing zoning policy.[82] Shortly thereafter, some suburbs began to invent a variety of exclusionary techniques. NIMBY forces, potent at the local level of government, are less potent at the state and national levels. In retrospect, Hoover's

79. See chapter 11.

80. Einstein et al., *Neighborhood Defenders* (2019).

81. See chapter 3.

82. See chapters 1 and 12.

panel made a major mistake. The panel's model statute should have more greatly constrained the policy choices of local governments.

Sociology: Esteem and Disesteem in the Eyes of Neighbors

Sociologists could fruitfully analyze how homeowners in a neighborhood of houses react to proposals that threaten densification. Most homeowners have social ties, some strong, some weak, with neighbors.[83] Parents of children long enrolled in local public schools are likely to be the most socially enmeshed. Residents with the most irreplaceable neighborhood ties likely would be the most fervent opponents of densification. At a public hearing, they would be prime candidates for assuming the role of neighborhood defender. A key sociological question is whether other neighbors would confer esteem, or disesteem, on those who had stepped into that role.[84] The existence of the zoning straitjacket suggests the usual answer: esteem.

The possibility of financial profit, however, complicates densification scenarios and heightens their sociological interest. In a neighborhood such as Professorville, the owner of a lot rezoned for higher density might benefit from a huge increase in the lot's market value. That prospect might induce some owners to act, not as neighborhood defenders, but as pro-densification profit-maximizers. A better understanding of the social dynamics would be enlightening.

Philosophy: Norms of Distributive Justice

Philosophers concerned with the fairness of rewards also may have something to contribute to the understanding of zoning politics. The beneficiaries of residential densification would include, among many others, housing consumers and construction workers. Opponents of a densification measure, however, would be wise to characterize the sole prospective beneficiaries as "greedy developers."[85] Monkkonen and Manville have found that this framing, with its implication of ill-gotten gains,

83. See, e.g., Fischer, *Dwell Among Friends* (1982); Gans, *Levittowners* (1982).

84. McAdams, "Development of Norms" (1997): 355–72.

85. This perception might have startled Joseph Eichler. In 1967, Eichler Homes filed for bankruptcy. See Joseph Eichler (2020).

tends to bolster public opposition to development proposals.[86] The fate of zoning proposals to bring greater urban density may turn on perceptions of who would benefit. YIMBYs—Yes In My Backyard advocates—should take note.

Proximity to a Transit Node May Flip Zoning Politics Toward Densification

Of this book's central findings, economists are apt to be least surprised that the availability of nearby mass transit can flip zoning politics to favor densification. The opening of the Courthouse Metro station in Arlington, Virginia, promised to bring financial riches to owners of houses located nearby. To cash in, these homeowners eventually supported the densification of their neighborhood, and county officials duly removed the single-family straitjacket.[87]

Yet why does zoning politics in a neighborhood such as Professorville—indeed, in most existing single-family neighborhoods—operate so differently? The work of Kahneman and Tversky currently provides the most penetrating insight. Status quo bias systematically influences homeowners, who undervalue all types of gains, including financial gains, that a rezoning for greater density would confer on them. In a world where local governments control zoning, the upshot has been a rampant NIMBYism.

In the United States, local zoning politics freezes land uses in a neighborhood of detached houses. This is true not only in a wealthy suburb, such as Palo Alto, Woodbridge, and West Lake Hills, but also in Euclid, Ohio, whose median household income is 25 percent of Palo Alto's. Homeowners in these neighborhoods, of course, commonly are free to raze their houses and replace them. With rare exception, however, local

86. Monkkonen and Manville, "Opposition to Developers?" (2019) (finding that a survey frame that highlighted developers' profits increased project opposition by 20 percent, twice the increase of a frame that highlighted traffic-congestion issues).

87. See chapter 6.

zoning rules forbid the construction of denser residential structures, even duplexes. The zoning straitjacket binds a solid majority of the nation's urbanized land, much of it in central cities. In the eyes of many zoning officials, a household can achieve the American Dream of homeownership only in a neighborhood of detached houses.

The rigidity of the zoning straitjacket inflicts major costs on the United States. Today's urban landscape will not be adapted to life a century from now. Real estate and labor markets, if freer to operate, would enable the nation to adjust to changes in what architects can design and in how households would prefer to live. The U.S. law of real property traditionally has included doctrines designed to keep land markets dynamic. Among them have been the Rule Against Perpetuities and the Rule Against Restraints on Alienation.[88] The zoning straitjacket goes against this sound legal tradition.

During the nineteenth century, the Manhattan real estate market may have been overly dynamic. Federal Hall, razed in 1812, had been the site of George Washington's initial inauguration, and it was arguably the nation's most historic building.[89] Today, the problem is not excessive dynamism, but excessive stasis. In the words of the immortal Jane Jacobs, "The purpose of zoning . . . should not be to freeze conditions and uses as they stand. That would be death."[90] Homeowners in neighborhoods of detached houses have learned how to do exactly what Jacobs dreaded. Life is better.

88. Brooks and Rose, *Saving the Neighborhood* (2013): 73–78.

89. Tauranac, "Lost New York" (1999).

90. Jacobs, *Great American Cities* (1992): 253. But cf. Schoenbaum, "Stuck or Rooted?" (2017) (stressing the benefits of rootedness).

8

Private Covenants: Often Valuable, But Inflexible

Landowners are compelled to comply not only with public regulations, such as zoning, but also with private promises to restrict land uses.[1] A century ago, private real estate covenants were relatively uncommon. Times have changed. Most city and suburban housing in the United States now comes saddled with covenants. These restrictions have many benefits, particularly when a development is young. As a development ages, however, covenants may significantly contribute, along with zoning practices, to the freezing of U.S. neighborhoods.

Consider Lakeside Village, a condominium complex in Culver City, a municipality that the City of Los Angeles largely surrounds. Many attorneys know the complex because it was the site of the famous "indoor cat" decision of the California Supreme Court.[2] Built in 1973, Lakeside Village contains 530 housing units in a dozen three-story buildings.[3] Spring ahead to the year 2100, when Lakeside Village, if it were still standing, likely would be well past its prime. For a number of reasons, a solid majority of residents might then desire to amend or terminate the Village's covenant scheme. By 2100, for example, many residents might consider the Village's facades and room layouts outmoded, regard the complex as

1. Brady, "Turning Neighbors into Nuisances" (2021): 1673; Van Hecke, "Zoning Ordinances and Restrictions" (1928).
2. Nahrstedt v. Lakeside Village Condominium Ass'n, 878 P.2d 1275 (Cal. 1994).
3. Id. at 1278.

an embarrassing energy hog, or seek conversion of some of the complex's buildings to commercial use. Lakeside Village's written declaration of covenants, however, likely would require that an extraordinary majority, perhaps 75 percent, of the condominium's membership approve any proposed covenant amendment allowing one of these changes. As the decades pass, real estate covenants thus threaten to freeze Lakeside Village's buildings as they are. Human inertia and status quo bias deepen this threat to the dynamism of real estate markets.

Covenants come in two basic forms: negative restrictions on the use of land and affirmative obligations to perform duties, especially that of paying an assessment to a homeowners association. In 2018, the Community Association Institute estimated that at least 61 percent of new dwellings produced in the United States came tethered with covenants.[4] That estimate included only dwellings in common-interest communities (CICs), that is, those where there is an affirmative duty to pay an assessment. In numerous additional developments, negative covenants also restrict a landowner's choices among land uses and building designs.

Covenants restricting land uses first appeared in the United States in the early nineteenth century. During the first half of the twentieth century, they gained notoriety as a mechanism for the exclusion of households from neighborhoods because of race and sometimes religion. In 1948, the Supreme Court famously held in *Shelley v. Kraemer*, however, that courts could not enforce these particular sorts of restrictions.[5] The Court's decision, however, did not forbid covenants limiting an owner's choices among land uses and building designs.[6] Since *Shelley*, these have become ubiquitous.

4. Community Association Institute, "Community Association Factbook" (2018): 3. CAI has an incentive to inflate its numbers. See McKenzie, *Privatopia* (1994): 105–20 (skeptically appraising CAI's activities).

5. 334 U.S. 1 (1948); see also Barrows v. Jackson, 346 U.S. 249 (1953) (denying remedy of damages). On the prior popularity of racial covenants, see U.S. Department of Justice, *Prejudice and Property* (1948); see also Brooks and Rose, *Saving the Neighborhood* (2013) (arguing that racial covenants, even if unenforceable, might continue to affect who lives in a neighborhood).

6. These constraints can have racially exclusionary effects. Berry, "Does Zoning Matter?" (2001) (finding no significant difference in residential racial segregation between Houston and Dallas, and attributing this result to potency of covenants in Houston); Strahilevitz, "Exclusionary Amenities" (2006).

Two Historical Snapshots

This chapter focuses on the history of developers' employment of covenants in the United States.[7] Because the book focuses on the risk that neighborhoods will become frozen, the chapter emphasizes how long a negative or affirmative covenant might bind an owner of land. Declarations of covenants lie scattered in tens of thousands of local land-records offices. This diffusion has discouraged empirical research into what the documents provide. To introduce the modest amount of current knowledge, this section first describes how covenants have frozen many land uses in Hancock Park, a famous subdivision in Los Angeles and site of the so-called Dead Mile. It then turns to a brief depiction of more current covenant practices, especially as they have evolved during the past few decades.

Hancock Park: Los Angeles in the 1920s

Downtown Los Angeles, originally sited where residents could readily access fresh water, lies fifteen miles east of the Pacific Ocean. One of Greater Los Angeles's major thoroughfares, Wilshire Boulevard, runs due west from downtown toward the ocean beaches. During the 1920s, a decade in which the population of the City of Los Angeles doubled, G. Allen Hancock subdivided Hancock Park, a rectangular tract of almost one-square mile. The rectangle's southern border was Wilshire Boulevard.[8] Hancock quickly succeeded in creating a high-end neighborhood of houses. He imposed covenants, running with the land, which restricted most lots to a single-family residence on a lot of at least 15,000 square feet. As was common in California at the time, Hancock also banned residency by non-Whites.[9] He set an explicit expiration date for the restrictions,

7. For histories of covenant practice in the United States, see Brady, "Turning Neighbors into Nuisances": 1617–23 (2021), and Fogelson, *Bourgeois Nightmares* (2005).
8. More precisely, the south side of the Hancock Park rectangle abuts Wilshire Boulevard; the west side, Highland Avenue; the north side, Melrose Avenue; and the east side, Rossmore Avenue. Wallach, *Miracle Mile in Los Angeles* (2013): 34.
9. Rodman, "Hancock Park" (2014). In the 1920s, California courts were willing to enforce racial restrictions on the identity of occupants, but not of land transferees. Los Angeles Inv. Co. v. Gary, 186 P. 596 (Cal. 1919). There are hints that, in the 1920s, subdividers in California especially favored racial covenants. Monchow, *Deed Restrictions* (1928): 47–50 (reporting that racial restrictions were present in 10 out of 11 California developments, compared to, in other states, 31 out of 73).

January 1, 1970. Hancock, unlike a handful of pioneering 1920s developers, did not establish a common-interest community (CIC) to govern Hancock Park. Many residents apparently now wish that he had. Competing neighborhood associations have arisen, but none has the power to compel a Hancock Park homeowner to pay an assessment.[10]

As the decades passed, public works departments substantially widened Wilshire Boulevard. A lot abutting that thoroughfare became too noisy to serve as an appropriate site for a single-family house. Owners of Hancock Park lots abutting Wilshire brought several lawsuits—some successful, some not—claiming that conditions had changed so much that courts should no longer enforce the single-family-use restriction.[11] Aware that the covenants would expire in 1970, some owners of vacant lots chose simply to wait until that date, in the hope that Los Angeles would then zone their lots for a more intensive use, such as a commercial office building. Thus evolved, prior to 1970, the Dead Mile on Wilshire, a stretch centered on Hancock Park (see figure 9).[12] The nickname highlights the stark difference between that underdeveloped stretch and Wilshire's so-called Miracle Mile, a commercial strip just to the west.[13]

How did Hancock's covenants interact with the City of Los Angeles's zoning?[14] Los Angeles had designated "residence" districts as early as 1909, well before New York City's more celebrated embrace of zoning in 1916.[15] In 1920, Los Angeles also became the U.S. pioneer in the mapping

10. In 1948, residents of Hancock Park created an informal association, which began asking homeowners to pay voluntary dues. In 2005, a transient rival entered. See Hancock Park Homeowners Ass'n Est. 1948 v. Hancock Park Home Owners Ass'n, 2006 WL 4532986 (C.D. Cal. 2006).

11. Compare Bolotin v. Rindge, 41 Cal. Rptr. 376, 377 (Cal. App. 1964) (holding conditions had not sufficiently changed to bar enforcement), with Hirsch v. Hancock, 343 P.2d 959 (Cal. App. 1959) (permitting an oil derrick on a Hancock Park lot).

12. Wallach, *Miracle Mile in Los Angeles* (2013): 70–71.

13. Id.

14. On the interaction of demand for the two devices, see Cheung and Meltzer, "Homeowners Associations" (2013) (finding that a greater number of CICs is associated with more local land use regulation).

15. Ex parte Quong Wo, 118 P. 714 (Cal. 1911); Whitnall, "History of Zoning" (1931): 10–12. New York City's first zoning ordinance also had regulated building bulks, particularly heights, which Los Angeles's initial ordinance had not.

Figure 9. Wilshire Boulevard's Dead Mile in 1971, just after Allen Hancock's covenants expired. The view is to the west. The white high-rise building in the distance stood at Wilshire Boulevard and South Rimpau Boulevard. (Los Angeles Times Photographs Collection. Courtesy of Special Collections, Charles E. Young Research Library, UCLA)

of districts solely for single-family detached houses.[16] Nonetheless, Hancock correctly envisioned that city zoning by itself would not be sufficient to create the high-end neighborhood of large single-family lots that he had in mind.[17] A century after Hancock dreamed of its creation and long after the covenants expired in 1970, the core of Hancock Park remains as he had originally conceived it. In 2020, the City of Los Angeles was zoning most of the neighborhood for single-family detached houses on lots

16. Whitnall, "History of Zoning" (1931): 12.

17. In the 1920s, Hancock also may have recognized that covenants were more reliable than zoning in furthering his goal of restricting occupancy to Whites. At the time, racial zoning was unconstitutional, but racial covenants were not. Compare Buchanan v. Warley, 245 U.S. 60 (1917) (holding that racial zoning unconstitutionally impaired property rights), with Corrigan v. Buckley, 271 U.S. 323 (1926) (holding private covenants did not entail state action). *Corrigan* met its demise in Shelley v. Kraemer, 334 U.S. 1 (1948).

of at least 15,000 square feet, exactly what Hancock's covenants had specified. This minimum lot-size requirement was three times greater than what Los Angeles was requiring in the single-family neighborhood just east of Hancock Park.[18]

In 2020, Zillow placed the median value of a Hancock Park house on a 15,000-sq.-ft. lot at around $5 million.[19] Despite this astronomic value, market pressure to densify this now centrally located neighborhood is intense. The City of Los Angeles has responded by rezoning some of the edges of Hancock Park for commercial and multifamily uses. For example, the city zones much of the neighborhood's frontage on Wilshire Boulevard for those uses, typically resulting in buildings less than four stories in height. In 2020, these rezonings represented about 5 percent of the total area of Hancock Park.[20] In short, covenants originally shaped land uses in Hancock Park, and, after they expired, zoning largely took over the task of freezing 95 percent of the neighborhood.

The Rise of Common-Interest Communities

The developer of a common-interest community, which Hancock Park is not, compels each purchaser to become a member of a private homeowners association and pay a periodic assessment to that entity.[21] In 1844, four purchasers of a Boston farm created the first CIC in the United States, Louisburg Square in the Beacon Hill neighborhood.[22] In that instance, owners of twenty-eight townhouses abutting a small park agreed

18. In 2020, Los Angeles's primary zone in Hancock Park, RE 15, required a minimum house-lot of 15,000 sq. ft. Arden Boulevard, one block east of Rossmore Avenue, Hancock Park's eastern boundary, then lay in the city's standard R1–1 zone, which required only a 5,000-sq.-ft. house-lot.
19. See Zillow.com. Search conducted in August 2020.
20. This estimate ignores the acreage of Wilshire Country Club and various schools.
21. The key judicial decision upholding the power of a CIC to impose mandatory assessments is Neponsit Property Owners' Ass'n v. Emigrant Indus. Sav. Bank, 15 N.E.2d 793 (N.Y. 1938).
22. Urban Land Institute, *Homes Association Handbook* (1964): 41–43. A map, id. at 42, indicates the layout. A private trust, not a CIC, governs Manhattan's Gramercy Park, established a decade earlier. Id. at 39.

to pay mandatory fees to maintain the park. Louisburg Square endures as an institution, evidence that covenants may produce value for centuries.

Nationally known CIC developments of recent vintage include the New Urbanist communities of Celebration and Seaside in Florida and Kentlands in Maryland.[23] Residential structures in these communities vary; they include detached single-family houses, townhouses, and higher-rise apartments and condominiums. Property owners, not tenants, elect the members of the executive board that governs the CIC association.[24] Covenants typically empower the board to adopt and enforce rules governing member conduct and to collect assessments to finance maintenance of the CIC's common property, such as recreation facilities and open space.[25] So thoroughgoing is board enterprise in Celebration and Seaside that the residents in both have declined to incorporate as municipalities.

The Community Associations Institute (CAI) represents CICs, the predominant subset of covenanted developments. CAI surveys assert, as mentioned, that in 2018 CICs accounted for 61 percent of new housing units built in the United States. There have been few studies of what CIC covenants typically provide. Susan French and Wayne Hyatt, two noted legal experts, nonetheless assert that the "modern documents" of a CIC typically handle covenant life in the following manner.[26] The declaration of covenants specifies an initial term, perhaps thirty to fifty years. The covenants then automatically renew for a shorter term, commonly ten years, unless opponents of renewal, by majority or supermajority vote, affirmatively vote to amend or terminate them. Specialists refer to this system as "automatic renewal with opt-out." This now-standard ap-

23. See Celebration, Florida; Seaside, Florida; Kentlands, Maryland. The latter is part of the City of Gaithersburg.

24. Ellickson, "Homeowners Associations" (1982a): 1539–63. The Uniform Common Interest Ownership Act (2008 rev.) uses *executive board* to refer to the group in charge. Id. at § 1–103 (18). Chapter 6 of the American Law Institute's *Restatement: Servitudes* (2000) recommends a special set of rules to govern CICs.

25. See Hyatt, *Homeowner Association Practice* (2000): 7–28 (reviewing a variety of CIC forms). On the potential power of CICs in local politics, see Dilger, *Neighborhood Politics* (1992): 104–30.

26. Hyatt and French, *Community Association Law* (2008): 503; see also French, "Modern Law of Servitudes" (1982): 1314.

proach stacks the deck in favor of the continuation of covenants. Unless loosened, these restrictions, coupled with zoning restrictions and historic preservation regulations, threaten to freeze land uses in urban America.

A History of the Use of Real Estate Covenants

Covenants can impose social costs, as racial covenants unquestionably did. Nonetheless, as pioneering developers realized, private restrictions also can confer tangible social benefits. Especially prior to the advent of zoning in the 1910s, urban homebuyers were uncertain about what the future would bring. A next-door neighbor might install an unneighborly use that courts would not deem noxious enough to constitute a nuisance. Some residential developers therefore began to employ covenants to assure buyers that a new development would be free of nonresidential uses.[27] Many early developers, including Allen Hancock, went further and imposed covenants to restrict land uses in their developments to single-family dwellings.[28] In the 1920s, public officials commonly followed the same practice and mapped single-family-only zones, an approach that Los Angeles invented.

The Crudeness of Early Covenants

During the 1920s, and sometimes even later, many state courts viewed covenants with hostility.[29] They inherited this bias partly from

27. In Helen Monchow's sample, about 80 percent of the covenant schemes permitted only residential uses. Monchow, *Deed Restrictions* (1928): 28–31. In suburban Milwaukee, Zigurds Zile found an even higher percentage, 86 percent. Zile, "Private Zoning" (1959): 464.

28. Covenants permitted only single-family houses in 63 percent of Monchow's sample, and in 74 percent of Zile's. Monchow, *Deed Restrictions* (1928): 28–31; Zile, "Private Zoning" (1959): 471.

29. Prior to the mid-twentieth century, if a state court deemed covenants ambiguous, it tended to interpret them to permit multifamily dwellings. Brady, "Turning Neighbors into Nuisances" (2021): 1644–53. See, e.g., Johnson v. Jones, 90 A. 649, 650 (Pa. 1914) (holding that "all doubts are to be resolved against the restriction and in favor of the free and unrestricted use of the property"). The Pennsylvania court accordingly interpreted a covenant allowing a "dwelling house" to enable construction of an apartment building.

English law. England lacked a general system of land records. Its courts rightly worried that the spread of enforceable restrictive covenants would surprise many purchasers of burdened land.[30] In the United States, by contrast, states have long mandated that local governments operate land-records systems. These recording systems enable title-insurance companies to shield land purchasers against the sorts of surprises that had worried English courts. As the twentieth century progressed, most state courts overcame their initial hostility to covenants and increasingly warmed to their potential.[31]

Even as late as the 1950s, the drafting of covenants tended to be amateurish.[32] Two basic problems recurred. First, drafters of covenants tended to be casual in identifying both the lot owners bound by the restrictions and those entitled to enforce them. Instead of prerecording a general declaration of covenants, the developer of a large subdivision might include covenants in only some deeds.[33] Some courts eventually tidied up these messes, perhaps unsoundly, by concluding, in some instances, that a "general plan" of covenants had burdened and benefited all lots.[34] As the twentieth century progressed, this problem lessened. By mid-century, both state and local governments had greatly increased the formality of their subdivision regulations. Once more formal regulations existed, a

30. Dnes and Lueck, "Servitudes Governing Land" (2009): 89. But cf. Tulk v. Moxhay, 3 Phillips 774, 41 Eng. Rep. 1143 (Ch. 1848) (enforcing negative covenant as an equitable servitude).

31. See, e.g., Brandon v. Price, 314 S.W.2d 521, 523 (Ky. 1958): "Under the modern view, restrictions are regarded more as a protection to the property owner and the public rather than as a restriction on the use of property, and the old-time doctrine of strict construction no longer applies"; Dixon v. Van Sweringen Co., 166 N.E. 887 (Ohio 1929). See also Brooks and Rose, *Saving the Neighborhood* (2013): 3.

32. Zile concluded that the covenants he examined, mostly imposed in the 1950s, were generally poor in quality. Zile, "Private Zoning" (1959): 483.

33. Monchow, *Deed Restrictions* (1928): 14–15.

34. The leading case is Sanborn v. McLean, 206 N.W. 496 (Mich. 1925). Other courts reject *Sanborn* because it jeopardizes the interests of purchasers who rely on the integrity of land records. See, e.g., Riley v. Bear Creek Planning Comm., 551 P.2d 1213 (Cal. 1976); Houghton v. Rizzo, 281 N.E.2d 577 (Mass. 1972). See generally American Law Institute, *Restatement: Servitudes* (2000) § 2.14 (reviewing the mixed case law).

developer's attorney could record, prior to the sale of the first subdivision lot, an overarching declaration of covenants that clarified the lots burdened and benefited.

Second, drafters of early covenants tended to be cavalier about how long the scheme of covenants would last. The approach that currently is predominant—automatic renewal with opt-out—was not concocted until the early twentieth century. Prior to its invention, drafters of covenants, as we shall see, took a variety of approaches to covenant life.

Key Innovators Who Shaped Covenant Practices

Three individuals and two institutions were major contributors to the evolution of U.S. covenant practices. The first was the little-heralded Edward H. Bouton of the Roland Park Company, a Baltimore land developer.[35] For site-planning, Bouton's company frequently hired the firm of the prominent landscape architect Frederick Law Olmsted, Jr.[36] Between 1891 and 1931, Bouton used covenants at several notable Baltimore subdivisions, all of which evolved into common-interest communities.[37] Bouton notably experimented with each of the four basic options for limiting the life of a covenant.[38] He first tried perpetual covenants. Because human foresight plainly is limited, Bouton soon cast aside that approach, just as both courts and legislatures would come to frown on it. Next, Bouton tried fixed-term covenants. That approach required him to select a precise ending date, perhaps thirty or fifty years in the future, despite the uncertain nature of unfolding events.[39] Third, Bouton turned to authorizing purchasers in his developments, by plebiscite, to determine covenant length. He initially specified that the covenants were to terminate at a fixed date, but he authorized lot owners to affirmatively vote to extend them. This approach assumed that, when covenants were

35. Urban Land Institute, *Homes Association Handbook* (1964): 43–46. Bouton receives mention in Power, "City Growth" (1988): 650–54.

36. Urban Land Institute, *Homes Association Handbook* (1964): 43. The junior Olmsted had a yet more famous father.

37. Id. at 43–46.

38. Id. at 43.

39. See French, "Modern Law of Servitudes" (1982): 1315–16 n.255 (referring to fixed time limits as "completely arbitrary").

valuable, members would be able to overcome the collective-action problems that might make it difficult to keep them in place. In 1924, Bouton used a fourth approach at Homeland, a Baltimore subdivision: covenants automatically renewed for successive periods of years unless opponents ever mobilized enough votes to end or amend them.[40] As noted, this technique—automatic renewal with opt-out—has become standard.

Bouton's subdivision designs and artfulness in using covenants influenced other American developers.[41] Bouton mentored the second individual notable in the history of covenants, J. C. Nichols, a man twenty years younger. Nichols began development of Kansas City's Country Club District in 1905.[42] The development proved a huge success, cementing Nichols's national prominence. In 1929, more than a decade after the advent of zoning, Nichols published a ringing endorsement of the continuing utility of covenant restrictions: ". . . I believe practically all subdividers agree that zoning, as desirable as it is for cities as a whole, cannot, at least for the present, supplant all the advantages gained by the use of deed restrictions."[43] Like Bouton, Nichols experimented with various approaches to the lifespan of covenants.[44] Several sources identify Nichols as

40. Urban Land Institute, *Homes Association Handbook* (1964): 43.

41. Bouton swayed, among others, the Van Sweringen brothers, developers of the famed Shaker Heights, Ohio. Harwood, *Van Sweringen Brothers* (2003): 15–16; Stilgoe, *Borderlands* (1988): 239–51; Korngold, "Large-Scale Subdivisions" (2001); Dixon v. Van Sweringen Co., 166 N.E. 887 (Ohio 1929).

42. Urban Land Institute, *Homes Association Handbook* (1964): 51–54; see also McKenzie, *Privatopia* (1994): 38–43 (discussing Nichols). At several developments, Nichols imposed covenants to bar occupancy or ownership by Blacks. Monchow, *Deed Restrictions* (1928): 47, 50.

43. Nichols, "A Developer's View" (1929): 142. But cf. Bassett, "Zoning" (1922): 324 (affirmatively favoring the use of covenants, but only as a supplement to zoning).

44. In some early subdivisions, Nichols's company required lot owners affirmatively to vote to extend the prior term. See Strauss v. J. C. Nichols Land Co., 37 S.W.2d 505 (Mo 1931) (sustaining legality of a vote-to-extend procedure in a 1912 subdivision). Nichols later switched to an opt-out, or vote-to-terminate, approach. See, e.g., Maurer v. J. C. Nichols Co., 485 P.2d 174, 176 (Kan. 1971) (involving 1924 covenants that required owner opt-out at least five years prior to the expiration of a term). Nichols later provided a rationale for this shift: "With the greater protection to property through such automatic extension of restric-

the inventor of automatic renewal with opt-out.[45] By the mid-1920s, both Bouton and Nichols were regularly employing that approach.

The 1930s saw the creation of two institutions that have greatly influenced covenant practices. The first was the Federal Housing Administration (FHA), a New Deal agency established in 1934.[46] FHA provides mortgage insurance, protecting lenders from borrower defaults. Its underwriting policies have greatly influenced how covenants are used. During its early decades, FHA favored developments of single-family detached houses in low-density neighborhoods, and it frowned on the mixing of different land uses.[47] By 1938, the agency was recommending that covenants have an initial term of at least twenty-five years.[48]

In 1936, J. C. Nichols helped found the Urban Land Institute (ULI), a nonprofit specializing in issues of land development. In 1947, both FHA and ULI explicitly endorsed automatic renewal with owner opt-out every ten years or so.[49] In that year, both institutions published sample forms

---

tions, particularly if they cover an area of considerable size, the original restriction period need not be so long. Perhaps 25- to 30-year periods are long enough to give reasonable assurance and yet short enough to permit readjustment of restrictions to changing modes of life." Nichols, "A Developer's View" (1929): 135.

45. Fogelson, *Bourgeois Nightmares* (2005): 108–9; Urban Land Institute, *Homes Association Handbook* (1964): 51. But cf. the prior footnote.

46. Weiss, *Rise of Community Builders* (1987): 141–58.

47. Enlightened opinion at the time favored the separation of land uses. Whittemore, "FHA and Zoning" (2012a): 626, 630 (affirming that FHA policies supported segregation of different land uses and promoted low-density single-family detached housing). See also Adams, *Design of Residential Areas* (1934): 7–8, 89 (asserting, at 89, that a detached house "is the best type for most people").

48. Federal Housing Administration, *Underwriting Manual* (1938): § 980 (3). During the New Deal, FHA notoriously supported the use of racially restrictive covenants. See id. at § 980 (3) (g) (favoring "[p]rohibition of the occupancy of properties except by the race for which they are intended"). In 1947, the agency dropped that explicit policy. Brooks and Rose, *Saving the Neighborhood* (2013): 108–9, 170–71.

49. Urban Land Institute, *Community Builders Handbook* (1947): 167–70 (reproducing "Protective Covenants Recommended" by FHA); Federal Housing Administration, *Underwriting Manual* (1947): § 1364 (1) (recommending an initial term at least as long as the term of FHA mortgage insurance and an automatic renewal term of ten years). In 1947, the term of an FHA-insured mortgage averaged 19.2 years. Pinto, "Housing Finance" (2015).

for covenants that included an *identical* paragraph on the issue of covenant length.[50] ULI likely copied the FHA version.

The federal agencies that regulate financial institutions encourage lawyers for developers to use boilerplate documents when creating covenants.[51] During the postwar homebuilding boom, attorneys relied heavily on the FHA-ULI form. A Westlaw search in 2020 uncovered 115 reported judicial decisions, overwhelmingly by state courts, that quote the exact words that FHA and ULI had offered in 1947 to govern the life of covenants.[52]

A third individual important in the history of American covenant law was Byron R. Hanke. Hanke served as FHA's national director of land planning from 1946 to 1972. In the decades after World War II, Hanke fought against then popular subdivision practices, such as the creation of rectangular house-lots situated within a grid of streets.[53] He came to favor Planned Unit Development (PUD) zoning that would enable the mixing of different land uses rather than single-use zones.[54] In the 1960s,

50. "These Covenants are to run with the land and shall be binding on all parties and all persons claiming under them until January 1, 19 , (twenty-five year period), at which time *said Covenants shall be automatically extended for successive periods of* 10[1] years unless by vote of a majority of the then owners of the building sites covered by these covenants it is agreed to change said covenants in whole or in part." Footnote 1 read, "Some developers recommend as high as a 40 year initial period with successive extensions of 25 years." Urban Land Institute, *Community Builders Handbook* (1947): 167, 174.
51. Winokur, "Promissory Servitudes" (1989): 58–59 nn.244–45.
52. The search, conducted on February 16, 2020, employed the ten-word phrase that footnote 50 places in italics. Of the 115 decisions, in 107 drafters had chosen 10 years as the length of the renewal period, 3 had chosen less than 10 years, and 5 had chosen either 20 or 25 years. In 1964, the Urban Land Institute published a successor handbook. The 1964 version of the ULI Handbook repeated the italicized words quoted in footnote 50, but added the requirement that at least two-thirds of the membership approve any amendment to the covenant scheme. See Urban Land Institute, *Homes Association Handbook* (1964): 392.
53. Hanke, "Planned Unit Development" (1965): 16.
54. Id. at 17. Hanke's article appeared as part of a symposium on PUDs, 114 U. Pa. L. Rev. 3–170 (1965). Publication of the symposium helped promote use of the PUD device. This technique has fallen into decline because some suburbs consider it overly pro-development. See Appendix.

FHA detailed Hanke to work for ULI. The upshot was the ULI's *Homes Association Handbook*, published in 1964.[55] This volume quickly became the bible of creators of mandatory-membership common-interest communities. After 1970, the number of CICs in the United States skyrocketed. The rising popularity of condominium ownership, an option generally not available in the United States prior to the 1960s, helped fuel the boom.[56]

The Declining Value of Covenants over Time

The many supporters of covenants were clear-eyed about their benefits, but they downplayed the negative features of aging covenants. Scholarly studies affirm that covenants can usefully constrain a landowner's choices among land uses and building designs.[57] In 2019, economists Wyatt Clarke and Matthew Freedman, marshaling data almost national in scope, published one of the most notable contributions.[58] Controlling for other variables, Clarke and Freedman found that the presence of a CIC increased the value of a house by about 8 percent when a development was new. The authors also found, however, that the premium decreased steadily over time and had disappeared, on average, once a development was forty years old.[59] Three other studies support the plausible intuition that the value of covenants tends to erode over time.[60] But

55. Urban Land Institute, *Homes Association Handbook* (1964). The volume identifies Hanke, whose name appears first on the authors' page, as "Study Director and Land Planner." The same page lists Jan Krasnowiecki, another major contributor to the *Handbook*, as "Legal Counsel." Krasnowiecki then was a member of the University of Pennsylvania law faculty.
56. Hansmann, "Condominium and Cooperative Housing" (1991): 61–62.
57. Richard Brooks and Carol Rose, authors of a book critical of racial covenants, agree that nonracial covenants potentially have utility. Brooks and Rose, *Saving the Neighborhood* (2013): 92, 101–2. See also Hughes and Turnbull, "Uncertain Neighborhood Effects" (1996b) (lauding potential of covenants); Monchow, *Deed Restrictions* (1928): 78 ("subdividers and purchasers are familiar with this method of control and feel confident of its permanency and soundness").
58. Clarke and Freedman, "Effects of Homeowners Associations" (2019) (examining only covenanted developments of single-family houses).
59. Id. at 11.
60. Hughes and Turnbull, "Restrictive Land Covenants" (1996a): 160; Meltzer

only on average. Townhouse owners at Louisburg Square, established in 1844, today undoubtedly would favor perpetuation of their association.[61]

Why covenants can enhance property values, especially early on, is hardly mysterious. A landowner's choices among land uses commonly generate both negative and positive externalities on neighbors. A variety of mechanisms can internalize these externalities, including informal norms, nuisance litigation, and public regulations. Compared to these other alternatives, developer-imposed covenants potentially have several advantages.[62] Builders can employ covenants to market communities with distinctive attributes, analogous to Tiebout competition among suburban municipalities.[63] Allen Hancock, for example, perceived that there would be demand in Los Angeles for a high-end community of houses, and, at Hancock Park, he employed covenants to deliver that product. Covenants decentralize the creation of land use restrictions from a monopolist, in that instance the City of Los Angeles, to entrepreneurs such as Hancock who operate on a more fine-grained level. In the words of the Supreme Court of California, "common interest developments are a more intensive and efficient form of land use that greatly benefits society and expands opportunities for home ownership."[64]

Whether the Hancock Park covenants—even ignoring their odious racial exclusions—in fact would have survived a cost-benefit analysis, however, is far from clear. On the positive side, an analyst would include the enhancement of consumer choice among neighborhood ambiances. By establishing a CIC, a developer can credibly promise the availability of specific facilities. These include not only the commonplace, such as tennis courts and gardenlike grounds, but also the exotic, such as bandstands and sculpture gardens. Contemporary covenants enable developers to create communities, such as Celebration and Seaside, which are more specialized than the ones that public authorities could bring into being.

---

and Cheung, "Homeowners Associations" (2014): 97; Rogers, "Impact of Covenant Restrictions" (2010).

61. Urban Land Institute, *Homes Association Handbook* (1964): 41–43.

62. Ellickson, "Alternatives to Zoning" (1973): 711–19.

63. Tiebout, "Theory of Local Expenditures" (1956).

64. Nahrstedt v. Lakeside Village Condominium Ass'n, 878 P.2d 1275, 1288 (Cal. 1994).

This likely enhances the bonding social capital of eventual residents.[65] Enthusiasts of covenanted communities, such as Fred Foldvary and Robert Nelson, stress these potential upsides.[66]

Covenants also, however, give rise to costs. Developers commonly employ them with the intent of excluding certain people.[67] At Hancock Park, Allen Hancock wanted to keep out not only non-Whites but also middle-income households of any race. The exclusiveness of Hancock Park might have added to the bonding social capital of its residents, but it simultaneously reduced bridging social capital across different income groups in Los Angeles.[68] Evan McKenzie, at times a severe critic of covenanted communities, emphasizes another social cost.[69] In his eyes, CICs, which allocate votes according to property ownership, tend to undermine traditions of democratic governance and reduce involvement in the affairs of local governments. In short, even when all the current residents of a covenanted community would like to perpetuate it, a benefit-cost analyst should attend to these potential diffuse social costs.

In most instances, nevertheless, exclusionary zoning is a far more serious problem than exclusionary covenants. Few covenant schemes bind more than 1 percent of the area of a municipality.[70] In a mass society,

65. See Putnam, *Bowling Alone* (2000): 22–24 (distinguishing between bonding and bridging social capital).
66. Foldvary, *Private Communities* (1994); Nelson, *Private Neighborhoods* (2005); see also Dilger, *Neighborhood Politics* (1992), a largely favorable assessment.
67. Strahilevitz, "Exclusionary Amenities" (2006) (emphasizing possible racial motives that may underlie a covenant scheme); Speyrer, "Homes in Houston" (1989): 128 (expressing concern for groups that covenants may economically exclude).
68. Putnam implies that bridging social capital is especially valuable. Putnam, *Bowling Alone* (2000): 23, 358, 363. See also Fennell, "Contracting Communities" (2004): 882–90 (discussing social capital in CICs).
69. McKenzie, *Privatopia* (1994): 21–23; McKenzie later muted his objections. McKenzie, *Beyond Privatopia* (2011): 118–19. Another work skeptical of private restrictions is Barton and Silverman, *Common Interest Communities* (1994). Gated communities, a minor fraction of CICs, have drawn the sharpest criticism. Blakely and Snyder, *Fortress America* (1997).
70. According to CAI's numbers, in 2018 an average CIC governed about eighty housing units. Community Association Institute, "Community Association Factbook" (2018): 1.

freedom of association has value in its own right. In addition, as a symbolic matter, governmental pursuit of economic segregation is more offensive than private pursuit of that same goal. Indeed, in a leading Pennsylvania decision striking down large-lot zoning, the court approvingly noted that landowners could employ covenants to assure that lots are spacious.[71]

Not only can covenants give rise to diffuse social costs, but they also can be costly to some nominal beneficiaries. This chapter emphasizes the collective-action problem that covenant beneficiaries may face when a restriction has become outmoded.[72] In addition, these covenants limit a landowner's freedom to choose among alternative land uses and building designs.[73]

Overall, do the benefits of covenants exceed their costs? Clarke and Freedman, who did not give weight to covenants' possibly negative social effects, assert that they increase home values, especially when young. Clay Gillette, a centrist observer, acknowledges that covenants tend to foster homogeneous sorting. Partly in light of the widespread human impulse to bond with others who are similar, at least within the constraints of fair-housing legislation, however, Gillette is unwilling to condemn covenanted communities across the board.[74] I agree. To repeat, the social costs of exclusionary zoning are far more serious than the social costs of exclusionary covenants.

In 1982, I published an article that strongly supported the potential of CICs as a decentralized source of land use regulation.[75] Since then, for

71. "'An owner of land may constitutionally make his property as large and as private or secluded or exclusive as he desires and his purse can afford. He may, for example, singly or with his neighbors, purchase sufficient neighboring land to protect and preserve by restrictions in deeds or by covenants inter se, the privacy, a minimum acreage, the quiet, peaceful atmosphere and the tone and character of the community which existed when he or they moved there.'" National Land & Inv. Co. v. Kohn, 215 A.2d 597, 612–13 (Pa. 1965), quoting Bilbar Constr. Co. v. Easttown Twp. Bd. of Adjustment, 141 A.2d 851, 867 (Pa. 1958) (dissenting opinion).

72. See also Korngold, *Private Land Use Arrangements* (2016): 323–31.

73. Winokur, "Promissory Servitudes" (1989): 62–66.

74. Gillette, "Courts, Covenants, and Communities" (1994): 1398, 1441. Fennell, "Contracting Communities" (2004), offers another centrist perspective.

75. Ellickson, "Homeowners Associations" (1982a); see also Ellickson, "Alternatives to Zoning" (1973): 711–19.

two reasons, my enthusiasm has cooled. First, it has become increasingly evident that the popularity of CICs is not entirely market-driven. To placate fiscally selfish Homevoters, a local government commonly insists that a developer create a CIC to provide services, such as street cleaning and trash collection, which the same government provides without charge in older neighborhoods.[76] This has come to be known as the "offloading" of costs to CICs.[77] Second, as Lee Anne Fennell and Paula Franzese have persuasively demonstrated, legal doctrines compel many CICs to be overly inflexible.[78] A famous California decision, now a staple of legal education, held that a CIC could enforce a no-pets policy against a resident whose "indoor cats" were unlikely ever to bother a neighbor.[79] In that instance, attorneys might have advised the CIC board that a failure to enforce the community's no-pets policy might lead to a judicial holding that it had waived the covenant.[80] Today, indoor cats; tomorrow, pit bulls. On balance, I nonetheless continue to regard covenants, particularly when they are new, as potentially cost-justified land use controls.

Three Actors Who Can Eliminate Stale Covenants

When covenants benefit only a dozen or so landowners, beneficiaries are unlikely to have much difficulty in consensually agreeing to modify or terminate them. In an Illinois case, *Cordogan v. Union*

76. Korngold, "Cutting Municipal Services" (2012).
77. Cheung, "Public and Private Governments" (2008) (on offloading practices in California).
78. Fennell, "Contracting Communities" (2004): 849–64, 891–95; Franzese, "Demise of Community" (2002). A large literature develops this theme. See, e.g., Fraser, "Condo Commandos" (2000) (asserting that male residents aged 70 and older have disproportionate power on CIC boards); Korngold, "Single Family Use Covenants" (1989); McKenzie, *Privatopia* (1994): 41, 131–32; Nelson, *Private Neighborhoods* (2005): 118–21 (noting, however, at 121, that a 1999 survey found that only 8 percent of CIC members deemed their rules to be either "not appropriate at all" or "somewhat inappropriate").
79. Nahrstedt v. Lakeside Village Condominium Ass'n, 878 P.2d 1275 (Cal. 1994). A subsequent California statute provided that no covenant that a CIC imposed after 2000 could bar an owner from having at least one pet. Cal. Civ. Code § 4715 (2020).
80. Hyatt, *Homeowner Association Practice* (2000): 164.

National Bank of Elgin, a developer had restricted lots in a small subdivision to single-family residences.[81] Unable to sell the lots because of nearby commercial uses, the developer persuaded the City of Elgin to rezone the land to allow duplexes. The Illinois appellate court, however, refused to terminate the covenant because of changed neighborhood conditions. Eduardo Peñalver later discovered that the developer eventually had succeeded in buying out all the covenant beneficiaries.[82] When covenant beneficiaries are more numerous, however, as they commonly are, stale covenants threaten to freeze urban neighborhoods.

Three distinct actors can address this potential rigidity. First, the attorneys who draft covenants at the behest of developers can explicitly anticipate the issue of staleness. Second, judicial bodies can create doctrines to limit the enforcement of outmoded covenants. Third, state legislatures, the chief creators of property law in the United States, have ample authority to prevent the enforcement of old restrictions. Each of these three actors is aware of the others' potential involvement. Susan French, a preeminent scholar of covenant law, served as Reporter for the *Restatement (Third) of Property: Servitudes.*[83] Her Restatement notes that attorneys drafting covenants might, instead of themselves addressing the issue of termination, leave "the matter open, anticipating that the law would extricate their successors from intractable problems that might arise in the future."[84]

Drafting Covenants in Anticipation of Change

There have been few studies of what covenants actually provide. Two scholars have assessed in detail how U.S. covenant schemes address issues of amendment and termination. Helen Monchow's survey, published in 1928, examined eighty-four U.S. covenant schemes in various states, mostly imposed in the 1920s.[85] Zigurds Zile's, which appeared in

81. 380 N.E.2d 1194 (Ill. Ct. App. 1978).
82. Ellickson et al., *Land Use Controls* (2021): 535.
83. I served as an Adviser to this Restatement, a position far less influential than Reporter.
84. American Law Institute, *Restatement: Servitudes* (2000) § 7.10 cmt. (a) (2000). See also id. at § 4.3, cmt. e.
85. Monchow, *Deed Restrictions* (1928): 27. Just over half originated in four states: California, Illinois, Massachusetts, and New York.

1959, examined one hundred in Waukesha County, Wisconsin, part of Greater Milwaukee.[86] Monchow found that most covenants had fixed lives of thirty to forty years.[87] Zile reported that 58 percent of the covenants in his sample also had a fixed end-date, with a median and mode of twenty-five years, but that 24 percent were perpetual.[88] Zile also found that drafters of covenants were beginning to authorize plebiscites among benefited owners. In 6 percent of Zile's sample, owners could affirmatively vote to extend covenant life. He also found that 12 percent embraced the current predominant approach, automatic renewal with opt-out.[89] In a more recent empirical study in Weld County, Colorado, William Rogers briefly treats the question of covenant length. He found that owners are more likely to amend covenants than to terminate them root-and-branch. Rogers states, "Some covenants require 90 percent agreement to any amendment in the first 10 years and 75 percent afterwards. Out of 220 covenants, in Weld, since the summer of 2003 only ten have been terminated, while there have been almost 100 amendments."[90]

Automatic renewal with opt-out, the system pioneered by Bouton and Nichols and later endorsed by FHA and ULI, puts the burden of collective action on those who want to amend or terminate a covenant scheme, not on those who want to perpetuate it.[91] This approach has one chief advantage. It works to reduce the transaction costs of decision-making in a community disposed to renew its covenants. When no opponents appear, the covenants march costlessly on.

86. Zile, "Private Zoning" (1959). Part I of Zile's article identifies Waukesha County. Developers had recorded most of the covenants in Zile's sample in the early 1950s.
87. Monchow, *Deed Restrictions* (1928): 57–60.
88. Zile, "Private Zoning" (1959): 459.
89. Id. at 460.
90. Rogers, "Market for Institutions" (2006): 506. Rogers does not discuss the longevity of the covenant schemes he examined.
91. ULI's *Homes Association Handbook* twice states that requiring owners to vote to renew covenants would be "extremely undesirable." Urban Land Institute, *Homes Association Handbook* (1964): 212, 336. "Although most home owners would rather see the covenants continue, a majority vote to reinstate them may be difficult to marshal. . . . " Id. at 212. Collective-action problems, however, also beset opponents of stale covenants.

Automatic renewal with opt-out, however, overly protects the status quo and threatens to freeze too large a fraction of American real estate. Researchers such as Clarke and Freedman have found that most covenants typically lose value after forty years. Individuals who favor perpetuation of existing covenants commonly control a CIC's executive board. Especially in the face of a supportive board, owners who wish to amend or terminate a covenant scheme confront heavy odds. First, a collective-action problem, the temptation to free ride on the activism of others, is likely to bedevil them. Second, and as important, most individuals have an innate preference for maintaining the status quo. Owners, when confronting the question of the amendment or termination of a covenant, tend to underestimate the gains from removing the restriction and to exaggerate the associated losses.[92] Outmoded covenants therefore are too likely to march onward.

A drafter of covenants should consider other systems less biased in favor of the status quo. Here are two possibilities, both with the virtue of simplicity. First, a drafter could require, after the initial fixed term, that a majority of beneficiaries periodically affirm the covenants—opt-in, as opposed to opting-out. Second, after forty or fifty years, the covenant scheme might prohibit specific performance of any negative covenant, thereby limiting an enforcer to the remedy of damages.[93] The widespread adoption of either of these drafting reforms would help unfreeze American neighborhoods.

There are numerous other options of greater complexity. One is worth spelling out in detail. The drafter of covenants using the system would specify an initial fixed term, say, fifty years, and thereafter require that beneficiaries vote every ten years. Unlike automatic renewal with opt-out, however, this variant would periodically place the burden of approving the scheme on covenant proponents. For example, the drafter might require that members affirmatively vote to endorse continuation of the covenant scheme in year 50, year 80, year 110, and so on. Opt-outs would remain available to members in years 60, 70, 90, 100, and so on. Susan French, an eminent scholar of covenants, has informed me that she would

92. See chapter 7.

93. A possibility discussed later in this chapter.

prefer this approach to the one most currently used, automatic renewal with opt-out.[94]

A drafter of any system of neighborhood voting invariably confronts various sub-issues. First, should a vote to amend or remove stale covenants require a bare majority of owners, or some sort of supermajority? Leading authorities now recommend that either action require a vote of at least two-thirds of the membership.[95] The Restatement even sees no problem with requiring 99 percent of owners to assent to amendment or termination.[96] Once covenants have become long-lived, these extraordinary majority requirements threaten to freeze neighborhoods. A drafter of a covenant scheme would be wise to reduce, as the years pass, the supermajority required. At the end of the initial term, for example, no more than 60 percent of the electorate should have to favor change, and, after eighty years, no more than a bare majority. A California statute recognizes the problems that a declaration's supermajority requirement may pose. It authorizes a covenant beneficiary to petition a court to reduce the required vote from a supermajority to fifty percent plus one.[97]

A second sub-issue is how long prior to the end of the initial term, or a renewal term, opponents of continuation would have to act. ULI's 1964 *Handbook* favors forcing opponents to take action at least three years prior to the end of a term.[98] J. C. Nichols, a stalwart proponent

94. In an e-mail message to me dated February 20, 2020, Susan French stated that she endorsed the procedure mentioned in the text, citing "our current struggles to build affordable housing."

95. Urban Land Institute, *Homes Association Handbook* (1964): 212; Uniform Common Interest Ownership Act (2008 rev.) § 2–117(a); cf. id. at § 2–118(a) (requiring 80 percent to approve a decision to terminate); see also Natelson, *Property Owners Associations* (1989): 698–99 (providing sample declaration that would require 75 percent of owners to agree to modify or terminate).

96. American Law Institute, *Restatement: Servitudes* (2000), § 7.10, cmt. (a): "If the servitudes provide a means for modification or termination by agreement of less than 100 percent of the servitude beneficiaries, a court should rarely intervene. . . . "

97. Cal. Civ. Code § 4275 (2020), applied in Ocean Windows Owners Ass'n v. Spataro, 2017 WL 1075056 (Cal. App. 2017). In that instance, at the time of the decision the covenanted community was forty-four years old.

98. Urban Land Institute, *Homes Association Handbook* (1964): 212, 392. The

of covenants, advocated requiring, in some instances, mobilization five years in advance.[99] Partly because most people are procrastinators, these approaches also help perpetuate existing restrictions. Especially for long-lived covenants, drafters should authorize members to amend or terminate no more than two years prior to the end of an extension period.

Authors of formbooks for covenants, in sum, should attune themselves to the risk of the straitjacketing of neighborhoods. If drafters of covenants do not reform their ways, a state legislature could consider mandating some of the reforms just mentioned.

Judicial Doctrines That Weed Out Stale Covenants

Richard Epstein has contended that the original developer should solely determine covenant length. In his view, the developer, when setting the lifespan of a restriction, can best consider all pertinent variables.[100] Virtually no one, and certainly not the Restatement, agrees with Epstein's analysis.[101] Stewart Sterk highlights some rationales for limiting a developer's freedom of covenant. Sterk stresses that covenants can impose negative externalities on outsiders, and he notes that a drafter may underestimate the transaction costs of later consensual modification.[102] As the next pages reveal, both courts and legislatures, contrary to Epstein's urgings, have taken steps to weed out stale covenants. These lawmakers assume that someone who knows how urban conditions actually have evolved rightly may be able to second-guess the developer's original judgment about covenant life. Attorneys who draft covenants, in fact, commonly draft them in the shadow of these judicial and legislative constraints. They do not assume, à la Epstein, that freedom of covenant is unfettered.

Many covenants created during the nineteenth century, and even thereafter, were explicitly or implicitly perpetual. Early on, courts pro-

---

handbook also would require that "written notice of the proposed agreement is sent to every Owner at least 90 days in advance of any action taken." Id. at 392.

99. Fogelson, *Bourgeois Nightmares* (2005): 109.

100. Epstein, "Freedom of Contract" (1982): 1358; Epstein, "Covenants and Constitutions" (1988): 919–26 (urging, at 919, authorization of a developer opt-out from the changed-conditions doctrine).

101. See, e.g., American Law Institute, *Restatement: Servitudes* (2000) § 7.10 (advocating a mandatory changed-conditions doctrine).

102. Sterk, "Law of Servitudes" (1988); Sterk, "Servitude Restrictions" (1985).

vided relief to landowners burdened by allegedly outmoded restrictions. State judiciaries developed a number of common-law doctrines to weed out stale covenants. Two warrant emphasis.[103]

Changed conditions. A case that arose in midtown Manhattan, *Trustees of Columbia College v. Thacher*, gave rise to the most important ground for judicial relief: change in neighborhood conditions.[104] In *Thacher*, an 1859 covenant had restricted uses at the corner of Sixth Avenue and 50th Street to dwelling houses. Two decades later, an elevated train was running along Sixth Avenue, with a stop at that exact corner. The highest New York court refused to order a landowner to honor the covenant on the ground that neighborhood conditions had changed sufficiently to make equitable enforcement inappropriate. The court noted, however, that the beneficiary arguably should be entitled to recover damages for breach of the covenant.[105]

Subsequent case law sheds light on the sorts of neighborhood change that are particularly salient in the application of this common-law doctrine.[106] A leading decision by the Supreme Court of Nevada understandably gives more weight to changes in use patterns within the covenanted subdivision than on private lands across the street from it.[107] *Thacher* held that a change in transportation options available on public streets might be sufficient to prevent covenant enforcement. This reasoning, however, is unsound in some instances. If California courts were to deem the widening of Wilshire Boulevard a decisive change for Hancock Park lots abutting that roadway, that neighborhood's covenant scheme could fall like dominos.[108]

103. Comprehensive discussions of grounds for covenant termination include Hyatt and French (2008): 426–53, and American Law Institute, *Restatement: Servitudes* (2000), chapter 7.

104. Trustees of Columbia College v. Thacher, 87 N. Y. 311 (1882) (unanimous).

105. Id. at 319.

106. See generally Robinson, "Obsolete Covenants" (1991).

107. Western Land Co. v. Truskolaski, 495 P.2d 624 (Nev. 1972). ULI's 1964 *Homes Association Handbook* explicitly criticizes the result in Downs v. Kroger, 254 P. 1101 (Cal. 1927). In that instance the court held that changes in land uses across the street from a covenanted community had vitiated covenant enforcement. Urban Land Institute, *Homes Association Handbook* (1964): 336.

108. See River Heights Assocs. Ltd. Partnership v. Batten, 591 S.E.2d 683 (Va. 2004) (widening of U.S. highway from two to eight lanes held not a sufficient change in conditions). But cf. American Law Institute, *Restatement:*

The Nevada decision also holds, on a knottier issue, that a decision of zoning authorities to rezone covenanted lands for more intense uses is *not* evidence of a change of conditions.[109] For fresh covenants, this reasoning typically is sound. It enables lot purchasers to rely on the enforceability of the covenant scheme, a set of controls independent of zoning. As covenants age, however, courts should be more open to accepting a rezoning as evidence that conditions indeed may have changed.[110]

An Albuquerque, New Mexico, case illustrates the point.[111] In that instance, applicable covenants had banned commercial uses in a residential subdivision. The declaration authorized the owners to amend the covenants after twenty years. Residents chafed at the absence of commercial uses. Twenty-four years after the developer had first imposed the covenants, 85 percent of the owners approved an amendment allowing commercial uses on two particular lots. Importantly, the City of Albuquerque also had agreed to rezone both lots from single-family to commercial. A New Mexico appellate court nonetheless struck down the covenant amendment because it did apply subdivision-wide. A more enlightened decision would have taken Albuquerque's rezoning as a signal that neighborhood change would be beneficial.[112]

A recent American Law Reports annotation includes almost four hundred reported cases involving the issue of covenant termination for changed conditions.[113] The source excludes cases involving racial covenants. The annotation indicates that case frequency has declined sharply,

---

Servitudes (2000) § 7.10, ill. 3 (implying that judges at times should not enforce covenants along a newly widened right-of-way that is attracting heavier traffic).

109. Western Land Co. v. Truskolaski, 495 P.2d 624, 627 (Nev. 1972).

110. Judges seldom do. Volume II of American Law Institute, *Restatement: Servitudes* (2000) cites twelve reported decisions in which a challenger to covenants introduced evidence of a zoning change to support a claim that conditions had changed. Id. at 416–18. The challenger won only one, Zimmerman v. Seven Corners Dev., Inc., 654 N.Y.S.2d 523 (App. Div. 1997) (limiting covenant beneficiaries to an award of damages).

111. Ridge Park Home Owners v. Pena, 544 P.2d 278 (N.M. 1975).

112. In this case, an award of damages would have been more sensible. See below.

113. On January 23, 2020, the ALR Annotation, "Change in Neighborhood" (2000) and its supplements included 394 reported cases. During the 2000s and 2010s, the covenant challenger lost three-quarters of these cases.

from about seventy per decade in the 1930s and 1940s to seventeen per decade in the 2000s and 2010s. One reason may be drafters' disinclinations to make covenants perpetual, as they choose instead to favor automatic renewal with opt-out.[114] More ominously, the decline may be evidence of the increasing ossification of U.S. urban real estate.

Waiver. Suppose covenants imposed in 1940 had restricted uses in a neighborhood of one hundred house-lots to single-family detached houses. As time has passed, seventeen scattered lot owners, in violation of the covenants, have converted their houses to duplexes, and three have opened commercial uses. A fact pattern of this sort commonly induces a court to terminate the covenants. Judges provide a variety of rationales. They may deem lot owners to have "waived" or "abandoned" the covenants.[115] Given that the use changes were internal to the subdivision, a court also could hold that conditions had changed, a doctrine just discussed.

However justified termination of these covenants might be *ex post,* this approach has a definite downside *ex ante.* The waiver doctrine tends to prompt a homeowners association to enforce all covenants strictly, forbidding "indoor cats," for instance, under the aegis of a no-pets policy.[116] Worried about a judicial finding of waiver, J. C. Nichols himself had urged

114. Judges perhaps would be less likely to find changed conditions when the drafter had set an express termination date not far in the offing. The decisional law, however, is not especially supportive. See, e.g., Hirsch v. Hancock, 343 P.2d 959 (Cal. App. 1959) (permitting, on account of changed conditions, violation of residential covenant eleven years prior to its termination date); Norris v. Williams, 54 A.2d 331 (Md. 1947) (holding a restriction with an express life of 50 years terminated after 30).

115. See, e.g., B.B.P. Corp. v. Carroll, 760 P.2d 519 (Alaska 1988) (holding that lot owners had abandoned a covenant requiring removal of trees but perhaps not a covenant against view-blockage); Antis v. Miller, 524 So.2d 71 (La. Ct. App. 1988) (ruling that twenty-year failure to object to multifamily uses had resulted in abandonment of entire covenant scheme). But cf. Swenson v. Erickson, 998 P.2d 807 (Utah 2000) (holding that installation of small storage sheds on 19 of 52 lots did not prevent lot owner from enforcing restriction on location of a somewhat larger secondary structure). American Law Institute, *Restatement: Servitudes* (2000) § 7.4 prefers the term *abandonment,* and, in comment b, it offers a distinction between waiver and abandonment.

116. Nahrstedt v. Lakeside Village Condominium Ass'n, 878 P.2d 1275 (Cal. 1994).

the strict enforcement of covenants.[117] In the eyes of many commentators, this has made life in a covenanted community overly regimented.

Courts have a third option to address the competing interests of litigants in a dispute stemming from dated covenants.

The advantages of a damage award for breach of covenant. As the *Thacher* court noted as early as 1882, courts have a way to split the baby when a landowner breaches a covenant.[118] In the Albuquerque case, the court considered only two options: either upholding or invalidating the covenant amendment that would have introduced commercial uses into a single-family neighborhood.[119] The court instead could have held the sponsors of the new commercial uses liable in damages to the objecting neighbors for any diminutions in the market values of their properties. This approach would have loosened the covenant straitjacket, which is what most of the Albuquerque homeowners wanted in that instance. It also would have acknowledged the special suffering of the owners of the houses abutting the new commercial uses.

Numerous commentators have urged courts, in appropriate cases, to use damages as the remedy for covenant breach.[120] Yet courts rarely opt for this compromise. I reviewed thirty-four changed-conditions cases decided between 2000 and 2019 and found that courts discussed the possibility of damages in only two.[121] A Massachusetts statute, however, commendably recognizes the merits of damages as a remedy.[122]

117. Nichols, "A Developer's View" (1929): 139. In 1964, ULI invoked this rationale to urge "prompt action" to enforce all covenants. Urban Land Institute, *Homes Association Handbook* (1964): 297–98. But see Fennell, "Contracting Communities" (2004): 849–64 (emphasizing "the problem of uniform rules").

118. Trustees of Columbia College v. Thacher, 87 N. Y. 311, 319 (1882).

119. Ridge Park Home Owners v. Pena, 544 P.2d 278 (N.M. 1975).

120. See, e.g., Ellickson, "Homeowners Associations" (1982a): 1535–39; French, "Modern Law of Servitudes" (1982): 1317–18; Winokur, "Promissory Servitudes" (1989): 83; see also American Law Institute, *Restatement: Servitudes* (2000) § 8.3(1); St. Lo Const. Co. v. Koenigsberger, 174 F.2d 25, 28–30 (D.C. Cir. 1949) (Edgerton, C.J., dissenting).

121. The source was ALR Annotation, "Change in Neighborhood" (2000), examined on January 23, 2020. Cf. Robinson, "Obsolete Covenants" (1991): 549 n.10 (finding one-seventh of changed-conditions cases referred to damages as a possible remedy).

122. Mass Gen. Laws Ann. ch. 184, § 30 (2020).

The standard measure of damages is diminution in the market value of the covenant beneficiary's land. This formula fails to recognize the possibility that a complainant may have subjectively perceived a greater loss. A party who deliberately breaches a covenant intentionally inflicts damage. In some instances of this stripe, legislatures have used multipliers to increase damage awards.[123] They might consider doing so in these cases as well.

Statutes That Limit Covenant Enforcement

State legislatures have authority to assume command of covenant law. In virtually all cases, they could override the policies of not only state courts, but also, and more importantly, the drafter of a set of covenants. For example, a state statute could mandate, despite express covenant language to the contrary, that covenant beneficiaries periodically had to reaffirm the restrictions by majority vote.

A handful of state legislatures have taken decisive steps to terminate aged covenants.[124] Charles Clark, the premier American legal scholar of covenant law in the first half of the twentieth century, favored the passage of a statute whose effects, contrary to his intentions, would have been ham-handed. He urged legislation to limit the life of a covenant to thirty years or an even shorter period once the covenant had ceased conferring substantial benefits on beneficiaries.[125] Clark asserted, "[t]he clog on titles which useless servitudes may offer is known to all, though, like the weather, we talk about it but do nothing."[126] Contrary to Clark's analysis, Louisburg Square and many other developments illustrate that covenants

123. See, e.g., Head v. Amoskeag Mfg. Co., 113 U.S. 9, 10 n.1 (1885) (citing New Hampshire statute that awarded a victim of intentional flooding 150 percent of market damages); Conn. Gen. Stat. § 52–560 (2020) (awarding victim of intentional taking of timber at least three times loss of market value).

124. Overviews of the various statutes include Sterk, "Servitude Restrictions" (1985): 654–56; Harvard Law Review Note, "Touch and Concern" (2009): 953 n.85. By one count, five states have statutes that terminate covenants that have ceased conferring substantial benefits on the party seeking enforcement. French, "Modern Law of Servitudes" (1982): 1318 n.264.

125. Clark, "Limiting Land Restrictions" (1941). Clark's proposed statute also would have limited the lives of most easements. Easements usually have far fewer beneficiaries. A negotiation over easement termination thus is far less likely to pose collective-action problems.

126. Clark, "Limiting Land Restrictions" (1941): 738.

can have value for more than a century.[127] Minnesota mistakenly followed Clark's advice and once limited covenant lives to thirty years.[128] Georgia legislators made a similar error. In a statute now considerably modified, Georgia once limited the duration of a servitude to twenty years in an area governed by zoning laws.[129] Although the Georgia enactment correctly detected the interrelationship between public and private land use controls, it ignored the advantages of authorizing developers to tailor their own long-lasting rules.

Massachusetts legislators have acted more soundly. They have restricted the life of a covenant to thirty years, but they authorize 50 percent of the restricted owners to affirmatively vote to extend the term.[130] This reform has two notable virtues. It recognizes that stale covenants indeed can impose significant costs, both on beneficiaries and the public at large, and that status quo bias tends to perpetuate the familiar. Once covenants have become aged, a legislature is wiser to place the burden of collective action, as Massachusetts has, on covenant proponents, not covenant opponents.[131] A second Massachusetts statute correctly recognizes that an

127. Urban Land Institute, *Homes Association Handbook* (1964): 41–43.

128. Minn. Stat. § 500.20(2) (1980); Haugen v. Peterson, 400 N.W.2d 723 (Minn. 1987). In 1982, Minnesota repealed this provision for CICs and certain other covenants. Minn. Stat. § 500.20 (2020). Minnesota continues, however, as Clark had suggested, to terminate covenants once they confer only nominal value. See id. at § 500.20 (1). Cf. R.I. Gen. Laws, Property § 34–4-21 (2020) (limiting to thirty years the lives of virtually all covenants that are facially perpetual); Harvard Law Review Note, "Touch and Concern" (2009): 953 (urging that lives of covenants be limited to thirty years, but authorizing beneficiaries unanimously to extend or modify them).

129. Ga. Code Ann. § 44–5-60(b) (1981), applied in McKinnon v. Neugent, 167 S.E.2d 593 (Ga. 1969).

130. Mass. Gen. Laws Ann. ch. 184, § 27(b) (West 2020) (applicable only when the number of bound lots is four or more). Sterk, "Servitude Restrictions" (1985): 658–59, analyzes this statute and argues that perhaps only 30 percent or 40 percent of the electorate should have to approve extension of the covenant term. But cf. Heller, "Boundaries of Private Property" (1999): 1185 (criticizing voting rules that give excessive veto power to minorities of unit owners). Why reject majority rule in this context?

131. When a covenant scheme has failed to provide procedures for modification and termination, a Louisiana statute authorizes owners of a majority of the af-

award of damages, especially after decades have passed, can be a useful compromise between the interests of those who want covenants to continue and those who want to be free of them.[132]

James Winokur has suggested an alternative way to defang the damage of overly restrictive covenants. He favors a state statute that, after twenty years, would limit the number of lot owners entitled to enforce a negative covenant to the eleven closest to the site.[133] This reform would shift enforcement powers away from the many, including the executive board, to a smaller group better able to work out a compromise. No state has taken up Winokur's innovative idea.

Constitutional issues lurk. A court conceivably might deem, for example, a statute that had terminated covenants earlier than the drafter intended an unconstitutional taking of the property of a covenant beneficiary.[134] A state or federal court ruling of this sort is highly unlikely.[135] Stale covenants inflict diffuse social costs by freezing neighborhoods and reducing housing supply. Just as a state legislature has broad authority to override local zoning decisions, it has wide berth to override covenants. California has largely preempted not only zoning restrictions that impair the building of accessory dwelling units (ADUs) but also covenants that have the same effect.[136]

---

fected land to amend or terminate the covenants fifteen years after their creation. La. Civ. Code § 780 (2019). This provision recognizes the potential obsolescence of restrictions. Unlike Massachusetts, however, Louisiana places the burden of collective action on covenant opponents.

132. Mass. Gen. Laws Ann. ch. 184, § 30 (2020), applied in Blakeley v. Gorin, 313 N.E.2d 903 (Mass. 1974). See also N.Y. Real Prop. Law § 1951 (2) (2020) (authorizing, in some instances, extinguishment of a covenant upon payment of damages). See generally Bell and Parchomovsky, "Pliability Rules" (2002) (reviewing advantages of various remedies).

133. Winokur, "Promissory Servitudes" (1989): 79–82.

134. See, e.g., Blakeley v. Gorin, 313 N.E.2d 903, 917–21 (Mass. 1974) (Quirico, J., dissenting).

135. If brought under the federal constitution, the sole remedy of a successful takings claimant would be an award of damages, not invalidation of the offending statute. First English Evangelical Lutheran Church v. Los Angeles County, 482 U.S. 304 (1987).

136. Cal. Civ. Code § 4751 (2020) (overriding covenants that unreasonably restrict ADUs). See generally Infranca, "New State Zoning" (2019): 857–70 (emphasizing instances of zoning overrides, not covenant overrides).

Some state statutes similarly have overridden single-family-only covenants that bar the opening of group homes.[137]

California and other states confronting a severe housing shortage might even consider the drastic step of an across-the-board invalidation of single-family-only covenants. That step would foster, at least where zoning also is not a barrier, the construction of "missing middle" units such as duplexes. There is a quasi-precedent for this step. A 2019 Oregon statute overrode single-family zoning in the state's most populous cities and suburbs. Oregon declined, however, to invalidate existing covenants that bar missing-middle housing. It instead chose to grandfather all existing single-family-only covenants, but it did prohibit developers from imposing new ones.[138]

Texas has enacted various statutes that, instead of overriding covenants, affirmatively promote their use.[139] Houston's reluctance to adopt zoning may have prompted this legislation. One Texas statute authorizes selected municipalities, among them the City of Houston, to deny a building permit for a commercial use that would violate a private covenant.[140] This shifts enforcement costs from property owners to taxpayers. A second statute authorizes at least 75 percent of covenant beneficiaries, in certain cities and counties including Houston's Harris County, to vote to extend, add to, or modify existing restrictions.[141] While covenants certainly can be useful tools, this second Texas statute is overly pro-covenant. Imagine that California had an equivalent statute. In upscale Hancock Park, where single-family-only covenants expired in 1970, 75 percent of lot

137. See, e.g., Cal. Health & Safety Code § 1566.5 (2020) (applicable only to post-1978 covenants); see generally Hubbard, "Group Homes" (1988).

138. Or. Rev. Stat. § 94.776 (2019). See also 27 Vt. Stat. Ann. § 545 (2020) (authorizing a municipality to override covenants imposed after 2021).

139. Hat-tip to Andrew Kull. According to one estimate, covenants constrain land uses in about two-thirds of Houston. Henderson, "Controls in Houston" (1987): 146 n.84.

140. Tex. Local Gov't Code § 214.161-.168 (2014); Berry, "Does Zoning Matter?" (2001): 262–63; Kapur, "Regulation in Houston" (2004): 10050–51.

141. Tex. Prop. Code §§ 201.006(b), 204.003(b)(1) (2020). See also Kapur, "Regulation in Houston" (2004): 10051–52. But see Brandwein v. Serrano, 338 N.Y.S.2d 192 (Sup. Ct. 1972) (refusing to allow extension of expired covenant that 62 of 73 owners had approved).

owners might well have voted to keep the lots along Wilshire Boulevard dead for additional decades.[142] Massachusetts has addressed the problem of stale covenants far more appropriately than Texas. This should puzzle political scientists. Exclusionary zoning has been vastly more prevalent in Massachusetts than Texas.

Concluding Remarks on Covenants

Institutional arrangements, once adaptive, may become outmoded. A central historical example is the open-field village, predominant in most of Europe for the millennium after 800 AD.[143] In England and elsewhere, open fields eventually were enclosed, either consensually or by act of Parliament. An enclosure permanently subdivided an arable open field into private parcels. In England, the promoters of enclosures typically emerged spontaneously, village by village.[144] Although historians have hotly debated the fairness of the enclosure movement, most rural residents appear to have recognized the greater efficiency of the new arrangement.

Aging covenanted communities, like aging open-field villages, are ripe for institutional change. Urban economists find that, after as few as forty years, the costs of covenants commonly exceed their benefits. Covenant enthusiasts—such as Edward Bouton, J. C. Nichols, and Byron Hanke—were innocent of these findings, discovered long after their lifetimes. By 2100, the covenants of Culver City's Lakeside Village, established in 1973, are likely to be long obsolete. Drafters of covenants, state courts, and state legislatures should anticipate that risk. They also should be aware of the status quo bias that tends to lock in existing institutional arrangements.

142. A California statute mimics Texas's by authorizing a majority of owners repeatedly to extend expired covenants, but only in a common-interest community. Cal. Civ. Code §§ 4265, 4270 (2020); see also American Law Institute, *Restatement: Servitudes* (2000) § 6.10(1)(a)(1). Because Hancock Park is not a CIC, this statute does not apply to it.

143. Ellickson, "Property in Land" (1993): 1388–92 (1993); Smith, "Semicommon Property Rights" (2000).

144. Sharman, "Enclosure Acts" (1989): 49–50.

For two reasons, however, the covenant straitjacket is likely to prove not as constraining as the zoning straitjacket. In 2018, as noted, common-interest communities in the United States contained an average of eighty dwelling units, far fewer than the number in most municipalities.[145] A small community is relatively close-knit, abetting cooperation among members. Promoters of reform in these communities are likely to emerge spontaneously, as they did in open-field villages. As in that case, the weeding out of an obsolete arrangement promises to enhance aggregate property value.[146]

In addition, both state courts and legislatures, despite their spotty record on covenant issues, are likely to be more helpful than historically they have been on zoning issues. When a zoning reform is proposed, state institutions commonly succumb to suburbs' concerns about infringements on local autonomy. Both state courts and state legislatures, by contrast, have less reason to sympathize with owners who are seeking to perpetuate outmoded covenants. The politics of stale covenants tends to be far less challenging than the politics of exclusionary zoning.

Nonetheless, the rigidity of land uses in much of urban America imposes colossal costs. It harms the national economy, inflates housing costs, and inhibits internal migration. Although public land use controls have been the primary cause, private covenants unquestionably also have contributed. Drafters, judges, and state legislators should come to recognize that while covenants commonly have value in their teens, they rarely do in their dotage.

145. Community Association Institute, "Community Association Factbook" (2018): 1.

146. There are shards of evidence that CICs indeed can succeed in revising their covenants. See Nelson, *Private Neighborhoods* (2005): 93 (citing a 1995 CAI survey that found that 28 percent of CICs had submitted covenant amendments to their memberships, winning approval in 67 percent of cases); Rogers, "Market for Institutions" (2006): 506 (finding that around 40 percent of covenant schemes in Weld County, Colorado, had been amended).

PART

Reforming Zoning Practices

9

Benefit-Cost Analysis of Land Use Policies

The remainder of the book grapples with what is to be done. This chapter introduces benefit-cost analysis and indicates both its merits and limitations in the assessment of land use policies. Most local governments have numerous reasons to embrace exclusionary policies, and few are likely to reform themselves. The two chapters that follow therefore explore what higher-level governments might do. I recommend that both the federal government and, more importantly, state governments pursue zoning reform. In chapter 10 I recommend that the federal government significantly expand its funding of housing vouchers. Chapter 11 addresses state reforms, the crucial frontier, and offers concrete reforms that a state might consider.

The normative yardstick behind most of these recommendations is benefit-cost analysis. There is a vast literature on this method of evaluation.[1] The federal government currently employs it as its default technique.[2] Most commentators on land use policy implicitly employ some version of this analytic method, including, tellingly, those who defend the use of zoning to slow neighborhood change.[3]

1. See, e.g., Adler and Posner, *Cost-Benefit Analysis* (2006); Sunstein, *Cost-Benefit Revolution* (2018).
2. Federal policymakers are required to subject a proposed policy to benefit-cost analysis. Exec. Order No. 12866 § 1 (1993), 3 C.F.R. 638–40 (1994).
3. See, e.g., Karkkainen, "Reply to Critics" (1994): 74 nn.110–11, 77; Serkin, "Case for Zoning" (2020): 749, 771, 775, 786; Steele, "Functions of Zoning" (1986): 747; see

Benefit-cost analysis of course has limitations. It is inherently difficult to execute. In addition, it commonly fails to include normative considerations that many regard as pertinent in policy analysis. A benefit-cost analyst traditionally would not consider the effects of a policy option on the achievement of, for example, horizontal equity (the like treatment of like individuals), distributive justice, and negative liberty.[4] In many instances, although not all, inclusion of these considerations actually would bolster the case for the positions I advance in the chapters to come. It is easier, for instance, to root out horizontal inequity from housing vouchers than from project-based housing subsidies. And state limits on exclusionary zoning plainly would improve the opportunities of lower-income households, enhancing distributive justice.

Despite its limitations, benefit-cost analysis is invaluable. As a method for assessing the advantages and disadvantages of, for example, the densification of the Palo Alto neighborhood of Professorville, it has no credible rival. From a benefit-cost perspective, the construction of more housing in portions of Professorville would be meritorious if the gainers from that policy, including housing consumers, housing suppliers, and the net beneficiaries of greater agglomeration, would gain enough to compensate the losers from the policy, including some Professorville homeowners and Silicon Valley commuters.[5] Virtually all studies by economists suggest that zoning practices, on balance, significantly harm the national economy.[6] These studies imply that the aggregate effect of public land use regulation is negative. The finding that zoning politics tends to freeze land uses in a developed neighborhood of detached houses supports that suspicion. A benefit-cost analyst who focused more narrowly, however, rightly might award many specific zoning measures a passing grade.

---

also Clowney, "Walk Along Willard" (2005): 137–71 (stressing risk of coordination failures in the absence of zoning).

4. See Symposium on Cost-Benefit Analysis (2000); Liscow, "Is Efficiency Biased?" (2018) (stressing attention to distributive consequences of policy choices); Nussbaum, "Costs of Tragedy" (2000) (on moral limits of cost-benefit analysis).

5. This is the standard Kaldor-Hicks yardstick, which itself has variations. See Craswell, "Incommensurability" (1998).

6. See chapter 1.

The Benefits of Public Land Use Controls

Land use policy is intriguing because there are sound reasons for doubting the coordinating capacities of both market forces and government planners. Not surprisingly, commentators on the zoning system disagree about its overall merits. Zoning has had both skeptics and boosters.[7] Even most critics of conventional planning and regulatory practices, however, agree that some zoning controls promise to generate benefits in excess of costs, by, for example, protecting views and limiting congestion.[8] William Fischel has usefully drawn a "zoning haystack" that rests, at bottom, on benefit-cost analysis.[9] The haystack depicts the costs of both too little and too much public regulation of a private landowner's choices. In Fischel's depiction, "good housekeeping" zoning would maximize the value of land within a community and would be more cost-justified than either, in his words, "zero zoning" or "no-growth zoning."[10] The economists who have criticized the macroeconomic consequences of zoning have tended to overlook its possible benefits.

In the nineteenth century, land use in the United States was mostly laissez-faire. The hoary law of nuisance provided landowners some protection against the most noxious uses, but it was limited in scope. In the absence of protective covenants, an urban landowner lived in fear that a next-door neighbor might build a livery stable, funeral parlor, or manufacturing plant that a court would find fell short of a nuisance. Although neighbors at times successfully engaged in Coasean bargaining, transaction costs commonly limited their capacity to internalize land use

7. Skeptics of zoning include Cappel, "Walk Along Willow" (1991); Epstein, "Externalities in Real Estate" (2018); Siegen, "Non-zoning in Houston" (1970); see also Ellickson, "Alternatives to Zoning" (1973). For commentary more admiring of zoning, see text accompanying notes 23–27.

8. See, e.g., Bertaud, *Order Without Design* (2018): 7; Glaeser et al., "Manhattan So Expensive?" (2005): 361–66; Malpezzi, "Housing Prices, Externalities" (1996): 210–13 (1996) (reviewing potential negative externalities of housing development); see also Span, "How Courts Should Fight" (2001): 9–15 (asserting that zoning might enhance the bonding social capital of a neighborhood's residents).

9. Fischel, *Zoning Rules!* (2015): 324–27.

10. Id. at 325.

externalities in that fashion.[11] The shortcomings of laissez-faire generated, prior to the twentieth century, demand for both pre-zoning public regulations and private covenants.[12] Nineteenth-century covenants typically assured a lot buyer that neighbors would use their lots for residential purposes, perhaps only single-family dwellings.[13]

That zoning had wide appeal in the early twentieth century is readily understandable. In an established neighborhood without covenants—that is, most of urban America—zoning and other forms of public land use control promised to supplement, and perhaps outperform, covenants. A zoning ordinance would cover far more territory and, even in a covenanted area, might provide longer-lasting protection.

The spread of apartment houses in the early twentieth century particularly alarmed urban residents. Nuisance law precedents did not protect homeowners from a multifamily structure.[14] A new apartment building might block light and air, aggravate traffic congestion and parking shortages, and disrupt the traditional scale of a low-rise neighborhood. In his famous *Euclid* opinion, Justice Sutherland rightly recognized that an apartment builder, if unconstrained, might site a structure suboptimally. In his words, "Under these circumstances, apartment houses, which in a different environment would be not only entirely unobjectionable but highly desirable, come very near to being nuisances."[15] Sutherland correctly concluded that an apartment building, like many other land uses, could impose negative externalities that bargaining among neighbors would be unlikely to internalize. His opinion, however, failed to mention less intrusive public regulations, such as mandatory setbacks or minimum lot-area requirements, that would have remedied many of the problems he associated with an apartment building. The Village of Euclid instead had forbidden the erection of multifamily structures in over half the village.

11. See Coase, "Problem of Social Costs" (1960).
12. On early regulatory efforts, see Ellickson and Been, *Land Use Controls* (2005): 74–75.
13. See chapter 8.
14. Lewyn, "Yes to Infill" (2015): 842, 846; Shoked, "Reinvention of Ownership" (2011): 110; City of Youngstown v. Kahn Bros. Bldg. Co., 148 N.E. 842, 845 (Ohio 1925) (dictum).
15. Village of Euclid v. Ambler Realty Co., 272 U.S. 365, 394–95 (1926).

During the 1920s, the zoning movement gained momentum, partly due to federal backing. Some U.S. cities in the Southern and Border States sought to use zoning to cement patterns of racial segregation. Many cities, however, had more defensible reasons for wanting to control unneighborly land uses. Zoning could reduce the risk that an urban lot owner would fall victim to, for example, a livery stable scam.[16] Even some land developers joined the zoning bandwagon.[17] Shertzer, Twinam, and Walsh assert that Chicago's first zoning ordinance, adopted in 1923, enhanced the city's single-family house values by segregating houses from industrial uses.[18] Other studies similarly find that a single-family zone can boost home values.[19] Zoning spread rapidly not only because it appealed to racists and classists, but also because it addressed the genuine problem of externalities that the laissez-faire approach had ignored.

Even an extreme land use control, one that denies a landowner the right to undertake an ordinary land use, may pass benefit-cost analysis. In Silicon Valley, some Santa Clara County zoning regulations require Stanford University to use a vast amount of its foothill lands along the I-280 corridor as open space.[20] Because these measures inflate regional housing prices and impair the attainment of agglomeration efficiencies, in many applications they would flunk a benefit-cost assessment. On some hillsides, however, they likely would not. Requiring a landowner to supply open space, however, commonly does warrant compensation, perhaps in the form of a tax break or government transfer payment.

Municipal historic protection efforts also may survive benefit-cost scrutiny. During the nineteenth century, the Manhattan real estate market was overly dynamic. In 1812, the owner of Federal Hall, one of the

16. See chapter 1.

17. Fischel, *Zoning Rules!* (2015): 178–80; Weiss, *Rise of Community Builders* (1987): 10–12.

18. Shertzer et al., "Economic Geography of Cities" (2018): 34; but see McMillen and McDonald, "First Chicago Zoning Ordinance" (1993): 168–69, 187 (finding no increase in residential property values after Chicago first adopted zoning).

19. Jud, "Effects of Zoning" (1980): 148, 150; Speyrer, "Homes in Houston" (1989).

20. See chapter 3.

nation's most historic buildings, unilaterally razed the structure.[21] Today, by contrast, many commentators worry that New York City's preservation efforts have gone too far.[22] But no one disputes that *some* historic preservation, perhaps cushioned by compensation, is cost-justified.

In 1986 and 1994, Eric Steele and Bradley Karkkainen separately published thoughtful articles that articulated the affirmative case for municipal zoning, especially the single-family zone. Steele, who had studied zoning in the City of Evanston, Illinois, saw zoning as a bulwark that might prevent overly rapid change that could destroy the solidarity and cohesion of an existing neighborhood, particularly one where detached houses predominated.[23] Karkkainen similarly asserted that homeowners are socially embedded in their neighborhoods and tend to value their homes at greater than market value. Karkkainen, while critical of exclusionary zoning practices, generally supported the use of public land use controls to protect this "subjective surplus."[24]

In a 2020 article, Christopher Serkin built on both Steele's and Karkkainen's defenses of zoning. Serkin contended that the benefits of zoning largely arise not from preventing incompatible land uses but rather from slowing the rate of neighborhood change. For him, a homebuyer buys not just a residence but also a set of neighborhood characteristics. Any increase in density or change in land uses nearby disrupts the buyer's expectations.[25] Commendably, Steele, Karkkainen, and Serkin all support only slowing, not stopping, the rate of neighborhood change. All three explicitly warn of the costs of freezing zoning designations.[26] None of

21. Tauranac, "Lost New York" (1999).
22. Ellen and McCabe, "Historic Preservation" (2017); Glaeser, "Preservation Follies" (2010).
23. Steele, "Functions of Zoning" (1986): 717. Serkin sees Steele's account as "process-oriented," and instead offers a substantive defense of zoning. Serkin, "Case for Zoning" (2020): 752 n.17.
24. Karkkainen, "Reply to the Critics" (1994): 73–74.
25. Serkin, "Case for Zoning" (2020): 771.
26. Steele, "Functions of Zoning" (1986): 747 ("The participatory purpose of zoning is to conserve communities by mediating change, not to overcome market forces and prevent development and change."); Karkkainen, "Reply to the Critics" (1994): 79 ("A zoning scheme also should not attempt to freeze a neighborhood in time."); Serkin, "Case for Zoning" (2020): 752–53 ("In-place property

the three, however, refers to the reality of status quo bias, the inherent human psychological disposition that inclines people to fear dynamic real estate markets.[27]

The Costs of Public Land Use Controls

Many costs, as well as many benefits, go into the hopper of benefit-cost analysis. Most legal commentators on zoning practices, apart from Steele, Karkkainen, and Serkin, have been critical of the system. The critics commonly emphasize the ubiquity of inefficient exclusionary practices. The costs of zoning include micro-distortions—for example, requirements that a subdivider offer a larger house-lot than a consumer would desire or the Palo Alto policies that push denser growth away from the city's downtown. Among the macro-distortions are costly shifts in patterns of interstate migration, for instance, from Silicon Valley to Texas. The studies of the Raj Chetty team imply that exclusionary zoning inflicts pervasive social harm by deterring households from upgrading their neighborhoods. Any set of public controls also invariably gives rise to administrative costs. These include the salaries and time of public servants and the burden on housing suppliers of learning the rules of the game.[28] A conscientious benefit-cost analyst would attempt to include all of these.

A locality may have a benign motivation, such as environmental protection, for limiting the development of small house-lots and multifamily housing.[29] The balance of this chapter deals, however, with four motivations that are inherently suspect: the promotion of racial segregation; the promotion of class segregation; the seeking of fiscal advantage; and the

owners should not be entitled to lock in the status quo, and they should expect some reasonable measure of change.").

27. See chapter 7.

28. Ellickson, "Alternatives to Zoning" (1973): 688–90.

29. Discussions of underlying motivations include Bogart, "Motivations for Exclusionary Zoning" (1993); Ihlanfeldt, "Exclusionary Land-Use Regulations" (2004): 272–75; and "Developments in the Law—Zoning" (1978): 1443–62 (discussing "legitimate objectives of zoning"). Been et al., "Overtaking the Growth Machine?" (2014): 234–38, summarize scholars' attempts, using regression analysis or otherwise, to measure the strength of the various motivations.

cartelization of housing markets. A benefit-cost analysis should give no weight to a locality's success in achieving any of these four objectives. Indeed, in many instances, a locality's pursuit of one of these objectives creates significant social costs. If so, an analyst rightly would attach a negative weight.

Zoning Motivated by Racial Discrimination

Racial discrimination violates core American ideals embodied in, most particularly, the Equal Protection Clause of the Fourteenth Amendment. In 1917, the Supreme Court of the United States struck down overt racial zoning on another constitutional ground.[30] In 1948, however, the Court did invoke the Equal Protection Clause in holding that courts could not enforce private covenants that restricted ownership by race.[31] The Fair Housing Act of 1968 is the primary federal statute that embodies the principle of nondiscriminatory access to housing.[32]

Racial tensions have been an enduring dilemma in the United States. In the early twentieth century, when many localities overtly sought to zone by race, the Supreme Court repeatedly held that they could not.[33] Both conscious and subconscious racial animus nevertheless likely continues to motivate local zoning practices.[34] According to recent precedent, a plaintiff asserting that a zoning policy violates the Equal Protection Clause must prove that the locality harbored a racially discriminatory intent.[35] As a result, city attorneys tend to advise local officials considering an exclusionary ordinance to avoid any mention of racial motivation. Social norms also deter the neighborhood defenders who appear at public hear-

30. Buchanan v. Warley, 245 U.S. 60 (1917).
31. Shelley v. Kraemer, 334 U.S. 1 (1948).
32. 42 U.S.C. §§ 3601–31 (2012).
33. Buchanan v. Warley, 245 U.S. 60 (1917); Harmon v. Tyler, 273 U.S. 668 (1927) (per curiam); City of Richmond v. Deans, 281 U.S. 704 (1930) (per curiam).
34. Rolleston, "Restrictive Suburban Zoning" (1987): 19; Trounstine, "Geography of Inequality" (2020).
35. Village of Arlington Heights v. Metropolitan Housing Dev. Corp., 429 U.S. 252 (1977); but cf. Texas Dep't of Housing & Community Aff. v. Inclusive Communities Project, Inc., 576 U.S. 519 (2015) (holding that, in challenge based on Fair Housing Act of 1968, disparate impact may be sufficient).

ings from speaking explicitly about race.[36] Nonetheless, at many public hearings on zoning issues, racial motivations no doubt continue to hover over the debate. I speculate that, in the three metros, racial animus currently is most influential in Greater New Haven and least in Silicon Valley.[37]

For many observers, disproportionately sociologists, zoning remains largely about race.[38] This may be valid in some instances. Numerous other motivations, however, also influence zoning policy. The American population has become far more racially diverse. Racial segregation in U.S. neighborhoods increased steadily through 1970, but it has declined significantly since.[39] The rate of interracial marriage increased from 3 percent in 1970 to 17 percent in 2015, with all groups sharing in the increase.[40] A zoning decision based mainly on race is less likely today than a half-century ago, and certainly less likely than a century ago.

Because racial animus violates American ideals, a benefit-cost analyst plainly should award no credit to a zoning measure's contribution to racial segregation. The harder and more pertinent question is the number an analyst should enter on the cost side of the ledger. A number of researchers have attempted to measure these costs, which indeed may be high.[41]

Discrimination by Social Class

In the ancient city of Rome, inhabitants of different social classes tended to cluster in different neighborhoods.[42] Today, in most cities in Europe and the United States, this pattern, if anything, has become more pronounced.[43] Greater Austin, although less racially segregated than the

36. Einstein et al., *Neighborhood Defenders* (2019): 137.
37. See chapter 5 on racial demography in the three metropolitan areas.
38. See, e.g., Massey and Denton, *American Apartheid* (1993).
39. See chapter 5.
40. Pew Research Center, "Social & Demographic Trends" (2017).
41. See, e.g., Gregory Acs et al., "Cost of Segregation" (2017); Huiping Li et al., "Residential Segregation" (2013); cf. Raj Chetty et al., "Race and Economic Opportunity" (2019): 756–63 (investigating the effects of neighborhood on social mobility).
42. Ellickson, "Ancient Rome" (2020): 164–65.
43. On Europe, see Musterd et al., "Socioeconomic Segregation" (2017). On U.S. patterns, see Jargowsky and Wheeler, "Economic Segregation" (2017): 22

average U.S. city, according to one source ranks third from the top in economic segregation.[44] Self-sorting contributes to these outcomes. Many households apparently desire to settle in a neighborhood with residents whose incomes and educations are similar to their own. A developer, aware of that tendency, commonly pitches different sections of a large development to households in different social classes.

Most suburbanites cannot afford private-school tuition and instead enroll their children in public schools. Zoning offers parents a crude mechanism for managing the quality of their children's classmates. It is plausible, although hardly certain, that a high-ability child would be more likely to reside in an expensive house on a large lot than in either an apartment building or a cheaper house on a smaller lot. Homevoters thus recognize that exclusionary zoning policies might enhance the quality of their children's peers at public school.[45] Love of children predictably leads to adult passion at zoning hearings.

Most zoning ordinances explicitly foster economic segregation. City councils typically vary, for example, their lot-size minimums from one single-family zone to another and limit multifamily housing to small areas of town.[46] Because the median incomes of Black and Hispanic households tend to be relatively low, these commonplace zoning policies have

---

(reporting sharp increase in economic segregation in most metros); Reardon and Bischoff, "Income Segregation" (2011): 1139 (reporting increase in 1970–1990 in income segregation among Black households). Neither of the latter two sources discusses the influence of zoning. Some sources that do provide less support for the link between zoning and class segregation. See, e.g., Berry, "Does Zoning Matter?" (2001) (finding that economic and racial segregation is no greater in zoned Dallas than in unzoned Houston).

44. Florida, "Economically Segregated Cities" (2015).

45. A number of studies indicate that classmates affect student performance. See, e.g., Burke and Sass, "Classroom Peer Effects" (2013): 77 (finding high-ability students benefit most from an increased share of high-ability classmates); Huang and Zhu, "Peer Effects" (2020) (finding, in China, negative effects in grade seven, but not in grade nine).

46. How much these policies actually prevent poor children from living in an upper income neighborhood is far from clear. See Lens and Monkkonen, "More Segregated by Income?" (2016) (finding that land use regulations contribute to the segregation of the rich from the middle class, but not the rich from the poor).

racially disparate impacts, possibly actionable under antidiscrimination statutes.[47] Nonetheless, the New Jersey Supreme Court, in its landmark *Mount Laurel I* decision limiting exclusionary policies, was willing to tolerate some use of zoning to this end: "[Municipalities] can have industrial sections, commercial sections and sections for every kind of housing from low cost and multifamily to lots of more than an acre with very expensive homes."[48]

Should the American tradition of promoting class segregation through zoning count on balance as a virtue or a vice? Prevailing legal norms do not provide a clear answer.[49] The three primary markers of social class are income, years of education, and vocation. For purposes of the Equal Protection Clause, none of these is a suspect classification, unlike race, national origin, and religion.[50] The texts of most civil rights statutes similarly fail to bar discrimination by either social class as such or by one of the three narrower markers that correlate with it. The clustering of households by social status conceivably has benefits. It might promote, for example, deeper social ties among neighbors. In a single-family area, a zoning ordinance that promoted equality in lot sizing conceivably might enhance bonding social capital among residents.[51]

Most commentators nonetheless conclude that residential class segregation, on balance, is socially costly.[52] Raj Chetty and his co-authors have

47. Texas Dep't of Housing & Community Aff. v. Inclusive Communities Project, Inc., 576 U.S. 519 (2015); Zasloff, "Disparate Impact" (2017).
48. Southern Burlington County N.A.A.C.P. v. Mount Laurel Township, 336 A.2d 713, 733 (N.J. 1975). On the *Mount Laurel* cases, see Chapter 11.
49. See Stahl, "Challenge of Inclusion" (2017) (arguing that, although some form of exclusion is inherent in any idea of community, the key normative variable is the scale—building, neighborhood, elementary school, city—at which a community excludes).
50. See, e.g., San Antonio Independent School District v. Rodriguez, 411 U.S. 1, 18–29 (1973) (holding that wealth is not an inherently suspect classification). Many have advocated expansion of Equal Protection protections. See, e.g., Peterman, "Socioeconomic Status Discrimination" (2018).
51. Cf. Schuck, *Diversity in America* (2003): 203–07 (arguing that Americans think that many forms of classism are legitimate).
52. See, e.g., Fennell, "Properties of Concentration" (2006) (concluding that the external costs of exclusionary policies exceed their benefits); Oliver, *Democracy in*

emphasized the damage done when children under age thirteen grow up in a predominantly poor neighborhood.[53] Because of these sorts of findings, a benefit-cost analyst should not credit a zoning system's promotion of segregation by social class. Distributive justice considerations support this conclusion.[54] As with racial segregation, a conscientious benefit-cost analyst in fact might attempt to measure the social costs of zoning policies that worsen economic segregation.

A developer who imposes covenants on a subdivision also typically promotes economic segregation. Chapter 8 describes how the developer of Los Angeles's Hancock Park deliberately sought to create a neighborhood of well-heeled homeowners. Especially when a covenanted community is small in area—Hancock Park is under a square mile—this typically should be legally permissible. Constitutional precedents regarding freedom of association, a right that the U.S. Constitution nowhere specifically mentions, indicate the value of allowing the institutions of civil society to differentiate themselves. The Supreme Court has held that freedom of association entitles parents to educate their children in a private school and to join with others in a civic association.[55] In most cases, a local government's efforts to use zoning to promote segregation by social class is more offensive than a private covenant aimed at the same end.[56]

Zoning to Reap Fiscal Benefits

As William Fischel has famously argued, homeowners generally seek to use zoning to enhance the value of their abodes.[57] For many

---

Suburbia (2001): 5–8, 208; Reich, "Secession of the Successful" (1991). See also Putnam, *Bowling Alone* (2000): 214 ("sprawl has been especially toxic for bridging social capital").

53. Chetty et al., "Exposure to Better Neighborhoods" (2016).

54. Cf. Calabrese et al., "Political Economy of Zoning" (2007) (asserting that exclusionary zoning adds to overall efficiency but disserves lower income households).

55. See, e.g., Pierce v. Society of the Sisters, 268 U.S. 510 (1925) (finding constitutional entitlement to send children to private school); NAACP v. Alabama ex rel. Patterson, 357 U.S. 449 (1958) (protecting the right of a group to refuse to disclose a list of members).

56. But cf. Serkin, "Case for Zoning" (2020): 793–98 (expressing concern that covenants may intensify racial and social segregation).

57. Fischel, *Homevoter Hypothesis* (2001): 4–6.

households, the home is a major asset, one not readily insurable against a loss in market value.[58] Suburbanites therefore tend to shape zoning to attract fiscal winners, that is, land uses that would generate more local tax revenue than they would cost the municipality to serve.[59] Zoning officials thus are eager to provide sites for light industry and housing developments restricted to the elderly. Conversely, suburbs make efforts to zone out fiscal losers. In a state where local property taxes finance most of the costs of public schools, a suburb tends to be particularly averse to allowing the construction of inexpensive dwellings that school-age children might occupy.[60] Politicians in Orange, Connecticut, for example, when advising their electorate on how to vote on the acquisition of the Hubbell property, rested their argument entirely on fiscal considerations.[61]

A state's fiscal structure may importantly influence its localities' exclusionary tendencies. In California, voter approval of Proposition 13 in 1976 sharply reduced a municipality's fiscal benefits from permitting housing construction.[62] In Texas, a state that lacks an income tax, housing construction promises to bring in more property tax revenue than it would in California (and perhaps Connecticut).[63]

Playing for fiscal advantage typically is a zero-sum game. In light of the administrative costs of local strategizing, it actually is a negative-sum game. The New Jersey Supreme Court's famous *Mount Laurel I* decision therefore rightly excoriated the practice of municipal zoning for fiscal advantage.[64] Two decades prior to *Mount Laurel,* the Supreme Court of

58. See id. at 268–70 (proposing a form of home equity insurance that might dampen interest in exclusionary zoning).
59. Hamilton, "Zoning and Property Taxation" (1975); Hanushek and Yilmaz, "Local Provision of Education" (2015); Rolleston, "Restrictive Suburban Zoning" (1987): 19 (finding evidence of fiscal zoning); see also Fischel, *Zoning Rules!* (2015): 129–62 (discussing link between land use regulation and fiscal considerations).
60. Gallagher, "Fiscal Externality" (2016), contends that units in a multifamily building actually are fiscal winners.
61. See chapter 4.
62. See chapter 5.
63. Proposition 13 also provides property tax savings to those who long remain in a dwelling unit. This has reduced house turnover in California. Wasi et al., "Lock-In Effect of Proposition 13" (2005).
64. Southern Burlington County N.A.A.C.P. v. Mount Laurel Township, 336 A.2d 713, 730–31 (N.J. 1975).

Connecticut also had condemned fiscal motivations for land use decisions.[65] Because the game of tax avoidance is negative-sum, a benefit-cost analyst of exclusionary zoning should not give weight to a locality's fiscal gains. Politicians at city hall, caught in a strategic dilemma, of course cannot.

Cartelization of Housing Supply

Some of the most enthusiastic proponents of growth controls commonly are those who have most recently purchased a house in a suburb. Consider a young couple who had marshaled all their savings to purchase a $2.5 million Eichler in south Palo Alto. Imagine that, shortly after their purchase, Palo Alto were to consider a rezoning that would significantly densify the city. By increasing housing supply, the new policy would tend to drive down the value of all Palo Alto houses, including the couple's Eichler. To protect their major financial asset, the couple likely would support city council candidates who would oppose the densification measure.

This scenario assumes that conventional housing economics is sound, namely that the construction of a large quantity of new housing typically causes house prices and rents to fall. Most housing specialists agree that a Palo Alto decision to densify would almost certainly have this result. A few observers, however, disagree.[66] They surmise, in some contexts, that the construction of housing would signal that a location is hot, perhaps causing an upward shift in the demand curve. The authors of a burst of recent empirical studies, however, affirm that greater housing production typically does reduce rents.[67] The history of housing prices in Silicon Valley also tends to refute the supply skeptics. The population of the region tripled between 1950 and 1970, yet house prices in 1970 remained barely above the national median. The escalation in prices after 1970 stemmed in part, as conventional housing economics would predict, from increasing restrictions on housing supply.[68]

65. Beach v. Planning & Zoning Comm'n, 103 A.2d 814 (Conn. 1954) (rejecting legitimacy of town's refusal to approve subdivision map for fiscal reasons). See generally "Developments in the Law—Zoning" (1978): 1457–62.
66. See, e.g., sources cited in Been et al., "Supply Skepticism" (2019): 29–31.
67. See Chapter 1.
68. See Chapter 3.

The wish of the hypothetical couple to curb housing supply in Palo Alto would be an effort to reap monopoly rents. A city hall that sought to fulfill the couple's wish would be managing a homeowners' cartel.[69] As a legal matter, municipal actions intended to cartelize housing supply would violate the spirit, if rarely the letter, of federal and state antitrust laws.[70] Conventional antitrust analysis holds that monopolization efforts inflict deadweight losses. If Palo Alto were to refuse to densify, eventual migrants to the city thus would suffer more than members of the homeowners' cartel would gain. A benefit-cost analyst therefore should ignore existing homeowners' benefits from monopoly housing prices. Indeed, the analyst should add, on the cost side of the ledger, the deadweight loss the homeowners' cartel had inflicted.

69. Ellickson, "Suburban Growth Controls" (1977): 400–01; Ortalo-Magné and Prat, "Homeownership Versus Affordability" (2014).

70. See, e.g., City of Columbia v. Omni Outdoor Advertising, Inc., 488 U.S. 365 (1991); Local Government Antitrust Act of 1984, codified at 15 U.S.C.A. §§ 34–36 (2018).

10

The Important Federal Role in Zoning Reform

States are the best reformers of abusive local zoning practices.[1] Nonetheless, the federal government has an essential role in complementing state efforts.[2] This chapter emphasizes what Washington, D.C. does best, appropriating funds. Here I urge the federal government to expand its housing voucher program and provide grants-in-aid to state agencies charged with extirpating exclusionary practices.

The standard federal perspective is hostility to local exclusionary practices. Specially appointed federal commissions on housing issues, for example, have uniformly criticized exclusionary zoning.[3] Some members of both the Obama and Trump administrations also have been overtly critical.[4] (As the 2020 election neared, however, candidate Trump reverted to a policy of protecting the status quo in the suburbs.[5]) Since 2000, the

1. But cf. Schill, "Federal Role" (1992): 726–29 (offering reasons why the federal government might be more likely than a state to preempt local powers).
2. See generally Glaeser and Gyourko, *Federal Housing Policy* (2008).
3. National Commission on Urban Problems, *Building the American City* (1969): 213–16; Committee on Urban Housing, *A Decent Home* (1969): 142–43; *Report of the President's Commission on Housing* (1982): 200–09; *Report of the Bipartisan Millennial Housing Commission* (2002): 20 and n.18.
4. Furman, "Barriers to Shared Growth" (2015); President Trump's Executive Order 13878, 84 Fed. Reg. 30853 (June 15, 2019), establishing a White House Council on Eliminating Regulatory Barriers to Affordable Housing.
5. Trump and Carson, "We'll Protect America's Suburbs" (2020) (rejecting "the ultra-liberal view that the federal bureaucracy should dictate where and how people live").

federal Department of Housing and Urban Development has maintained a Regulatory Barriers Clearinghouse.[6] Viewed from inside the Beltway, the large national costs of exclusionary policies seem to swamp the possible advantages of local control of land use decision-making.

Greater Federal Funding of Housing Vouchers

Congress can assist the battle against exclusionary zoning by appropriating additional funds for Housing Choice Vouchers, commonly known as Section 8.[7] A national government has a comparative advantage in funding any welfare program intended to cushion its citizens from economic insecurity.[8] If subnational entities instead were to finance them, a wealthier household, to reduce its tax burdens, might move out of a relatively generous state, and a less wealthy household might move in. National governments therefore fund most welfare programs. Most developed nations have chosen to dispense in-kind housing subsidies, not just transfer cash to a household deemed worthy of assistance. This approach, while paternalistic, does help assure some pass-through of benefits to children present in recipient households.[9]

Like legislatures in many other nations, Congress has seesawed between two competing forms of in-kind housing assistance: (1) portable housing vouchers and (2) aid to specific projects in which some or all of the dwelling units benefit from subsidized rents.[10] The voucher approach requires a recipient household to locate, in the large private stock of housing, both a dwelling and a landlord willing to rent.[11] Section 8 traditionally has

6. In recent years, however, the work of the Clearinghouse has not been conspicuous.

7. 42 U.S.C. 1437f (2021). See generally Rosen, *Voucher Promise* (2020) (investigating implementation of Section 8 in Park Heights neighborhood of Baltimore).

8. Musgrave and Musgrave, *Public Finance* (1976): 623; Ellickson, "Homeowners Associations" (1982a): 1554–55.

9. Olsen, "Housing Programs" (2003): 368–70. See generally Glaeser and Gyourko, *Federal Housing Policy* (2008): 54–56 (identifying possible benefits of in-kind housing assistance).

10. On the relative merits of these approaches, and the preferences of states for project-based subsidies, see Kazis, "Failed Federalism" (forthcoming).

11. Some states offer their own housing vouchers. Connecticut calls them RAPs.

required a voucher recipient to pay 30 percent of income toward rent, with the federal government paying the balance, subject to a ceiling. Project-based assistance, by contrast, aims to reduce rents in specific buildings. The traditional federal public housing program, begun in 1937, relied on a public housing authority, a local public entity, to erect buildings in which federal and local subsidies enabled below-market rents. More recently, the federal government has authorized private limited-profit firms to develop most subsidized projects. The number of units aided under the Low Income Housing Tax Credit (LIHTC) program, which Congress first approved in 1986, now far exceeds units in public housing.[12]

None of the current federal housing assistance programs is an entitlement program. According to one federal estimate, in 2015 only about one-quarter of low-income households eligible for some form of federal housing assistance actually received it.[13] The horizontal inequity is manifest. The households receiving either vouchers or project-based housing subsidies are no different from the households on waiting lists. As a cure, Edgar Olsen has urged the federal government to entitle all eligible applicants to receive housing vouchers, a reform he thinks would require some reduction in average voucher amounts.[14]

Tellingly, most urban economists deem housing vouchers far superior to any form of project-based assistance, including a mixed-income project in which only a fraction of rents are subsidized.[15] The left-leaning Center on Budget and Policy Priorities similarly supports housing vouchers.[16] No form of housing assistance, of course, is problem-free. The most

---

Connecticut Rental Assistance Program (2020). At times, Connecticut has closed its waitlist for these transfer payments.

12. Schwartz, *Housing Policy* (2010): 103.

13. Congressional Budget Office, "Federal Housing Assistance" (2015): 10.

14. Olsen, "Reforming Housing Assistance" (2015): 28–30; Olsen, "Housing Policy Reform" (2006): 109–12.

15. See, e.g., Olsen, "Reforming Housing Assistance" (2015); Weicher, *Privatizing Subsidized Housing* (1997). Vouchers usually have a minor effect on rent levels. Eriksen and Ross, "Housing Vouchers" (2015). See also Ellen, "Housing Choice Vouchers" (2020) (praising vouchers but noting that recipients tend to remain in poor neighborhoods, and that some landlords refuse to accept vouchers). There is little evidence that voucher holders worsen crime rates in the neighborhoods where they use their vouchers. Ellen et al., "Vouchers Cause Crime?" (2011).

16. Fischer, "Housing Vouchers Work" (2017).

prominent criticism of vouchers is that a landlord might decline to rent to a tenant tendering one.[17] Some states, including California and Connecticut, and some cities as well, prohibit a landlord from acting in this fashion, although perhaps not effectually.[18]

Although not free of the risk of horizontal inequity, vouchers have four significant, and inherent, advantages over project-based housing assistance. First, and perhaps most important, researchers have found that subsidized housing projects of all types are inordinately expensive to build.[19] Per dollar spent, housing vouchers confer substantially more benefits on tenants. HOPE VI, the program used to finance replacement of obsolete public housing projects, has been the most profligate drain on federal tax dollars.[20] Although the per-square foot construction costs of new LIHTC units have been lower than those for HOPE VI units, even LIHTC projects are about 20 percent more expensive than market-rate equivalents.[21] When a LIHTC project includes unsubsidized units, syndication fees and other administrative costs per assisted unit invariably rise.

Second, when a recipient tenant can find another private landlord willing to lease, a housing voucher is portable.[22] A tenant who vacates a unit in a subsidized project, by contrast, typically loses the subsidy. Project-based subsidies thus inherently impair tenants' geographic mobility, lead

17. Thomas, "Separated by Design" (2020).

18. See, e.g., Cal. Gov't Code § 12927 (2021); Conn. Gen. Stat. Ann. § 46a-64c(a)(1) (2021). For discussion, see Oliveri, "Vouchers and Affordable Housing" (2019).

19. DiPasquale et al., "Comparing Costs" (2003); Mayo, "Inefficiency in Subsidized Housing" (1986): 244 (estimating that tenant benefits, per dollar spent, were 82 percent for vouchers, as opposed to a median of 48 percent for projects); Olsen, "Reforming Housing Assistance" (2015): 27–29; see also Fuller, "Cost $750,000" (2020).

20. DiPasquale et al., "Comparing Costs" (2003): 148, 152; cf. Kinnaird, "Public Housing: Abandon HOPE " (1994) (concluding that vouchers would be far superior to HOPE I, a program to sell public housing units to tenants).

21. Eriksen, "Market Price" (2009): 145; see also Eriksen and Lang, "Proposed Reforms" (2020): 4 n.18 (providing examples of exceptionally costly LIHTC projects); U.S. General Accounting Office, "Federal Housing Assistance" (2002): 29 (estimating that LIHTC costs 30 percent more than vouchers).

22. Compare Rubinowitz and Rosenbaum, *Class and Color Lines* (2000) (analyzing the *Gautreaux* program in Greater Chicago, another program designed to enable tenant mobility).

to mismatches between households and housing units, and dull a landlord's incentives to respond to tenant complaints.[23]

Third, vouchers are far better at achieving the economic integration of neighborhoods. Raj Chetty and his co-authors have shown that poor children under age thirteen benefit significantly from a move to a higher-income neighborhood. It is notable that Chetty's research team has used housing vouchers, not rentals in subsidized projects, to permit tenants to upgrade their neighborhoods. Vouchers enable quiet integration. A household with a housing voucher can arrive in the neighborhood inconspicuously and, if both landlord and tenant keep mum, even anonymously. The newcomers also would have the advantage of being flesh-and-blood individuals, not the hypothetical intruders that project opponents at a public hearing might imagine in advance. Integration by subsidized project is far more strident. Prior to approving construction of a subsidized project, a suburb commonly would hold one or more public hearings. Homevoter protests at these sessions are almost a certainty.[24] New York once authorized its Urban Development Corporation, initially headed by Edward Logue, to override local zoning when it built a subsidized project. New York suburbs strongly objected and persuaded the state legislature to withdraw the power to override.[25] In practice, many LIHTC developers avoid the approval gauntlet and instead site their subsidized projects in high-poverty neighborhoods.[26]

Fourth, an administering government can deliberately shape a voucher program to encourage a recipient in a low-income neighborhood to move where neighbors would be somewhat more prosperous. Chetty's team has explored a number of options.[27] The provision of counseling services, for example, might encourage some voucher recipients to seek out

23. Ellickson, "Mixed-Income Housing Project" (2010): 998–99.
24. Cf. Diamond and McQuade, "Low-Income Property Development" (2019) (finding that a LIHTC project tends to increase the value of nearby property in a poor neighborhood, but decrease it in a wealthy neighborhood).
25. Briffault, "Our Localism" (1990): 69.
26. Glaeser and Gyourko, *Rethinking Federal Housing Policy* (2008): 110; Saito, "LIHTC" (2020): 467–71 (providing maps of LIHTC project locations in selected metropolitan areas).
27. Bergman, Chetty et al., "Creating Moves to Opportunity" (2021).

neighborhoods with better public schools. Another possibility is to alter the formula for voucher aid. For a higher-cost zip code, for instance, Congress could authorize HUD to raise the maximum permissible rent, thereby upping the federal share of the rent payment.[28] Project-based housing subsidies, of any stripe, are far less flexible.

Greater federal funding of vouchers, by itself, hardly would enable a lower-income household to access a wealthy exclusionary suburb. The next chapter outlines a necessary complementary action: the state legislature's paring back of the regulations that exclusionary localities use to prevent the construction of least-cost housing. Implementation of both prongs of the reform would enable, over time, the emergence of diverse housing stocks in most urban neighborhoods.

The goal, however, is not to make all neighborhoods physically and socially identical. Many households prefer neighborhoods where many people like themselves live. Within the constraints of fair housing legislation, developers tend to cater to this taste. Because of both covenants and the inclination of like households to cluster, even in the absence of exclusionary zoning, American neighborhoods are destined to be heterogeneous.

Federal Grants-In-Aid to State Agencies That Limit Exclusionary Zoning

The next chapter recommends that a state afflicted with local exclusionary practices establish a specialized state agency to reduce barriers to the building of least-cost housing. Numerous researchers have found that exclusionary practices significantly damage the national economy. Congress therefore would be justified in providing grants-in-aid to encourage states to establish these agencies. During his 2020 presidential bid, candidate Joe Biden indeed proposed $300 million in federal aid for this exact purpose.[29]

28. On adjustments of this sort, see Collinson and Ganong, "Housing Voucher Design" (2018); NYU Furman Center, "Small Area Fair Market Rents" (2018).

29. Biden, "Investing in Our Communities" (2020): "Biden will . . . invest $300 million in Local Housing Policy Grants to give states and localities the technical

These grants-in-aid would be both more direct and more symbolically powerful than various alternatives that other reformers have advanced. Senator Cory Booker has proposed, for example, conditioning local and state eligibility for Community Development Block Grants (CDBG) on progress on zoning reform.[30] Booker's approach is indirect and does not threaten the loss of federal grants that local politicians are likely to most value.[31] More effective would be Edward Glaeser's proposal that the federal government tie all highway grants to state progress on removing barriers to housing production.[32] Glaeser and Joseph Gyourko have urged Congress to amend the Internal Revenue Code to place a cap on the deductibility of mortgage interest payments in counties where housing production has been subpar.[33] That proposal, if adopted, might generate some political pressure on local officials. A program of direct federal grants-in-aid to state anti-exclusion agencies, as candidate Biden proposed, however, would be far more potent than one of these lesser measures.

A Revised Standard Zoning Enabling Act

In some hands, the federal pulpit can be bully. In the early 1920s, Herbert Hoover, then secretary of commerce, helped convene a panel that drafted the Standard State Zoning Enabling Act (SZEA).[34] Hoover's action helped spur the spread of zoning. By 1925, nineteen states had adopted some version of the act, with most other states soon to follow.[35] The SZEA's drafters apparently did not anticipate exclusionary practices, which did not emerge until a few years after the panel had completed its work.[36]

---

assistance and planning support they need to eliminate exclusionary zoning policies and other local regulations that contribute to sprawl."

30. Housing, Opportunity, Mobility, and Equity Act of 2018, S. 3342, 115th Cong. (2018).
31. Schuetz, "Withholding CDBG Funds" (2018a).
32. Glaeser, "America's Urban Frontier" (2020b): 15–16.
33. Glaeser and Gyourko, *Federal Housing Policy* (2008): 128–32, 143–44, 161–65.
34. See chapters 1 and 12.
35. National Commission on Urban Problems, *Building the American City* (1969): 201.
36. See chapter 2.

The pertinent federal department now is HUD, not the Department of Commerce.[37] The HUD secretary might consider appointing a panel to draft a revised SZEA. The revised version, unlike the original, ideally would include constraints on local exclusionary practices. HUD's sponsorship of a rewrite certainly would shine a national spotlight on the issue of exclusionary zoning.

Any HUD effort to revise the SZEA, however, would risk interest-group capture. The main threat likely would come from professional housers, the developers who specialize in the building of subsidized projects.[38] A mix of social idealism and economic self-interest motivates these specialists. In 1993, professional housers were potent enough to persuade Congress to make the mediocre LIHTC program permanent.[39] As members of the HUD panel, they might push for mandatory inclusionary zoning, an expensive form of project-based housing assistance that would serve their interests. Housing vouchers, as noted, are vastly superior to any form of project-based subsidy.

The Role of the Federal Courts

In 1967, Lawrence Sager published in the *Stanford Law Review* a landmark article on suburban land use policies.[40] Sager used *exclusionary zoning* in his title, helping establish that phrase as the standard shorthand for describing suburban proclivities.[41] Sager's article twice nominated none other than the Supreme Court of the United States to take charge

37. The Census Bureau, a fount of data on American life, remains in the Department of Commerce. It conducts, among other endeavors, the Census of Governments. Because zoning is the principal discretionary policy of local governments, the Census Bureau might consider including, in the Census of Governments, questions that would help reveal patterns of local zoning.
38. Ellickson, "Mixed-Income Housing Project" (2010): 1016–17 (describing various initiatives of professional housers).
39. The successful lobbying effort included Grogan, "Points of Urban Light" (1992). Paul Grogan then was president of the nonprofit Local Initiatives Support Corporation (LISC), a major syndicator of LIHTCs.
40. Sager, "Exclusionary Zoning" (1969).
41. Although Sager was not the first to use the phrase exclusionary zoning, his article helped bury "snob zoning," "exclusionary zoning's" main competitor at the time.

of rooting out exclusionary practices.[42] Sager contended that the Court should interpret the Equal Protection Clause of the Fourteenth Amendment, the clause the Court had relied on to bar racial segregation in public schools, to bar land use practices that have racially discriminatory effects. Subsequent Court decisions interpreting the Equal Protection Clause dashed this hope.[43]

Federal judges certainly have an important, if limited, role to play. As mentioned, the Supreme Court struck down both overt racial zoning in 1917 and overt racial covenants in 1948.[44] Legal commentators have universally acclaimed both these rulings. Historically, however, in contexts where intentional racial discrimination has not been present, federal judges have tended to resist both landowner and consumer claims that zoning policies have violated federal constitutional rights.[45] As Judge Richard Posner put it, "If the plaintiffs can get us to review the merits of [this] decision under state law, we cannot imagine what zoning dispute could not be shoehorned into federal court in this way, there to displace or postpone consideration of some worthier object of federal judicial solicitude."[46] In general, federal judges sense that state judges, who have

42. Id. at 799, 800.
43. See, e.g., Village of Arlington Heights v. Metropolitan Dev't Corp., 429 U.S. 252 (1977) (requiring showing that racially discriminatory intent motivated local zoning); Lindsey v. Normet, 405 U.S. 56 (1972) (holding that housing is not a "fundamental right" under Equal Protection Clause); San Antonio Ind. Sch. Dist. v. Rodriguez, 411 U.S. 1 (1973) (holding that wealth is not necessarily a "suspect classification" under Equal Protection Clause).
44. Buchanan v. Warley, 245 U.S. 60 (1917); Shelley v. Kraemer, 334 U.S. 1 (1948).
45. See, e.g., Warth v. Seldin, 422 U.S. 490 (1975) (denying, in a 5-to-4 decision, standing to challenge a suburb's exclusionary practices to, among others, minority residents and a homebuilders association whose members lacked an interest in a proposed project); see also, e.g., Construction Industry Ass'n v. City of Petaluma, 522 F.2d 897 (9th Cir. 1975) (holding that an annual limit on housing starts did not violate Due Process Clause of Fourteenth Amendment; "it is the state legislature's and not the federal courts' role to intervene" (id. at 908)); Ybarra v. Town of Los Altos Hills, 503 F.2d 250 (9th Cir. 1974) (denying Equal Protection Clause challenge to town's one-acre minimum for a single-family lot).
46. Coniston Corp. v. Village of Hoffman Estates, 844 F.2d 461, 467 (7th Cir. 1988).

better knowledge of both zoning law and the local topography, are better equipped to take on the burden of policing local abuses.

For two reasons, Sager's nomination of a central role for the federal courts was dubious. First, the capacity and legitimacy of any court, relative to a legislature or administrative agency, is inherently limited.[47] Second, and more important, the American commitment to federalism in governance calls for states to take the lead in preventing zoning abuses.[48]

In some contexts, a federal statute might provide a ground for a successful attack on exclusionary practices. The main candidate is the Fair Housing Act of 1968.[49] In 2015, a closely divided Supreme Court held that the Act potentially reaches any policy that has a racially discriminatory impact.[50] Virtually any zoning policy, such as a routine minimum lot-size requirement, could meet this test. It is unclear how this body of case law will evolve and whether Congress will amend the statute. Several federal court decisions since 2015 suggest that the Fair Housing Act may become a potent weapon against exclusionary practices.[51] Most federal judges, however, have traditionally been deeply averse to active involvement in zoning issues.[52] That reluctance likely will limit the eventual impact of the Fair Housing Act.

47. See chapter 11.

48. Id.

49. 42 U.S.C. § 3601–31 (2012).

50. Texas Dep't of Housing & Community Aff. v. Inclusive Communities Project, Inc., 576 U.S. 519 (2015) (Kennedy, J.) (5–4 decision).

51. See, e.g., MHANY Management, Inc. v. County of Nassau, 2017 WL 4174787 (E.D. N.Y. 2017) (holding that a rezoning that prevented construction of multi-family housing violated Fair Housing Act); Avenue 6E Investments, LLC v. City of Yuma, 818 F.3d 493 (9th Cir. 2016) (holding city may have violated Act by refusing to reduce minimum lot-size for a detached house from 8,000 to 6,000 sq. ft.).

52. I have long urged federal judges to avoid federalizing zoning law. Ellickson, "Suburban Growth Controls" (1977): 471, 511. The best counterargument rests on the life tenure of a federal judge, a form of job security far greater than that of a state judge.

11

The Central Role of States in Zoning Reform

In the United States, the media are obsessed with political events occurring inside the Beltway. In many contexts, this attention misses the mark. *State* governments, not the federal government, largely shape many central areas of law, including criminal law, family law, inheritance law, and property law. Most relevantly, states are key players in the field of land use law. In this chapter, I contend that a state should preempt many of the land use choices that its local governments now are free to make. This would correct the error that the Herbert Hoover panel made in the 1920s when it recommended that states delegate almost unbridled zoning authority to local governments.[1] Subject to these selective preemptions, localities would retain substantial power to regulate land uses.

Decentralizing Power in a Federal System of Government

The United States Constitution displays a deep commitment to the rights of states. The Tenth Amendment provides, "The powers not delegated to the United States by the Constitution, nor prohibited by it to the States, are reserved to the States respectively, or to the people." The vast size of the nation and the variety of its terrain support decentralization of many key governing functions. Authorizing a state to shape local land use policies enables state officials to take advantage of their local

1. See chapters 1 and 12.

knowledge of the territory and the distinct preferences of their residents. As Justice Brandeis famously observed, having the states function as laboratories also offers a systemic advantage.[2] A state can learn by observing the results of what other states have done.

Local control of zoning, the aim of Herbert Hoover's model act, makes perfect sense in some contexts. A municipality's residents typically know its terrain better than the electorate of the state or county that includes the municipality. Placing localities in charge also seems to accord, on its face, with the principle of subsidiarity: the wisdom of allocating responsibility for handling an issue to the smallest unit competent to manage it.[3] A former three-term mayor of Beverly Hills, California, explicitly invoked the principle of subsidiarity when opposing state preemption of local land use decisions.[4] In American law and politics, the legal notion of "home rule" best captures the benefits of decentralized governmental authority. When a local policy has little or no effect on outsiders, home rule and subsidiarity are splendid principles. There is a rub, however, and it is a serious one. In 1922, Hoover's panel had no inkling that localities would begin to use zoning for exclusionary purposes, harming outsiders with no voice in the adoption of the injurious policies. As early as the 1930s but especially since 1970, suburbs and cities have increasingly used zoning policies to inflict massive damage on both regional housing consumers and the national economy.

In 1953, Harvard law professor Charles Haar fired the first prominent scholarly salvo against suburban exclusion.[5] He scathingly criticized a New Jersey Supreme Court decision that had upheld the constitutionality of a suburb's mandate that a residential housing unit have a floor area greater than a specified minimum. Haar rightly contended that this

2. New State Ice Co. v. Liebmann, 285 U.S. 262, 311 (1932) (Brandeis, J., dissenting).
3. On subsidiarity, see, e.g., Hills, "Localist Case" (2005): 189–90.
4. Mirisch, "Protecting Communities" (2018).
5. Haar, "Zoning for Minimum Standards" (1953) (criticizing Lionshead Lake, Inc. v. Township of Wayne, 89 A.2d 693 (N.J. 1952) (5–2 opinion by Vanderbilt, C.J.), *appeal dismissed,* 344 U.S. 919 (1953)). But cf. Builders Service Corp. v. Planning & Zoning Comm'n of Town of East Hampton, 545 A.2d 530 (Conn. 1988) (holding that state zoning enabling act did not authorize town to impose a minimum required floor area for a residence).

zoning provision would injure regional housing consumers. In his view, judicial deference to the policy therefore had been unwise. Val Nolan and Frank Horack, two Indiana University law professors, promptly responded. They discounted Haar's argument about negative effects on housing consumers, and they invoked a localist line of defense: "It is . . . altogether characteristic . . . for a state to deal with new and complex problems locally, through the experimental probings of the smallest units of government acting voluntarily under enabling legislation."[6] Haar refused to retreat, however, and soon clarified his position. In a 1957 article, he primarily urged state legislatures to take the lead in zoning reform.[7]

Haar's 1957 article also advocated that states create regional planning bodies to prepare "regional master plans."[8] The merits of this second recommendation are doubtful. Because municipalities are prone to misuse zoning powers, a sub-state entity larger in area than a locality—perhaps a regional body, county, or council of governments—conceivably might play a useful role. In practice, however, state policymakers usually are wise to choose among the set of governments that already exists.[9] Few *regional* governments exist and virtually none has the power to override local planning policies. In many metropolitan areas, counties are too small to take into account the interests of regional housing consumers. Because representatives of local governments tend to dominate councils of governments, those entities plainly are not trustworthy protectors of regional interests.[10] On most land use questions, state control is preferable to

6. Nolan and Horack, "Minimum Space Requirements" (1954): 985.
7. Haar, "Realism in Land-Use Planning" (1957): 531–37. Compare Haar, *Suburbs Under Siege* (1996): xiv, 4, 129–33 (lauding activism of state supreme courts on land use issues).
8. Haar, "Realism in Land-Use Planning" (1957): 536–37.
9. In my younger days, I did not consistently recognize this practical constraint. See Ellickson, "Alternatives to Zoning" (1973): 762–71 (recommending that states establish metropolitan nuisance boards). Others have called for the creation of new sets of regional institutions. See, e.g., Camacho and Marantz, "Toward Metropolitan Governance" (2020).
10. Councils of Governments, that is, federations of localities, are ubiquitous. Northern California has ABAG (Association of Bay Area Governments), Greater New Haven has SCRCOG (Southern Connecticut Regional Council of Govern-

both local and, *pace* Haar, regional control. In general, states are spacious enough and their politics broad-minded enough to take into account the negative effects of local land use policies on housing consumers.

Indeed, on some issues, states arguably are territorially too small. Positive and negative externalities from both land uses and land use policies can spill over state borders. A towering smokestack can cause interstate pollution. California's Environmental Quality Act and Hawaii's state land controls may have significantly impaired the housing prospects of housing consumers in other states.[11] Policymakers, however, have to make a rough cut. Haar's central recommendation in 1957—that states are the optimal reformers of local exclusionary practices—remains sound.

State Legislatures, the Architects of Land Use Law

Haar's 1957 recommendation was far more cogent than Lawrence Sager's, a dozen years later. Sager urged the Supreme Court of the United States to take the lead in zoning reform.[12] Although the federal government has recently legislated in a few pockets of land use law—for example, in cases involving religious land uses and wireless communication towers—zoning law in the United States is largely state and local law.[13] In somewhat smaller nations, such as France and Japan, by contrast, national governments have commonly established parameters that severely constrain local choices among land use policies.[14] The American tradition of federalism counsels against both a centralized national land use policy and federal court activism.

---

ments), and Greater Austin, CAPCOG (Capital Area Council of Governments). Beginning in the 1960s, the federal government helped incentivize the creation of these entities. See Council of Governments (2020).

11. See respectively Hernandez, "CEQA Lawsuits" (2018), and Ellickson, "Suburban Growth Controls" (1977): 434 and n.133.

12. See chapter 10.

13. On the exceptions mentioned, see Religious Land Use and Institutionalized Persons Act of 2000, 42 U.S.C. §§2000cc to 2000cc-5 (Supp. 2018); Telecommunications Act of 1996, 47 U.S.C. § 332(c)(7)(B)(i) (Supp. 2019). See also Sterk, "Federal Land Use Intervention" (2019).

14. See chapter 7.

The Legal Powers of States, Even in the Teeth of Home Rule

As Herbert Hoover's panel recognized, state legislatures have fulsome power over land use regulation.[15] In its 1983 *Mount Laurel II* opinion articulating constraints on exclusionary practices, the New Jersey Supreme Court recognized the breadth of legislative powers and pleaded with the state legislature to act.[16] In most contexts, a state legislature has the power to preempt local zoning controls. Oregon, for example, recently commanded its more populous localities to permit the building of a fourplex in any area that they zone for some residential use.[17] Since 1982, California, with increasing success, has ordered its local governments to permit the owner of a single-family house to build an accessory dwelling unit (ADU, or granny flat).[18] Eighteen states preempt local restrictions that bar the opening of home-based daycare operations.[19] Because property law is mostly state law, state courts and legislatures also have the power to alter nuisance law and the law of covenants, potential complements of public regulatory measures. To enable the opening of a group care facility in a single-family neighborhood, for example, some states have chosen not only to preempt local zoning but also to override private covenants.[20]

Localities have a possible legal ground for challenging a state's action to limit exclusionary zoning. A large majority of states have embraced

15. See also Lemar, "Role of States" (2019) (reviewing history of state overrides of local zoning, for example, in the siting of group care homes, child-care facilities, and accessory dwelling units).
16. Southern Burlington County NAACP v. Township of Mount Laurel, 456 A.2d 390, 417 (N.J. 1983) [hereinafter *Mount Laurel II*] ("a brief reminder of the judicial role in this sensitive area is appropriate, since powerful reasons suggest, and we agree, that the matter is better left to the Legislature").
17. H.B. 2001, 80th Leg. Assembly, Reg. Sess. § 2 (Or. 2019) (enacted).
18. Local compliance was grudging at first. Brinig and Garnett, "ADU Reforms" (2013): 546–66 (describing how a majority of California's most populous cities initially undermined the state legislature's efforts to encourage production of ADUs). California, however, eventually had greater success. Schleicher, "Constitutional Law for NIMBYs" (2020): 907–8.
19. Lemar, "Role of States" (2019): 308.
20. See, e.g., Cal. Health & Safety Code § 1566.5 (Supp. 2020); Korngold, "Single Family Use Covenants" (1989): 969 n.100.

home rule, commonly by incorporating some version of that principle in the state constitution.[21] Local governments have been the staunchest backers of home rule protections. Preventing state incursions on local power is a principle that unites them. Localities have long been lobbyists, individually and collectively, in statehouses. Between 1997 and 2007, the national increase in local government lobbying outstripped that of traditional lobbyists, such as industry and labor.[22] In California, local governments currently spend more to lobby Sacramento than any other group.[23] In almost all states, local governments have allied with one another to create an association. There is a League of California Cities, a Connecticut Conference of Municipalities, and a Texas Municipal League. Despite the state's small population, the annual meeting of the Connecticut Conference of Municipalities typically attracts over a thousand attendees.[24] State legislators tend to be reluctant to offend these potent interest groups.[25]

Even in a constitutional home-rule state, however, home rule seldom stands in the way of state legislative reform of exclusionary zoning. State courts, not federal courts, hear litigation over the scope of home rule powers. Most have held that a state legislature can override a local policy when the legislature has asserted a "statewide interest."[26] Protecting the interests of nonresident housing consumers to enjoy less costly housing

21. Baker et al., *Local Government Law* (2015): 316–64. See, e.g., Cal. Const. art. XI, § 5 (Supp. 2020); Tex. Const. art. XI, § 5 (Supp. 2020). See also Conn. Const. art. X, § 1 (2021) and Conn. Gen. Stat. § 7–148 (2008) (on local government powers in Connecticut). Baker and Rodriguez, "Constitutional Home Rule" (2009): 1374–1424, provide an appendix that indicates the extent of home rule in each of the states. In some states, a municipality's voters must approve a charter before it can exercise home rule powers.
22. Lowery et al., "Public Sector Lobbying" (2013).
23. Meyers, "Lobbying in Sacramento" (2017). A city that individually lobbies commonly is seeking to increase its share of discretionary state grants. Payson, "Local Governments Use Lobbyists" (2020).
24. Connecticut Conference of Municipalities (2020).
25. See Babcock and Bosselman, "Apartment Boom" (1963): 1084–85 (expressing the "futile hope that state legislatures will suddenly resist the power of the municipal leagues").
26. Baker et al., *Local Government Law* (2015): 342–55.

typically would suffice.[27] If a state statute, for example, were to put the burden on a zoning government to prove the regional cost-effectiveness of a zone requiring a house-lot in excess of 10,000 square feet, state courts likely would uphold it.[28]

Ongoing State Efforts to Combat Exclusionary Zoning

The pioneer has been Oregon, long unconventional in its land use policies.[29] In 1973, Oregon established a powerful statewide planning agency, the Land Conservation and Development Commission (LCDC), and, a few years later, a specialized land use court.[30] With the encouragement of 1000 Friends of Oregon, a watchdog group, the agency generally has used its powers to promote urban densification.[31] LCDC rules currently require a locality, with some exceptions, to authorize the building of as many housing units in its non-single-family residential zones as in its single-family zones.[32] In most states, exclusionary suburbs would flatly flunk this Oregon directive.

Oregon has taken another major step to increase urban densities. In 2019, its legislature, as mentioned, abolished the single-family zone. The 2019 statute compels a city with a population of at least 25,000 to permit

27. See, e.g., Floyd v. New York State Urban Dev. Corp., 300 N.E.2d 704, 706 (N.Y. 1973) (stating, in upholding power of UDC to override local zoning, "Housing is a matter of State-wide concern"); Anderson v. City of San Jose, 255 Cal.Rptr.3d 654, 671–74 (Cal. App. 2019) (asserting statewide dimension of the affordable housing shortage); San Francisco Bay Area Renters Federation v. City of San Mateo (Cal. App. 2021) (rejecting city's assertion that California statute violated home rule provision of California constitution). See also Infranca, "New State Zoning" (2019); Stahl, "State Preemption" (2020).
28. See Schoenbrod, "Large Lot Zoning" (1969): 1437–41 (proposing this reform).
29. See generally Sullivan, "Oregon Planning Program" (2012).
30. Id. at 367–72.
31. See, e.g., Seaman v. City of Durham, 1 LCDC 283, 290–91 (1978) (striking down city's attempt to reduce permitted densities in both single-family and multifamily zones). See also Liberty, "Abolishing Exclusionary Zoning" (2003): 591–95; Span, "How Courts Should Fight" (2001): 74.
32. Or. Admin. Rules § 660–007–0030 (2020) (excepting only "small developed cities").

the building of fourplexes in all areas where the city permits some form of residential use.[33] This reform greatly increases prospects for the construction of "missing middle" housing.

Oregon's policies, however, are perverse in some ways. LCDC has articulated over a dozen unweighted goals for the agency to pursue.[34] The agency's articulation of multiple unweighted goals suggests a naïve faith in the potential of comprehensive planning. Two of the LCDC's goals, preserving prime agricultural lands and drawing urban growth boundaries, commonly are in tension with the goal of making housing affordable. This complexity may have contributed to the tardiness of LCDC decision-making.[35] The state agency whose establishment I recommend, by contrast, would focus more narrowly on removing local and state regulatory barriers that inefficiently stymie housing production.

Oregon is not alone in opposing exclusionary policies. In 2020, the Vermont legislature enacted a statute authorizing fourplexes throughout that state, not just in populous areas.[36] Vermont also chose to preempt local lot-size requirements in excess of one-quarter acre where municipal water is available, and in excess of one-eighth acre where both municipal water and sewer are available.[37]

California is another potential hotbed of zoning reform. There, state policies such as the California Environmental Quality Act (CEQA) and local zoning practices have combined to generate the nation's highest housing prices. The legal crazy quilt in California is as complex as any state's.[38] To date, labor union and environmentalist opposition has blocked CEQA reform. Former governor Jerry Brown has stated that, "You can't change CEQA. . . . The unions won't let you because they use it as a hammer to get project labor agreements. The environmentalists

33. H.B. 2001, 80th Leg. Assembly, Reg. Sess. § 2 (Or. 2019) (enacted). The Oregon statute also requires a city with a population between 10,000 and 25,000 residents to allow duplexes in all its residential zones.
34. Sullivan, "Oregon Planning Program" (2012): 370–71.
35. Id. at 374–77, 392–93.
36. 24 Vt. Stat. Ann. § 4412(a)(D) (2020).
37. 24 Vt. Stat. Ann. § 4412(b)(A) (2020).
38. See chapter 3.

like it because it's the people's document that you have to disclose all the impacts."[39] California voters' approval of Proposition 13 in 1976 reduced a locality's fiscal incentive to allow housing construction.[40]

California nonetheless has enacted a number of modestly helpful statutes, including one that entitles a homeowner to add an ADU, or granny flat.[41] Out of self-interest, many Homevoters ended up supporting this measure. This small reform has led to the construction of thousands of ADUs in California, although not yet enough to make a measurable dent on the state's astronomic housing prices.[42] California state senator Scott Wiener, the most conspicuous advocate of expanding housing production, has introduced several other highly publicized bills of greater potential importance. The most controversial, SB 50, would preempt local controls that prevent the construction of mid-rise multifamily housing near a transit station.[43]

Several states have gone down a far less promising path. Christopher Elmendorf calls it the "Northeastern Model."[44] Massachusetts pioneered the model in 1970 when it enacted an anti-snob zoning law.[45] A developer triggers the Northeastern Model by proposing to build a project in which some or all housing units will have below-market rents, commonly thanks to federal housing subsidies. The state then helps the developer obtain local approvals that otherwise might not be forthcoming. The California legislature, in enacting another of Senator Wiener's bills, went down

39. Newton, "Gov. Jerry Brown" (2016).
40. Quigley and Raphael, "Housing in California" (2005): 323.
41. Cal. Gov't Code § 65852.2 (West 2019), requires a local government to permit construction of an ADU on a residentially zoned lot, including a single-family lot.
42. According to California ADU (2020), localities in the state issued permits for almost 16,000 ADU units in 2019. See also Sisson, "Backyard Building Boom?" (2019).
43. Wick, "Demise of SB 50" (2019). Legislators have introduced similar measures in Oregon and Washington. Elmendorf and Shanske, "Auctioning the Upzone" (2020): 518 n.22.
44. Elmendorf, "Beyond the Double Veto" (2019): 94–100.
45. Low and Moderate Income Housing Act, Mass. Gen. Laws ch. 40B, §§ 20–23 (West Supp. 2021). The Massachusetts statute influenced the drafting of the Connecticut Appeals Act, discussed in chapter 4.

a path that similarly emphasizes project-based housing subsidies.[46] The Northeastern Model fails to keep its eye on the main goal of zoning reform, namely removal of constraints on the building of least-cost, market-rate housing. For reasons presented in the discussion of federal subsidies, housing vouchers help tenants far more, per dollar spent, than any form of project-based assistance, the mainstay of the Northeastern Model.[47]

What States Should Do

In a state where local exclusionary practices have boosted housing prices, the legislature has a multitude of reform options.[48] On many dimensions, Oregon serves as a role model.[49] My core recommendation is that the legislature establish a state agency but charge it with a mission narrower than that of the Oregon LCDC. The state agency's sole mission would be to eliminate local regulatory barriers that impede the production of housing, particularly least-cost market-rate dwellings.[50] That would focus the agency's attention on the chief problem that local zoning abuses create.

An administrative agency could be potent, especially if its staff is capable. The state anti-exclusion agency might begin by collecting data and issuing reports that publicize existing regulatory barriers. The legislature's preemptive statute should require a locality to forward to the agency basic data, including its zoning ordinance, zoning map, and housing-start statistics. Many metrics for measuring the extent of exclusionary policies

46. See Cal. Gov't Code § 65913.4 (2020); 40 Main Street Offices, LLC v. Los Altos (2020). This Wiener statute authorizes the California Department of Housing and Community Development to require some localities to streamline their administrative approvals, primarily for projects that would include income-restricted units. By encouraging conferral of project-based housing subsidies, the statute embraces what Elmendorf calls the Northeastern Model.

47. See chapter 10.

48. For a concise summary of possible reforms at all levels of government, see Shoag, "Removing Barriers" (2019): 13–20.

49. While most states have established state housing and planning agencies with varying mandates, only Oregon has effectively targeted exclusionary zoning.

50. See Span, "How Courts Should Fight" (2001): 38 (preferring that a state agency, not a state court, undertake this mission).

are available.[51] The agency could calculate and publicize findings about how various metrics apply within the state.

The state also should order the agency to preempt most local regulations that pertain to public health. Paul and Linda Davidoff made this recommendation a half-century ago.[52] Suburbs commonly invoke public health concerns to justify their minimum lot-size requirements. In a neighborhood lacking sanitary sewers to remove wastewater, a house's septic tank indeed may contaminate a nearby water well. Some exclusionary suburbs, to obtain legal cover, have deliberately refused to install sanitary sewers.[53] To foil that ploy, the legislature should mandate that the new state agency, working in conjunction with the state public health agency, preempt local regulations governing the design of wastewater systems. State preemption would help unloose the potential of package plants and other decentralized treatment systems.[54]

Mild and strong forms of preemption. A state's internal politics invariably will constrain its legislature's options. Of the many possible legislative preemptions, I mention two. One is mild, and therefore more politically feasible, and one stiffer. A state legislature adopting the mild version would adopt one of the Oregon LCDC's current substantive rules: *a locality's zoning policies must permit, as of right, in its non-single-family zones the construction of as many housing units as it permits in its single-family zones.*[55] This mild reform confers an abundance of planning options on a locality that acts in good faith. And rightly so. Local zoners, although inclined to ignore the interests of regional housing consumers, typically do have superior knowledge of both resident tastes and the affected terrain. Note that this mild reform would not abolish the single-family zone, as the Oregon legislature recently has.[56] Nor would it limit the power of developers to use covenants to produce small specialized

51. See chapter 2.
52. Davidoff and Davidoff, "Opening the Suburbs" (1971): 529. The Davidoffs also recommended that state health officials preempt local regulations that specify a dwelling unit's minimum habitable floor area. Id.
53. See chapter 4.
54. Id.
55. Or. Admin. Rules § 660–007–0030 (2020).
56. H.B. 2001, 80th Leg. Assembly, Reg. Sess. § 2 (Or. 2019) (enacted).

neighborhoods. A local government acting in bad faith, however, could readily evade this mild state command. The next section of this chapter addresses how to deter that temptation.

A distinct advantage of this mild approach is that it is simple. The Oregon legislation abolishing the single-family zone in the state's populous cities was a blunderbuss intervention, but easy to understand. Simplicity is an advantage, both when state legislators debate a proposal and when a state agency implements it.

Stronger interventions, if state politics were to permit, would reduce local options far more. The state legislature could require a suburb, for example, to zone at least 10 percent of its total land area, in relatively central locations, to permit multifamily housing up to a density of at least sixteen units per acre.[57] Because a bulky multifamily structure can have negative spillover effects, the preemptive legislation could authorize a locality to impose on any new apartment building reasonable design requirements, such as a height limit and minimum setbacks from property boundaries. At first blush, this preemptive reform might seem a draconian incursion on local autonomy. The proposed reform, however, would merely turn back the regulatory clock, for a tenth of the town, to the era prior to the advent of zoning. Then a developer was free to site an apartment house in any location, unless a covenant barred it. Moreover, in most suburbs, demand for dense multifamily structures is minimal. In most towns, few developers in fact would build them. Households of modest income deserve this reform.

Numerous other stiffer state preemptions come readily to mind. To expedite the development of missing middle housing, for example, the preemptive statute could require a locality to allow these uses in an additional 20 percent of its total land area. To enable development of

57. Suggestions to free up the supply of multifamily housing include Boudreaux, "Infill" (2018) (advocating a state statute requiring localities to expand their multifamily districts, perhaps with a requirement that an apartment builder compensate nearby homeowners (id. at 654–55)); Gottlieb, "Minimum Zoning Mandates" (2019) (proposing a state mandate that a locality allow, as of right, row-houses and small apartment buildings virtually everywhere); Hills, "Saving *Mount Laurel*" (2013): 1629 (urging a state to require each locality to permit the same percentage of multifamily units that is present in the state's housing stock).

single-family houses on lots no greater than 8,000 square feet, the legislation could mandate that a locality allow these on yet an additional 30 percent, subject to the state agency's public health regulations. A strong reform package also might limit developers' use of covenants. In a development greater than one square mile in area, for example, the legislature could limit to half the covenanted area any covenant requiring a house-lot greater than 10,000 square feet.

State certification and the need to deter bad faith. The legislature should empower the agency periodically to decide whether a locality's zoning policies satisfy the state mandates. The Oregon LCDC has similar enforcement powers. The Oregon legislature has authorized the LCDC to "acknowledge" a local policy, but also to decline to do so.[58]

Some localities are likely to comply with both statutory and agency directives in good faith. Others may be tempted to flout them. To deter misconduct, the reform statute *must* include penalties for bad-faith noncompliance. A locality acting in bad faith has a huge toolkit. To thwart residential density, it might require, for example, fifty-foot side yards, four on-site parking spaces per dwelling unit, mandatory solar heating, or an endless series of public hearings. A recalcitrant suburb might be tempted to evade even the mild form of state preemption presented above. The mild alternative would require a locality to permit, in its non-single-family zones, as many units as it permits in its single-family zones. A bad-faith suburb could nominally comply with that requirement by rezoning a single block for infinite density. Or it could authorize duplexes in half its currently developed single-family neighborhoods, where demand for duplexes might be infinitesimal.

Examples abound of localities responding in bad faith to state efforts to curb exclusionary policies. The Township of Mount Laurel, whose policies prompted two famous New Jersey Supreme Court opinions on exclusionary zoning, dragged out its response to the court's decisions for more than twenty years.[59] Orange, Connecticut, after losing a lawsuit brought under the Connecticut Appeals Act, sought to use its eminent

58. Or. Rev. Stat. §§ 197.015(1), 197.251 (2019); Sullivan, "Oregon Planning Program" (2012): 370–71.

59. See text accompanying note 109 in this chapter.

domain powers to take the site where a developer had proposed erecting multifamily housing.[60]

State legislators bent on zoning reform therefore must anticipate local evasion and take steps to deter those actions. A legislature could start by instructing the state anti-exclusion agency to refuse to certify the policies of a locality acting in bad faith. In addition, however, the agency would have to apply sanctions to violators. Homevoters tend to respond to fiscal risks. After an agency finding of local bad faith—a finding reviewable in court—the legislature could authorize the agency to recover from the offending locality both attorney fees and a large monetary sum. More boldly, the legislature could authorize a court, in the event of local bad faith, to award those amounts to a self-nominated "private attorney general."[61] A precedent in Westchester County, New York, suggests the potency of this potential sanction.[62] In that instance, the eventual settlement required the defendant county to pay the plaintiff $2.5 million in attorney fees and a $7.5 million share of the damage award.[63] By authorizing private-attorney-general enforcement, the state legislature also would help thwart efforts by local governments to capture the state anti-exclusion agency.

Rulemaking and adjudication. A standard agency function is rulemaking to flesh out attainment of the legislature's objectives. Another is adjudication. An example, in this context, of adjudication would be the agency's periodic decisions about whether localities' policies had complied with both the preemptive statute and agency rules. I propose below that state legislators consider authorizing landowners on a specific blockfront to opt out of local land use regulations.[64] If landowners were to opt out, they then would be subject to controls that the state agency had crafted. To implement that proposal, the state anti-exclusion agency likely would have to engage in both rulemaking and adjudication.

60. See chapter 4.
61. See generally Rubenstein, "Private Attorney General" (2004).
62. United States ex rel. Antidiscrimination Center of Metro New York, Inc. v. Westchester County, 2009 WL 1108517 (S.D. N.Y. 2009). In that case, the plaintiff had successfully invoked the federal False Claims Act.
63. Relman Colfax, "Anti-Discrimination Center" (undated).
64. See text accompanying notes 86–88.

Using Wealth Currently Forgone to Spur Zoning Reform

The prevalence of exclusionary policies poses a deep puzzle. Although many economists have found that these policies inflict massive losses, entrepreneurs and politicians have seldom been able to broker deals to reduce the waste.

Consider again the Palo Alto neighborhood of Professorville.[65] It lies within easy walking distance of both downtown Palo Alto and a CalTrain station. Palo Alto currently permits in Professorville only a single-family detached house on a 10,000-sq.-ft. lot. As in other Palo Alto neighborhoods of single-family houses, this zoning designation is essentially frozen. Rezoning parts of Professorville to permit, as of right, sixteen residential units per acre in mid-rise buildings would attract the interest of numerous multifamily developers. If zoning were to be relaxed in this fashion, some bidders likely would offer to buy a Professorville house for, say, triple the value it commands under current zoning.[66] Silicon Valley is hardly short on entrepreneurs. Why has none of them been able to persuade Palo Alto to unlock the value now forgone in Professorville?[67]

In the 1940s, the English began to use the word *betterment* to describe the increase in land value that would accompany the loosening of land use regulations.[68] Some of the most creative land use scholars—among them Chris Elmendorf, Rick Hills, and David Schleicher—have considered how zoning reformers might use forgone betterment to help build a political coalition that would rezone the Professorvilles of this world for higher residential density.[69]

65. See chapter 7.
66. The Arlington, Virginia, homeowners near the Courthouse Station were able to sell for three times market value. See chapter 6. Housing demand is far more fervent in Palo Alto than in Arlington.
67. Political ideologies and psychological dispositions also influence the popularity of local land use policies. See chapter 7. The stickiness of Professorville's current single-family zoning further demonstrates the strength of local preferences for maintaining the status quo.
68. In England, the Uthwatt Report, "Compensation and Betterment" (1942) helped popularize the notion of betterment.
69. Several of Hills and Schleicher's joint works have offered insights into the dynamics of zoning politics. See, e.g., Hills and Schleicher, "Balancing 'Zoning Budget'" (2011) (emphasizing tendency of local governments to make zoning

In Professorville, the three most plausible candidates to enjoy a share of the betterment would be (1) the City of Palo Alto itself; (2) neighbors, that is, the owners of Professorville lots that Palo Alto would continue to zone only for single-family use; and (3) the owners of Professorville lots that Palo Alto would rezone to allow denser development.[70] I treat these possibilities in turn.

Zoning normally is not for sale.[71] In a creative analysis, Elmendorf and Darien Shanske nonetheless propose that a city that rezones for higher density should be entitled to reap a major fraction of the betterment. They urge enactment of a state statute that would enable local governments to sell to developers, at auction, rights to build denser structures.[72] Indeed, São Paolo has gone down this path, raising almost $2.8 billion in this fashion.[73] Elmendorf and Shanske contend that many localities in fact are already selling zoning, although they are doing so through procedures far more administratively wasteful.[74] The prospect of greater municipal revenue likely would pique the interest of many Palo Alto politicians and interest groups, perhaps enough to persuade them not to succumb to Professorville NIMBYs. Elmendorf and Shanske observe that their proposal also would encourage localities to streamline their land use procedures in order to pocket greater revenue.[75] The two authors propose that an auction winner have the right to transfer, within a multi-block territory, the development rights it had purchased.[76] Some transferability may be necessary to reduce public perceptions of insider dealing.[77] Elmendorf and Shanske's proposal, while inventive, is complex. Were it

decisions seriatim, not citywide, an approach that empowers NIMBY neighbors); Hills and Schleicher, "Transferable Development Rights" (2020).

70. Furth, "Development Dividends" (2019), proposes that neighborhood tenants also share in the forgone betterment.

71. See Mun. Art Soc'y v. City of New York, 522 N.Y.S.2d 800, 803–04 (N.Y. Sup. Ct. 1987).

72. Elmendorf and Shanske, "Auctioning the Upzone" (2020). The authors also would require that a state agency approve the auction. Id. at 533, 536–42.

73. Sandroni, "Value Capture in São Paulo" (2010).

74. Elmendorf and Shanske, "Auctioning the Upzone" (2020): 522–32.

75. Id. at 536.

76. Id. at 559–60.

77. If a sale of zoning was site-specific, it would be an ad hoc bargain between

to be in effect, the authors recognize that a locality might be tempted to zone more strictly in order to induce higher bids at auction.[78] They therefore recommend that the legislature establish a baseline of development entitlements that a locality has to honor.[79] The reform of zoning seldom is simple.

Other reform options are available. Suppose Palo Alto were to upzone a single block of Professorville but retain single-family zoning for the rest of the neighborhood. In that event, David Schleicher has proposed that the city transfer a large fraction of the forgone betterment to the Professorville homeowners who had not been upzoned.[80] Palo Alto, for example, could voluntarily rebate portions of their property taxes. This sort of system of financial rewards, Schleicher surmises, would foster more neighborhood support for rezonings to permit multifamily housing and potentially sow division in NIMBY ranks.[81] Although Schleicher's insight is penetrating, some details of his proposal are debatable.[82] He recognizes that there are other, perhaps simpler, options for lessening NIMBYs' concerns about the coming of nearby apartments.[83] If the densification of a single block of Professorville would lower home values nearby, for example, a California statute could entitle a homeowner to collect from the developer damages equal to the drop in market value.

---

two monopolists, the landowner and the zoning government. Perceptions of corruption might abound.

78. Id. at 539 (marshaling examples of abuses by São Paolo and Culver City, California).

79. Id. at 533.

80. Schleicher, "City Unplanning" (2013): 1725–32.

81. See also Fischel, "Comment on Elmendorf" (2019): 45 (recommending that Homevoters be entitled to a share of the betterment).

82. Schleicher calls his system Tax Increment Local Transfers (TILTs). He provides an example where the city would grant property tax reductions to owners of land within a "community board district." Schleicher, "City Unplanning" (2013): 1726–27. In Manhattan, these districts average two square miles in area. Because residential densification typically inflicts far more localized costs, inducements targeted at a smaller area might be more effective. Schleicher also recognizes that an owner of land in a commercial or industrial zone is not likely to act as a NIMBY and thus is not a plausible candidate for property tax relief. Id. at 1728 n. 210.

83. Id. at 1728–31.

The third basic option is to leave some or all of the betterment with the owners of the Professorville lots rezoned for greater density. The opening of the Metro Courthouse Station in Arlington, Virginia, mobilized homeowners near the station to support the upzoning of their neighborhood.[84] In that rare instance, a rezoning loosened the straitjacket that encases most American single-family neighborhoods. Some Professorville homeowners, by analogy, might turn out to be members of pro-density sleeper cells. A rezoning that would triple the market value of their houses might eventually persuade some of them to support the upzoning. For a full century, however, the City of Palo Alto has almost never upzoned any of its existing single-family neighborhoods for greater density.[85]

The State of California, as part of its preemptive efforts, could aid the pro-density sleeper cell. The state could entitle the owners of a majority, or supermajority, of the land on a particular blockfront in a neighborhood such as Professorville to vote to opt out of all local land use regulation.[86] After a favorable blockfront vote, power to control land uses on that blockfront would pass from Palo Alto to the state anti-exclusion agency. A vote favoring the opt-out thus would not eliminate public regulatory measures but instead substitute state controls for local controls. The opt-out option would encourage entrepreneurs to assemble either lots or assents to opt out from lot owners along particular blockfronts. Following an affirmative vote to opt out, the state agency would convene a public hearing at which both skeptical neighbors and those opting out could express their views. The dense residential development of a blockfront that had opted out of local control might well reduce the value of properties nearby. A state legislature therefore might consider making a densifying developer civilly liable for losses inflicted.[87] A state also could adopt Donald Shoup's idea of "graduated density zoning." This would

84. See chapter 6.

85. Id.

86. Cf. Myers and Hendrix, "Make Zoning Hyperlocal" (2021). Lots on a blockfront are those that face a street on both sides. The state anti-exclusion agency would have to issue rules governing the mechanics of blockfront voting.

87. Cf. Boudreaux, "Infill" (2018): 654–55. A damage award might include a bonus payment that increased with the length of the claimant's ownership of a home. Ellickson, "Alternatives to Zoning" (1973): 731 n. 224.

compel a local government to allow an owner who had assembled several lots into a larger parcel to develop that parcel more densely.[88] This reform would transform local zoning practices everywhere, particularly in Greater New Haven, where many spacious parcels already exist.

All the reforms just discussed would attempt to deploy betterment now left on the table to transform zoning outcomes. The efficiency and fairness of the various approaches vary. If the states reforming zoning practices were to go down different paths, they indeed would serve as laboratories. That was Justice Brandeis's hope.

Assembling a Political Coalition to Support State Zoning Reform

The difficulty of mobilizing political support for the reform of exclusionary practices varies from state to state. Part of the pro-reform base would be the numerous firms and individuals, from real estate brokers to moving companies, that would profit from increased residential construction. Most real estate developers probably would be part of the coalition, but perhaps not those with special political connections to zoning officials. In a state where exclusionary zoning has been rife, employers, both large and small, often worry about the burdens of housing costs on employees. Reform proponents could fan those flames. Housing consumers, the principal beneficiaries of zoning reform, typically are difficult to organize. YIMBY activists, if that movement proves able to sustain itself, are obvious candidates to join the pro-reform movement. Housing producers are unlikely to succeed politically without conspicuous help from housing consumers.

In many states, a successful campaign for zoning reform would have to win support from three key groups: construction unions, environmentalists, and civil rights organizations. Leaders of the construction trades standardly aspire to assure that employers pay prevailing wages at a project site. That policy is hardly conducive to the reduction of housing costs.[89] To keep construction unions on board, however, zoning reform proponents might have to compromise on that front. Ideological concerns,

88. See Shoup, "Graduated Density Zoning" (2008).

89. Kessler and Katz, "Prevailing Wage Laws" (2001).

not pocketbook concerns, tend to motivate members of environmental groups. Many resist most proposed housing developments, regardless of location. A thoughtful environmentalist should recognize, however, that current zoning practices promote sprawl and auto-dependence, and they worsen the nation's carbon footprint. Those realities might persuade some environmental activists to join a reform coalition. Members of civil rights groups also might find themselves conflicted. Zoning reform promises to reduce housing costs and to open more city and suburban neighborhoods to access by members of racial minority groups. Incumbent elected officials who are members of a minority group, however, might worry that zoning reform would diffuse their electoral base.

When a state legislature debates zoning reform, proponents should hammer at the costs, to both the national economy and regional housing consumers, of unbridled local discretion. Opponents predictably will invoke principles of subsidiarity and home rule. Given the intensity of status quo bias in local politics, few mayors are likely to support establishment of a state agency to review local land use policies. State and federal politicians, however, are less likely to vote to keep things as they are.[90]

In many regulatory contexts, there is a risk that one or more interest groups will capture the regulating agency. One set of candidates, in this context, are professional housers. They would profit if the state anti-exclusion agency were to require an exclusionary suburb to build the wasteful projects in which they specialize.[91] Developers of market-rate housing also might benefit from agency capture. If the agency, for example, was to promulgate a cost-justified rule governing the design of decentralized package plants, unscrupulous developers might seek to further relax that rule. By far the greatest danger, however, is that local officials would succeed in capturing the state anti-exclusion agency. Freedom from state control is a principle that unites localists. In Oregon, the LCDC thus far has staved off local capture. As mentioned, to reduce the risk of any form of capture, the state legislature could authorize a self-appointed private attorney general to enforce its preemptive statute.

90. See chapter 7.
91. See chapter 10.

The Role of State Courts

Federal judges commonly duck cases that pose exclusionary zoning issues. State judges, by contrast, understandably recognize that they have a somewhat more prominent role to play. Between 1965 and 1985, several state supreme courts, California's and Connecticut's conspicuously not among them, struck down exclusionary practices on a variety of grounds.[92] As nearly all law students learn, the New Jersey Supreme Court was the most activist of these state courts, perhaps because the tenure of its members is unusually secure.[93] The New Jersey Supreme Court rendered a slew of pertinent decisions, the most conspicuous involving a township in southern New Jersey. In *Mount Laurel I* in 1975 and *Mount Laurel II* in 1983, two unanimous decisions, the court held that the Township of Mount Laurel's zoning ordinance had overly limited the housing options of low- and moderate-income housing consumers.[94] In a bow to federalism, the court based both decisions not on the U.S. Constitution, but on a broad provision of the state constitution. The court held that the New Jersey constitution required that a local zoning measure promote the "general welfare" of the state, and it found that Mount Laurel's ordinance had not done so.[95] This state constitutional grounding constrained the options of the New Jersey legislature. In 1985, it enacted a statute that the New Jersey Supreme Court quickly found passed state

92. Ellickson et al., *Land Use Controls* (2021): 691–92 (describing judicial decisions in Pennsylvania—a state with several prominent anti-exclusion decisions—New Hampshire, and New York).

93. Span, "How Courts Should Fight" (2001): 70–71 (indicating that New Jersey reviews appointed judges only after seven years on the bench, and traditionally has reappointed them).

94. Southern Burlington County NAACP v. Township of Mount Laurel, 336 A.2d 713 (N.J. 1975), *appeal dismissed & cert. denied,* 423 U.S. 808 (1975) [hereinafter *Mount Laurel I*]; *Mount Laurel II,* 456 A.2d 390 (N.J. 1983).

95. *Mount Laurel I,* 336 A.2d 713, 724–25 (N.J. 1975). Cf. Sutton, *Who Decides?* (2022) (urging development of state constitutional law); Linde, "States' Bills of Rights" (1980) (contending that a state supreme court should review the constitutionality of a statute under the state constitution prior to applying the federal constitution).

constitutional muster.[96] To date, the consequences of the court's *Mount Laurel* decisions have been modest.[97]

Mount Laurel Township, as it happens, is less exclusionary than about a third of the suburbs in Silicon Valley, Greater New Haven, and Greater Austin. The *Mount Laurel I* opinion itself mentioned that the township was fast-growing, partly because it had approved several relatively dense PUD developments. The township's median household income is middling for a New Jersey suburb near Philadelphia. In 2016, two immediate neighbors, Moorestown Township and Medford Township, had median incomes at least 25 percent higher than Mount Laurel Township's.

The *Mount Laurel* decisions have spawned several books and countless commentaries.[98] In my view, the New Jersey Supreme Court's performances were mixed. My assessment owes much to the work of others, especially Rick Hills and Henry Span.[99] There were some genuine positives. New Jersey legislators had been reluctant to confront the difficult issue of exclusionary zoning, a practice in the narrow interest of many suburbanites.[100] As Richard Babcock and Fred Bosselman correctly have observed, "In the current political posture, neither the communities nor the state legislatures will undertake this disquieting job [of reforming exclusionary practices] unless the courts compel them to do so." In effect, the New Jersey Supreme Court's decisions teed up the issue, thereby starting a potentially productive dialogue between the court and the state legislature.[101] Even commentators who stress limits on the legitimacy and

96. Hills Dev't Co. v. Township of Bernards, 510 A. 2d 621 (N.J. 1986).

97. Marantz and Zheng, "Limits of Judicial Impact" (2018); Mitchell, "Increase Suburban Housing Choice?" (2004); Wish and Eisdorfer, "Impact of *Mount Laurel*" (1997); but see Haar, *Suburbs Under Siege* (1996): 129–33.

98. In addition to Haar, *Suburbs Under Siege* (1996), discussions of the *Mount Laurel* decisions and their aftermath include Boudreaux, *Housing Bias* (2011): 103–15, and Kirp et al., *Our Town* (1995). Kirp et al. praise the decisions, but less effusively than Haar does.

99. Hills, "Saving *Mount Laurel*" (2013); Span, "How Courts Should Fight" (2001).

100. Babcock and Bosselman, "Apartment Boom" (1963): 1091.

101. Cf. Bickel, *Least Dangerous Branch* (1962); Calabresi, *Age of Statutes* (1982)

legal capacity of courts agree that the New Jersey Supreme Court had been right to press the issue, certainly in the early years.[102]

I also applaud the court for basing its decisions on a provision in the New Jersey constitution. Law professors in the United States pay great attention to the federal constitution but little to state constitutions. As Henry Span has sagely suggested, a state constitutional decision can provide political cover for a legislature confronting a difficult political issue, which exclusionary zoning unquestionably is.[103] In the *Mount Laurel* decisions, the New Jersey Supreme Court also properly refused even to cite a provision in the New Jersey constitution of 1947 that resoundingly endorses the principle of local home rule.[104] As Charles Haar first noted in 1953, when a local government's exclusionary zoning practices affect the interests of outsiders, state institutions have adequate reason to second-guess local policies.[105]

The New Jersey Supreme Court, however, made three serious errors, particularly in *Mount Laurel II.* First, it insisted on a set of housing policy reforms that would have been both wasteful and certain to arouse the ire of suburbanites. Between 1975 and 1983, the dates of the two *Mount Laurel* opinions, the court vacillated in its legal mandates, partly because four of the court's seven members changed between those years. Justice Frederick Hall, the author of *Mount Laurel I,* resigned from the court in 1975 just prior to the release of that opinion. A 1977 decision, *Oakwood at Madison,* helps clarify how *Mount Laurel II* eventually went off track.[106]

102. Span, "How Courts Should Fight" (2001): 86–104; Tarr and Harrison, "State Supreme Court Policymaking" (1984): 567.
103. Span, "How Courts Should Fight" (2001): 85.
104. N.J. Const., art. IV, § 7, ¶ 11 (Supp. 2019): "The provisions of this Constitution and of any law concerning municipal corporations formed for local government, or concerning counties, shall be liberally construed in their favor." In Vickers v. Gloucester Township, 181 A.2d 129 (N.J. 1962), the majority opinion cited this provision and held that its broad language justified the majority's refusal to strike down a ban on mobile home parks in industrial districts. But cf. id. at 142–43 (Hall, J. dissenting) (interpreting the provision as solely intended to overturn New Jersey's judicial tradition of narrowly construing the powers of municipalities).
105. Haar, "Zoning for Minimum Standards" (1953).
106. Oakwood at Madison, Inc. v. Madison Township, 371 A.2d 1192 (N.J. 1977).

In *Oakwood,* the New Jersey Supreme Court soundly had asserted that its objective was to prevent the erection of barriers to the building of "least-cost" housing.[107] That statement correctly identifies both the basic problem—the excessive regulation of housing production—and the best solution, the paring back of zoning restrictions on the production of market-rate housing.

The New Jersey court, however, soon abandoned its *Oakwood* analysis. In 1979, Governor Byrne appointed Chief Justice Robert Wilentz, who would author the 1983 *Mount Laurel II* decision. *Mount Laurel II* emphasized a different solution to the problem of housing affordability not deregulation, but production of project-based subsidized housing.[108] In 2000, the Township of Mount Laurel eventually did agree to allow the construction, on a cul-de-sac, of the first phase of the Ethel Lawrence Homes, a 100-unit rental project in which all units were subsidized.[109] The Black and Hispanic population of Mount Laurel Township increased from roughly 4 percent in 1970 to 15 percent in 2016. The Ethel Lawrence Homes project, counting all its phases, accounted for no more than 10 percent of the increase in the presence of Blacks and Hispanics in the township. The Lawrence townhouses, clustered in the center of their tract, are accessible solely by means of a single dead-end road. This "pod"

Partly because *Oakwood* failed to provide a credible remedy, many have viewed the decision as a retreat from *Mount Laurel I.* See, e.g., Haar, *Suburbs Under Siege* (1996): 33: Kirp et al., *Our Town* (1995): 89; Span, "How Courts Should Fight" (2001): 49–50. Indeed, the New Jersey Supreme Court did as well See *Mount Laurel II,* 456 A.2d 390, 438 (N.J. 1983) (" . . . in spite of our intentions, *Madison* has led to little but a sigh of relief from those who oppose *Mount Laurel*").

107. 371 A.2d 1206–8. The following year, Oregon's LCDC cited *Oakwood at Madison* and invoked the notion of "least-cost housing" in one of its most influential anti-exclusion decisions, Seaman v. City of Durham, 1 LCDC 283 (1978).

108. *Mount Laurel I,* 336 A.2d 713 (N.J. 1975), made a similar error. The opinion referred, anachronistically, to the moral duty of a suburb to establish a public housing authority. Id. at 734. By 1975, the year *Mount Laurel I* was decided, the federal government had largely switched away from public housing and toward either housing vouchers or private subsidized projects.

109. Massey et al., *Climbing Mount Laurel* (2013): 51–64. Most occupants of the development were households headed by single mothers. Id. at 62.

design tends to isolate residents, contrary to the integrationist intentions of many of the project's proponents.

New Jersey has continued to promote the production of subsidized projects.[110] The state supreme court's decision to choose the subsidized-project path, what Elmendorf calls the Northeastern Model, was a mistake. On many dimensions, housing vouchers, possibly even state-funded or locally funded housing vouchers, are far superior to project-based subsidies.[111] The court should have stuck to the goal that *Oakwood* had articulated: the elimination of zoning restrictions on the building of least-cost housing.[112] That approach would have been far cheaper for taxpayers, less stigmatizing and immobilizing for subsidy recipients, and less controversial in its method of integrating neighborhoods.

Second, the New Jersey Supreme Court failed to identify a legal remedy that would have induced the state's suburbs voluntarily to comply with its rulings. *Mount Laurel II* claimed that it was bringing some "steel" to its enforcement efforts.[113] Steel it proved not to be. Although the Township of Mount Laurel eventually did agree to permit construction of the Ethel Lawrence Homes, the township succeeded in delaying completion of that project until 2000. *Mount Laurel II* introduced the so-called builder's remedy, which may entitle a New Jersey builder proposing 20 percent subsidized units on a specific site to have an effective hammer against a suburb. That remedy, however, necessarily entails project-based housing subsidies, an inherently mediocre approach. The Supreme Court of New Jersey instead should have articulated a remedy that would have successfully deterred a suburb from overly restricting the production of least-cost housing. Authorization by the court of a self-nominated private attorney general to enforce violations of the court's mandates would have been a real showing of steel.[114] So would have been a ruling that a municipality, so long as it refused to allow sufficient least-cost housing, had to allow,

110. See, e.g., In re Declaratory Judgment Actions Filed by Various Municipalities, 152 A.3d 915 (N.J. 2017).
111. See chapter 10.
112. See Hills, "Saving *Mount Laurel*" (2013): 1631–32.
113. *Mount Laurel II*, 456 A.2d 390, 410 (N.J. 1983).
114. See text accompanying notes 61–63; Payne, "Lawyers, Judges" (1998): 1691, 1700–1702 (1998) (urging empowerment of public-interest groups as plaintiffs).

as of right, the construction, in a zone permitting residential uses, of *any* proposed residential use. Either of those remedies would have prompted quicker suburban compliance.

Third, *Mount Laurel II* mistakenly required the calculation of each suburb's fair share of regional housing need.[115] In the court's view, the New Jersey constitution did not permit "numberless" resolution of the problem of exclusionary zoning. This additional requirement spawned an outpouring of consultants' studies and lawsuits, paperwork of little value. The state agency charged with making fair-share calculations eventually gave up on the task.[116] The court had a far simpler, but numberless, solution. It could have continued to embrace the *Oakwood* standard that each suburb had to permit ample least-cost housing and coupled that directive with a more effective sanction.

State courts have limited legitimacy and limited capacity.[117] State judges can only deal with the cases that attorneys bring to them. Partly because their staffs are small, they are far less able than an administrative agency to gather data and engage in rulemaking and systematic adjudication. In *Mount Laurel II,* the New Jersey Supreme Court held that the general welfare clause of the state constitution implied that a developer who had provided subsidies for 20 percent of a project's units warranted a builder's remedy.[118] That judicial holding was pure invention, and it cast doubt on the legitimacy of the court's entire decision. In many contexts, a legislature can generate numbers more credibly than a court. Tax codes are full of numbers. It is significant that the New Jersey Supreme Court eventually deferred to the fair housing statute enacted by the New Jersey legislature.[119] It also is significant that no other state supreme court has emulated the two *Mount Laurel* decisions.

115. *Mount Laurel II,* 456 A.2d 390, 436–42 (N.J. 1983). Hills, "Saving *Mount Laurel*" (2013): 1618–29, discusses this judicial misstep.

116. See In re Adoption of N.J.A.C. 5:96 and 5:97 ex rel. New Jersey Council on Affordable Housing, 110 A.3d 31, 34 (N.J. 2015) (asserting that the Council had not updated its fair share rules since 1999).

117. Tarr and Harrison, "State Supreme Court Policymaking" (1984): 526–56; see also Tarr and Porter, *State Supreme Courts* (1988).

118. *Mount Laurel II,* 456 A.2d 390, 452 n.37 (N.J. 1983).

119. Hills Dev't Co. v. Township of Bernards, 510 A. 2d 621 (N.J. 1986).

Perhaps as a result of the court's three central mistakes, many New Jersey politicians and voters eventually came to doubt the legitimacy of the *Mount Laurel* decisions. In a 1984 interview, New Jersey governor Thomas Kean, a political moderate, stated that *Mount Laurel II*'s effort to force economic mixing derived from a "communist concept."[120] Kean, who had won the governorship in a squeaker in 1981, won reelection in 1985 with 70 percent of the popular vote. In 1986, however, Kean nominated Robert Wilentz, author of *Mount Laurel II,* for a second term. The state senate approved the nomination narrowly, by a 21–19 vote.[121]

Nonetheless, despite the inherent limits on what they can accomplish, state judges unquestionably have a substantial role in the development of land use law. They routinely make rulings that involve zoning and local government powers. In deciding these cases, they should be alert to the risk that Charles Haar highlighted in the 1950s: a suburb's land use decision may negatively affect outsiders, particularly regional housing consumers. In ruling on, for example, the scope of a suburb's home-rule protections, a state judge should recognize that local governments are unlikely to be trustworthy guardians of regional interests. Similarly, in light of suburbs' inherent exclusionary tendencies, state courts should not invariably presume that local zoning and planning decisions are valid.[122]

Self-Reform by Local Governments

A local government that formerly embraced exclusionary policies conceivably could reform itself. Grand Rapids, Michigan, and Minneapolis, Minnesota, two central cities, have won headlines by abolishing, à la Oregon, the single-family zone.[123] Of the forty-one jurisdictions studied, only a handful have reformed their zoning practices. Two California cit-

120. Hanley, "Some Jersey Towns" (1984).

121. Stout, "Robert Wilentz" (1996).

122. See Elmendorf, "Beyond the Double Veto" (2019): 110–13 (criticizing laws and decisions, in California and other states, that presume validity of local actions).

123. Brey, "Zoning in Grand Rapids" (2018); Schuetz, "Minneapolis 2040" (2018b). Both Grand Rapids and Minneapolis require, however, that a new building respect the scale of nearby single-family structures.

ies, Redwood City and the City of San Jose, have significantly increased permitted residential densities, but they did so only in non-single-family neighborhoods.[124] Leander, Texas, reduced the required size of houselots in some single-family zones.[125] The City of Austin did consider CodeNEXT, a proposal that would have densified parts of the city, but it retreated in the face of neighborhood opposition.[126] The existence of a zoning straitjacket protecting single-family neighborhoods underscores scholars' claims that exclusionary suburbs are unlikely to undertake significant reform on their own.[127] At city hall, YIMBY lobbying efforts to support dense housing are most likely to succeed in a non-single-family neighborhood. At a state capital, however, where status quo bias is less pronounced, prospects for YIMBY lobbyists improve.[128]

Some local politicians, of course, do empathize with regional housing consumers. When establishing zoning procedures and voting on specific substantive proposals, these individuals have countless opportunities to honor these concerns. A decision that affects the structuring of a local government, for example, can powerfully influence a suburb's exclusionary tendencies. Several researchers have found that a shift from at-large elections to elections by district tends to prompt a city to issue fewer

124. See chapter 3.

125. See chapter 2, especially figure 2.

126. See chapter 6.

127. Babcock and Bosselman, "Apartment Boom" (1963): 1091 (emphasizing opposition to multifamily dwellings); Span, "How Courts Should Fight" (2001): 22–26.

128. I once exaggerated the possibility of local zoning reform. Ellickson, "Suburban Growth Controls" (1977): 409–10, 434. In those passages, I emphasized the risk that a homeowner cartel might succeed in capturing state lawmaking. That remains a genuine concern. CEQA, the environmental-impact statute California enacted in 1970, exemplifies the danger of a state providing a legal tool for slowing housing development in all localities. My 1977 article wrongly predicted, however, that pro-development interests would succeed, in most metropolitan areas, in controlling enough local governments to forestall damage to housing consumers. In 1977, I had in mind the likes of Emeryville, California, a pro-development locality just southwest of Berkeley. My analysis underestimated both the impact of statutes such as CEQA and the strength of localities' incentives to engage in exclusionary zoning. Schleicher, "City Unplanning" (2013): 1693, rightly took my analysis to task.

housing permits, especially for multifamily housing.[129] In 1975, a New York City charter revision created fifty-nine "Community Boards" in subareas of the city. Although these boards nominally possess only "advisory" powers, in practice their creation likely has crimped housing production.[130] These examples illustrate how local opponents of exclusion, commonly handicapped by a paucity of allies, must be vigilant.

The Institutions of Civil Society

Various foundations and nonprofits have supported studies of, and challenges to, exclusionary zoning. In 1962, three foundations helped finance the Regional Plan Association's *Spread City,* a sterling depiction of zoning practices in Greater New York.[131] Between 1969 and 1975, lawyers had great hope, soon dashed, that the courts would find a federal constitutional basis for limiting exclusionary practices. During that period, as many as eleven foundations helped fund litigation efforts.[132] The Suburban Action Institute, which Paul Davidoff and Neil Gold founded in 1969, was a prominent recipient.[133] The reform efforts of this period largely went for naught. In many regions during ensuing years, exclusionary practices spread and housing prices spiraled upward. Decades later, two nonprofit think tanks helped fund a landmark 2006 study of zoning practices in Greater Boston.[134] Edward Glaeser and Jenny Schuetz, two preeminent analysts of exclusionary zoning, both were involved. In New Jersey, the Fair Share Housing Center continues to pursue enforcement

129. Hankinson and Magazinnik, "Effect of District Representation" (2019) (focusing on California); Mast, "Warding Off Development" (2020) (reporting similar results nationwide); see also Louthen, "Legislator Vetoes" (2020) (attacking aldermanic privilege on housing issues).

130. Schleicher, "City Unplanning" (2013): 1706–7, 1712; cf. Foster and Glick, "Integrative Lawyering" (2007): 2032–34 (describing community board's opposition to expansion of Columbia University campus in West Harlem).

131. Regional Plan Association, *Spread City* (1962). The Ford Foundation, the Rockefeller Brothers Fund, and the Taconic Foundation provided financial support. Harvard economist Raymond Vernon helped manage the endeavor.

132. Shields and Spector, "Movement for Social Change" (1972): 313.

133. Id. at 301–2.

134. Glaeser et al., "Eastern Massachusetts" (2006).

of the *Mount Laurel* decisions. To date, foundation support of the center has been modest.[135]

Two diffuse and opposing groups of activists warrant mention. NIMBYs typically self-organize spontaneously to oppose a particular development proposal. Status quo bias, fiscal concerns, and genuine environmental worries commonly fuel their passion, coupled by, in some instances, preferences for class and racial segregation. The geographic propinquity of the members of a NIMBY group reduces their costs of organizing and enhances their political power. In 2018, California NIMBYs created an umbrella organization, Livable California.[136] They have yet to organize nationally.

YIMBYs, a countervailing set of activists, emerged during the 2010s.[137] In 2020, the organization claimed several dozen local chapters in the United States.[138] The alliance convened its first national convention in 2016. YIMBYs are particularly prominent in California, where soaring prices have especially nettled housing consumers. Silicon Valley tech firms have provided the YIMBY movement some financial support.[139] The growth of the internet appears to have helped YIMBYs more than NIMBYs. YIMBYs tend to be younger and more technologically adept. Some NIMBYs have accused YIMBYs of being shills for developers, a widely hated group.[140] Whether the YIMBY movement will flower, or even endure, is far from certain.

A few bloggers have emerged as influential voices on exclusionary zoning practices. Jenny Schuetz, whom the Brookings Institution hired as a fellow in 2017, has become a prominent spokesperson on housing and land use issues.[141] Issi Romem has contributed an invaluable statistical study documenting the freezing of land uses in many American neighborhoods.[142] In the mass media, Conor Dougherty of the *New York Times*

135. Marek, "Fund for New Jersey" (2014).
136. Livable California (2020).
137. Stahl, "Yes in My Backyard" (2018).
138. YIMBY Action (2020).
139. Stahl, "Yes in My Backyard" (2018): 7.
140. See, e.g., Meronek, "YIMBYs Exposed" (2018).
141. Schuetz (2020).
142. Romem, "Dormant Suburban Interior" (2018).

has authored lucid articles depicting local constraints on housing production.[143] In 2020, Dougherty published *Golden Gates,* a well-received popular book on housing politics in the Bay Area.[144]

Scholars and think tanks also have contributed to zoning reform. Through the 1980s, much of the valuable commentary on exclusionary practices appeared in U.S. law journals. In recent decades, by contrast, economists have outperformed those trained in law. Among the standout economists have been Edward Glaeser and Joseph Gyourko.[145] Economist William Fischel's classic, *The Homevoter Hypothesis,* is the finest study of the politics of exclusion.[146]

Researchers in three other disciplines could contribute more to the understanding of exclusionary zoning. Political scientists traditionally have focused largely on national politics and neglected, in particular, local politics.[147] In the 2010s, valuable works by Katherine Einstein, Michael Hankinson, Eric Oliver, and others indicate that political scientists indeed have much to contribute on zoning questions. They would be particularly qualified to determine whether, as I hypothesize, politicians in different levels of government in fact vary in their inclinations to support NIMBYism.[148]

Sociologists have been the foremost analysts of racial segregation, which exclusionary zoning unquestionably tends to abet. Yet sociologists have done little to illuminate the social dynamics of NIMBYism on the one hand and YIMBYism on the other. I have yet to unearth a sociological field study of neighbors' reactions to a proposal to densify a particular neighborhood.[149] Sociologists could help identify, for example, the

143. See, e.g., Dougherty, "Anti-Growth Sentiment" (2016).
144. Dougherty, *Golden Gates* (2020), favorably reviewed in Mari, "Fight for Housing" (2020).
145. Among their co-authored works are Glaeser and Gyourko, "Zoning's Steep Price" (2002), *Rethinking Federal Housing Policy* (2008), and "Implications of Housing Supply" (2018).
146. Fischel, *Homevoter Hypothesis* (2001).
147. Berry and Howell, "Local Elections" (2007): 845 n.3.
148. See chapter 7.
149. The modest sociological literature on NIMBYism occasionally focuses on opposition to residential densification. See, e.g., Eranti, "Re-visiting NIMBY" (2017) (discussing proposed housing developments in Helsinki, Finland).

factors that helped enable homeowners near the new Metro station in Arlington, Virginia, to support the upzoning of their neighborhood.[150]

A third underperforming discipline has been psychology and, relatedly, behavioral economics. Chapter 7 asserts that neighbors, because of status quo bias, exaggerate the costs of neighborhood change and, conversely, undervalue the benefits of change. Psychologists could test the truth of these assertions. All else equal, would Manhattanites gauge the loss of a long-standing land use, such as the World Trade Center, as more grievous than the loss of a newer one, such as the Freedom Tower, the building that replaced the twin towers? Would the building of duplexes and triplexes in an Oregon neighborhood of single-family houses in fact traumatize nearby homeowners? Psychologists plainly have much to contribute to the understanding of zoning issues.

150. Clary and Rasmussen, "Buyout Phenomenon" (1985).

12

The Case for Greater Urban Density

This brief chapter argues that state governments should compel local governments to allow somewhat greater residential density. California, for example, should force Palo Alto to enable the densification of portions of Professorville, the single-family neighborhood near Palo Alto's downtown. The construction of more housing in Professorville, of course, would clash with other worthy goals, particularly, in that instance, historic preservation. As before, my basic normative yardstick is benefit-cost analysis.[1] I assume that the benefits of densifying parts of Professorville would exceed the accompanying costs.[2]

The case for densification assumes that adding people to a metropolis would benefit most of its current residents. Large metropolitan areas unquestionably are the workhorses of national economies. Productivity per capita rises by 15 percent worldwide when a metropolitan area doubles in headcount.[3] The densest U.S. metropolitan area, Greater New York City, is about twice as dense as the runner-up, Greater Los Angeles, which in turn is three times denser than Greater Atlanta.[4] The average densities of U.S. metros, however, are markedly lower than most abroad. Euro-

1. See chapter 9.
2. On the net benefits of density, see Downs, *New Visions for Metropolitan America* (1994): 142–61.
3. Bertaud, *Order Without Design* (2018): 145 (interpreting Bettencourt and West, "Unified Theory" [2010]).
4. Bertaud, "Smart Growth" (2003): 382–83.

pean metros are roughly four times more dense and Asian metros roughly eight times.[5]

An invisible hand does not assure the optimality of a metropolitan area's total population, nor its average population density, nor the slope of the density gradient from the area's center. Absent binding public land use regulations, households' decisions on where to reside and developers' decisions about where to build largely determine the extent of a metropolitan area's expansion. These private choices have pervasive spillover effects, both positive and negative. Each of the institutions that might respond to these externalities is imperfect.[6] In some contexts, private parties might be able to employ covenants, norms, and other nongovernmental mechanisms to internalize the externalities of urban growth.[7] These tools of private ordering, however, are nearly always ineffectual in their control of metropolitan form. The private decisions that influence a metropolitan area's size and density are simply too numerous, and their effects too complex. In the language of law and economics, transaction costs are too high. That the invisible hand faces shortcomings, of course, does not imply that a government would necessarily handle the problem more satisfactorily. A government well might worsen urban form. A suburb's exclusionary zoning practices, for example, can themselves generate new negative externalities, for example, by restricting the housing opportunities of nonresidents.

A half-century ago, urban specialists tended to emphasize the negative effects of metropolitan growth. George Tolley, a University of Chicago economist, stressed in a notable 1974 article the deleterious impact of residential densification on air quality and vehicular congestion.[8] Correctly recognizing that an invisible hand would not correct these diffuse externalities, Tolley concluded that big cities tend to be too big. Since 1974, levels of air pollution in most U.S. metros have improved markedly, thanks to environmental regulations.[9] Traffic congestion, however,

5. Id. at 382.
6. Komesar, *Imperfect Alternatives* (1996).
7. Ellickson, "Alternatives to Zoning" (1973).
8. Tolley, "City Bigness" (1974) (discussing optimal "city size," a phrase that conflates a metropolitan area's total population and the density of its settlement).
9. Kahn, "Cost of Urban Agglomeration" (2010): 347–49.

remains a salient concern for many urbanites.[10] In Professorville, opponents of a residential densification might sincerely ground their opposition on fears of negative effects on commuting times and parking options. Some problems that Tolley did not emphasize, such as crime, housing costs, and risks during a pandemic, also tend to increase with density.[11]

Tolley's emphasis on the net detrimental effects of metropolitan growth, however, is passé.[12] Beginning in the 1980s, many economists began stressing agglomeration efficiencies, a term capacious enough to encompass the positive effects of both an increase in a metropolitan area's total population and the density of its residential neighborhoods. Edward Glaeser, a preeminent urban economist, is one of the scholars most closely associated with the idea.[13] David Schleicher warrants credit for importing agglomeration theory into the legal literature.[14] Schleicher credits Alfred Marshall, a nineteenth-century economist, as the theory's earliest progenitor, and Glaeser, Paul Krugman, Robert Lucas, and David Romer as the principal economists who elaborated the theory.[15]

Agglomeration theorists identify three principal benefits of density.[16] Together, these potentially could outweigh the undoubted downsides of increased city bigness.[17] All three stem from the fact that closer physical

10. Bertaud, *Order Without Design* (2018): 143–218 (discussing mobility and congestion issues).
11. On crime, see Garnett, "Planning for Density" (2017): 17–22. As land becomes scarcer, the price of real estate tends to mount. On the spread of infectious disease, see Glaeser, "Cities and Pandemics" (2020a).
12. Also pertinent is the literature on Henry George Theorem, largely impenetrable to non-economists. See, e.g., Arnott, "Optimal City Size" (2004); Kanemoto et al., "Optimal City Sizes" (1996) (discussing whether Tokyo is too populous).
13. Glaeser, *Agglomeration and Spatial Equilibrium* (2008): 116–64. Another much-cited work is Duranton and Puga, "Urban Agglomeration Economies" (2004).
14. Schleicher, "City as Economic Subject" (2010).
15. Id. at 1509 n.9, 1516.
16. Id. at 1513–29 (providing a fuller discussion).
17. Density can bring other benefits. There may be economies of scale in the provision of urban infrastructure. See Bettencourt and West, "Unified Theory" (2010): 912. Because large metros tend to be rich, they also generate positive fiscal externalities when taxes are progressive. Albouy, "Burden of Federal Taxation" (2009).

proximity tends to lower transportation costs and thus increase chances of human interaction. First, urban density tends to reduce the costs both of transporting goods and of consumer access to services. In Detroit, manufacturers of auto parts traditionally clustered together. High density similarly increases ease of access to medical specialists, restaurants, and other service providers.[18] Second, higher density fosters specialization of capital assets and, more importantly, human capital. Major sports stadiums tend to cluster in metropolitan areas, as do teaching hospitals, high-powered law firms, and innovative technology companies. Third, greater density increases knowledge spillovers. Information-technology specialists seek to live in Silicon Valley because they anticipate learning from one another, both on and off the job. In addition, they may recognize that living in Silicon Valley would spark among them sharper competition for status.[19]

With rare exception, specialists in urban economics and related fields—the persons most knowledgeable about urban externalities of all sorts—currently are boosters of urban density. These specialists span a broad ideological spectrum and include, among many others, Vicki Been, William Fischel, Edward Glaeser, Paul Krugman, David Schleicher, and Jenny Schuetz.[20] Fischel and Glaeser indeed have explicitly urged greater densification of Silicon Valley.[21] There are, of course, dissenters, perhaps most notably Joel Kotkin, who contends that most Americans prefer less dense environments.[22] Kotkin should recognize, however, more frequently than

18. Schleicher, "City as Economic Subject" (2010): 1518, invokes the example of Detroit.
19. See Mitchell, "London Calling?" (2019) (finding that authors significantly enhanced their productivity by moving to London).
20. See, e.g., Been et al., "Overtaking the Growth Machine?" (2014) (supporting state overrides of local decisions that exclude locally unpopular uses); Fischel, "Rise of the Homevoters" (2017): 30 (favoring population growth in both the Boston-Washington corridor and larger West Coast cities); Glaeser, *Triumph of the City* (2011): 34 (asserting that Silicon Valley "is allowing too much space between its innovators"); Krugman, "Cities for Everyone" (2016); Schleicher, "City Unplanning" (2013): 1673–74; Schuetz, "Minneapolis 2040" (2018b) (lauding densification).
21. See note 20.
22. See, e.g., Kotkin, *Human City* (2017); Kotkin, "Densification Efforts" (2015).

he does, that zoning regulations substantially constrain what homebuilders can supply.[23]

All of the authors of the widely heralded economic critiques of zoning cited in chapter 1, such as Hsieh and Moretti, and Herkenhoff, Ohanian, and Prescott, are implicitly pro-density. These authors are economists and surely aware that zoning controls might successfully curb some negative externalities. Their uniform willingness to proclaim that the zoning system is harming the national economy implies that they regard the benefits of zoning to be minor.

A handful of urban economists, most notably David Albouy and Edward Glaeser and their co-authors, have published analyses that explicitly attempt to take into account *both* positive and negative externalities of densification. Each concludes that current zoning practices, on balance, are overly anti-density.[24] In addition, Gabriel Ahlfeldt and Elisabetta Pietrostefani have thoroughly reviewed the pertinent economic literature on urban form. They assert that most investigators conclude that increases in urban density, on balance, usually have positive welfare effects.[25]

The case for densification thus is potent. Uncertainties certainly remain, and debate rightly will continue. Benefit-cost analysis, my approach, surely is not a magic solvent.[26] It is notable, however, that most

23. Another apparent skeptic of density is J. B. Wogan, a former member of the staff of the periodical *Governing*. Wogan has focused on the consequences of metropolitan population growth, not increases in metropolitan density. In "Population Growth" (2017), he relies principally on a Brookings paper by Paul Gottlieb, an economist at Rutgers. Gottlieb found that a U.S. metro's rate of population growth in the 1990s was only weakly associated with increases in its residents' prosperity. Gottlieb hardly is a fan of restrictive land use regulations. See Gottlieb et al., "Local Housing Growth" (2012): 297 (confirming "the widespread belief that there is too much large-lot zoning in northwestern New Jersey relative to market demand").
24. Albouy and Ehrlich, "Cost of Land-Use Restrictions" (2018); Glaeser et al., "Manhattan So Expensive?" (2005) (asserting that, while land use regulations in Manhattan generate some benefits, their costs are greater). See also Cheshire and Sheppard, "Welfare Economics" (2002) (claiming that land use controls in Reading, England, on balance reduced local incomes by 3.9 percent).
25. Ahlfeldt and Pietrostefani, "Effects of Density" (2019).
26. See chapter 9.

urban economists now reject George Tolley's view that metropolitan densification brings net costs. Urban crowdedness is back in favor.

Since the early days of public land use regulation, the United States has let local governments assume leading roles. The most notable event occurred in 1922, when Herbert Hoover appointed a panel that recommended that states delegate broad zoning authority to local governments. Local officials certainly do have the best knowledge of both local preferences and the local landscape. Crucially, however, local officials lack incentives to use zoning in a regionally appropriate fashion. In 1947, Greenwich, Connecticut, homeowners wielded large-lot zoning to enrich themselves by preventing developers from erecting dwelling units that would compete with the ones they occupied.[27] Greenwich's policy boosts housing prices and lengthens commuting times for numerous commuters. It impairs the ability of Greater New York City to reap the many benefits of agglomeration. Large-lot zoning overtly fosters segregation by social class and likely aggravates racial segregation. In addition, status quo bias particularly afflicts local decision-making, increasing the power of NIMBYists.[28] In retrospect, the Hoover panel was wrong to give local government a blank check.

The principle of subsidiarity endorses the decentralization of a governmental function to the smallest government capable of handling it. Local zoning, if constrained, certainly can be beneficial, and a state legislature should not prohibit its use. When land use policies affect a region, however, Greenwich and the like are the wrong decision-makers. The Hoover panel erred in recommending that states grant suburbs virtually unfettered zoning powers. The State of Connecticut, not the Town of Greenwich, could better weigh the effects of zoning policies on the density gradient of Greater New York City. The history of Oregon's land use policies demonstrates that a state is far less likely than a locality to act in parochial fashion. States should correct Hoover's error. Leviathan can do mischief at city hall. Excessive home rule has damaged the nation.

27. See chapter 1.
28. See chapter 7.

Appendix

The Cornucopia of Big Data and Its Potential

Advances in information technology greatly facilitate the study of municipal zoning. This section publicizes possibilities that researchers might exploit.

In writing this book, I examined the zoning ordinances and zoning maps of forty-one scattered local governments. Twenty years ago, a would-be researcher likely would have recoiled from the task of gathering these documents. Today, it is simple. Virtually all municipalities make both documents available online. A suburb's planning department typically posts its zoning map. The providers of ordinances are more varied. A municipality commonly hires a private firm to post its entire code of ordinances.

Since the 1960s, electronic Geographical Information Systems (GIS) have revolutionized the field of geography. The leader of the industry, ESRI, a firm based in Redlands, California, has developed ArcGIS Desktop software, the most popular available option. ArcGIS Desktop enables a user to view various "layers" of geographic phenomena that specialists have developed and posted. The boundaries of a suburb's land use zones are a prime candidate for a layer.

Millions of Americans are familiar with GIS mapping technologies. Innocents should take the plunge. A particularly unintimidating GIS site is that of the blue-collar town of East Haven, Connecticut, findable at http://easthaven.mapxpress.net/portal.asp. Try it. First, click on the "interactive mapping" button. Then click on the + button to zoom in. Those actions will generate a detailed map of East Haven that shows both the boundaries of each lot and the footprint of each building. Click on a parcel of choice. Your most recent click will have generated, among other things, the name of the owner of the property chosen, the zoning of that parcel, and various photos of the premises. An additional click or two would reveal the parcel's property tax assessment and the book and page numbers in the town's land records where the most recent deed transferring the property has been recorded.[1] Next, click on "Map Layers" in the upper right of the screen and select "zoning." These actions will reproduce the town's full zoning map. A suburb's other GIS layers might show, for example, the location of its utility poles and water mains.

The present study required, for each suburb, calculation of the acreage placed in various residential zones. ArcGIS Desktop can greatly ease these sorts of calculations. Not all suburbs have prepared zoning layers, but more and more are doing so. A researcher can download a zoning layer, if available, into an ArcGIS map and then use "queries" to isolate the parcels placed in a particular zone. A tool in the ArcGIS Desktop "attribute table" utility can automatically sum the acreages of the subset of parcels chosen. Voila! Note also that East Haven's basic GIS map includes an "area measure" tool that might assist alternative methods of calculating acreage in a specific zone.

Facility with ArcGIS Desktop takes practice. The good news is that the library staffs of major U.S. universities now include specialists capable of training professors and students in the use of these systems. Some legal scholars have been aware of GIS, but most seem oblivious to its advent and potential.[2] As of 2019, Harvard's and Yale's flagship law journals, for example, had yet to publish an article that referred to ArcGIS, ESRI, or, indeed, GIS itself.

Technical Issues Involved in Various Calculations

The book presents summary information derived from a boatload of raw data on zoning practices of suburbs in three particular metros. To

1. Less information is available in California, where a privacy statute has deterred state and local agencies from posting information about owners online. See Cal. Gov't Code § 6254.21 (2019) (restricting agencies from posting home addresses of government officials without their permission).
2. Exceptions include Ng et al., "Using GIS in Research" (2016); Salkin, "Mega-Pixels" (2010–2011): 18–20.

simplify data gathering and enable the preparation of the tables in chapter 2, I used various rules of thumb. This section identifies what they were.

Chapter 2 focuses primarily on minimum lot-size requirements in residential subdivisions and constraints on the building of multifamily housing. Zoning regulations control many other aspects of development, for example, the permitted height of a building, its setback from a lot-line, and the parking spaces required. Unless noted, these ancillary controls were ignored.

I started gathering data, largely from online sources, in 2015. The New Haven suburbs were examined first. For them, I relied heavily on a 2010 "build-out" study that the South Central Regional Council of Governments had commissioned from consultants Milone & MacBroom, Inc.[3] Chris Rappa of SCRCOG generously made available the pertinent databases. I gathered data for Austin's suburbs largely in 2016 and Silicon Valley's in 2017. The date of the present study thus is a bit of a blur. The picture provided is roughly accurate for, to nominate a specific year, 2016.

For each suburb, I used the most recent zoning map it had posted online to calculate the acreages in each of its zones. Some suburbs, particularly small ones, are slow to update their zoning maps. Portola Valley, California, the worst offender of those studied, was posting in 2020 a zoning map dated 2007. The published texts of suburbs' zoning ordinances usually are more up-to-date. Portola Valley, for example, publishes updated ordinances almost every year. The calculations relied on the most recent zoning map and on the most recent ordinance text, sources that commonly bear different dates. In a few instances, to resolve ambiguities, I partly divined a suburb's land use policies from other documents, most commonly, a formally approved general or specific plan. A zone that appears in a locality's zoning ordinance may not appear on its map. For simplicity, I treated a suburb's published zoning map as conclusive evidence of what it permits.

The calculation of the acreage in a particular zone at times entailed complications. Many suburbs entitle developers to cluster housing units on smaller lots.[4] This possibility, which ordinarily fails to increase the gross density of development, was ignored. Also ignored were most

3. Milone & MacBroom, Inc., *Regional Build-Out Analysis* (2010).

4. See chapter 2.

overlay zones, unless massive in area, such as Woodbridge, Connecticut's "public watershed" overlay that increases to two acres the required minimum lot size for more than half the town. I also declined to tally potential accessary dwelling units, projects that might mildly densify a single-family neighborhood.[5] Because I regarded the zoning map as definitive, I ignored nonconforming uses and uses allowed by variance. Also ignored was the possibility that a locality might allow by special permit a residential use in a nonresidential zone.

These simplifications potentially distort the impacts of zoning policies. Chapter 2 mentions, for example, possible distortions in Orange, Connecticut, and Round Rock, Texas. On balance, however, partly because some of the potential distortions offset, the zoning metrics offered here are in many ways superior to prominent alternatives.

Central to the study was calculation of the acreage that a municipality's zoning map places in a given residential zone. In a municipality with a downloadable zoning layer, the ArcGIS program permits ready calculations of those figures. A majority of localities, however, have yet to publish a zoning layer. For these laggards, I used one of two alternative systems. A municipality may publish a .pdf version of its zoning map that enables use of the Adobe area-measurement tool. If so, the area of a zone can be measured, in square inches, on the map itself. With modest ingenuity, a researcher then can convert those square inches into acres. The more burdensome approach involved use of Google Earth. A particular residential zone can be replicated on a Google Earth map, and its area can be measured through use of the Google Earth measuring tool.

Rights-of-way for local streets commonly make up from 10 percent to 30 percent of a suburb's total area. On most zoning maps and zoning layers, zone acreages include rights-of-way as well as lots. My reported results also include rights-of-way in the zone totals. The databases of fifteen of the thirty-seven municipalities, however, excluded street rights-of-way from their zone-area totals. To improve the quality of interjurisdictional comparisons, I adjusted the zone areas of each of the fifteen upward, using a multiplier of 1.1, 1.2, or 1.3, applying the higher multipliers to the denser municipalities. Excluded from zone area totals in all metros were

5. See chapter 11.

the areas of lakes greater than five acres, state parks, and rights-of-way of limited-access highways.

A major purpose of the study was determination of how commonly suburbs zone to permit multifamily development. That phrase is ambiguous. As chapter 2 states, I deemed a zone to permit multifamily construction only if the zone permitted *both* a residential density of *at least eight dwelling units per gross acre* and multifamily use *as of right*. *As of right*, in this context, means that

- even though the locality requires a developer to apply for a special permit, the title of the zone in the zoning ordinance includes a word such as *multifamily, apartments, townhouses, condominiums, elderly housing, affordable,* or *mobile home*; or
- the locality insists only on site-plan review, and land uses in the zone are not explicitly limited to single-family detached housing, duplexes, and triplexes; or
- the name of the zone is *planned unit development* (PUD) or *planned development* (PD), and extrinsic sources provide a means for measuring the zone's potential for multifamily development.

This definition enabled me to divide a suburb's residential zones into three categories: those permitting multifamily development ≥8 units per acre (including sets of four or more adjacent townhouses); those allowing only single-family detached houses; and those permitting uses in between, such as duplexes and triplexes. This last category is roughly equivalent to what has come to be known as the "missing middle."[6]

Some suburbs in all three metros have PUD (or PD) zones, a deal-making approach invented in the 1960s.[7] These arrangements greatly complicate assessment of the impact of zoning. A locality that employs the PUD approach permits a developer who controls a largish tract to propose a mix of land uses, perhaps including multifamily buildings and commercial uses. After bargaining, the locality signs off on the deal. The PUD technique tends to be pro-development. The popularity of PUDs therefore has been declining in exclusionary communities such as Palo Alto and most New Haven suburbs.[8]

6. Parolek, *Missing Middle Housing* (2020).
7. See chapter 4.
8. See, e.g., Sheyner, "'Planned Community' Projects" (2014) (describing Palo Alto's suspension of PUDs).

Fast-growing Round Rock, Texas, has placed 30 percent of its residentially zoned land in PUD zones, the most of any suburb studied. Leander, Texas, with 25 percent, ranked second. In Silicon Valley, Mountain View and the City of Santa Clara were the most notable users of PUDs, each placing about one-sixth of their residential acreage in these zones. No New Haven suburb, by contrast, uses PUDs for more than 3 percent of its land area. A PUD designation requires a researcher to dig deeper. For example, Round Rock's online records revealed that the city had authorized some residential development in fifty of its PUDs, occasionally including apartments and townhouses. After examining Round Rock's public records regarding these PUDs and viewing them in Google Earth, I tallied 93 percent of Round Rock's PUD acreage as single-family and 7 percent as multifamily.

A small but telling part of chapter 2 addresses the ownership and zoning of undeveloped land parcels between 20 and 40 acres in area. To locate parcels of that size, I used the parcel layers that California and Texas counties post, and, in Connecticut, I drew on the SCRCOG "build-out" report.[9] Simple ArcGIS queries enabled the pinpointing of parcels of the specified size. Tax assessors' records revealed the names of owners.

The most complex zoning ordinances encountered—with "complex" not intended as a compliment—were those of San Mateo County, California, and the City of Austin. The most unconventional—meant neither as a compliment nor a condemnation—were those of Leander, Texas, which has adopted what it calls "composite" zoning, and Hamden, Connecticut, which has embraced transect zoning.[10]

Prior Empirical Studies of Zoning Practices

Many others have sought to plumb local zoning practices. This section briefly describes some of the most noteworthy ventures.[11]

Two previous undertakings most closely resemble the current one. In 2021, Sara Galvin, then a professor at the University of Connecticut School of Law, published, in cooperation with the Regional Plan Associa-

9. Milone & MacBroom, Inc., *Regional Build-Out Analysis* (2010).

10. See Garnett, "Redeeming Transect Zoning?" (2013).

11. See also Rothwell, "Housing Costs" (2012): 7–8 (summarizing zoning metrics that various researchers have employed).

tion, the invaluable *Connecticut Zoning Atlas*. This source maps zoning practices throughout the state of Connecticut. A user can apply various filters to reveal, for example, variations in lot-size requirements and zones that permit multifamily housing.

The other notable study examined zoning practices in Greater Boston.[12] It bears the fingerprints of Edward Glaeser, a preeminent zoning scholar. Amy Dain of the Pioneer Institute and Jenny Schuetz, then a doctoral student, supervised a large team of researchers. They assembled, beginning in 2004, a database far larger than mine. It included more localities—a total of 187 cities and towns—and covered a wider variety of land use regulations, such as wetland controls. The authors of the Boston study used regression analyses to weigh the importance of the variables affecting the probability of a locality's embrace of various exclusionary techniques. The Boston study did not compare, however, zoning practices across different metropolitan areas.

The Boston study generated a number of articles, of which the most cited is Glaeser and Ward.[13] At times, that pair of authors used methods that differ from mine. Glaeser and Ward focused on a locality's average minimum lot-size requirement for a single-family house.[14] Although an average can be revealing, it ignores variations that some of my metrics take into account. For example, housing in a suburb that required one-acre lots everywhere likely would be more expensive than housing in a suburb that insisted on two-acre house-lots in some parts of town but allowed 5,000-sq.-ft. lots in many other areas.

Two empirical studies of zoning practices have been nationwide in scope.[15] The best known and most influential has been the Wharton Residential Land Use Regulatory Index. In 2008, the Wharton team published a summary of local officials' responses to a questionnaire, and, in 2019, a

12. Glaeser et al., "Eastern Massachusetts" (2006). See also Massachusetts Municipalities, Housing Regulation Database (2005), reproducing some of the data collected.
13. Glaeser and Ward, "Evidence from Greater Boston" (2009). Jenny Schuetz also used the database for two articles on the exclusion of multifamily housing. Schuetz, "Multifamily Housing" (2008) and "Rental Housing" (2009).
14. Glaeser and Ward, "Evidence from Greater Boston" (2009): 268–69.
15. An ampler summary of these national studies appears in O'Neill et al., "California's Housing Policy Debates" (2019): 20–25.

reconstituted team began working to update the Index using responses to a more recent questionnaire.[16] While the Wharton indexes are a major achievement, their creators no doubt would concede some shortcomings, in particular the low local response rates to both questionnaires.[17]

The other nationwide survey, undertaken in 2003 by a Brookings Institution team, canvassed the land use policies of 1,800 local governments in the fifty most populous metropolitan areas.[18] Although the Brookings study included a number of probing questions, it shed little light on the acreages that municipalities place in their various residential zones.

In 1992, Glickfeld and Levine studied the number of regulatory instruments used by localities in California, the state with the nation's highest housing prices.[19] This helped stimulate a California-specific study by John Quigley and his co-authors.[20] Recent California investigations include ones by Kristoffer Jackson and Mawhorter and Reid.[21] Furth and Gonzalez have built on the latter.[22] In the Bay Area, Moira O'Neill et al. have examined how cities have processed projects with five or more dwelling units.[23]

Also notable are studies of zoning changes, including ones by Vicki Been, Josiah Madar, and Simon McDonnell in New York City, C. J. Gabbe in Los Angeles, and Andrew Whittemore in both Durham, North Carolina, and Los Angeles.[24] Alexander von Hoffman has described in detail the zoning histories of two Boston suburbs.[25]

16. Gyourko et al., "Wharton Index" (2008); Gyourko et al., "New Wharton Index" (2019).
17. See chapter 2.
18. Pendall et al., "Land Use Regulations" (2006).
19. Glickfeld and Levine, *Local Growth Control* (1992).
20. Quigley et al., "Measuring Land Use Regulations" (2009).
21. Jackson, "Land Constraints" (2018); Mawhorter and Reid, "Housing Policies Across California" (2018).
22. Furth and Gonzalez, "California Zoning" (2019).
23. O'Neill et al., "California's Housing Policy Debates" (2019). O'Neill et al. review various California-specific studies at 25–27.
24. Been et al., "Overtaking the Growth Machine?" (2014); Gabbe, "Why Are Regulations Changed?" (2018); Whittemore, "Zoning Los Angeles" (2012b); Whittemore, "Racial Bias" (2018). See also Munneke, "Zoning Change" (2005).
25. Von Hoffman, "Wrestling with Growth in Acton, Massachusetts" (2010b); "Land Use Regulations in Weston, Massachusetts" (2010a). Weston is the wealthiest municipality in Massachusetts.

Bibliography

Acs, Gregory, et al. 2017. "The Cost of Segregation: National Trends and the Case of Chicago, 1990–2010." Urban Institute, Mar. 29.

Adams, Thomas. 1934. *The Design of Residential Areas: Basic Considerations, Principles, and Methods.* Harvard University Press, a volume in Harvard City Planning Studies.

Adler, Matthew D., and Eric Posner. 2006. *New Foundations of Cost-Benefit Analysis.* Harvard University Press.

Agatstein, Jessie. 2015. "The Suburbs' Fair Share." 44 *Real Est. L.J.* 219.

Ahlfeldt, Gabriel M., and Elisabetta Pietrostefani. 2019. "The Economic Effects of Density: A Synthesis." 111 *J. Urb. Econ.* 93.

Albouy, David. 2009. "The Unequal Geographic Burden of Federal Taxation." 117 *J. Pol. Econ.* 635.

Albouy, David, and Gabriel Ehrlich. 2018. "Housing Productivity and the Social Cost of Land-Use Restrictions." 107 *J. Urb. Econ.* 101.

ALR Annotation. 2000. "Change in character of neighborhood as affecting validity or enforceability of restrictive covenant." 76 ALR 5th 337.

Altshuler, Alan A., Arnold M. Howitt, and José A. Gómez-Ibáñez. 1993. *Regulation for Revenue: The Political Economy of Land Use Exactions.* Brookings Institution Press.

American Law Institute. 2000. *Restatement (Third) of Property: Servitudes.*

American Society of Planning Officials. 1967. "New Directions in Connecticut Planning Legislation." Feb.

Apicella, Coren L., et al. 2014. "Evolutionary Origins of the Endowment Effect: Evidence from Hunter-Gatherers." 104 *Am. Econ. Rev.* 1793.

Arnold, Craig Anthony. 1998. "Planning Milagros." 76 *Denv. U. L. Rev.* 1.

Arnott, Richard. 2004. "Does the Henry George Theorem Provide a Practical Guide to Optimal City Size?" 63 *Am. J. Econ. & Soc.* 1057.

Atherton, California, Zoning Map. 2011. Available at www.ci.atherton.ca.us/DocumentCenter/View/286/Zoning24x36_001?bidId.

Ayres, Ian. 2000. "Disclosure Versus Anonymity in Campaign Finance." In 42 *Nomos: Designing Democratic Institutions* 19. NYU Press.

Babcock, Richard F., and Fred P. Bosselman. 1963. "Suburban Zoning and the Apartment Boom." 111 *U. Pa. L. Rev.* 1040.

Badger, Emily, and Quoctrung Bui. 2019. "Cities Start to Question an American Ideal: A House with a Yard on Every Lot." *N.Y. Times,* June 18.

Badger, Emily, Kevin Quealy, and Josh Katz. 2021. "A Close-Up Picture of Partisan Segregation, Among 180 Million Voters." *N.Y. Times,* Mar. 17.

Baker, Lynn A., Clayton P. Gillette, and David Schleicher. 2015. *Local Government Law: Cases and Materials.* 5th ed. Foundation Press.

Baker, Lynn A., and Daniel B. Rodriguez. 2009. "Constitutional Home Rule and Judicial Scrutiny." 86 *Denver U. L. Rev.* 1337.

Balcones Canyonlands Preserve. Undated. Available at www.austintexas.gov/bcp.

Baldassare, Mark, and Georjeanna Wilson. 1996. "Changing Sources of Suburban Support for Local Growth Controls." 33 *Urb. Stud.* 459.

Barth, Brian. 2019. "The Double-Edged Sword of Preemption." *Planning* 17, Nov.

Barton, Stephen E., and Carol J. Silverman, eds. 1994. *Common Interest Communities: Private Governments and the Public Interest.* Institute of Governmental Studies Press, Berkeley, California.

Bassett, Edward M. 1922. "Zoning." National Municipal League. Supplement, 317.

Bates, Laurie J., and Rexford E. Santerre. 2001. "The Public Demand for Open Space: The Case of Connecticut Communities." 50 *J. Urb. Econ.* 97.

Bayer, Patrick, Hanming Fang, and Robert McMillan. 2014. "Separate When Equal? Racial Inequality and Residential Segregation." 82 *J. Urb. Econ.* 32.

Beach, Patrick. 2018. "Saddling the Colorado." *Austin American-Statesman.* Sept. 25.

Been, Vicki, Ingrid Gould Ellen, and Katherine O'Regan. 2019. "Supply Skepticism: Housing Supply and Affordability." 29(1) *Housing Pol'y Debate* 25.

Been, Vicki, Josiah Madar, and Simon McDonnell. 2014. "Urban Land-Use Regulation: Are Homevoters Overtaking the Growth Machine?" 11 *J. Empirical Legal Stud.* 227.

Béland, Daniel, and Robert Henry Cox, eds. 2011. *Ideas and Politics in Social Science Research.* Oxford University Press.

Bell, Abraham, and Gideon Parchomovsky. 2002. "Pliability Rules." 101 *Mich. L. Rev.* 1.

Bergin, Thomas F. 1972. "Price Exclusionary Zoning: A Social Analysis." 47 *St. Johns L. Rev.* 1.

Bergman, Peter, Raj Chetty, et al. 2021. "Creating Moves to Opportunity: Experimental Evidence on Barriers to Neighborhood Choice." Working paper. Mar.

Berry, Christopher. 2001. "Land Use Regulation and Residential Segregation: Does Zoning Matter?" 3 *Am. L. & Econ. Rev.* 251.

Berry, Christopher R., and William G. Howell. 2007. "Accountability and Local Elections: Rethinking Retrospective Voting." 69 *J. Pol.* 844.

Bertaud, Alain. 2018. *Order Without Design: How Markets Shape Cities.* MIT Press.

———. 2003. "Clearing the Air in Atlanta: Transit and Smart Growth or Conventional Economics?" 54 *J. Urb. Econ.* 379.

Berube, Alan, and Cecile Murray. 2018. "America's Older Industrial Cities Are Key to an Inclusive Economy." Brookings Institution. Available at www.brookings.edu/research/older-industrial-cities/#09009.

Bettencourt, Luis, and Geoffrey West. 2010. "A Unified Theory of Urban Living." 467 *Nature* 912.

Bickel, Alexander M. 1962. *The Least Dangerous Branch: The Supreme Court at the Bar of Politics.* Yale University Press.

Biden, Joe. 2020. "The Biden Plan for Investing in Our Communities Through Housing." Available at https://joebiden.com/housing/.

Bird, Amy. 1985. "Stanford Faces Demand for Affordable Housing." *Stanford Daily*, Apr. 19.

Bishop, Bill. 2008. *The Big Sort: Why the Clustering of Like-Minded America Is Tearing Us Apart.* Mariner Books.

Bitters, Janice. 2020. "Controversial Vallco Project Can Continue Under SB 35, Judge Rules." *San Jose Spotlight,* May 6.

Blakely, Edward J., and Mary Gail Snyder. 1997. *Fortress America: Gated Communities in the United States.* Brookings Institution Press.

Blumgart, Jake. 2019. "Minneapolis Evicts Single-Family Zoning." *Planning* 12 Mar.

Bogart, William T. 1993. "'What Big Teeth You Have!': Identifying the Motivations for Exclusionary Zoning." 30 *Urb. Stud.* 1669.

Boggs, Erin, and Lisa Dabrowski. 2017. "Out of Balance: Subsidized Housing, Segregation, and Opportunity in Connecticut." Sept. Available at https://d33euwcbjqojuo.cloudfront.net/documents/Out_Of_Balance_Report_-_Final-rev_1.pdf.

Bonica, Adam, Adam Chilton, and Maya Sen. 2016. "The Political Ideologies of American Lawyers." 8 *J. Legal Analysis* 277.

Bosselman, Fred P. 1992. "The Commodification of 'Nature's Metropolis': The Historical Context of Illinois' Unique Zoning Standards." 12 *N. Ill. U. L. Rev.* 527.

Boudreaux, Paul. 2018. "Infill: New Housing for Twenty-First-Century America." 45 *Fordham Urb. L.J.* 595.

———. 2016. "Lotting Large: The Phenomenon of Minimum Lot Size Laws." 68 *Me. L. Rev.* 1.

———. 2011. *The Housing Bias: Rethinking Land Use Laws for a Diverse America.* Palgrave MacMillan.

Brady, Maureen E. 2021. "Turning Neighbors into Nuisances." 134 *Harv. L. Rev.* 1609.

Branford Land Trust Timeline. Undated. Available at http://branfordlandtrust.org/wp-cont3nt/uploads/2014/01/OpenSpace-Timeline.pdf.

Brey, Jared. 2018. "A Decade Without Single-Family Residential Zoning in Grand Rapids." Next City blog. Dec. 26.

Briffault, Richard. 1990. "Our Localism: Part I—The Structure of Local Government Law." 90 *Colum. L. Rev.* 1.

Brinig, Margaret F., and Nicole Stelle Garnett. 2013. "A Room of One's Own? Accessory Dwelling Unit Reforms and Local Parochialism." 45 *Urb. Law.* 519.

Britschgi, Christian. 2019. "Virginia Bill Would End Single-Family-Only Zoning in the Old Dominion." Reason blog. Dec. 31.

Bronin, Sara C. 2019. "Comprehensive Rezonings." 2019 *BYU L. Rev.* 725.

Brooks, Andree. 1982. "Town Reversing Stand on Condos." *N.Y. Times,* June 20.

Brooks, Leah, and Byron Lutz. 2016. "From Today's City to Tomorrow's City: An Empirical Investigation of Urban Land Assembly." 8 *Amer. Econ. J.: Econ. Pol'y* 69.

Brooks, Richard R. W., and Carol M. Rose. 2013. *Saving the Neighborhood: Racially Restrictive Covenants, Law, and Social Norms.* Harvard University Press.

Bumgardner, David, and Keyavash Hemyari. 2017. "Dodging Mud Slingers: An Analysis and Defense of Texas Municipal Utility Districts." 21 *Tex. Rev. L. & Pol.* 377.

Burke, Mary A., and Tim R. Sass. 2013. "Classroom Peer Effects and Student Achievement." 31 *J. Labor Econ.* 51.

Bussemaker, Nathalie. 2019. "Up Close: Picking up the Pieces of Connecticut's Economy." *Yale Daily News,* Apr. 11.

Calabrese, Stephen, Dennis Epple, and Richard Romano. 2007. "On the Political Economy of Zoning." 91 *J. Pub. Econ.* 25.

Calabresi, Guido. 1982. *A Common Law for an Age of Statutes.* Harvard University Press.

California ADU. 2020. Available at adu.california.org.

Camacho, Alejandro E., and Nicholas Marantz. 2020. "Beyond Preemption, Toward Metropolitan Governance." 39 *Stan. Envt'l L.J.* 125.

Campanella, Thomas J. 2018. "Long Before Levittown, Brooklyn Boasted Mass-Produced Housing." CityLab blog. Jan. 4.

Cappel, Andrew J. 1991. "Note, A Walk Along Willow: Patterns of Land Use Coordination in Pre-Zoning New Haven (1870–1926)." 101 *Yale L.J.* 617.

Card, David, and Jesse Rothstein. 2007. "Racial Segregation and the Black-White Test Score Gap." 91 *J. Pub. Econ.* 2158.

Carroll, Robert D. 2001. "Note, Connecticut Retrenches: A Proposal to Save the Affordable Housing Appeals Procedure." 110 *Yale L.J.* 1247.

Celebration, Florida. 2020. Available at https://en.wikipedia.org/wiki/Celebration,_Florida.

Chambers, Marcia. 2006. "The Boss of Branford." *Branford Eagle,* Oct 6.

Charles, Eleanor. 2001. "Apartment Developer with the Law in Its Toolbox." *N.Y. Times,* July 22.

Cheshire, Paul, and Stephen Sheppard. 2002. "The Welfare Economics of Land Use Planning." 52 *J. Urb. Econ.* 242.

Chetty, Raj, et al. 2019. "Race and Economic Opportunity in the United States: An Intergenerational Perspective." 135 *Q. J. Econ.* 711.

Chetty, Raj, Nathaniel Hendren, and Lawrence F. Katz. 2016. "The Effects of Exposure to Better Neighborhoods on Children: New Evidence from the Moving to Opportunity Experiment." 106 *Am. Econ. Rev.* 855.

Cheung, Ron. 2008. "The Interaction Between Public and Private Governments: An Empirical Analysis." 63 *J. Urb. Econ.* 885.

Cheung, Ron, and Rachel Meltzer. 2013. "Homeowners Associations and the Demand for Local Land Use Regulation." 53 *J. Reg. Sci.* 511.

Cho, Wendy K. Tam, James G. Gimpel, and Iris S. Hui. 2019. "Migration as an Opportunity to Register Changing Partisan Loyalty in the United States." 25 *Population, Place & Space* 1.

Clark, Charles E. 1941. "Limiting Land Restrictions." 27 *Am. Bar Ass'n J.* 737.

Clarke, Wyatt, and Matthew Freedman. 2019. "The Rise and Effects of Homeowners Associations." 112 *J. Urb. Econ.* 1.

Clary, Thomas A., and Paul W. Rasmussen. 1985. "The Buyout Phenomenon." *Planning* 18. Oct.

Cleveland Annexation Map. Undated. Available at https://upload.wikimedia.org/wikipedia/commons/9/93/Cleveland_Annexation_Map_4-Color_Final.png.

Clingermayer, James. 1993. "Distributive Politics, Ward Representation, and the Spread of Zoning." 77 *Pub. Choice* 725.

Clowney, Stephen. 2005. "Note, A Walk Along Willard: A Revised Look at Land Use Coordination in Pre-Zoning New Haven." 115 *Yale L.J.* 116.

Coase, R. H. 1960. "The Problem of Social Costs." 3 *J. L. & Econ.* 1.

Collinson, Robert, and Peter Ganong. 2018. "How Do Changes in Housing Voucher Design Affect Rent and Neighborhood Quality?" 10(2) *Am. Econ. J.: Econ. Pol'y* 62.

Committee on Urban Housing. 1969. *A Decent Home*. Government Printing Office.

Community Association Institute. 2018. "Community Association Factbook." Available at https://foundation.caionline.org/publications/factbook/.

Congressional Budget Office. 2015. "Federal Housing Assistance for Low-Income Households." Available at www.cbo.gov/sites/default/files/114th-congress-2015–2016/reports/50782-lowincomehousing.pdf.

Connecticut Commission on Fiscal Stability and Economic Growth. 2018. Draft of final report. Mar. Available at www.cga.ct.gov/fin/tfs/20171205_Commission%20on%20Fiscal%20Stability%20and%20Economic%20Growth/20180301/Draft%20Report.pdf.

Connecticut Conference of Municipalities (2020). Available at www.ccm-ct.org/convention.

Connecticut Department of Economic and Community Development. 2020. Housing & Income Data. Available at https://portal.ct.gov/DECD/Content/About_DECD/Research-and-Publications/01_Access-Research/Exports-and-Housing-and-Income-Data.

Connecticut Land Conservation Council (2018). Available at www.ctconservation.org/land-trusts-by-town.

Connecticut Rental Assistance Program. 2020. Available at https://portal.ct.gov/DOH/DOH/Programs/Rental-Assistance-Program.

Connecticut State Parks History. 2016. Available at https://portal.ct.gov/DEEP/State-Parks/History/State-Parks-History.

Connecticut Zoning Atlas. 2021. Available at www.desegregatect.org/atlas.

Cook, Stephen F. 1982. "Redwood City: High Housing Prices and No Growth." 4 *Stan. Envt'l L. Ann.* 68.

Cortright, Joe. 2018. "The Persistence of Residential Segregation." CityCommentary blog. May 6. Available at https://cityobservatory.org/the-persistence-of-residential-segregation/.

Council of Governments. 2020. Available at https://en.wikipedia.org/wiki/Council_of_governments.

Couture, Victor, and Jessie Handbury. 2020. "Urban Revival in America." 119 *J. Urb. Econ.* 103267.

Cox, Wendell. 2018. "California's Dense Suburbs and Urbanization." New Geography blog. Mar. 14. Available at www.newgeography.com/content/005908-californias-dense-suburbs-and-urbanization.

Coyle, Stephen. 1982. "A Far Cry from *Euclid.*" 4 *Stan. Envt'l L. Ann.* 83.

Craswell, Richard. 1998. "Incommensurability, Welfare Economics, and the Law." 146 *U. Pa. L. Rev.* 1419.

Cutler, David M., and Edward L. Glaeser. 1997. "Are Ghettos Good or Bad?" 112 *Q. J. Econ.* 827.

Cutler, Kim-Mai. 2015. "East of Palo Alto's Eden: Race and the Formation of Silicon Valley." TechCrunch blog. Jan. 10. Available at https://techcrunch.com/2015/01/10/east-of-palo-altos-eden/.

Dahl, Robert. 1961. *Who Governs? Democracy and Power in an American City.* Yale University Press.

Dana, David A. 2009. "Exclusionary Eminent Domain." 17 *Sup. Ct. Econ. Rev.* 7.

Davidoff, Paul, and Linda Davidoff. 1971. "Opening the Suburbs: Toward Inclusionary Land Use Controls." 22 *Syracuse L. Rev.* 509.

Davis, Gregg C. 1982. "Portola Valley: A Tale of Two Subdivisions." 4 *Stan. Envt'l L. Ann.* 40.

Dericks, Gerard H., and Hans R.A. Koster. 2018. "The Billion Pound Drop: The Blitz and Agglomeration Economics in London." CEP Discussion Paper No. 1542. Apr.

"Developments in the Law—Zoning." 1978. 91 *Harv. L. Rev.* 1427.

Devine-Wright, Patrick. 2009. "Rethinking NIMBYism: The Role of Place Attachment and Place Identity in Explaining Place-Protective Action." 19 *J. Community & Applied Soc. Psychol.* 426.

Diamond, Rebecca, and Tim McQuade. 2019. "Who Wants Affordable Housing in Their Backyard? An Equilibrium Analysis of Low-Income Property Development." 127 *J. Pol. Econ.* 1063.

Dilger, Robert Jay. 1992. *Neighborhood Politics: Residential Community Associations in American Governance.* NYU Press.

DiMento, Joseph, et al. 1980. "Land Development and Environmental Control in the California Supreme Court: The Deferential, the Preservationist, and the Preservationist-Erratic Eras." 27 *UCLA L. Rev.* 859.

DiPasquale, Denise, Dennis Fricke, and Daniel Garcia-Diaz. 2003. "Comparing the Costs of Federal Housing Assistance Programs." 9 *Econ. Pol'y Rev.* 147.

Diversity and Disparities. Undated. Available at https://s4.ad.brown.edu/projects/diversity/segregation2010/Default.aspx?msa=41940.

Dnes, Antony, and Dean Lueck. 2009. "Asymmetric Information and the Law of Servitudes Governing Land." 38 *J. Legal Stud.* 89.

D'Onfro, Jillian. 2018. "Google Has Huge Plans for Its Home City." CNBC. Dec. 9. Available at www.cnbc.com/2018/12/09/google-reveals-north-bayshore-mountain-view-development-plan.html.

Doremus, Holly. 2003. "Takings and Transitions." 19 *J. Land Use & Envt'l L.* 1.

Dougherty, Conor. 2020. *Golden Gates: Fighting for Housing in America.* Penguin Press.

———. 2016. "How Anti-Growth Sentiment, Reflected in Zoning Laws, Thwarts Equality." *N.Y. Times,* July 3.

Downs, Anthony. 1994. *New Visions for Metropolitan America.* Brookings Institution and Lincoln Institute for Land Policy.

———. 1973. *Opening Up the Suburbs: An Urban Strategy for America.* Yale University Press.

Dubin, Jon C. 1993. "From Junkyards to Gentrification: Explicating a Right to Protective Zoning in Low-Income Communities of Color." 77 *Minn. L. Rev.* 739.

Duranton, Gilles, and Diego Puga. 2019. "Urban Growth and Its Aggregate Implications." NBER Working Paper #26591. Dec.

———. 2004. "Micro-Foundations of Urban Agglomeration Economies." In *Handbook of Regional and Urban Economics,* vol. 4, 2063. Elsevier.

Ebersold, Thomas. 2016. "Seaside Avenue Affordable Housing Plan Denied." *Milford Mirror,* Apr. 6. Available at www.milfordmirror.com/58144/seaside-avenue-affordable-housing-plan-denied/.

Echeverria, John D., and Thekla Hansen-Young. 2009. "The Track Record on Takings Legislation: Lessons from Democracy's Laboratories." 28 *Stan. Envt'l L.J.* 439.

Einstein, Katherine Levine, David M. Glick, and Maxwell Palmer. 2019. *Neighborhood Defenders: Participatory Politics and America's Housing Crisis.* Cambridge University Press.

Ellen, Ingrid Gould. 2020. "What Do We Know About Housing Choice Vouchers?" 80 *Reg. Sci. & Urb. Econ.* #103380.

Ellen, Ingrid Gould, Michael C. Lens, and Katherine O'Regan. 2011. "Memphis Murder Revisited: Do Housing Vouchers Cause Crime?" Feb. Available at www.huduser.gov/publications/pdf/ellen_memphismurder_assistedhousingrcr07_v2.pdf.

Ellen, Ingrid Gould, and Brian J. McCabe. 2017. "Balancing the Costs and Benefits of Historic Preservation." In *Evidence and Innovation in Housing Law and Policy* 87. Lee Anne Fennell and Benjamin J. Keys, eds. Cambridge University Press.

Ellen, Ingrid Gould, Katherine O'Regan, and Ioan Voicu. 2009. "Siting, Spillovers, and Segregation: A Reexamination of the Low-Income Housing Tax Credit Program." In *Housing Markets and the Economy: Risk, Regulation, and Policy* 233. Edward L. Glaeser and John M. Quigley, eds. Lincoln Institute of Land Policy.

Ellickson, Robert C. 2022. "Stale Real Estate Covenants." 63 *Wm. & Mary L. Rev.* 1831.

———. 2021a. "Zoning and the Cost of Housing: Evidence from Silicon Valley, Greater New Haven, and Greater Austin." 42 *Cardozo L. Rev.* 1611.

———. 2021b. "The Zoning Straitjacket: The Freezing of American Neighborhoods of Single-Family Houses." 96 *Ind. L.J.* 395.

———. 2020. "Ancient Rome: Legal Foundations of the Growth of an Indispensable City." In *Roman Law and Economics,* vol. 2, 159. Giuseppe Dari-Mattiacci and Dennis P. Kehoe, eds. Oxford University Press.

———. 2010. "The False Promise of the Mixed-Income Housing Project." 57 *UCLA L. Rev.* 983.

———. 2006. "The Puzzle of the Optimal Social Composition of Neighborhoods." In *The Tiebout Model at Fifty: Essays in Public Economics in Honor of Wallace Oates* 199. William A. Fischel, ed.

———. 1993. "Property in Land." 102 *Yale L.J.* 1315.

———. 1982a. "Cities and Homeowners Associations." 130 *U. Pa. L. Rev.* 1519.

———. 1982b. "The Effect of Growth Controls on Housing Prices on the San Francisco Peninsula." 1982 *Stan. Envt'l L. Ann.* 3.

———. 1981. "The Irony of Inclusionary Zoning." 54 *S. Cal. L. Rev.* 1167.

———. 1977. "Suburban Growth Controls: An Economic and Legal Analysis." 86 *Yale L.J.* 385.

———. 1973. "Alternatives to Zoning: Covenants, Nuisance Rules, and Fines as Land Use Controls." 40 *U. Chi. L. Rev.* 681.

Ellickson, Robert C., and Vicki L. Been. 2005. *Land Use Controls,* 3rd ed. Wolters Kluwer, Aspen Casebook Series.

Ellickson, Robert C., Vicki Been, Roderick M. Hills, Jr., and Christopher Serkin. 2021. *Land Use Controls,* 5th ed. Wolters Kluwer, Aspen Casebook Series.

Elliott, Rebecca, and Rob Copeland. 2021. "Tesla to Move Headquarters from California to Texas, Elon Musk Says." *Wall St. J.*, Oct. 7.

Elmendorf, Christopher S. 2019. "Beyond the Double Veto: Land Use Plans as Preemptive Intergovernmental Contracts." 71 *Hastings L.J.* 79.

Elmendorf, Christopher S., Eric Biber, Paavo Monkkonen, and Moira O'Neill. 2020. "Making It Work: Legal Foundations for Administrative Reform of California's Housing Framework." 46 *Ecology L. Q.* 973.

Elmendorf, Christopher S., and Darien Shanske. 2020. "Auctioning the Upzone." 70 *Case W. Res. L. Rev.* 513.

Emporis, Palo Alto. 2020. Available at www.emporis.com/statistics/tallest-buildings/city/101892/palo-alto-ca-usa.

Epstein, Richard A. 2018. "Positive and Negative Externalities in Real Estate Development." 102 *Minn. L. Rev.* 1493.

———. 1988. "Covenants and Constitutions." 73 *Cornell L. Rev.* 906.

———. 1982. "Notice and Freedom of Contract in the Law of Servitudes." 55 *S. Cal. L. Rev.* 1353.

Eranti, Veikko. 2017. "Re-visiting NIMBY: From Conflicting Interests to Conflicting Valuations." 65 *Soc. Rev.* 285.

Eriksen, Michael D. 2009. "The Market Price of Low-Income Housing Tax Credits." 66 *J. Urb. Econ.* 141.

Eriksen, Michael D., and Bree J. Lang. 2020. "Overview and Proposed Reforms of the Low-Income Housing Tax Credit Program." 80 *Reg. Sci. & Urb. Econ.* #103379.

Eriksen, Michael D., and Anthony W. Orlando. 2020. "Returns to Scale in Residential Construction: The Marginal Impact of Building Height on Affordability." Working paper.

Eriksen, Michael D., and Amanda Ross. 2015. "Housing Vouchers and the Price of Rental Housing." 7 *Am. Econ. J.: Econ. Pol'y* 154.

Euclid Village Zoning Map. 1922. Available at http://codesproject.asu.edu/sites/default/files/1922%20Zoning%20Map_0.jpg.

Evenson, Bengte, and William C. Wheaton. 2003. "Local Variation in Land Use Regulations." Brookings-Wharton Papers on Urban Affairs 221.

Faturechi, Robert. 2016. "The Fire Sprinkler War, State by State." ProPublica blog. June 22.

Federal Housing Administration. 1947. *Underwriting Manual.* Jan. Government Printing Office.

———. 1938. *Underwriting Manual.* Feb. Government Printing Office.

Feeley, Malcolm M., and Edward Rubin. 2008. *Federalism: Political Identity and Tragic Compromise.* University of Michigan Press.

Fennell, Lee Anne. 2017. "Searching for Fair Housing." 97 *B.U. L. Rev.* 349.

———. 2006. "Properties of Concentration." 73 *U. Chi. L. Rev.* 1227.

———. 2004. "Contracting Communities." 2004 *U. Ill. L. Rev.* 829.

Fernandez, Ryan. 2020. "San Jose Finalizes Win-Win Plan for Winchester Ranch Mobile Home Park." *Silicon Valley Bus. J.* Jan. 17.

Field, Ben. 1993. "Why Our Fair Share Housing Laws Fail." 34 *Santa Clara L. Rev.* 35.

Fischel, William A. 2019. "Comment on Elmendorf." *Regulation*, 44. Summer

———. 2017. "The Rise of the Homevoters: How the Growth Machine Was Subverted by OPEC and Earth Day." In *Evidence and Innovation in Housing Law and Policy* 13. Lee Anne Fennell and Benjamin J. Keys, eds. Cambridge University Press.

———. 2015. *Zoning Rules! The Economics of Land Use Regulation.* Lincoln Institute of Land Policy.

———. 2001. *The Homevoter Hypothesis: How Home Values Influence Local Government Taxation, School Finance, and Land-Use Policies.* Harvard University Press.

———. 1999. "Does the American Way of Zoning Cause the Suburbs of U.S. Metropolitan Areas to Be Too Spread Out?" In *Governance and Opportunity in Metropolitan America* 151. Alan A. Altshuler, William K. Morrill, Harold Wolman, and Faith Mitchell, eds. National Academies Press.

———. 1985. *The Economics of Zoning Laws.* Johns Hopkins University Press.

Fischer, Claude S. 1982. *To Dwell Among Friends: Personal Networks in Town and City.* University of Chicago Press.

Fischer, Will. 2017. "Housing Vouchers Work: Efficiently Helping Families Afford Homes." Center on Budget and Policy Priorities blog. May 2. Available at www.cbpp.org/blog/housing-vouchers-work-efficiently-helping-families-afford-homes.

Florida, Richard. 2015. "America's Most Economically Segregated Cities." Bloomberg CityLab blog. Feb. 23.

Fogelson, Robert M. 2005. *Bourgeois Nightmares: Suburbia 1870–1930*. Yale University Press.

Foldvary, Fred. 1994. *Public Goods and Private Communities: The Market Provision of Social Services.* Edward Elgar.

40 Main Street Offices, LLC v. Los Altos. 2020. Available at www.coxcastle.com/Templates/media/files/Los-Altos.pdf.

Foster, Sheila R., and Brian Glick. 2007. "Integrative Lawyering: Navigating the Political Economy of Urban Redevelopment." 95 *Calif. L. Rev.* 1999.

Franzese, Paula A. 2002. "Does It Take a Village? Privatization, Patterns of Restrictiveness, and the Demise of Community." 47 *Vill. L. Rev.* 553.

Fraser, Charles E. 2000. "Condo Commandos: An Abuse of Power." In *Trends and Innovations in Master-Planned Communities* 46. Urban Land Institute.

Freeman, Lance, and Jenny Schuetz. 2017. "Producing Affordable Housing in Rising Markets: What Works?" 19 *Cityscape* 217.

Freemark, Yonah. 2020. "Upzoning Chicago: Impacts of a Zoning Reform on Property Values and Housing Construction." 56 *Urb. Aff. Rev.* 752.

French, Susan F. 1982. "Toward a Modern Law of Servitudes: Reweaving the Ancient Strands." 55 *S. Cal. L. Rev.* 1261.

Frey, William H. 2012. "Population Growth in Metro America Since 1980." Brookings Institution. Mar. Available at www.brookings.edu/wp-content/uploads/2016/06/0320_population_frey.pdf.

Frieden, Bernard J. 1979. *The Environmental Protection Hustle.* MIT Press.

Fuller, Thomas. 2020. "Why Does It Cost $750,000 to Build Affordable Housing in San Francisco?" *N.Y. Times,* Feb. 20.

Furman, Jason. 2015. "Barriers to Shared Growth: The Case of Land Use Regulation and Economic Rents." Speech to Urban Institute by Chair of President Obama's Council of Economic Advisors. Nov. 20. Available at https://obamawhitehouse

.archives.gov/sites/default/files/page/files/20151120_barriers_shared_growth_land_use_regulation_and_economic_rents.pdf.

Furth, Salim. 2019. "Development Dividends: Sharing Equity to Overcome Opposition to Housing." Mercatus Center Policy Brief. July.

Furth, Salim, and Olivia Gonzalez. 2019. "California Zoning: Housing Construction and a New Ranking of Local Land Use Regulation." Mercatus Center at George Mason University. August.

Gabbe, C. J. 2018. "Why Are Regulations Changed? A Parcel Analysis of Upzoning in Los Angeles." 38 *J. Planning Educ. & Res.* 289.

Gallagher, Ryan M. 2016. "The Fiscal Externality of Multifamily Housing and Its Impact on the Property Tax: Evidence from Cities and Schools, 1980–2010." 60 *Reg. Sci. & Urb. Econ.* 249.

Galvan, Sara C. 2007. "Wrestling with MUDs to Pin Down the Truth About Special Districts." 75 *Fordham L. Rev.* 3041.

Ganong, Peter, and Daniel Shoag. 2017. "Why Has Regional Income Convergence in the U.S. Declined?" 102 *J. Urb. Econ.* 76.

Gans, Herbert J. 1982. *The Levittowners: Ways of Life and Politics in a New Suburban Community.* Columbia University Press.

Garnett, Nicole Stelle. 2017. "Planning for Density: Promises, Perils, and a Paradox." 33 *J. Land Use & Envt'l L.* 1.

———. 2013. "Redeeming Transect Zoning?" 78 *Brook. L. Rev.* 571.

Gikas, Petros, and George Tchobanoglous. 2009. "The Role of Satellite and Decentralized Strategies in Water Resources Management." 90 *J. Envt'l Mgmt.* 144

Gilbert, Michael D. 2013. "Campaign Finance Disclosure and the Information Tradeoff." 98 *Iowa L. Rev.* 1847.

Gillette, Clayton P. 1994. "Courts, Covenants, and Communities." 61 *U. Chi. L. Rev.* 1375.

Glaeser, Edward. 2014. "Land Use Restrictions and Other Barriers to Growth." Cato Online Forum. Dec. 1. Available at www.cato.org/publications/cato-online-forum/land-use-restrictions-other-barriers-growth.

———. 2011. *Triumph of the City: How Our Greatest Invention Makes Us Richer, Smarter, Greener, Healthier, and Happier.* Penguin Random House.

Glaeser, Edward L. 2020a. "Cities and Pandemics Have a Long History." 30 *City J.* 22. Spring.

———. 2020b. "The Closing of America's Urban Frontier." 22 *Cityscape* 5.

———. 2010. "Preservation Follies: Excessive Landmarking Threatens to Make Manhattan a Refuge for the Rich." 20 *City J.* 62. Spring.

———. 2008. *Cities, Agglomeration, and Spatial Equilibrium.* Oxford University Press.

Glaeser, Edward, and Joseph Gyourko. 2018. "The Economic Implications of Housing Supply." 32 *J. Econ. Persp.* 3.

———. 2008. *Rethinking Federal Housing Policy: How to Make Housing Plentiful and Affordable.* AEI Press.

———. 2002. "Zoning's Steep Price." *Regulation* 24. Fall.

Glaeser, Edward L., Joseph Gyourko, and Raven Saks. 2005. "Why Is Manhattan So Expensive? Regulation and the Rise in Housing Prices." 48 *J. L. & Econ.* 331.

Glaeser, Edward L., and Matthew E. Kahn. 2010. "The Greenness of Cities: Carbon Dioxide Emissions and Urban Development." 67 *J. Urb. Econ.* 404.

Glaeser, Edward, Jenny Schuetz, and Bryce Ward. 2006. "Regulation and the Rise of Housing Prices in Greater Boston: A Study Based on New Data from 187 Communities in Eastern Massachusetts." Pioneer Inst. for Pub. Pol'y Res. & Rappaport Inst. for Greater Boston.

Glaeser, Edward L., and Jesse M. Shapiro. 2003. "Urban Growth in the 1990s: Is City Living Back?" 43 *J. Reg'l Sci.* 139.

Glaeser, Edward L., and Kristina Tobio. 2008. "The Rise of the Sunbelt." 74 *S. Econ. J.* 610.

Glaeser, Edward L., and Bryce A. Ward. 2009. "The Causes and Consequences of Land Use Regulation: Evidence from Greater Boston." 65 *J. Urb. Econ.* 265.

Glickfeld, Madelyn, and Ned Levine. 1992. *Regional Growth . . . Local Reaction: The Enactment and Effects of Local Growth Control and Management Measures in California.* Lincoln Institute of Land Policy.

Goldberg, Ted, and Raquel Maria Dillon. 2018. "Arson Probed as Cause of 5-Alarm Fire at New West Oakland Development." KQED, Oct. 23.

Goldsberry, Kirk. 2015. "It's Foolish to Define Austin by Its City Limits." FiveThirtyEight blog. Jan. 26. Available at https://fivethirtyeight.com/features/austin-city-limits-population-growth/.

Gordon, Robert J. 2016. *The Rise and Fall of American Growth: The U.S. Standard of Living Since the Civil War.* Princeton University Press.

Gottlieb, Joshua D. 2019. "How Minimum Zoning Mandates Can Improve Housing Markets and Expand Opportunity." In *Expanding Economic Opportunity for More Americans* 214. Melissa S. Kearney and Amy Ganz, eds. Feb. Aspen Institute.

Gottlieb, Paul D., et al. 2012. "Determinants of Local Housing Growth in a Multi-Jurisdictional Region, Along with a Test for Nonmarket Zoning." 21 *J. Housing Econ.* 296.

Graham, Bryan S. 2018. "Identifying and Estimating Neighborhood Effects." 56 *J. Econ. Lit.* 450.

Greater Austin School District Map. Undated. Available at https://independencetitle.com/wp-content/uploads/AustinDistMap.pdf.

The Greatest Grid: The Master Plan of Manhattan 1811–2011. 2012. Hilary Ballon, ed. Columbia University Press.

Green, Jason. 2013. "Voters Reject Affordable Senior Housing Project in Palo Alto." *Mercury News,* Nov. 5.

Grogan, Paul. 1992. "Points of Urban Light." Op-Ed. *Wash. Post,* July 19, p. C3.

Guilford Land Trust, Land Acquisition. 2020. Available at https://guilfordlandtrust.org/wordpress/about/how-can-you-protect-your-land.

Gyourko, Joseph, Jonathan Hartley, and Jacob Krimmel. 2019. "The Local Residential Land Use Regulatory Environment Across U.S. Housing Markets: Evidence from a New Wharton Index." Dec. NBER Working Paper 26573.

Gyourko, Joseph, and Raven Molloy. 2015. "Regulation and Housing Supply." In *Handbook of Regional and Urban Economics,* vol. 5b, 1289. Gilles Duranton, Vernon Henderson, and William Strange, eds. Elsevier.

Gyourko, Joseph, Albert Saiz, and Anita Summers. 2008. "A New Measure of the Local Regulatory Environment for Housing Markets: The Wharton Residential Land Use Regulatory Index." 45 *Urb. Stud.* 693.

Haar, Charles M. 1996. *Suburbs Under Siege: Race, Space, and Audacious Judges* Princeton University Press.

———. 1957. "Regionalism and Realism in Land-Use Planning." 105 *U. Pa. L. Rev.* 515

———. 1953. "Zoning for Minimum Standards: The Wayne Township Case." 66 *Harv. L. Rev.* 1051.

Hall, Andrew B., and Jesse Yoder. 2020. "Does Homeownership Influence Political Behavior? Evidence from Administrative Data." Working paper. Mar. 8.

Hamilton, Bruce W. 1975. "Zoning and Property Taxation in a System of Local Governments." 12 *Urb. Stud.* 205.

Hamilton, Emily. 2020. "Nebraska Housing Reform Bill Fails to Go Far Enough." Mercatus Center blog. Mar. 20.

Hamilton, Emily, and Eli Dourado. 2018. "The Premium for Walkable Development Under Land Use Regulations." Mercatus Center at George Mason University.

Hanke, Byron R. 1965. "Planned Unit Development and Land Use Intensity." 114 *U. Pa. L. Rev.* 15.

Hankinson, Michael. 2018. "When Do Renters Behave Like Homeowners? High Rent, Price Anxiety, and NIMBYism." 112 *Am. Pol. Sci. Rev.* 473.

Hankinson, Michael, and Asya Magazinnik. 2019. "Aggregating Voters and the Electoral Connection: The Effect of District Representation on the Distributive Equity of the Housing Supply." Working paper. Aug. 21.

Hanley, Robert. 1984. "Some Jersey Towns, Giving in to Courts, Let in Modest Homes." *N.Y. Times,* Feb. 29, p. A1.

Hansmann, Henry. 1991. "Condominium and Cooperative Housing: Transactional Efficiency, Tax Subsidies, and Tenure Choice." 20 *J. Legal Stud.* 25.

Hanushek, Eric A., and Kuzey Yilmaz. 2015. "Land-Use Controls, Fiscal Zoning, and the Local Provision of Education." 43 *Pub. Fin. Rev.* 559.

Hargrove, Brantley. 2019. "Could a Tug-of-War Between Two Central Texas Counties Leave Residents Without Drinking Water?" *Texas Monthly.* Apr.

Harris, Connor. 2018. "Lone Star Slowdown? How Land-Use Regulation Threatens the Future of Texas." Manhattan Institute report. Dec. Available at https://media4.manhattan-institute.org/sites/default/files/R-CH-1218.pdf.

Hart Research Associates. 2014. "MacArthur How Housing Matters Survey #11127," question 23, Apr.

Harvard Law Review Note. 2009. "Note, Touch and Concern: The Restatement (Third) of Property: Servitudes, and a Proposal" 122 *Harv. L. Rev.* 938.

Harwood, Herbert H., Jr. 2003. *Invisible Giants: The Empires of Cleveland's Van Sweringen Brothers.* Indiana University Press.

Hasse, John, John Reiser, and Alexander Pichacz. 2011. "Evidence of Persistent Exclusionary Effects of Land Use Policy Within Historic and Projected Development Patterns in New Jersey: A Case Study of Monmouth and Somerset Counties." June.

Heller, Michael A. 1999. "The Boundaries of Private Property." 108 *Yale L.J.* 1163.

Heller, Michael, and Rick Hills. 2008. "Land Assembly Districts." 121 *Harv. L. Rev.* 1465.

Henderson, Archie. 1987. "Land Use Controls in Houston: What Protection for Owners of Restricted Property?" 29 *S. Tex. L. Rev.* 131.

Herkenhoff, Kyle F., Lee E. Ohanian, and Edward C. Prescott. 2018. "Tarnishing the Golden and Empire States: Land-Use Restrictions and the U.S. Economic Slowdown." 93 *J. Monetary Econ.* 89.

Hernandez, Jennifer. 2018. "California Environmental Quality Act Lawsuits and California's Housing Crisis." 24 *Hastings Envt'l L.J.* 21.

Hertz, Daniel. 2016. "The Illegal City of Somerville." CityObservatory blog. June 15. Available at https://cityobservatory.org/the-illegal-city-of-somerville/.

Higgs, Robert. 1975. "Urbanization and Inventiveness in the United States, 1870–1920." In *The New Urban History* 247. Leo F. Schnore and Eric E. Lampard, eds. Princeton University Press.

Hills, Roderick M., Jr. 2013. "Saving *Mount Laurel*." 40 *Fordham Urb. L.J.* 1611.

———. 2005. "Is Federalism Good for Localism? The Localist Case for Federal Regimes." 21 *J. L. & Politics* 187.

Hills, Roderick M., Jr., and David Schleicher. 2020. "Building Coalitions Out of Thin Air: Transferable Development Rights and 'Constituency Effects' in Land Use Law." 12 *J. Legal Analysis* 79.

———. 2015. "Planning an Affordable City." 101 *Iowa L. Rev.* 91.

———. 2010. "The Steep Costs of Using Noncumulative Zoning to Preserve Land for Urban Manufacturing," 77 *U. Chi. L. Rev.* 249.

Hills, Roderick M., Jr., and David N. Schleicher. 2011. "Balancing the 'Zoning Budget.'" 62 *Case W. Res. L. Rev.* 81.

Hirt, Sonia. 2014. *Zoned in the USA: The Origins and Implications of American Land-Use Regulation.* Cornell University Press.

History of Atherton. 2020. Available at www.ci.atherton.ca.us/96/History-of-Atherton.

Hodara, Susan. 2005. "Weekender: Branford, Conn." *N.Y. Times,* Aug. 26.

Holahan, David. 2016. "Greater New Haven's 'Most Italian' Roots Run Deep." *Hartford Courant,* Apr. 21.

Hornbeck, Richard, and Daniel Keniston. 2017. "Creative Destruction: Barriers to Urban Growth and the Great Boston Fire of 1872." 107 *Am. Econ. Rev.* 1365.

Kolko, Jed. 2016. "'Normal America' Is Not a Small Town of White People." FiveThirtyEight blog. Apr. 28.

Komesar, Neil K. 1996. *Imperfect Alternatives: Choosing Institutions in Law, Economics, and Public Policy*. University of Chicago Press.

Korngold, Gerald. 2016. *Private Land Use Arrangements: Easements, Real Covenants, and Equitable Servitudes*, 3rd ed. Juris Publishing.

———. 2012. "Cutting Municipal Services During Fiscal Crisis: Lessons from the Denial of Services to Condominium and Homeowner Association Owners." 15 *N.Y.U. J. Legis. & Pub. Pol'y* 109.

———. 2001. "The Emergence of Private Land Use Controls in Large-Scale Subdivisions." 51 *Case W. Res. L. Rev.* 617.

———. 1989. "Single Family Use Covenants: For Achieving a Balance Between Traditional Family Life and Individual Autonomy." 22 *U.C. Davis L. Rev.* 951.

Korobkin, Russell B., and Thomas S. Ulen. 2000. "Law and Behavioral Science: Removing the Rationality Assumption from Law and Economics." 88 *Calif. L. Rev.* 1051.

Kotkin, Joel. 2019. "Densification Efforts Like SB50 Are the Wrong Fix to California's Housing Problem." May 13. Available at https://joelkotkin.com/densification-efforts-like-sb50-are-the-wrong-fix-to-californias-housing-problem/.

———. 2017. *The Human City: Urbanism for the Rest of Us*. Agate.

Krugman, Paul. 2016. "Cities for Everyone." *N.Y. Times*, Apr. 4.

Kurhi, Eric. 2017. "$40 Million Purchase Saves Palo Alto's Buena Vista Mobile Home Park." *Mercury News*, May 18.

Ladera, California. 2020. Available at https://en.wikipedia.org/wiki/Ladera,_California.

Lambert, Bruce. 1997. "At 50, Levittown Contends with Its Legacy of Bias." *N.Y. Times*, Dec. 28.

Lee, Hyojung. 2020. "Are Millennials Coming to Town? Residential Location Choice of Young Adults." 56 *Urb. Aff. Rev.* 565.

Lee, Kwan Ok. 2017. "Temporal Dynamics of Racial Segregation in the United States: An Analysis of Household Residential Mobility." 39(1) *J. Urb. Aff.* 40.

Lemar, Anika Singh. 2019. "The Role of States in Liberalizing Land Use Regulations." 97 *N.C. L. Rev.* 293.

———. 2015. "Zoning as Taxidermy: Neighborhood Conservation Districts and the Regulation of Aesthetics." 90 *Ind. L.J.* 1525.

Lens, Michael C., and Paavo Monkkonen. 2016. "Do Strict Land Use Regulations Make Metropolitan Areas More Segregated by Income?" 82 *J. Am. Planning Ass'n* 6.

Levine, Jonathan. 2006. *Zoned Out: Regulation, Markets, and Choices in Transportation and Metropolitan Land Use*. RFF Press.

Lewyn, Michael E. 2015. "Yes to Infill, No to Nuisance." 42 *Fordham Urb. L.J.* 841.

Li, Huiping, Harrison Campbell, and Steven Fernandez. 2013. "Residential Segregation, Spatial Mismatch, and Economic Growth Across U.S. Metropolitan Areas." 50 *Urb. Stud.* 2642.

Li, Xiaodi. 2020. "Do New Housing Units in Your Backyard Raise Your Rents?" Working paper. June 13. Available at www.fanniemae.com/media/35821/display.

Liberty, Robert L. 2003. "Abolishing Exclusionary Zoning: A Natural Policy Alliance for Environmentalists and Affordable Housing Advocates." 30 *B.C. Envt'l Aff. L. Rev.* 581.

LIHTC Database Access. 2020. Available at https://lihtc.huduser.gov/.

Linde, Hans A. 1980. "First Things First: Rediscovering the States' Bills of Rights." 9 *U. Balt. L. Rev.* 379.

Lindsay, Ira K. 2021. "In Praise of Nonconformity." 81 *Santa Clara L. Rev.* 745.

Liscow, Zachary D. 2018. "Is Efficiency Biased?" 85 *U. Chi. L. Rev.* 1649.

———. 2017. "The Efficiency of Equity in Local Government Finance." 92 *N.Y.U. L. Rev.* 1828.

Livable California. 2020. Available at www.livablecalifornia.org/.

Logan, John R. 2013. "The Persistence of Segregation in the 21st Century Metropolis." 12(2) *City & Community* 160.

Loh, Tracy Hadden. 2019. "How Well Is the Region Doing at Planning for Growth Near Metro?" Greater Greater Washington blog. Jan. 30. Available at https://ggwash.org/view/70464/transit-oriented-development-are-we-upzoning-near-metro-rail-washington-region.

Lopez, Russ, and H. Patricia Hynes. 2003. "Sprawl in the 1990s." 38 *Urb. Aff. Rev.* 325.

Louthen, Elliot. 2020. "Note, Prerogative and Legislator Vetoes." 115 *Nw. U. L. Rev.* 549.

Lowery, David, et al. 2013. "Explaining the Anomalous Growth of Public Sector Lobbying in the American States, 1997–2007." 43 *Publius* 580.

Lynch, Kevin. 1981. *Good City Form*. MIT Press.

Malone, Terry. 2017. "5-Over-2 Podium Design." *Structure Mag.*, Jan. Available at www.structuremag.org/?p=10934.

Malpezzi, Stephen. 1996. "Housing Prices, Externalities, and Regulation in U.S. Metropolitan Areas." 7 *J. Housing Res.* 209.

Mandelker, Daniel R. 2008. "Legislation for Planned Unit Developments and Master-Planned Communities." 40 *Urban Lawyer* 419.

Mangin, John. 2018. "Ethnic Enclaves and the Zoning Game." 36 *Yale L. & Pol'y Rev.* 419.

Manville, Michael, Paavo Monkkonen, and Michael Lens. 2020. "It's Time to End Single-Family Zoning." 86 *J. Am. Planning Ass'n* 106.

Marantz, Nicholas J., and Paul G. Lewis. 2021. "Jurisdictional Size and Residential Development: Are Large-Scale Local Governments More Receptive to Multifamily Housing?" *Urb. Aff. Rev.* 1.

Marantz, Nicholas J., and Huixin Zheng. 2018. "Exclusionary Zoning and the Limits of Judicial Impact." *J. Planning Educ. & Res.* 1.

Marble, William, and Clayton Nall. 2021. "Where Self-Interest Trumps Ideology: Liberal Homeowners and Local Opposition to Housing Development." 83 (4) *J. Politics* 1747.

Marek, Kiersten. 2014. "Behind the Fund for New Jersey's Support of a Housing Rights Group." Inside Philanthropy blog. Oct. 7.

Mari, Francesca. 2020. "Where America's Fight for Housing Is an All-Out War." *N.Y. Times,* Feb. 14.

Martin, Dolores Tremewan, and Richard E. Wagner. 1978. "The Institutional Framework for Municipal Incorporation: An Economic Analysis of Local Agency Formation Commissions in California." 21 *J. L. & Econ.* 409.

Massachusetts Executive Office of Environmental Affairs. 2016. MassGIS data layers. Available at https://docs.digital.mass.gov/dataset/massgis-data-layers.

Massachusetts Municipalities, Housing Regulation Database. 2005. Available at www.masshousingregulations.com/index.asp.

Massey, Douglas S., et al. 2013. *Climbing Mount Laurel: The Struggle for Affordable Housing and Social Mobility in an American Suburb.* Princeton University Press.

Massey, Douglas S., and Nancy A. Denton. 1993. *American Apartheid: Segregation and the Making of the Underclass.* Harvard University Press.

Mast, Evan. 2021. "The Effect of New Market-Rate Housing Construction on the Low-Income Housing Market." *J. Urb. Econ.* (forthcoming).

———. 2020. "Warding Off Development: Local Control, Housing Supply, and NIMBYs." Upjohn Inst. working paper 20–330. Apr.

Mawhorter, Sarah, and Carolina Reid. 2018. "Local Housing Policies Across California," Terner Center for Housing Innovation, U.C. Berkeley.

Mayo, Stephen K. 1986. "Sources of Inefficiency in Subsidized Housing Programs." 20 *J. Urb. Econ.* 229.

McAdams, Richard H. 1997. "The Origin, Development, and Regulation of Norms." 96 *Mich. L. Rev.* 338.

McCloskey, Deirdre N. 2017. *Bourgeois Equality: How Ideas, Not Capital or Institutions, Enriched the World.* University of Chicago Press.

McConnell, Virginia, and Margaret Walls. 2005. *The Value of Open Space.* Resources for the Future. Jan.

McCready, Brian. 2011. "Orange Residents Overwhelmingly OK $7.1M Hubbell Land Purchase." *New Haven Register,* July 12.

McDonald, Jason. 2012. *Racial Dynamics in Early Twentieth-Century Austin, Texas.* Rowman & Littlefield.

McDonald, John F., and Daniel P. McMillen. 1998. "Land Values, Land Use, and the First Chicago Zoning Ordinance." 16 *J. Real Est. Fin. & Econ.* 135.

McGlinchy, Audrey. 2019. "After More Than a Yearlong Hiatus, Austin's Code Rewrite Returns." KUT, Oct. 4.

———. 2017. "Residents of East Austin, Once a Bustling Black Enclave, Make a Suburban Exodus." NPR Cities Project, July 12. Available at www.npr.org/2017/07/12/536478223/once-a-bustling-black-enclave-east-austin-residents-make-a-suburban-exodus.

McKenzie, Evan. 2011. *Beyond Privatopia: Rethinking Residential Private Government.* Rowman & Littlefield.

———. 1994. *Privatopia: Homeowner Associations and the Rise of Residential Private Government.* Yale University Press.

McLaughlin, Nancy A. 2013. "Perpetual Conservation Easements in the 21st Century." 2013 *Utah L. Rev.* 687.

McLoughlin, Pam. 2020. "Affordable Housing Project Approved in Orange Gets Praise from Town Officials." *New Haven Register,* Sept. 13.

Meltzer, Rachel, and Ron Cheung. 2014. "How Are Homeowners Associations Capitalized into Property Values?" 46 *Reg. Sci. Urb. Econ.* 93.

Menlo-Atherton High (2020). "School Boundaries Map." Available at https://california.hometownlocator.com/schools/profiles,n,menlo-atherton%20high,z,94025,t,pb,i,1007127.cfm.

Mensinger, Susan. 1982. "Los Altos Hills: The Statutory Scheme." 4 *Stan. Envt'l L. Ann.* 21.

Meronek, Toshio. 2018. "YIMBYs Exposed: The Techies Hawking Free Market 'Solutions' to the Nation's Housing Crisis." *In These Times,* May 21.

Meyers, John. 2017. "Political Road Map: No One Spends More on Lobbying in Sacramento Than Local Governments." *L.A. Times,* Aug. 6.

Michael Van Valkenburgh Associates, Inc. Undated. Available at www.mvvainc.com/project.php?id=13.

Midpeninsula Regional Open Space District. Available at www.openspace.org/sites/default/files/district_map.pdf.

Milone & MacBroom, Inc. 2015. Guilford Plan of Conservation and Development Update, July 15. Available at www.ci.guilford.ct.us/wp-content/uploads/FINAL-Guilford-PoCD-2015.pdf.

———. 2010. South Central Regional Council of Governments, *Regional Build-Out Analysis,* June.

Minor, Beth. 2018. E-mail to author from City Clerk, City of Palo Alto, Cal. Dec. 30.

Mirisch, John. 2018. "The Protecting Communities and Local Rights Amendment—A Not-So-Modest Proposal." *Fox & Hounds,* Apr. 9. Available at www.foxandhoundsdaily.com/2018/04/protecting-communities-local-rights-amendment-not-modest-proposal/.

Mitchell, James L. 2004. "Will Empowering Developers to Challenge Exclusionary Zoning Increase Suburban Housing Choice?" 23 *J. Pol'y Analysis & Mgmt.* 119.

Mitchell, Sara. 2019. "London Calling? Agglomeration Economies in Literature Since 1700." 112 *J. Urb. Econ.* 16.

Mokyr, Joel. 2016. *A Culture of Growth: The Origins of the Modern Economy.* Princeton University Press.

Molotch, Harvey. 1976. "The City as a Growth Machine: Toward a Political Economy of Place." 82 *Am. J. Soc.* 309.

Monchow, Helen C. 1928. *The Use of Deed Restrictions in Subdivision Development.* Institute for Research in Land Economics and Public Utilities.

Monkkonen, Paavo, and Michael Manville. 2019. "Opposition to Development or Opposition to Developers? Survey Evidence from Los Angeles County on Attitudes Towards New Housing." 41 *J. Urb. Aff.* 1123.

Morris, Allie. 2019. "Texas Has Third-Highest Property Tax Rate for Single-Family Homes, Study Finds." *San Antonio Express-News,* Apr. 9.

Mummolo, Jonathan, and Clayton Nall. 2017. "Why Partisans Do Not Sort: How Quality and Resource Constraints Prevent Political Segregation." 79 *J. Pol.* 45.

Munneke, Henry J. 2005. "Dynamics of the Urban Zoning Structure: An Empirical Investigation of Zoning Change." 58 *J. Urb. Econ.* 455.

Musgrave, Richard A., and Peggy B. Musgrave. 1976. *Public Finance in Theory and Practice,* 2d ed. McGraw-Hill.

Musterd, Sako, et al. 2017. "Socioeconomic Segregation in European Capital Cities: Increasing Separation Between Poor and Rich." 38 *Urb. Geography* 1062.

Myers, John, and Michael Hendrix. 2021. "To Create More Affordable Housing, Make Zoning Hyperlocal." CityLab, Feb. 19.

Nasri, Arefeh, and Lei Zhang. 2014. "The Analysis of Transit-Oriented Development (TOD) in Washington, D.C. and Baltimore Metropolitan Areas." 32 *Transport Pol'y* 172.

Natelson, Robert G. 1989. *Law of Property Owners Associations.* Little Brown & Co.

National Advisory Commission on Civil Disorders. 1968. *Report.* Government Printing Office.

National Commission on Urban Problems. 1969. *Building the American City.* Government Printing Office.

Nelson, Robert H. 2005. *Private Neighborhoods and the Transformation of Local Government.* Rowman & Littlefield.

Newton, Jim. 2016. "Gov. Jerry Brown: The Long Struggle for the Good Cause." *UCLA Blue Print.* Spring.

Ng, Michael T., Edwin Chow, and David W. S. Wong. 2016. "Geographical Dimension of Colonial Justice: Using GIS in Research on Law and History." 34 *L. & Hist. Rev.* 1027.

Nguyen, Mai Thi, Victoria Basolo, and Abhishek Tiwari. 2013. "Opposition to Affordable Housing in the USA: Debate Framing and the Responses of Local Actors." 30 *Housing, Theory & Soc'y* 107.

Nichols, J. C. 1929. "A Developer's View of Deed Restrictions." 5 *J. Land & Pub. Util. Econ.* 132.

Noguellou, Rozen. 2016. "La règle d'urbanisme et les PLU—Où se trouve la règle d'urbanisme?" *Revue française de droit administratif* 872, Sept.-Oct.

Nolan, Val, Jr., and Frank E. Horack, Jr. 1954. "How Small a House—Zoning for Minimum Space Requirements." 67 *Harv. L. Rev.* 967.

Norton, Sam. 2017. "Costco Gives Up on Branford Plans." *New Haven Register,* Feb. 16.

Nussbaum, Martha C. 2000. "The Costs of Tragedy: Some Moral Limits of Cost-Benefit Analysis." 29 *J. Legal Stud.* 1005.

NYU Furman Center. 2018. "How Do Small Area Fair Market Rents Affect the Location and Number of Units Affordable to Voucher Holders?" Jan. 5. Available at https://furmancenter.org/files/NYUFurmanCenter_SAFMRbrief_5JAN2018_1.pdf.

O'Leary, Mary E. 2020. "Civil Rights Group Files Challenge to Woodbridge Zoning Excluding Multi-Family Units." *New Haven Register*, Sept. 29.

O'Leary, Mary, Ed Stannard, and Shahid Abdul-Karim. 2017. "1967 Riots: Four Tense Days that Began 'Evolution' of Blacks." *New Haven Register*, Apr. 12.

Oliver, J. Eric. 2012. *Local Elections and the Politics of Small-Scale Democracy*. Princeton University Press.

———. 2001. *Democracy in Suburbia*. Princeton University Press.

———. 2000. "City Size and Civic Involvement in Metropolitan America." 94 *Am. Pol. Sci. Rev.* 361.

Oliveri, Rigel C. 2019. "Vouchers and Affordable Housing: The Limits of Choice in the Political Economy of Place." 54 *Harv. C.R.-C.L. L. Rev.* 795.

Olsen, Edgar O. 2015. "Reforming Housing Assistance." 38 *Regulation* 26. Summer.

———. 2006. "Achieving Fundamental Housing Policy Reform." In *Promoting the General Welfare: New Perspectives on Government Performance* 100. Alan S. Gerber and Eric M. Patashnik, eds. Brookings Institution Press.

———. 2003. "Housing Programs for Low-Income Households." In *Means-Tested Transfer Programs in the United States* 365. Robert A. Moffitt, ed. University of Chicago Press.

Olson, Mancur. 1982. *The Rise and Decline of Nations: Economic Growth, Stagflation, and Social Rigidities*. Yale University Press.

Olzak, Susan, Suzanne Shanahan, and Elizabeth H. McEneaney. 1996. "Poverty, Segregation, and Race Riots: 1960 to 1993." 61 *Am. Soc. Rev.* 590.

O'Neill, Moira, Giulia Gualco-Nelson, and Eric Biber. 2019. "Developing Policy from the Ground Up: Examining Entitlement in the Bay Area to Inform California's Housing Policy Debates." 25 *Hastings Envt'l L.J.* 1.

Oppenheimer, Mark. 2008. "It's a Wonderful Block." *N.Y. Times Magazine*. Oct. 5, p. 70.

Orange Conservation Commission. Circa 2012. "A Guide to the Open Spaces of Orange, Connecticut."

Orfield, Myron. 2012. "How the Suburbs Gave Birth to America's Most Diverse Neighborhoods." CityLab blog. July 20. Available at www.citylab.com/equity/2012/07/how-suburbs-gave-birth-americas-most-diverse-neighborhoods/2647/.

Ortalo-Magné, François, and Andrea Prat. 2014. "On the Political Economy of Urban Growth: Homeownership Versus Affordability." 6(1) *Am. Econ. J.: Microeconomics* 154 (2014).

Page & Turnbull. 2016. "Professorville Historic District Design Guidelines." Oct. Available at www.cityofpaloalto.org/civicax/filebank/documents/61618.

Palo Alto Forward. 2020. Website at www.paloaltoforward.com/.

Parolek, Daniel G. 2020. *Missing Middle Housing: Thinking Big and Building Small to Respond to Today's Housing Crisis*. Island Press.

Payne, John M. 1998. "Lawyers, Judges, and the Public Interest." 96 *Mich. L. Rev.* 1685. Reviewing Charles Haar, *Suburbs Under Siege* (1996).

Payson, Julia A. 2020. "Cities in the Statehouse: How Local Governments Use Lobbyists to Secure State Funding." 82 *J. Politics* 403.

Pendall, Rolf. 1999. "Opposition to Housing: NIMBY and Beyond." 35 *Urb. Aff. Rev.* 112.

Pendall, Rolf, Robert Puentes, and Jonathan Martin. 2006. "From Traditional to Reformed: A Review of the Land Use Regulations in the Nation's 50 Largest Metropolitan Areas." Brookings Institution.

Peterman, Danieli Evans. 2018. "Socioeconomic Status Discrimination." 104 *Va. L. Rev.* 1283.

Pew Research Center. 2017. "Social and Demographic Trends." May 18. Available at www.pewsocialtrends.org/2017/05/18/1-trends-and-patterns-in-intermarriage/.

Pinto, Edward J. 2015. "Housing Finance Fact or Fiction?" American Enterprise Institute blog. June 24.

Plott, Charles R., and Kathryn Zeiler. 2007. "Exchange Asymmetries Incorrectly Interpreted As Evidence of Endowment Effect Theory and Prospect Theory?" 97 *Am. Econ. Rev.* 1449.

Postrel, Virginia. 1999. *The Future and Its Enemies: The Growing Conflict over Creativity, Enterprise, and Progress.* Free Press.

Power, Garrett. 1988. "The Unwisdom of Allowing City Growth to Work Out Its Own Destiny." 47 *Md. L. Rev.* 626.

Professorville Historic District. 1979. City of Palo, California. Application to National Park Service. Apr. 17. Available at www.cityofpaloalto.org/civicax/filebank/documents/61616.

PropertyShark. 2020. "Most Expensive U.S. Zip Codes in 2020." Available at www.propertyshark.com/Real-Estate-Reports/most-expensive-zip-codes-in-the-us.

Putnam, Robert D. 2000. *Bowling Alone: The Collapse and Revival of American Community.* Touchstone Books.

Quigley, John M., and Steven Raphael. 2005. "Regulation and the High Cost of Housing in California." 95 *Am. Econ. Rev.* 323.

Quigley, John, Steven Raphael, and Larry A. Rosenthal. 2009. "Measuring Land Use Regulations and Their Effects in the Housing Market." In *Housing Markets and the Economy: Risk, Regulation, and Policy* 271. Edward L. Glaeser & John M. Quigley, eds. Lincoln Institute of Land Policy.

Rae, Douglas W. 2003. *City: Urbanism and Its End.* Yale University Press.

Ramniceanu, Nicolas. 1982. "Mountain View: From Pro-Growth to No-Growth." 4 *Stan. Envt'l L. Ann.* 50.

Rappoport, Jordan. 2007. "Moving to Nice Weather." 37 *Reg. Sci. & Urb. Econ.* 375.

Reardon, Sean F., and Kendra Bischoff. 2011. "Income Inequality and Income Segregation." 116 *Am. J. Soc.* 1092.

Reddit. 2014. "Austin Annexations by Decade." Available at www.reddit.com/r/Austin/comments/2asmct/austin_annexations_by_decade_map/.

Regional Plan Association. 1962. *Spread City: Projections of Development Trends and the Issues They Pose: The Tri-State New York Metropolitan Region, 1960–1985.* Bulletin 100. Sept.

Reich, Robert B. 1991. "The Secession of the Successful." *N.Y. Times Magazine.* Jan. 20.

Reid, Carolina K., Carol Galante, and Ashley F. Weinstein-Carnes. 2017. "Addressing California's Housing Shortage: Lessons from Massachusetts Chapter 40B." 25 *J. Affordable Housing* 241.

Relman Colfax PLLC. Undated. "Anti-Discrimination Center v. Westchester County." Available at www.relmanlaw.com/cases-westchester.

Report of the Bipartisan Millennial Housing Commission. 2002. Government Printing Office.

Report of the President's Commission on Housing (1982). Government Printing Office.

Resseger, Matthew. 2013. "The Impact of Land Use Regulation on Racial Segregation: Evidence from Massachusetts Zoning Borders." Working paper. Nov. 26.

Richman, Barak D., and Christopher Boerner. 2006. "A Transaction Cost Economizing Approach to Regulation: Understanding the NIMBY Problem and Improving Regulatory Responses." 23 *Yale J. Reg*. 29.

Robinson, Glen O. 1991. "Explaining Contingent Rights: The Puzzle of Obsolete Covenants." 91 *Colum. L. Rev*. 546.

Rodman, Edmon J. 2014. "Let My People Go . . . to Hancock Park." Jewish Journal blog. Apr. 9. Available at https://jewishjournal.com/mobile_20111212/128273/.

Rogers, William H. 2010. "The Housing Price Impact of Covenant Restrictions and Other Subdivision Characteristics." 40 *J. Real Est. Fin. & Econ*. 203.

———. 2006. "A Market for Institutions: Assessing the Impact of Restrictive Covenants on Housing." 82 *Land Econ*. 500.

Rolleston, Barbara Sherman. 1987. "Determinants of Restrictive Suburban Zoning: An Empirical Analysis." 21 *J. Urb. Econ*. 1.

Rome, Adam. 2013. *The Genius of Earth Day*. Hill & Wang.

Romem, Issi. 2018. "America's New Metropolitan Landscape: Pockets of Dense Construction in a Dormant Suburban Interior." BuildZoom blog. Feb. 1. Available at www.buildzoom.com/blog/pockets-of-dense-construction-in-a-dormant-suburban-interior.

Romem, Issi, and Elizabeth Kneebone. Undated. "Disparity in Departure: Who Leaves the Bay Area and Where Do They Go?" BuildZoom blog & Terner Center. Available at http://ternercenter.berkeley.edu/uploads/Disparity_in_Departure.pdf.

Rose, Carol M. 1983. "Planning and Dealing: Piecemeal Land Controls as a Problem of Local Legitimacy." 71 *Calif. L. Rev*. 837.

Rosen, Eva. 2020. *The Voucher Promise: "Section 8" and the Fate of an American Neighborhood*. Princeton University Press.

Rosenthal, Stuart S. 2014. "Are Private Markets and Filtering a Viable Source of Low-Income Housing? Estimates from a 'Repeat Income' Model." 104 *Am. Econ. Rev*. 687.

Ross, Justin M. 2018. "Fiscal Zoning and Fiscal Externalities." 71 *Nat'l Tax J*. 45.

Rothstein, Richard. 2017. *The Color of Law: A Forgotten History of How Our Government Segregated America*. Liveright.

Rothwell, Jonathan T. 2012. "Housing Costs, Zoning, and Access to High-Scoring Schools." Brookings Metropolitan Policy Program.

———. 2011. "Racial Enclaves and Density Zoning: The Institutionalized Segregation of Racial Minorities in the United States." 13 *Am. L. & Econ. Rev.* 290.

Rothwell, Jonathan, and Douglas S. Massey. 2009. "The Effect of Density Zoning on Racial Segregation in U.S. Urban Areas." 44 *Urb. Aff. Rev.* 779.

Round Rock, Texas. 2019. "City Limits, ETJ, & MUDs." Feb. Available at www.roundrocktexas.gov/wp-content/uploads/2015/01/cl_etj_muds.pdf.

Rubenstein, William B. 2004. "On What a Private Attorney General Is—and Why It Matters." 57 *Vand. L. Rev.* 2129.

Rubinowitz, Leonard S., and James E. Rosenbaum. 2000. *Crossing the Class and Color Lines: From Public Housing to White Suburbia.* University of Chicago Press.

Sager, Lawrence Gene. 1969. "Tight Little Islands: Exclusionary Zoning, Equal Protection, and the Indigent." 21 *Stan. L. Rev.* 767.

Saito, Blaine G. 2020. "Collaborative Governance and the Low-Income Housing Tax Credit." 39 *Va. Tax Rev.* 451.

Saiz, Albert. 2010. "The Geographic Determinants of Housing Supply." 125 *Q. J. Econ.* 1253.

Salkin, Patricia E. 2010–11. "From Bricks and Mortar to Mega-Bytes and Mega-Pixels." 43 *Urb. Law.* 11.

Saltonstall, Gus. 2019. "Here Are the Best Pizza Places in America." Patch blog. Oct. 2.

San Jose, California. Undated. North San Jose Development Policy. Available at www.sanjoseca.gov/your-government/departments/planning-building-code-enforcement/planning-division/citywide-planning/area-plans/north-san-jose-area-development-policy.

Sandroni, Paulo. 2010. "A New Financial Instrument of Value Capture in São Paulo: Certificates of Additional Construction Potential." In *Municipal Revenues and Land Policies* 218. Gregory K. Ingram and Yu-Hung Hong, eds. Lincoln Institute of Land Policy.

Saratoga, California, History. 2020. Available at www.saratoga.ca.us/271/History.

Schelling, Thomas C. 1978. *Micromotives and Macrobehavior.* Norton.

Schill, Michael H. 1992. "The Federal Role in Reducing Regulatory Barriers to Affordable Housing in the Suburbs." 8 *J. L. & Pol.* 703.

Schleicher, David. 2020. "Constitutional Law for NIMBYs: A Review of 'Principles of Home Rule for the 21st Century' by the National League of Cities." 81 *Ohio St. L.J.* 883.

———. 2017a. "How Land Use Law Impedes Transportation Innovation." In *Evidence and Innovation in Housing Law and Policy* 38. Lee Anne Fennell and Benjamin J. Keys, eds. Cambridge University Press.

———. 2017b. "Stuck! The Law and Economics of Residential Stagnation." 127 *Yale L.J.* 78.

———. 2013. "City Unplanning." 122 *Yale L.J.* 1670.

———. 2010. "The City as a Law and Economic Subject." 2010 *U. Ill. L. Rev.* 1507.

Schmidt, Stephan, and Kurt Paulsen. 2009. "Is Open-Space Preservation a Form of Exclusionary Zoning?" *45 Urb. Aff. Rev.* 92.

Schmitt, Eric. 1989. "Connecticut's Condo Capital Deals with Boom Gone Bust." *N.Y. Times,* Sept. 3.

Schmitt, William E. 1985. "Homeowners Unite in Selling to Developers." *N.Y. Times,* Jan. 16, p. 1.

Schoenbaum, Naomi. 2017. "Stuck or Rooted? The Costs of Mobility and the Value of Place." 127 *Yale L.J. F.* 458.

Schoenbrod, David S. 1969. "Note, Large Lot Zoning." 78 *Yale L.J.* 1418.

School + State Finance Project. 2020. "Weights." Available at http://ctschoolfinance.org/ecs-formula/ecs-weights.

Schragger, Richard C. "The Perils of Land Use Deregulation." *U. Pa. L. Rev.* (forthcoming).

———. 2009. "Mobile Capital, Local Economic Regulation, and the Democratic City." 123 *Harv. L. Rev.* 482.

Schuck, Peter H. 2003. *Diversity in America: Keeping Government at a Safe Distance.* Harvard University Press.

Schuetz. 2020. Available at www.brookings.edu/experts/jenny-schuetz/.

Schuetz, Jenny. 2018a. "HUD Can't Fix Exclusionary Zoning by Withholding CDBG Funds." Brookings Institution blog. Oct. 15.

———. 2018b. "Minneapolis 2040: The Most Wonderful Plan of the Year." Brookings Institution blog. Dec. 12.

———. 2009. "No Renters in My Suburban Backyard: Land Use Regulation and Rental Housing." 28 *J. Pol'y Analysis & Mgmt.* 296.

———. 2008. "Guarding the Town Walls: Mechanisms and Motives for Restricting Multifamily Housing in Massachusetts." 36 *Real Est. Econ.* 555.

Schuetz, Jenny, Rachel Meltzer, and Vicki Been. 2011. "Silver Bullet or Trojan Horse? The Effects of Inclusionary Zoning on Local Housing Markets in the United States." 48 *Urb. Stud.* 297.

Schwartz, Alex F. 2010. *Housing Policy in the United States,* 2nd ed. Routledge.

Schwartz, Jonathan. 1997. Note, "Prisoners of Proposition 13: Sales Taxes, Property Taxes, and the Fiscalization of Municipal Land Use Decisions." 71 *S. Cal. L. Rev.* 183.

Seaside, Florida. 2020. Available at https://en.wikipedia.org/wiki/Seaside,_Florida.

Seifter, Miriam. 2021. "Countermajoritarian Legislatures." Working paper available at SSRN-id3782224.pdf.

Selmi, Daniel P. 2010. "The Contract Transformation in Land Use Regulation." 63 *Stan. L. Rev.* 591.

Serkin, Christopher. 2020. "A Case for Zoning." 96 *Notre Dame L. Rev.* 749.

———. 2010. "Entrenching Environmentalism: Private Conservation Easements over Public Land." 77 *U. Chi. L. Rev.* 341.

———. 2009. "Existing Uses and the Limits of Land Use Regulation." 84 *N.Y.U. L. Rev.* 1224.

Sharman, Frank A. 1989. "An Introduction to the Enclosure Acts." 10 *J. Legal Hist.* 45.

Shaw, Randy. 2018. *Generation Priced Out: Who Gets to Live in the New Urban America*. University of California Press.

Shertzer, Allison, Tate Twinam, and Randall P. Walsh. 2018. "Zoning and the Economic Geography of Cities." 105 *J. Urb. Econ.* 20.

Sheyner, Gennady. 2016. "Palo Alto Mulls Raising the Height Limit for New Buildings." *Palo Alto Weekly*. Nov. 25.

———. 2014. "Palo Alto Suspends 'Planned Community' Projects." *Palo Alto Weekly*, Feb. 4.

———. 2011. "Stanford Offers City $173M in Hospital Expansion 'Benefits.'" Palo Alto Online. Jan. 19. Available at www.paloaltoonline.com/news/2011/01/19/stanford-offers-city-173m-in-hospital-expansion-benefits.

Shields, Geoffrey, and L. Sanford Spector. 1972. "Opening up the Suburbs: Notes on a Movement for Social Change." 2 *Yale Rev. L. & Soc. Action* 300.

Shipman & Goodwin LLP. 2006. "Housing Land Use Appeals." PowerPoint presentation. Oct. 30.

Shoag, Daniel. 2019. "Removing Barriers to Accessing High-Productivity Places." Brookings Institution.

Shoked, Nadav. 2011. "The Reinvention of Ownership: The Embrace of Residential Zoning and the Modern Populist Reading of Property." 28 *Yale J. Reg.* 91.

Shoup, Donald. 2008. "Graduated Density Zoning." 28 *J. Planning Educ. & Res.* 161.

Shultz, Michael M., and Frank Schnidman. 1990. "The Potential Application of Land Readjustment in the United States." 22 *Urb. Lawyer* 197.

Siegen, Bernard H. 1970. "Non-zoning in Houston." 13 *J. L. & Econ.* 71.

Sims, Katharine R. E., and Jenny Schuetz. 2009. "Local Regulation and Land-Use Change: The Effects of Wetlands Bylaws in Massachusetts." 39 *Reg. Sci. & Urb. Econ.* 409.

Siniavskaia, Natalia. 2017. "Lot Size Is at a New Record Low." NAHB *Eye on Housing*. Oct. 3. Available at http://eyeonhousing.org/2018/08/lot-size-remains-record-low/?_ga=2.164146239.124965040.1549063508–511468845.1549063508.

Sisson, Patrick. 2019. "Will California's New ADU Laws Create a Backyard Building Boom?" Curbed blog. Oct. 11.

Smith, Henry E. 2000. "Semicommon Property Rights and Scattering in the Open Fields." 29 *J. Legal Stud.* 131.

Smith, Jonathan, and Alan Pendleton. 1998. "San Francisco Bay Conservation and Development Commission: Challenge and Response After 30 Years." 28 *Golden Gate U. L. Rev.* 269.

Smith, Merritt Roe. 2018. "Eli Whitney and the American System of Manufacturing." In *Technology in America: A History of Individuals and Ideas* 43. Carroll Pursell, ed. 3d ed. MIT Press.

Softky, Marion. 2005. "Los Trancos Woods on Track to Get Sewers." Almanac blog. June 15. Available at www.almanacnews.com/morgue/2005/2005_06_15.trancos.shtml.

Sorens, Jason. 2018. "The Effects of Housing Supply Restrictions on Partisan Geography." 66 *Pol. Geography* 44.

Sorensen, André, Junichiro Okata, and Sayaka Fujii. 2010. "Urban Renaissance as Intensification: Building Regulation and the Rescaling of Place Governance in Tokyo's High-rise Manshon Boom." 47 *Urb. Stud.* 556.

South Central Connecticut Regional Water Authority. 2018. "Annual Report." Available at www.rwater.com/media/3459/fy-2018-rwa-annual-report.pdf.

Southern Connecticut Regional Council of Governments. 2009. "Plan of Conservation and Development." Available at http://scrcog.org/wp-content/uploads/reports/AmendedPOCDfinal21July2009withMaps.pdf.

Span, Henry A. 2001. "How the Courts Should Fight Exclusionary Zoning." 32 *Seton Hall L. Rev.* 1.

Sparber, Sami. 2021. "Austin Is Capital of Homes Selling at Super Premiums." *Wall St. J.*, Aug. 18.

Speck, Jeff. 2012. *Walkable City: How Downtown Can Save America, One Step at a Time.* North Point Press.

Spence, David B. 2014. "The Political Economy of Local Vetoes." 93 *Tex. L. Rev.* 351.

Speyrer, Janet Furman. 1989. "The Effect of Land-Use Restrictions on Market Values of Single-Family Homes in Houston." 2 *J. Real Est. Fin. Econ.* 117.

Stahl, Kenneth A. 2020. "Home Rule and State Preemption of Local Land Use Control." 50 *Urban Lawyer* 179.

———. 2018. "'Yes in My Backyard': Can a New Pro-Housing Movement Overcome the Power of NIMBYs?" 41(3) *Zoning & Planning L. Rep.* 1.

———. 2017. "The Challenge of Inclusion." 89 *Temp. L. Rev.* 487.

———. 2010. "The Artifice of Local Growth Politics: At-Large Elections, Ballot-Box Zoning, and Judicial Review." 94 *Marq. L. Rev.* 1.

Stanford Community Plan Issues and Policies. Undated. Available at www.sccgov.org/sites/dpd/DocsForms/Documents/SU_CP.pdf.

Stanford Lands. 2020. Available at http://facts.stanford.edu/about/lands/.

Stanford News Service. 1998. "Sand Hill Road Project Gets Green Light." Available at https://news.stanford.edu/pr/98/980924sandhill.html.

Stanford University Terrace. 2020. Available at https://universityterrace.stanford.edu/community/interactive-map.

Starkey, Patrick. 2013. *Stuck in Place: Urban Neighborhoods and the End of Progress Toward Racial Equality.* University of Chicago Press.

Steele, Eric H. 1986. "Participation and Rules—The Functions of Zoning." 1986 *Am. B. Found. Res. J.* 709.

Sterk, Stewart E. 2019. "Federal Land Use Intervention as Market Restoration." 99 *B.U. L. Rev.* 1577.

———. 1988. "Foresight and the Law of Servitudes." 73 *Cornell L. Rev.* 956.

———. 1985. "Freedom from Freedom of Contract: The Enduring Value of Servitude Restrictions." 70 *Iowa L. Rev.* 615.

Stern, Robert A. M., David Fishman, and Thomas Mellins. 1997. *New York 1960: Architecture and Urbanism Between the Second World War and the Bicentennial*. Monacelli Press.

Stilgoe, John R. 1988. *Borderlands: Origins of the American Suburb, 1820–1939*. Yale University Press.

Stout, David. 1996. "Robert Wilentz, 69, New Jersey Chief Justice, Dies; Court Aided Women and the Poor." *N.Y. Times*, July 24.

Strahilevitz, Lior Jacob. 2006. "Exclusionary Amenities in Residential Communities." 92 *Va. L. Rev.* 437.

Strahilevitz, Michal A., and George Loewenstein. 1998. "The Effect of Ownership History on the Valuation of Objects." 25 *J. Consumer Res.* 276.

Suarez, Christopher A. 2010. "Sliding Towards Educational Outcomes." 15 *Mich J. Race & L.* 477.

Sullivan, Edward J. 2012. "The Quiet Revolution Goes West: The Oregon Planning Program 1961–2011." 45 *J. Marshall L. Rev.* 357.

Sunstein, Cass R. 2020. "Back to Mill? Behavioral Welfare Economics." *J. Benefit-Cost Analysis* (forthcoming).

———. 2018. *The Cost-Benefit Revolution*. MIT Press.

———. 2003. "Beyond the Precautionary Principle." 151 *U. Pa. L. Rev.* 1003.

Sutton, Jeffrey S. 2022. *Who Decides? States as Laboratories of Constitutional Experimentation*. Oxford University Press.

Symposium on Cost-Benefit Analysis. 2000. 29 *J. Legal Stud.* 837–1177.

Talen, Emily. 2012. *City Rules: How Regulations Affect Urban Form*. Island Press.

Tarr, G. Alan, and Russell S. Harrison. 1984. "Legitimacy and Capacity in State Supreme Court Policymaking: The New Jersey Court and Exclusionary Zoning." 15 *Rutgers L.J.* 513.

Tarr, G. Alan, and Mary Cornelia Aldis Porter. 1988. *State Supreme Courts in State and Nation*. Yale University Press.

Tauranac, John. 1999. "Lost New York, Found in Architecture's Crannies." *N.Y. Times*, Feb. 12.

Terner Center. 2018. "Local Housing Policies Across California." Dec. Available at http://californialanduse.org/download/Terner_California_Residential_Land_Use_Survey_Report.pdf.

Texas Almanac. 2018. "Major Aquifers of Texas." Available at https://texasalmanac.com/topics/environment/aquifers-texas.

Theis, Michael. 2017. "Austin Urbanist Group Slams Draft CodeNEXT Map for Perceived Lack of Density." *Austin Bus. J.*, Apr. 20. www.bizjournals.com/austin/news/2017/04/20/austin-urbanist-group-slams-draft-codenext-map-for.html.

Thomas, Jacqueline Rabe. 2020. "Separated by Design: How Wealthy Towns Keep People with Housing Vouchers Out." *Connecticut Mirror*, Jan. 9. Available at https://ctmirror.org/2020/01/09/separated-by-design-how-wealthy-towns-keep-people-with-housing-vouchers-out/.

Thompson, Derek. 2017. "What on Earth Is Wrong with Connecticut?" *Atlantic.* July 5.

Thorp, Victoria. 2014. "Palo Alto 101: What Is a 'Residentialist'?" Palo Alto Pulse blog. Oct. 1. Available at www.paloaltopulse.com/2014/10/01/palo-alto-pulse-asks-what-is-a-residentialist/.

Thoubboron, Kerry. 2019. "An Overview of the California Solar Mandate." Energysage blog. Nov. 7.

Tiebout, Charles M. 1956. "A Pure Theory of Local Expenditures." 64 *J. Pol. Econ.* 416.

Tolley, George S. 1974. "The Welfare Economics of City Bigness." 1 *J. Urb. Econ.* 324.

Tondro, Terry J. 2001. "Connecticut's Affordable Housing Appeals Statute: After Ten Years of Hope, Why Only Middling Results?" 23 *W. New Eng. L. Rev.* 115.

Torres, Gerald. 2012. "Liquid Assets: Groundwater in Texas." 122 *Yale L.J.F.* 143.

Travis County, Texas. 2020. "Balcones Canyonlands Conservation Plan." Available at www.traviscountytx.gov/tnr/bccp.

Tretter, Eliot. Undated. "Austin Restricted: Progressivism, Zoning, Private Racial Covenants, and the Making of a Segregated City." Available at https://repositories.lib.utexas.edu/handle/2152/21232.

Trounstine, Jessica. 2020. "The Geography of Inequality: How Land Use Regulation Produces Segregation." 114 *Am. Pol. Sci. Rev.* 443.

———. 2018. *Segregation by Design: Local Politics and Inequality in American Cities.* Cambridge University Press.

Trump, Donald J., and Ben Carson. 2020. "We'll Protect America's Suburbs." *Wall St. J.,* Aug. 16.

Turmelle, Luther. 2018. "Fix to Regional Water Authority Delivery System in North Branford Was Challenging." *New Haven Register*, Nov. 4.

Turner, Matthew A. 2005. "Landscape Preferences and Patterns of Residential Development." 57 *J. Urb. Econ.* 19.

Tyson, Christopher J. 2012. "Localism and Involuntary Annexation." 87 *Tul. L. Rev.* 297.

Urban kchoze. 2014. Available at http://urbankchoze.blogspot.com/2014/04/japanese-zoning.html.

Urban Land Institute. 1964. *Homes Association Handbook.* Technical Bulletin No. 50.

———. 1947. *Community Builders Handbook.*

U.S. Bureau of the Census. 2020a. "Characteristics of New Housing." Available at www.census.gov/construction/chars/.

———. 2020b. "State-to-State Migration Flows." Available at www.census.gov/topics/population/migration/guidance/state-to-state-migration-flows.html.

———. 2019. American Housing Survey, "Occupied Units." Available at www.census.gov/programs-surveys/ahs/data/interactive/ahstablecreator.html?s_areas=00000&s_year=2017&s_tablename=TABLE1&s_bygroup1=3&s_bygroup2=18&s_filtergroup1=1&s_filtergroup2=1.

———. Undated. American Community Survey 2012–2016.

U.S. Department of Commerce, Advisory Committee on Zoning. 1924. "A Standard State Zoning Enabling Act." Government Printing Office.

U.S. Department of Justice. 1948. *Prejudice and Property: An Historic Brief Against Racial Covenants.* Government Printing Office.

U.S. Energy Information Administration. 2020. "State Electricity Profiles." Nov. 2.

U.S. Environmental Protection Agency. 2004. "Decentralized Wastewater Treatment Systems: A Program Strategy." Available at https://wastewatereducation.org/watertowaste/epa_septic_program_strategy.pdf.

U.S. General Accounting Office. 2002. "Federal Housing Assistance: Comparing the Characteristics and Costs of Housing Programs." GAO-02-76.

Uthwatt Report. 1942. "Expert Committee on Compensation and Betterment: Final Report." Cmd. 6386.

Van Hecke, M. T. 1928. "Zoning Ordinances and Restrictions in Deeds." 37 *Yale L.J.* 407.

van Holm, Eric Joseph, and Christopher K. Wyczalkowski. 2019. "Gentrification in the Wake of a Hurricane: New Orleans After Katrina." 56 *Urb. Stud.* 2763.

van Wee, Bert. 2015. "Viewpoint: Toward a New Generation of Land Use Transport Interaction Models." 8 *J. Transport & Land Use* 1.

Vigdor, Jacob L., and Edward L. Glaeser. 2012. "The End of the Segregated Century: Racial Separation in America's Neighborhoods, 1890–2010." Manhattan Institute. Jan. 22.

Von Hoffman, Alexander. 2010a. "To Preserve and Protect: Land Use Regulations in Weston, Massachusetts." Joint Center for Housing Studies, Harvard University.

———. 2010b. "Wrestling with Growth in Acton, Massachusetts." Joint Center for Housing Studies, Harvard University.

Wagner, Kurt. 2017. "Facebook Is Building a New Campus that Includes 1,500 Apartments and a Grocery Store." Vox, July 7.

Wallach, Ruth, 2013. *Miracle Mile in Los Angeles: History and Architecture.* History Press.

Wanerka, Christine E. 1994. "The Branford Land Trust: History." In *Branford 350th Celebration.* Available in Branford Town Library.

Warner, Robert A. 1940. *New Haven Negroes: A Social History.* Yale University Press.

Wasi, Nada, et al. 2005. "Property Tax Limitations and Mobility: Lock-In Effect of California's Proposition 13." *Brookings-Wharton Papers on Urban Affairs* 59.

Wegmann, Jake. 2020. "Death to Single-Family Zoning . . . and New Life to the Missing Middle." 86 *J. Am. Planning Ass'n* 113.

Weicher, John C. 1997. *Privatizing Subsidized Housing.* American Enterprise Institute.

Weiss, Brandon. 2018. "Locating Affordable Housing: The Legal System's Misallocation of Subsidized Housing Incentives." 70 *Hastings L.J.* 215.

Weiss, Marc A. 1987. *The Rise of the Community Builders: The American Real Estate Industry and Urban Land Planning.* Beard Books.

Welch, Terrence S. 2008. "Containing Urban Sprawl: Is Reinvigoration of Home Rule the Answer?" 9 *Vt. J. Envt'l L.* 131.

White, James R. 1988. "Large Lot Zoning and Subdivision Costs: A Test." 23 *J. Urb. Econ.* 370.

Whitnall, Gordon. 1931. "History of Zoning." 155 *Annals Am. Acad. Pol. & Soc. Sci.* 1.

Whittemore, Andrew H. 2018. "The Role of Racial Bias in Exclusionary Zoning: The Case of Durham, North Carolina, 1945–2014." 50 *Env't & Planning A: Econ. & Space* 826.

———. 2012a. "How the Federal Government Zoned America: The Federal Housing Administration and Zoning." 39 *J. Urb. Hist.* 620.

———. 2012b. "Zoning Los Angeles: A Brief History of Four Regimes." 27 *Planning Persp.* 393.

Whyte, William H. 1964. *Cluster Development.* American Conservation Association.

Wick, Julia. 2019. "Inside the Demise of SB 50, the State's Most Talked-About Bill." *L.A. Times,* May 17.

Willingboro Township Zoning Map. 2017. Burlington County Department of Resource Conservation, Map 4M-38. Available at www.co.burlington.nj.us/DocumentCenter/View/6714/Map4M-38?bidId.

Wilson, James Q. 2006. "How Divided Are We?" *Commentary,* Feb. 15.

Winokur, James L. 1989. "The Mixed Blessings of Promissory Servitudes." 1989 *Wis. L. Rev.* 1.

Winslow, Ward. 1993. *Palo Alto: A Centennial History.* Palo Alto Historical Association.

Wish, Naomi Bailin, and Stephen Eisdorfer. 1997. "Impact of *Mount Laurel* Initiatives: An Analysis of the Characteristics of Applicants and Occupants." 27 *Seton Hall L. Rev.* 1268.

Wogan, J. B. 2017. "Population Growth Means a City Is Thriving, or Does It?" 30 *Governing* 24. Sept.

Wolf, Michael Allan. 2008. *The Zoning of America: Euclid v. Ambler.* University Press of Kansas.

Wong, Weihuang. 2018. "Our Town: Support for Housing Growth When Localism Meets Liberalism." MIT Pol. Sci. Dep't Res. Paper No. 2018–11. May 2.

Worley, William S. 1990. *J. C. Nichols and the Shaping of Kansas City.* Univ. of Missouri Press.

YIMBY Action. 2020. Searched Dec. 21. Available at https://yimbyaction.org/directory/.

Zasloff, Jonathan. 2017. "The Price of Equality: Fair Housing, Land Use, and Disparate Impact." 48 *Colum. Hum. Rts. L. Rev.* 98.

Zehr, Dan. 2020. "History of Austin's Racial Divide in Maps." *Austin American-Statesman.* Available at http://projects.statesman.com/news/economic-mobility/.

Zile, Zigurds L. 1959. "Private Zoning on Milwaukee's Metropolitan Fringe, Problems of Drafting—Part II." 1959 *Wisc. L. Rev.* 451.

Zillow.com. www.zillow.com/home-values/.

Zweig, Jason. 2020. "Why Invest? A 22-Year-Old's Tough Questions About Capitalism." *Wall St. J.,* Jan. 24.

Index

Figures, notes, and tables are indicated by f, n, and t following the page number.